Interactions

Collaboration Skills for School Professionals

FIFTH EDITION

Marilyn Friend

University of North Carolina, Greensboro

Lynne Cook

California State University, Dominguez Hills

PEARSON

Boston • New York • San Francisco
Mexico City • Montreal • Toronto • London • Madrid • Munich • Paris
Hong Kong • Singapore • Tokyo • Cape Town • Sydney

Executive Editor: Virginia Lanigan
Editorial Assistant: Matthew Buchholz
Development Editor: Christien Shangraw
Marketing Manager: Kris Ellis-Levy
Production Editor: Janet Domingo
Editorial Production Service: Omegatype Typography, Inc.
Composition Buyer: Linda Cox
Manufacturing Buyer: Megan Cochran
Electronic Composition: Omegatype Typography, Inc.
Interior Design: Lisa Devenish
Photo Researcher: Annie Pickert
Cover Administrator: Linda Knowles

For related titles and support materials, visit our online catalog at www.ablongman.com.

Between the time website information is gathered and then published, it is not unusual
for some sites to have closed. Also, the transcription of URLs can result in typographi-
cal errors. The publisher would appreciate notification where these errors occur so
that they may be corrected in subsequent editions.

ISBN 0-205-48351-8

Printed in the United States of America

10 9 8 7 6 5   RRD-VA   10   09   08

To Joseph Percy Price
1934–2001
An extraordinary educator who lives on through those,
like us, who were blessed by his life and teachings.

Contents

5   *Co-Teaching   111*

8 *Interpersonal Communication   200*

Features at a Glance

Putting Ideas into Practice

A Basis in Research

Preface

Collaboration has been a central element of successful education for many years. As we put the final touches on this fifth edition of *Interactions: Collaboration Skills for School Professionals*, we recognize clearly the changes in the field and the increasing emphasis on collaboration in educating all students. In the first edition we described the concerns we had about the direction the field of special education was taking regarding the way professionals worked together to provide services to students with disabilites. As we now reflect on the fifteen years that have passed since the first edition of *Interactions* was published, we are gratified to see a much greater understanding and appreciation of collaborative relationships and programs. When we first began working together, collaboration was acknowledged as important but was still primarily a small concern pertaining mostly to special educators; it was viewed by many as a luxury within the context of classroom instruction, and its study within a broader education framework was somewhat limited.

Much has changed since then. The Individuals with Disabilities Education Act (IDEA), the legislation governing the provision of services for students with disabilities, now carries a clear expectation that most students will be educated in typical classrooms with their peers. Furthermore, access to the general education curriculum for students with special needs has become a requirement at the same time that accountability for all students' learning has continued to grow. As a result, special education services delivered collaboratively to students within the general education classroom have become more and more common. Collaboration also has moved far beyond the school setting. There is increasing recognition that all of the agencies that serve families and children must share their efforts and resources in order to have any long-lasting positive impact on the lives of children and their families. The vastly increased breadth of concern for collaboration and depth of its examination are evidenced by the sharp rise in attention paid to collaboration in professional literature and conferences.

This fifth edition of *Interactions* responds to the changes in school policies and practices that have led to today's focused attention on collaboration as an essential skill for meeting the ever-increasing diversity of student needs. It is a guide for preprofessionals and professionals to help them understand and participate effectively in their interactions with other professionals and parents. This book was written for a broad audience, but especially for preservice and in-service special educators, general educators, and related services professionals who educate students with disabilities. Although the examples and activities focus on providers of special services, they are not unique to that group. We continue to believe that the principles for effective interaction are not dependent on roles or settings—they are universal. Our experiences in schools tell us that the concepts and skills in *Interactions* are thus equally applicable to individuals who educate English language learners, to those who work in early intervention and preschool programs, to site-based school management groups, to middle school teams, and to many other situations in which educators come together to work toward a common goal.

Over the past fifteen years, we have received much positive feedback about the pragmatic nature of this book and many helpful suggestions for improvement. In this edition, we continue to use the principles we believe lead to instructional effectiveness: a measured amount of theory and conceptual foundations heavily seasoned with examples, cases, and applied activities. *Interactions* was written specifically to enable readers to quickly use the knowledge and skills they acquire in their professional settings. We intend for the book to be a useful tool for practitioners in improving their skills and deepening their understanding—whether they are engaged in formal instructional settings, a study group, or independent study. Moreover, because many interaction situations are complex with many possible variations and outcomes, we have tried to present possibilities yet still leave the reader thinking critically about personal applications and alternative options.

Overview of the Book

We have had the good fortune of working and learning with talented teachers, administrators, parents, paraprofessionals, and providers of related services as they developed collaboration skills and developed specific applications of collaboration. We have benefitted immensely from our interactions with diverse educators who are implementing collaborative practices, and we believe that much of what we have learned together is reflected in the pages of this fifth edition of *Interactions*. Specifically, we have maintained our core of information about collaboration concepts, communication, and interaction process skills; we have expanded and deepened some material from the fourth edition; we have omitted a few topics that have taken on a lower priority in today's schools; we have reorganized the order of the chapters in response to student and instructor feedback; and we have again augmented the practical applications of the textbook's ideas.

We have eliminated the chapter on families and included much of the information in illustrations throughout the book and in Chapter 12, "Perspectives and Issues." We increased the emphasis on diversity by eliminating the special diversity feature in each chapter and instead incorporating discussions of diversity throughout the twelve chapters. Specially identified sections of each chapter also highlight important considerations for cross-cultural interaction and collaboration.

Chapter 1 presents a conceptual foundation for understanding collaborative interactions and activities as well as the settings and structures that support them. In this chapter we define collaboration and highlight its benefits and risks. In addition, we distinguish *collaboration* from other terms that are sometimes used interchangeably, and we explore the development of collaboration as it relates to special education, including the current trend to educate students with disabilities in general education classrooms.

Chapter 2 introduces interpersonal problem solving as the most central interaction process in which collaboration is applied and one in which effective communication skills must be used to achieve successful outcomes. It draws on but differs from professionals' skills for individual problem solving. The chapter has been moved forward to become the first application presented so that readers will understand the problem-solving process that they will use later as they learn about services for students.

The next three chapters of *Interactions* explore school services and applications in which success relies heavily on collaboration. Chapter 3 addresses the topic of teaming, including ideas for establishing and maintaining teams and problem solving to help teams work effectively. Teaming is addressed in a more pragmatic manner than in previous editions and is less theoretical. Chapter 4 considers consultation as a service delivery approach. It examines the various models through which consultation can be delivered, and it also offers a variety of suggestions for making consultation a viable means of supporting students and teachers. Chapter 5 takes up the topic of co-teaching, the service delivery option in which two educators share instructional responsibility in a single classroom. The prominent placement of this chapter signals the increased interest and acceptance of this type of service. Suggestions for setting up co-teaching programs and specific information about how such arrangements should function are provided.

Chapter 6 focuses on the use of paraeducators in providing services to students with disabilities. This chapter outlines appropriate and inappropriate roles for paraeducators, professionals' supervisory responsibilities when working with paraeducators, and issues that may arise when paraeducators are part of an educational team. Chapter 7 pulls together many of the practical matters that are of concern to those beginning to implement collaborative pratices. Topics include finding and managing time for planning, scheduling, program development and evaluation, and staff development. The chapter emphasizes the issues that arise when professionals collaborate "in the real world." We have found that the material in this chapter may be needed earlier for some learners. For readers struggling in situations in which collaboration seems nearly impossible because of constraints on logistics, this chapter may be an appropriate starting point.

The next three chapters of the book comprise a unit on communication skills. These chapters existed in the previous editions, but they have been updated and moved to follow the programmatic applications. While the skills are basic and quite essential to any effort to implement practical applications of collaboration, many students prefer to learn about and get answers to their questions regarding service delivery and collaborative programs before they tackle the requisite interpersonal skills. Chapter 8 serves as an introduction and overview of principles of clear and constructive communication. Concepts are presented that underlie communication and interaction skills, including recognizing diverse frames of reference and preparing to listen. This chapter also summarizes the principles of interpersonal communication, both verbal and nonverbal. An in-depth discussion of verbal communication occurs in the next two chapters. Chapter 9 provides the reader with knowledge and skills regarding using statements. Chapter 10 provides similar information about asking questions. In these two chapters, verbal strategies in using statements or asking questions are examined according to their intent to provide, solicit, or clarify information.

A somewhat different direction is taken in Chapter 11, which deals with awkward and adversarial interactions by focusing on both conflict and resistance. Strategies such as negotiation and persuasion are emphasized. These require the use of many of the interactive processes and communication skills addressed in the previous interpersonal communication section of the text. In Chapter 12 perspectives and special issues related to collaboration in specific contexts are outlined. Collaborative efforts are influenced by the roles of the persons who collaborate as well as the contexts in which they work, and these topics are explored in the chapter. For example, collaboration with families is examined and special attention is paid to the unique perspectives that families from various cultures may bring to school environments, and facilitating family participation in decision making about their children. Additionally, student collaboration and collaboration for transition planning are explored. Also included in Chapter 12 is a discussion of some of the critical ethical issues that arise when professionals collaborate.

The features in the fifth edition include most of those from previous editions of *Interactions,* and others have been added. The features include the following:

- **Orienting Graphic.** At the opening of each chapter is a graphic that depicts five components of collaboration and their relationship to one another. The components consist of personal commitment, communication skills, interaction processes, programs or services, and context. These are components of the framework described in Chapter 1. The components most relevant to the content are shaded in the icons at the opening of each chapter.
- **Connections.** Each chapter begins with a section titled Connections, which is designed to assist the reader in understanding how the specific chapter content relates to material in other chapters and to the overall organization of the book.
- **Learner Objectives.** Each Connections section is followed by Learner Objectives, which inform the reader about the main purposes of the chapter. The objectives also help the reader to set expectations for what he or she will be able to do after studying the chapter.
- **Photographs.** In the fifth edition, photographs are used generously to more clearly illustrate collaboration in action.

- **Case Materials.** Case descriptions and vignettes are presented at the opening of each chapter and throughout the text to illustrate relevant concepts and principles. These often include descriptions of specific school situations and extended dialog between professionals or parents.
- **Putting Ideas into Practice.** In each chapter, additional elaboration of concepts or skills practice is offered in Putting Ideas into Practice boxes. These boxes are another means of making written ideas come to life for application in real school settings.
- **A Basis in Research.** A research base is developing in the area of collaboration and, increasingly, research-based practices are called for. Each chapter contains a feature titled A Basis in Research, which highlights pertinent research findings.
- **Chapter Summaries.** Each chapter concludes with a summary in which the major points addressed in the chapter are recapped. The summaries are intended to assist the reader in reviewing his or her understanding of the primary concepts within each chapter.
- **Activities and Assignments.** Application items are found at the end of each chapter; they assess the reader's understanding of important information in the chapter and provide suggestions for skill development activities. These exercises may be used independently or as part of organized training experiences.
- **For Further Reading.** A brief list of additional readings is included at the end of each chapter. These references enable the reader who wants more detailed information about a particular topic to access that information quickly.

As with the previous edition, *Interactions* is accompanied by an **Instructor's Manual,** which is available electronically at the Instructor's Resource Center www.ablongman.com/irc. The manual includes chapter outlines, overhead transparency masters, additional activities and cases, and a test bank. It provides many more resources for teaching about collaboration than can be placed within the pages of the book itself.

We hope the fifth edition of *Interactions: Collaboration Skills for School Professionals* is useful to you and that you enjoy reading it. We continue to hold to our belief that collaboration is the foundation on which successful contemporary public schools are based, as well as the most effective means by which to provide services to students with disabilities and other special needs. We hope this edition of *Interactions* helps you further understand collaboration as it occurs in your workplace and enables you to refine your skills as a collaborative educator.

Acknowledgments

We often tell our students that collaboration is the best way to ensure one's lifelong learning, and we are reminded of this fact ourselves when we work with teachers, administrators, related-service personnel, families, paraeducators, and others in schools. We are indebted to them and to our students and colleagues who have contributed in many direct and indirect ways to the creation of this book and to the ideas that run through it. Even though we cannot name them all, we hope they see their influence reflected in this volume and know of our appreciation.

We would also like to thank the following colleagues who provided professional reviews of the fourth edition of *Interactions* to make suggestions for the fifth edition: Christine Allred, High Point University; Daniel Y. Kelly, SUNY Geneseo; Nancy Niemi, Nazareth College; and Philip Nordness, Western Illinois University. We appreciate the time and care it takes to review a manuscript and recognize the challenges of fitting an additional commitment in your busy schedules. We sincerely appreciate the detailed and insightful comments and suggestions you provided.

Throughout the development of this edition of *Interactions,* we received guidance, encouragement, and advice from the professional staff at Allyn and Bacon. We are very appreciative of Virginia Lanigan, who encouraged us during the writing process. We thank her for her patience, her tactful prodding, careful reviews, and unfailing support. We also feel fortunate indeed to have worked with Christien Shangraw, our development editor, and Janet Domingo, our production editor. They managed to guide all stages of development and production expertly, keep track of our whereabouts, correct our errors, and provide us with strong support.

Our families, as always, provided incredible support to us at every stage of this project. Our moms, Mary Ellen Penovich and Florence Cook, in the characteristic manner they share, proved again to be wonderful moms. They listened as we agonized over decisions and deadlines, consoled us when we were discouraged, often fretted about whether we were working too hard, and always encouraged us to succeed. They offered to help however they could; we hope they know that just caring and being there and putting up with our often unpredictable schedules was sometimes what we needed most. Thanks, Moms.

Bruce Brandon (Marilyn's spouse) and Fred Weintraub (Lynne's spouse) once more demonstrated the kindness, support, talent, and patience that allow us to maintain our productive long-distance collaboration. They put up with the long hours we spent in our respective offices; they listened as we sorted out difficult concepts; and they helped us maintain a healthy perspective on our work and our lives. Bruce took it upon himself to become the moderator of Internet humor to ensure we both had several humor breaks each day. Fred kept us grounded by critiquing our concepts and providing different perspectives from his administrative work. He also kept us well fed with his gourmet cooking during our brief times together. We don't tell them often enough how much we appreciate their support and help. Thanks, Fred and Bruce—we know we could not have done this without you.

Marilyn Friend
Lynne Cook

Foreword

Prior to the appearance of the first edition of this book in 1992, Nancy Waldron and I were working with teams of teachers from several schools in southern Indiana to develop and implement school improvement plans. These plans addressed improving academic and social outcomes for all students, and ensuring that students with disabilities were included in general education classrooms for a large part of the school day. We met on numerous occasions with these teams to plan these changes. As these meetings progressed, everyone realized that teachers didn't have all of the knowledge and skills that were necessary to support the changes that were being proposed. To address this need, we worked collaboratively with the teams from each school to plan professional development activities. Each of the teams readily agreed that at least some teachers in each school would need professional development related to topics such as behavior management, social skills training, class-wide peer tutoring, cooperative learning, accommodations and adaptations to meet the needs of all students, and so forth.

Once this list of professional development topics was developed, we realized that collaboration was conspicuously absent. We brought this up with the teams, and they were unanimous in taking the perspective that they "already know how to work together," and this would not be an issue for the teachers in their respective schools. We made it clear to the teachers on more than one occasion that we thought professional development on collaboration would be quite useful, but to no avail.

During the fall of the following year, each of the schools implemented their school change activities. We then met regularly with the teams to discuss what was going well and what was not working. A major topic that arose from the beginning of these meetings related to problems with collaboration. More than one special education teacher has said, "she treats me like an aide when I'm in her class," or "the classroom teacher won't give up any control over instruction or curriculum." Classroom teachers had similar concerns regarding how to work effectively with another teacher in "their classroom." Grade-level teams also brought up issues related to working together successfully to modify teacher schedules, adapt curriculum, and so forth.

After less than a month into the fall semester, all of the teams agreed that professional development related to collaboration was needed to address these issues. They also were critical of us as facilitators for not recommending professional development related to this topic. How quickly they forget! We agreed that this concern should be addressed, and arranged for professional development related to collaboration. These activities went a long way toward ameliorating the collaboration issues the teachers faced. And it was Marilyn Friend who provided this professional development based on the concepts she and coauthor Lynne Cook had already advanced.

In hindsight, it may seem astounding that we failed to convince a group of teachers that professional development related to collaboration was needed to support a major school change activity. How things have changed! Perhaps the greatest single reason this change has occurred is that over the last fifteen years, the demands on teachers to address the needs of an increasingly diverse range of students have increased exponentially. Furthermore, within this context of increasing student diversity, teachers are expected to increase the achievement levels of students to unprecedented levels. It is safe to say that most teachers have realized that no single teacher is prepared to address these challenges alone. Moreover, addressing the learning and behavioral needs of students from a range of backgrounds requires—better yet, demands—the combined knowledge, skills, and creative efforts of many teachers if student needs are to be successfully addressed and state-mandated outcomes achieved.

The first edition of this text appeared at a perfect time to fill a critical need, and perhaps more importantly, served to frame the discussion regarding collaboration that has occurred over the ensuing fifteen years or so . . . what collaboration is, why it is important, when and where is it useful, how we make it work, and so forth. In 2006, collaboration has become an accepted part of the vernacular of all educators, and continues to grow in importance as schools strive to meet increasingly higher demands related to outcomes for all students.

Today's schools accept that knowledge, skills, and dispositions related to collaboration are necessary to meeting their students' needs. And Marilyn Friend and Lynne Cook have provided us with a literate, practical, highly useful text that helps us traverse this minefield with some level of success. From the appearance of the first edition of this text, it has been apparent that Marilyn and Lynne have used what they have learned from working with teachers to ensure that this text is grounded in real-world problems, as well as solutions to problems that are teacher tested and effective.

This is the fifth edition of this text, and each edition has been marked by significant improvements to ensure that a cutting-edge perspective on collaboration is provided, which is grounded in current research and made applicable to teachers, counselors, school psychologists, administrators, and a range of other school professionals who work together to address student needs. Changes in this edition include vignettes to open each chapter that serve to invite the reader into the topic, an increased emphasis on the evolution of inclusion in Chapter 1, a more practical approach to teaming in Chapter 3, increased emphasis on research-based practices through the use of A Basis in Research features, and more emphasis on critical topics such as diversity and ethics. In addition to these changes, Chapter 1 includes an up-to-date discussion of collaboration in the context of IDEA 2004.

While these changes are important, the core of the text that has served us so well in understanding and applying collaboration as a style of interaction remains largely intact. As any reader will recognize, collaboration continues to present challenges, even under the best of circumstances. We are fortunate that this text continues to provide us with the best available information for addressing the difficulties faced by teachers and other professionals in addressing these challenges, as we seek to meet the academic and social needs of all students in classrooms and schools across America.

James McLeskey, Professor and Chair
Department of Special Education, University of Florida

CHAPTER 1

The Fundamentals of Collaboration

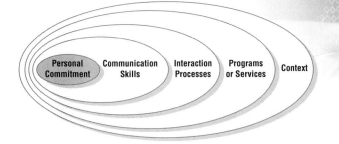

Personal Commitment | Communication Skills | Interaction Processes | Programs or Services | Context

Connections

Chapter 1 provides an overview of collaboration and lays the groundwork for all the information contained in the subsequent chapters. In this chapter you will learn what collaboration is (and is not), why it can be challenging, and how it fits into broader societal and school contexts. You will also find out about a framework for studying collaboration that serves as the structure for this textbook.

Learner Objectives

After reading this chapter you will be able to:

1. Provide examples of formal and informal collaboration occurring in schools that demonstrate the growing importance of collaboration for professional educators.
2. Express how you will use collaboration as a tool for working in twenty-first–century schools.
3. Define collaboration and describe its critical characteristics.
4. Outline the importance of collaboration from the perspectives of disciplines outside education, including business, health, and human services.
5. Describe the place of collaboration within the context of the No Child Left Behind Act of 2001 and other reform initiatives.

6. Explain how the 2004 reauthorization of the Individuals with Disabilities Education Act and related special education policy fosters collaboration among professionals and between professionals and parents/families.

7. Describe a framework for studying collaboration.

Staff members at John F. Kennedy Elementary School are holding a meeting in August to discuss priorities for the upcoming school year. Mr. Bauer, the principal, begins by congratulating the staff members on their hard work and the wonderful results of it: An impressive 95 percent of students in the school reached last year's goal for adequate yearly progress (AYP). To help orient the four new teachers at the meeting, several general and special education teachers, the speech language therapist, and the nurse share some of the factors that they believe contributed to the school's success. Their comments include grade-level planning meetings, the schoolwide commitment to using positive behavior supports, and the Family Partners project that increased the number of volunteers who read with students as well as participated in other school–home initiatives such as open house, conferences, and Reading Round-Up. As the conversation moves to resolving scheduling dilemmas from the previous year, the group engages in a spirited discussion—the professionals clearly disagree about what to do, but all voices are heard. A tentative plan is agreed on, and the group stops to retrieve their lunches. Until the meeting resumes, the conversation becomes a mix of follow-up from the morning session and catch-up from the summer break.

Introduction

Of all the many complex challenges facing schools in the first decade of the twenty-first century, none is as demanding nor as critical as creating in education a culture of collaboration and ensuring that everyone who works there has the dispositions, knowledge, and skills to collaborate. The preceding vignette illustrates this point for one situation. Here are more examples of the many ways in which collaboration is emerging in education settings:

■ Wednesday is a busy day for Ms. Maharrin, a middle school social studies teacher. In addition to her daily teaching responsibilities and all the work that surrounds that most critical part of her job, she is a member of her school's leadership team, and so she has agreed to meet from 7:30 to 8:15 AM to discuss several issues, including the staff development plan for the next school year. At lunch, Ms. Maharrin has arranged to meet with Mr. Newby, the school psychologist, to design an intervention for the new student who is experiencing much frustration in the classroom. During her team preparation period, Ms. Maharrin knows the upcoming field trip will be the primary topic for discussion, while during her individual preparation period, she needs to call two parents and touch base with Mrs. Knox, the special education teacher. After school, she plans to meet with her assistant principal, Mr. Okolo, to plan next week's pep rally for the beginning of the fall sports season. At the end of the day Ms. Maharrin wryly thinks to herself that teaching her students seems to be the smallest part of her day on Wednesdays—something she never would have imagined when she entered the teaching profession 19 years ago.

■ Mr. Mendez is a second-year student support teacher (SST) at Hawthorne High School. Last year, he was called a special education resource teacher, but his job title was changed to reflect his changed job responsibilities. Mr. Mendez begins each day touching base with his colleagues in the English department and working on paperwork. Once classes begin at 7:50 AM, he spends the morning co-teaching in two sections of English and teaching one section of a study skills class. During his preparation period, he meets with two students and the counselor about problems the students are experiencing in their classes. Mr. Mendez has time in his schedule for his assessment and IEP responsibilities, and this afternoon begins with the annual review meeting for one of the students on his caseload. During the last period, he again teaches a study skills class. After school, he works on lesson plans, meets briefly with Ms. Meyers, the social studies teacher with whom he co-chairs the school's inclusive practices task force, and makes a parent phone call. Mr. Mendez often notes that a large part of his job is public relations. He considers himself an advocate for students on his caseload, but he also knows that he influences teachers' thinking about students who are at risk. He finds that he must pay close attention to the personalities of the teachers with whom he works; if he establishes a strong working relationship with them, the students are the beneficiaries.

■ Mrs. Penny is a literacy facilitator at Eisenhower Elementary School. Her primary responsibility is to help teachers increase student achievement in reading and writing. However, her job usually does not include directly teaching students unless it is to model a technique or demonstrate a strategy. Thus, Mrs. Penny spends her time observing in classrooms, meeting with teachers individually and in small groups, advising the principal about needs she identifies related to literacy, conducting staff development on specific strategies and approaches, and analyzing and sharing literacy data with school staff members. She also works closely with the school's parent advisory group on working with families to foster literacy at home. Sometimes Mrs. Penny misses her days as a classroom teacher with its clear patterns and the joy of seeing her students succeed, but she also comments that she believes that she helps more students now by working with all the teachers and families and that her job now brings a different kind of satisfaction.

Each of the professionals just described has adult–adult interactions as a significant job responsibility. As a classroom teacher, Ms. Maharrin, whose primary responsibility is instruction, also is expected to work with colleagues and parents. Mr. Mendez's job title has changed in order to overcome some of the traditional and potentially stereotypical thinking sometimes associated with being a special educator in a high school. Half of his teaching occurs in partnership with general education teachers in that setting. Mrs. Penny's job is relatively new. As school administrators work to ensure that all students access the general curriculum and reach high standards, the need for professionals to support teachers as they instruct their students has grown. Taken together, these professional interactions illustrate three critical points for understanding the premise of this text.

First, collaboration has become an integral part of today's schools (Murray, 2004; Powers, Winters, Person, & Kim, 2004). In the past, educators who were not very effective in working with other adults were often excused with a comment such as, "But she's really good with students." Although working effectively with students obviously is still the most important aspect of educators' jobs, it is not enough. Everyone in schools, including general education teachers, needs the knowledge and skills to work with colleagues, paraprofessionals, and parents. This is true in early childhood programs, in elementary schools, and in middle and high schools. It is true in schools that are still regarded as traditional in terms of programs and services as well as in those leading the way in educational innovation. Part of the reason for the importance of collaboration is the general trend of increased responsibilities that are more realistically addressed when professionals pool their talents (e.g., Houser, 2005; Leimu & Koricheva, 2005; Neus & Scherf, 2005). Part of it is the No Child Left Behind Act of 2001, which has set high standards and created clear accountability systems for all students (e.g., Hourcade, Parette, & Anderson, 2003; *No Child Left Behind Alert*, 2005; Peck & Scarpati, 2004), and part of it is the continued trend toward inclusive practices (Henderson, 2002; McLaughlin, 2002; Patterson, 2005).

Second, the examples of professionals' collaborative activities demonstrate that such interactions occur both formally and informally. School leadership teams, middle school teams, co-teaching, and consultative meetings are representative of the growth of formal structures and activities in schools that rely on collaboration for success. Models emphasizing collaboration such as these are described in detail later in this text. Meetings to respond to particular student needs and phone calls to parents are examples of informal collaboration. Both types of collaboration are important. However, informal collaboration often occurs whether or not a context for collaboration has been fostered and whether or not any formal structures needing collaboration are in place. Formal collaboration typically requires that strong leadership has ensured that a collaborative school culture—one that values collegial interactions—has been created.

Third, this text is based on the belief that collaboration is the common thread in the many current initiatives for school reform. Collaboration is crucial as educators move to differentiate curriculum, meet standards of accountability for student achievement as measured through high-stakes testing, design local professional development plans, meet the requirements for highly qualified teachers, and work with increasingly diverse students and their families, a point illustrated in Putting Ideas into Practice. Collaboration also is part of special education through intervention teams, multifactored assessments, IEP development, in-class service delivery approaches, and parent participation.

PUTTING IDEAS INTO PRACTICE

Working with Diverse Families

Nearly all educators want to collaborate with families, but they may not be thinking of the diversity that exists in today's families. Here are some challenges families may face:

- *Single-parent families* may experience a great deal of stress and isolation, and the children from these families are more likely than other children to live in poverty.
- *Blended families,* in which parents each have children from former relationships, may need time to bond and to resolve issues related to child rearing (e.g., discipline). Sibling rivalry also may occur.
- Multigenerational families, in which grandparents or other relatives care for children, may face economic challenges, and the energy required to raise children may be daunting for the caregiver.
- *Foster families* are, by nature, temporary, and so the bonds may be a bit different from those in other families; children in foster families may experience stress because of not knowing exactly what the next steps in their lives may be.
- Homosexual families often face societal discrimination, and some teachers may feel uncomfortable interacting with these parents. Legal issues related to topics such as access to school records also may arise.

Here are a few ideas for working effectively with diverse families:

- Be sure to know the correct last names of every parent, regardless of the family structure.
- Avoid language that implies that "family" refers only to traditional family structure.
- For recently formed families, offer information on their children's strengths and abilities.
- Avoid making requests that may place parents in an uncomfortable position related to time or money. Some families cannot afford to contribute materials for classrooms, and some parents cannot come to conferences during typical school hours or on a specific day; therefore, options and alternatives should be offered.
- Remember that projects and activities that presume students are part of a traditional family may not be appropriate—for example, alternatives to creating a family tree and making Mother's Day gifts may be in order.
- In some cases—for example, when grandparents are raising children—you may need to explain school procedures when parents are unfamiliar with them.
- Perhaps most important, all educators should reflect on their own beliefs about nontraditional families and set aside any assumptions they may have about them. Being positive with students and families and being alert to and stopping teasing of students from these families are important responsibilities that you have.

Source: Adapted from J. A. Ray, "Family-friendly teachers: Tips for working with diverse families," *Kappa Delta Pi Record, 41* (2005): 72–76.

This book, then, is about effective interactions. It presents the generic concepts, principles, skills, and strategies that all school professionals can use to enhance their shared efforts to educate their students. Although many of the examples relate to special education, the information definitely is not limited to those applications.

Collaboration Concepts

The term *collaboration* has become something of an educational buzzword. One can easily get the sense that collaboration is viewed as the preferred approach in nearly any school situation. It is touted as the mechanism through which school reform can be accomplished (Dowell et al., 2004) and the instrument through which full-service schools can be created (Boulter, 2004; Hill, 2004). Principals are admonished to use a collaborative leadership style (Krajewski, 2005; Owings & Kaplan, 2005), and teachers are encouraged to use collaboration to address diverse student needs (e.g., Brighton, 2001; Friend & Pope, 2005; McDonnell, Thorson, Disher, Mathot-Buckner, Mendel, & Ray, 2003). Unfortunately, the term *collaboration* often is carelessly used and occasionally misapplied, as suggested in Figure 1.1.

Despite all the current discussion about collaboration, few clear definitions of it have been presented, and this has contributed to confusion about its character and implementation. In fact, some dictionary definitions of *collaboration* include reference to treason or working together for sinister purposes! In education literature and practice, you may find that collaboration is used as a synonym for related but distinctly different concepts addressed elsewhere in this book, including teaming, consultation, and inclusion, or is not defined

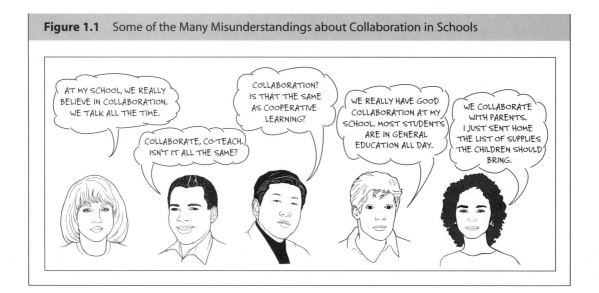

Figure 1.1   Some of the Many Misunderstandings about Collaboration in Schools

at all beyond a sense of working together (e.g., Dettmer, Dyck, & Thurston, 2005; Idol, Nevin, & Paolucci-Whitcomb, 2000). Since we firmly believe that a precise understanding of the term *collaboration* is far more than semantics, we begin by carefully defining it. Knowing what collaboration is and is not and how it applies to school initiatives can help you articulate your practices, set appropriate expectations for yourself, and positively influence others to interact collaboratively.

Definition

Given our commitment to presenting key concepts clearly, we begin our discussion of interpersonal collaboration with a technical definition that characterizes it as a unique concept:

> Interpersonal *collaboration* is a style for direct interaction between at least two co-equal parties voluntarily engaged in shared decision making as they work toward a common goal.

Notice that we call collaboration a *style*. In the same way that writers use various styles to convey information to readers so, too, do individuals use interpersonal styles or approaches for their interactions with one another (Pugach & Johnson, 2002). Some professionals may choose to be directive when they interact; others may choose to be accommodative or facilitative; still others may choose to be collaborative. At first glance, referring to collaboration as a style may appear to detract from its significance by equating it to something ephemeral and seemingly lacking in substance. However, using this term enables you to distinguish the nature of the interpersonal relationship—that is, collaboration—occurring during shared interactions from the activities themselves, such as teaming or problem solving.

As just implied, because collaboration is a style of interaction it cannot exist in isolation. It can occur only when it is used by people who are engaged in a specific process, task, or activity. To clarify this point, consider the following: If colleagues mentioned to you that they were collaborating, would you know what they were doing? Probably not. They could be collaboratively planning an educational program for a student with a disability, sharing the responsibilities for an academic lesson in a co-teaching arrangement, or planning a school social event. What the term *collaboration* conveys is *how* the activity is occurring—that is, the nature of the interpersonal relationship occurring during the interaction and the ways in which individuals communicate with each other.

Defining Characteristics for Collaboration

Considered alone, the definition we have presented only hints at the subtleties of collaboration. Through our writing (e.g., Friend, 2000; Friend & Cook, 1990; Friend & Cook, 2004), our own ongoing collaboration, and our experience facilitating the collaboration of others, we have identified several elements of collaboration that we call *defining characteristics* since they more fully explain the basic definition.

Collaboration Is Voluntary

It is not possible to force people to use a particular style in their interactions with others. States may pass legislation, school districts may adopt policy, and site administrators may implement programs, but unless school professionals and their colleagues choose to collaborate, they will not do so. Perhaps the best illustration of this notion is the current trend for schools to mandate that professionals collaborate in designing and implementing programs for students with special needs in general education classes. If you are familiar with such a situation, you are probably also aware that some individuals are unwilling to collaborate, regardless of the mandate. For example, a professional may spend a significant amount of time complaining about the demands of teaching certain students, time that otherwise could be spent collaboratively designing instruction that would help the students succeed. If that professional attends meetings as required but undermines the special educator's efforts to support the students, he or she is not collaborating in the sense outlined in this chapter. The professional relationship is constrained, the students are still in the classroom, and the special educator bears most responsibility for making accommodations. Alternatively, a professional unsure about inclusive practices can express anxiety and uncertainty, but that person may also work closely with others to support students with disabilities. In essence, education agencies can mandate administrative arrangements that require staff to work in close proximity, but only the individuals involved can decide if a collaborative style will be used in their interactions. In our work in schools, we frequently find ourselves emphasizing that there is no such thing as collaboration by coercion.

In today's school climate of high standards and accountability, collaboration is more important than ever before.

Does this mean that people *cannot* collaborate if programs are mandated? Not at all. Consider the situation at Jefferson High School, where classroom teachers have been notified that they will probably need to increase collaboration to support the growing number of students with disabilities who will be enrolling in their courses the next year. An algebra teacher might say, "I think there may be possibilities for student success in my classes, but I'm not sure about this. I'm worried that some of the students won't have the background to be successful here. I'm glad I'll have another teacher to work with as we try to make this work." The mandate is present, but so is the teacher's voluntariness to carry out the mandate, even though others may be voicing objections to it or ignoring it.

Collaboration Requires Parity among Participants

Parity is a situation in which each person's contribution to an interaction is equally valued, and each person has equal power in decision making; it is fundamental to collaboration. If one or several individuals are perceived by others as having significantly greater decision-making power or more valuable knowledge or information, collaboration cannot occur. To illustrate, think about a principal's participation on a multidisciplinary team. If the principal is considered to have equal, not disproportionately greater, power in the decision-making process, other team members may disagree with the principal's position, and the team's ultimate decision may be one the principal did not support. Without parity, it is likely that some team members will acquiesce to the principal's preferences because of concern about repercussions for disagreeing. Another example can provide further illustration: In an interdisciplinary teaching team, when one content-area (e.g., biology) teacher believes that another (e.g., English) does not have expertise to contribute to the instructional planning, parity is unlikely to develop. The characteristic of parity is very clear among the teachers introduced in the opening story about Kennedy Elementary School.

Keep in mind that individuals may have parity as they work together on a specific collaborative activity even though they do not have parity in other situations. For example, you may have parity in interactions with a paraprofessional to plan a community-based activity, but may interact directively and with appropriately greater authority and decision-making power when giving instructions to the same paraprofessional about working with students. Similarly, administrators and staff on a curriculum committee may have parity; outside of the committee, though, the relationship among the members may be markedly different.

Collaboration Is Based on Mutual Goals

Individuals who collaborate must share at least one goal. Imagine a meeting at which a decision must be reached about what specialized services a student should receive and the setting in which those services should be delivered. In one sense, the mutual goal of designing an appropriate education program seems to be obvious. In reality, however, at least two goals may be under consideration. The parents, social worker, and principal might think that the student should be in a general education setting for most of the day, whereas the special education teacher, classroom teacher, and psychologist might believe, because of professional literature they have read and their interactions with the student, that great care needs to be taken before there is any discussion of inclusion. In this case, a collaborative group will look at the greater goal of designing a program in the best interests of the student and will resolve their differences. In a group without a strong commitment to collaboration, the focus is likely to remain on the apparently disparate goals, and the matter may become contentious.

Professionals do not have to share many or all goals in order to collaborate, just one that is specific and important enough to maintain their shared commitment. They may differ in their opinions about a student's achievement potential, but share the goal of arranging convenient transportation for the student. Their differences can be set aside as not being essential to the immediate issue. They may agree that a student with multiple needs coming to the school should spend most of the school day with typical peers, but disagree about who should have primary teaching responsibility for the student and how appropriate supports should be arranged.

Collaboration Depends on Shared Responsibility for Participation and Decision Making

If you collaborate with a colleague, you are assuming the responsibility of actively engaging in the activity and the decision making it involves. We have found it useful to distinguish between responsibility for completing tasks associated with the collaborative activity and responsibility for the decision making involved in that activity. Shared participation in task completion does *not* imply that the individuals involved must divide tasks equally or participate fully in each task required to achieve their goal. In fact, participation in the activity often involves a convenient division of labor. For instance, as a speech and language therapist, you might collaborate with a kindergarten teacher to plan a series of language lessons for all the students. You volunteer to outline the concepts that should be addressed and to prepare several activities related to each. The teacher agrees to locate needed materials and to plan student groupings and instructional schedules for the lessons. In this case, you and the teacher are both actively participating in accomplishing the task, even though the division of labor may not be equal.

The second component of responsibility concerns *equal* participation in the critical decision making involved in the activity. In the example just described, you and the teacher had different responsibilities for the task, but to be collaborative you must participate equally in deciding the appropriateness of and possible needed modifications in the material you prepare, and you are equally responsible for deciding if the grouping and proposed schedule are workable.

Individuals Who Collaborate Share Resources

Each individual engaged in a collaborative activity has resources to contribute that are valuable for reaching the shared goal. The type of resources professionals have depends on their roles and the specific activity. Time and availability to carry out essential tasks may be the critical contribution that one person offers. Knowledge of a specialized technique may be another's resource. Access to other individuals or agencies that could assist in the collaborative activity may be a third person's contribution. If professionals cannot contribute a specific resource, they may be perceived as less serious about the collaborative goal, and they may encounter difficulty establishing parity.

For a different type of situation in which resources are shared, think of working with parents. For example, sharing resources often occurs when parents and school professionals collaboratively plan home reward programs for students. The parent is likely to have access to rewards to which the student responds (e.g., video games, computer access, special meals, access to a bicycle or car). The special services providers may be able to recommend the number of positive behaviors the student should display, the frequency of rewards, and the plan for systematically phasing out the rewards once success has been achieved. The program would not be possible without the contributions that everyone makes.

You may have found that sharing resources is sometimes the key motivator for individuals to collaborate. In fact, pooling the available—but too often scarce—resources in schools can lead to tremendously satisfying efforts on behalf of students; at the same time, it enhances the sense of ownership among the professionals. Unfortunately, the reverse also may occur: A scarcity of resources sometimes causes people to hoard the ones they control. Collaboration becomes unlikely when that happens. Ultimately, when resources are limited, the choice becomes this: Come together through collaboration and make the best of what is available, or fall apart as individuals compete to obtain resources that may even be inconsequential in terms of value.

Individuals Who Collaborate Share Accountability for Outcomes

Whether the results of collaboration are positive or negative, all the participating individuals are accountable for the outcome. Suppose you and several colleagues plan a parent information meeting. One person arranges for a room, another makes arrangements to provide coffee, and a third reserves a video and projector for the presentation. Shortly before the meeting is to begin, you realize that no one has remembered to pick up the video. In a collaborative effort, all the professionals share the resulting need to change the program at the last minute or to arrange to have someone dash to retrieve the video. Similarly, if a school leadership team is meeting to discuss the results of the evaluation data collected but one member has not finished compiling the results, the team is accountable for rescheduling the meeting date or for assisting the member aggregating the information.

A BASIS IN RESEARCH

Collaboration in Exemplary Schools

What are critical features of schools that foster high levels of achievement for all students? That question is an important one in an era of high standards and accountability, and it is one of the questions asked in the Beacons of Excellence project in which researchers from the University of Maryland studied six elementary and middle schools to determine factors that contributed to their success with students. Although not specifically studying the topic of collaboration, what these researchers found was that collaboration was a dominant feature of these schools.

Using a case study design, interviewing 12 special education teachers and 17 general education teachers and conducting focus groups with other educators, the researchers found that practices varied among schools but included these:

- Opportunities for collaborative planning with time devoted to this activity
- Co-teaching as part of the services available to students
- Informal collaboration and consultation
- Use of technology including voice mail and e-mail
- Strong leadership that included sharing decision making
- An overall culture of collaboration that included high levels of trust, high expectations for all students, and a sense of professional community

The researchers noted that their findings leave many related topics still to be explored. How are schools such as these different from schools that are not exemplary—is collaboration missing from those struggling schools? If an opportunity to delve more deeply into these schools' practices were possible, what would collaborative practices look like on a day-to-day basis? Perhaps most important, how can the collaborative features of these schools be described in a way that they can be applied in other schools?

Source: Adapted from E. A. Caron & M. J. McLaughlin, "Indicators of Beacons of Excellence schools: What do they tell us about collaborative practices?" *Journal of Educational and Psychological Consultation, 13* (2002): 285–313.

A second type of discussion of outcomes is important for today's professionals—that is, outcomes related to students. One question sometimes asked is whether collaboration makes a difference for students. The study described in A Basis in Research helps to address that question.

Emergent Characteristics

Several characteristics of collaboration can have multiple functions—they are mentioned both as prerequisites for as well as outcomes of collaboration. We refer to these as *emergent characteristics*. These characteristics must be present to some discernible degree at the outset of collaborative activity, but they typically grow and flourish from successful experience with collaboration. Additional specific ideas for fostering collaboration in schools are included in the following Putting Ideas into Practice.

Individuals Who Collaborate Value This Interpersonal Style

Collaboration is difficult but rewarding. Professionals who anticipate collaborating must believe that the results of their collaboration are likely to be more powerful and significant than the results of their individual efforts, or else they are unlikely to persevere. Typically, success in collaboration leads to increased commitment to future collaboration, and so beliefs and attitudes become increasingly positive. As a former graduate student once reported, "I used to work in a school where there was no collaboration. I worked very hard, but it was like beating my head against a wall. Now I work in a place where collaboration is the norm. I work even harder than I used to, but now it's fun." Individuals who collaborate truly believe that two (or even more) heads are better than one.

Professionals Who Collaborate Trust One Another

Even if you firmly believe in the beneficial outcomes of collaboration, you cannot suddenly introduce it, fully developed, into your professional interactions. If you recall your experiences as a new employee of a school district or agency, you probably remember experiencing a phase in which you learned about your colleagues, the norms of the school setting, and the manner in which to approach the other professionals with whom you worked most closely. And even though you interacted with other professionals during that time, the extent to which you could collaborate was limited. Only after a period of time in which trust and, subsequently, respect are established can school professionals feel relatively secure in fully exploring collaborative relationships. Once begun, however, those relationships may be strengthened until trust of colleagues becomes one of the most important benefits of collaboration. This scenario describes the emergence of trust: At the outset, enough trust must be present for professionals to be willing to begin the activity, but with successful experiences the trust grows. Conversely, trust is most fragile when a collaborative relationship is relatively new. If a colleague violates a shared confidence, fails to contribute to the activity, or communicates inaccurately, trust is likely to be damaged.

A Sense of Community Evolves from Collaboration

In collaboration, participants know that their strengths can be maximized, their weaknesses can be minimized, and the result will be better for all. The concept of community is receiving significant attention in contemporary professional literature (e.g., John-Steiner, 2000; Kronick, 2000; Wallace, Anderson, & Bartholomay, 2002). What is increasingly recognized is that the development of a

> **PUTTING IDEAS INTO PRACTICE**
>
> *Creating a Collaborative Culture*
>
> To what extent does your school have a collaborative culture? That is, to what extent are teachers encouraged to work collegially—by grade levels, instructional teams, teaching teams, and so on? Does collaboration extend to all school staff members, including related services providers, bilingual educators, and paraprofessionals? What happens if people disagree—is it a reason to end a discussion or an opportunity for building understanding? If you are trying to enhance the collaborative culture of your school, these activities could help build a strong foundation for it:
>
> 1. Work with your administrator or school leadership to schedule social activities for school staff. Friday morning treats that everyone gathers to share in the teachers' lounge, quarterly pitch-in lunches, or even occasional evening or weekend gatherings at someone's home or another location are examples of social events that encourage individuals to get to know each other better, thus laying the foundation for professional collaboration.
>
> 2. Try having professionals trade jobs for short periods of time so that everyone builds a better understanding of each other's roles and responsibilities. For example, a special educator might teach an eighth-grade English class while that teacher co-teaches a science class in which the special educator normally would be. This strategy often leads staff members to comment to one another, "Gee, you really work hard!" The increase in respect contributes to strong collaboration.
>
> 3. Suggest to your administrator or school leadership team that optional study groups be formed at school. Perhaps one group could address the general topic of collaboration while others find reading material on and discuss co-teaching, teaming, communication, and other pertinent topics. These groups could meet at lunch or before or after school, with the goal of clarifying ideas and looking for new strategies. The groups could then update other staff members by sending brief summary e-mail messages to the entire staff.
>
> 4. Work with your colleagues and administrator to create a plan for building a collaborative school culture. What is your overall goal (remembering that collaboration is never a goal in itself but rather the catalyst for achieving other goals)? What goals and activities might be appropriate for the current school year? Next year? What would you and your colleagues like to see happen over the next three years?

sense of professional community leads to better outcomes for students and satisfaction and support for educators (Mujis, Harris, Chapman, Stoll, & Russ, 2004). Perhaps you have experienced the sense of community in a faith-based, social, or student group. The willingness to work toward a common goal is accompanied by a decrease in concern about individual differences.

Taken together, these emergent characteristics highlight the opportunities you have and the risks you take when you begin to collaborate. You may attempt to establish trust and either succeed or be rebuffed; you may attempt to communicate an attitude supportive of collaboration and find that some but not others share your beliefs. Collaboration certainly is not easily accomplished, nor is it appropriate for every situation. More than anything, the emergent characteristics capture the powerful benefits of accepting the risks of collaboration. When collaborative efforts result in higher levels of trust and respect among colleagues and between professionals and parents/families, and working together results in more positive outcomes for students, the risks seem minor compared to the rewards.

The Dilemmas of Collaboration

Exploring the definition and characteristics of collaboration can lead to the impression that collaboration is unequivocally the best way to approach all of today's complex educational problems. However, a number of issues arise when school professionals attempt to establish collaborative relationships. These issues pertain to school structure, professional socialization, and logistics. You can explore other issues related to collaboration and possible solutions for addressing them by visiting websites such as those described in Putting Ideas into Practice on page 16.

School Structure

It has long been recognized that professionals in schools typically do their substantive work in isolation from others (e.g., Lortie, 1975; Pomson, 2005; Sarason, 1982), and this recognition and concern about its implications for the teaching profession continue even today (e.g., Milner & Hoy, 2003). This structure of professional isolation is contrary to the concept of collaboration, and its drawbacks are becoming clearer even as the pressure to create schools with a collaborative culture mounts. Within this physical isolation from other adults, each school professional sets about working with students. How do the professionals accomplish this? Essentially, they take charge. In their classrooms or offices, they are the experts who hold authority and power over students, and so they typically use a directive style to promote student learning, which is appropriate. However, constant use of this style with students may interfere with professionals' ability to switch to a collaborative style for interactions with colleagues and parents. As school leaders increasingly recognize the need to change school structure to foster collaboration, they should be aware of the companion need to facilitate constructive interactions among professionals.

Professional Socialization

Physical isolation and the use of a directive style with students are part of what contributes to the wide variation in emphasis on collegial relationships. However, a norm of isolation sometimes is still fostered through professional socialization. First, in some teacher and other professional preparation programs, you might discover that as you are successfully completing your student teaching,

PUTTING IDEAS INTO PRACTICE

Internet Resources for Collaboration

As most professionals know, the Internet is a tremendous source of information on almost any topic. Although only a few sites specifically address the professional collaboration that occurs among school staff members, the following sites include collaboration and pertinent related topics:

www.beachcenter.org

The Beach Center on Disability at the University of Kansas has as a goal working with all stakeholders to enhance the quality of life for individuals with disabilities and their families. This family-focused site contains many articles of interest and links to other sites emphasizing family collaboration.

http://teachnet.edb.utexas.edu/~Lynda_Abbott/teacher2teacher.html

Teacher-to-Teacher Collaboration is a website sponsored by the University of Texas. It includes links to sites that focus on assisting teachers to connect with and interact with one another. It also includes links to information about professional development, instructional matters, student behavior, and other topics of interest to educators.

http://ericec.org/faq/regsped.html

This ERIC document produced by the Council for Exceptional Children directs readers to topics that often include a collaboration component, including inclusive practices, multicultural education, and gifted education.

www.powerof2.org

Power of 2 is a website developed as part of a federally funded project to assist teachers and other educators to work together on behalf of students in inclusive schools. It includes a wide variety of material focused on accommodating the educational needs of students with disabilities.

www.middleweb.com

As you might guess, Middleweb is a website devoted to topics of interest to middle school educators. However, because collaboration is so integral to middle school models, you'll find many helpful resources on this site. Some recent discussions included collaborating about grades and considerations related to working on a team instead of as an individual.

One other suggestion: As you seek information related to collaboration and related topics, don't forget to check your own state department of education's website. Many have information that is practical and directly related to state policies as well as links to other valuable local and national sites.

practicum, or internship experiences, your supervisor leaves you alone to work with students. In other words, your professional training itself might encourage a belief that working in isolation is the role of the professional.

Second, this socialization of isolation may continue as you enter your profession and gain experience. Even for some teachers who participated in collaborative preparation programs, school cultures of independence or self-reliance are so strong that what evolves is a belief that you should handle your professional problems yourself. If you seek help, it is often only after you have decided that whatever is occurring is no longer your problem; your goal becomes seeking another to take ownership of it.

This discussion of structural isolation and individual characteristics of professionals in schools may leave the impression that collaboration is seldom likely in school settings. That certainly is not always the case, as was illustrated by the teachers from Kennedy Elementary introduced at the beginning of the chapter. In fact, we find that attention to collaboration in school clearly is increasing. We mention the issue of structural isolation only to raise your awareness of the difficulties in collaborating and to stress that even if you have learned about the importance of collaboration and embrace its value, you still may work with colleagues who do not. We also want to convey some of the resulting challenges that you will undoubtedly experience as you attempt to collaborate. These challenges are not unique to your specific school setting or professional relationships; they result from many factors that are part of all school professionals' experiences. Ultimately, these dilemmas provide the rationale for exploring the skills described later in the text because it is those skills that can enable school professionals to complement their other professional skills with collaborative ones.

Pragmatic Issues

When we described the defining characteristics of collaboration, we noted that resource sharing is essential, and we mentioned items such as time, space, and materials. We consider the topic of such pragmatic issues further in Chapter 7 with the extensive attention they merit; we mention the topic here just to acknowledge that pragmatic issues are another type of dilemma facing those who collaborate.

This discussion of the dilemmas that school structure, professional socialization, and pragmatic issues present for collaboration could have a somewhat sobering effect on your enthusiasm for it. In part, we hope this is so. Collaboration can be a powerful vehicle for accomplishing professionals' goals of educating students, but it can also be overused and misused. Collaborative efforts should be implemented only with a realistic understanding of their complexities and difficulties, because such understanding will lead to careful consideration of the extent to which collaborative efforts are feasible and recommended.

Collaboration in a Contemporary Context

How has collaboration come to be so important in special education that it is the subject of entire books and courses in professional preparation programs? What is fostering the development of so many collaborative structures in schools? Why is so much attention now devoted to the quality of the working relationships among professionals, paraprofessionals, and parents/families? What is occurring for students with special needs is simply a reflection of the direction of many endeavors in society and their application in education (Friend & Cook, 2004; Glazer, 2004; Lacey, 2001). By examining the larger context for collaboration, you can better understand its pervasiveness in today's world and its necessity for today's schools.

Societal Trends

Consider the world in which you now live. A valuable starting point is the arena of work: The vast majority of jobs available in the early twenty-first century are in service industries in which individuals interact with clients or customers to meet their needs (e.g., retail sales, telecommunications). This is a sharp contrast to preceding eras in which many workers toiled in isolation on assembly lines. Contemporary life also is characterized by an accelerated flow of information: People are inundated with it, whether through the Internet, the deluge of advertising that arrives each day, the seemingly endless array of television talk shows, or the stacks of publications that pile up, often unread, in many homes,

The growing significance of collaboration in education reflects its importance across many fields, including business and health services.

offices, and classrooms. Few individuals can hope to keep up with even the most crucial events occurring in their communities and their professions, much less throughout the world. Headline news programs and online summaries often have to suffice.

One response to the pressures of contemporary society's changing labor needs and its information explosion is an increasing reliance on collaboration (Nelson, 2001). For example, business managers, much more so now than in the past, are involving employees in decision making as a strategy for improving organizational effectiveness. Furthermore, employees report they find their jobs more satisfying if they participate in reaching decisions. Researchers agree that a sense of ownership and commitment appears to evolve through participation in such activity, and cutting-edge employers target team approaches that foster shared decision making as a major training topic for employees at many levels (Bassi & Van Buren, 1999; Hymowitz, 2006; Medved, 2001). All of these ideas, coming not from education but from business and industry, are directly related to collaboration.

Business is not the only domain in which collaboration is essential. In fact, collaboration seems to have become a standard for much that is worthwhile in contemporary professional culture. For example, Bennis and Biederman (1997), in their examination of the most significant innovations of the twentieth century, including the personal computer, aviation technology, and feature-length animated films, conclude that none of them would have been possible if not for a high degree of collaboration among very talented people. Fullan (2001) contends that the ability to bring people together to form professional relationships is a fundamental skill that enables leaders to help people develop commitment and tackle the exceedingly complex problems facing many disciplines, whether business management, industry, or computer or biological sciences.

Collaboration also has become increasingly important in the area of human services. For example, it is viewed as a means through which welfare, mental health, and other services can be more effectively provided to children and their families (Baum, 2003; Crow & Smith, 2003; Maurasse, 2004). In health care, collaboration is a means of bringing together medical and health care providers to integrate the delivery of services (Houser, 2005), a means of increasing the community's health (Institute of Medicine, 1996), a means of improving public health agency performance (Lovelace, 2000), and a means of improving services in intensive care (Orlovsky, 2005).

School Collaboration

Beginning with the premise that schools are a reflection of larger society, the current trend toward collaboration in the United States and around the world makes it quickly apparent why collaboration is such a significant trend in schools. Many examples of the trend are evident. For example, teachers are being asked to team with each other and with other school professionals, including media specialists, science consultants, literacy coaches, and speech/language therapists (Dole, 2004; Hadley, Simmerman, Long, & Luna, 2000; Kew, 2000). In all these efforts, the goal is to provide enhanced instruction to improve student learning, particularly in urban and rural areas. Middle school approaches are an especially interesting application of teacher–teacher collaboration (e.g., Achinstein, 2002; Clark & Clark, 2002) because they are premised on strong collaboration among teaching teams in core academic areas. Teachers in middle schools have regularly scheduled shared planning time so that they can integrate curricula, coordinate assignments and other major activities such as field trips, and discuss issues related to their shared students.

A second type of collaboration emphasized in the general school literature concerns school–university partnerships, often under the guise of school reform (Dallmer, 2004; Muchmore, Cooley, Marx, & Crowell, 2004). One common example of partnership for preprofessional preparation is a professional development school (PDS) model (Johnston, Tulbert, Sebastian, Devries, & Gompert, 2000; Leonard, Lovelace-Taylor, Sanford-DeShields, & Spearman, 2004) in which university faculty members work in school settings and school professionals serve as instructors in a highly collaborative manner to prepare future teachers. However, other partnerships also have formed, including the infusing of technology into K–12 settings (Sherry & Chiero, 2004), the creation of high school–community college dual enrollment programs (Gomez, 2001), and the development of strong and constructive relationships among school counselors, administrators, teachers, and families (Amatea, Daniels, Bringman, & Vandiver, 2004).

A third type of general school collaboration receiving renewed attention is peer collaboration. Researchers are finding that when students work with partners on various instructional tasks, they generally learn more than if they had worked alone (e.g., Samaha & DeLisi, 2000). Further, professionals have come to value peer interactions as a means of preparing students for their likely roles in the world of work (e.g., Van Meter & Stevens, 2000).

Finally, collaboration has not been ignored by school administrators. Principals are forming school leadership teams and collegial work groups to share decision making on critical school issues (Wesson & Kudlacz, 2000). They also are working collaboratively with teachers to help them set professional goals for each year and to make judgments about their schools' reform efforts (e.g., Johnson, 2004). They are emphasizing that teachers work with each other to solve problems about students experiencing difficulty, to establish and assess academic standards, and to create positive working relationships with parents and family members. School as a collaborative community of learners is now a consistent theme for administrators.

Special Education Collaboration

Although special education collaboration might be considered a subset of school collaboration, it has such a rich history and has become so much a part of policy and practice that it merits separate attention. For example, even before the first federal special education law was passed in 1975, special educators were providing indirect services to students with disabilities by working with their general

Teachers' informal collaboration is valuable, but schools also need to have in place more formal structures and procedures for collaboration.

education teachers in a model called *consulting teaching* (McKenzie, 1972). Likewise, school psychologists had long been urged to multiply their impact by helping teachers who could then better address the learning and behavior problems of several students (Tharp & Wetzel, 1969). Then, when P.L. 94-142 became law, collaboration was firmly integrated into special education with the provisions of parent participation and the mandate for the least restrictive environment. With each revision of special education law, the place of collaboration has been strengthened. In fact, the 2004 reauthorization of IDEA has, in essence, made collaboration a required part of special education services. As shown in Figure 1.2, collaboration either is mandated specifically or strongly implied in the entire process of identifying students who receive special services, delivering their instruction, and interacting with parents.

Unfortunately, considerable confusion has accompanied the evolution of collaboration in special education, especially since the increasing adoption of inclusive practices. For example, in some schools the terms *collaboration* and *inclusion* are used interchangeably, even though one is a style of interaction and the other is the belief system that creates a foundation for how students are educated. In others, collaboration is considered a way to deliver services, often confused with co-teaching, a service delivery approach that is discussed in detail in Chapter 5.

A discussion of special education collaboration would not be complete without mention of early childhood programs, where collaboration generally is integral (e.g., Hunt, Soto, Maier, Liboiron, & Bae, 2004). For example, early intervention services are based on the beliefs that parents or other caregivers are the primary teachers of young children and that professionals can foster their

---

Figure 1.2 Direct and Indirect Expectations of Collaboration in IDEA-04

- *IEP teams.* As has been true since federal special education law was first passed, each student's educational program must be designd by an IEP team that includes special education and general education professionals as well as parents. You should be aware, though, that parents may decide that a team member (e.g., the general education teacher) need not be present.

- *Least restrictive environment.* The law presumes that students should receive education in a general education setting, and it requires justification for any placement that is not general education. This presumption strongly suggests that classroom teachers and special educators will need to work together on behalf of students.

- *Highly qualified teacher requirement.* Special educators who teach core academic content (e.g., math, social studies, science, English) to students not taking alternate assessments must be highly qualified in those areas. However, if a highly qualified general education teacher and a special educator share teaching responsibilities, the special educator may not have to have the content area licensure. This requirement of the law can foster collaborative service delivery.

- *Assessment process.* Parents are integral to the assessment process. They must give permission for their children to be assessed, and they also must have a voice in the decision making that occurs as a result of assessment. Even more communication responsibility occurs when students are reevaluated. Because a decision may be made in some cases to omit standardized testing, parent involvement in decision making is even more critical.

- *Transition.* Because transition must be addressed for students beginning at age 16, strong collaboration is necessary and should involve students as well as parents. Further, transition plans often require the involvement of professionals from other agencies, and so interprofessional collaboration may be required.

- *Discipline and behavior support plans.* For any student with behavior problems, a functional assessment and behavior support plan is required. The process of gathering data, identifying the problem, designing alternative interventions, implementing them, and evaluating the outcomes typically will include participation by several professionals, paraprofessionals, and parents/family members.

- *Paraprofessionals.* Paraprofessionals, teaching assistants, and other individuals in similar roles should receive appropriate training for their jobs and supervision of their work. Although not all interactions with paraprofessionals may be collaborative, the specific expectation for teacher–paraprofessional interactions can foster collaboration.

- *Mediation and dispute resolution.* Unless declined by parents, states must make no-cost mediation available to parents as a strategy for resolving disagreements concerning their children with special needs. Further, and new in IDEA-04, prior to a due process hearing, the district must convene the IEP team members and parents in an attempt to informally resolve the dispute. The implication is that a strong bias exists for all parties, working together on behalf of students, to design the most appropriate education rather than escalating conflicts.

---

participation through collaboration. Further, early intervention programs are mandated to coordinate services among all providers (e.g., educators, social service agencies, medical professionals), and this mandate exists within a context of collaboration (Fowler, Donegan, Lueke, Hadden, & Phillips, 2000). Although

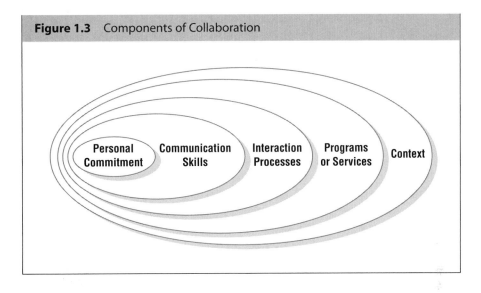

Figure 1.3   Components of Collaboration

Personal Commitment | Communication Skills | Interaction Processes | Programs or Services | Context

you will learn more about collaboration in early childhood special education in Chapter 12, for now you should realize that many professionals point to this area when seeking exemplary practices in school collaboration.

A Framework for Learning about Collaboration

The importance of collaboration in society, schools, and special education forms a rationale for focusing on the study of it. The complexity and subtlety of collaboration (Friend, 2000) suggest that in order to learn to form effective partnerships with others, you should strive for as complete an understanding of collaboration as possible. To accomplish this purpose, we offer a framework for learning about collaboration in Figure 1.3 that presents the components of collaboration and their relationships to one another. This framework shapes the material presented in this textbook as well as its organization, and you will find that each chapter opens with a graphic to remind you which part of the framework is addressed in that chapter.

The first component of the study of collaboration concerns your *personal commitment* to collaboration as a tool for carrying out the responsibilities of your job, including your beliefs about the benefits of working closely with colleagues and parents/families and the added value of learning from others' perspectives. Although it is difficult to offer specific skill training related to this commitment and no chapter is devoted solely to this component of collaboration, you will find that throughout this textbook you are asked to reflect on the importance of and merit in collaborating with others. For example, the teachers introduced at the beginning of the chapter demonstrated in the discussions they held that they were committed to their collaborative efforts.

The second component of collaboration is *communication skills*, the basic building blocks of collaborative interactions. Although most educators have relatively strong communication skills in order to be in their professions, the skills needed for collaboration are somewhat more technical and are best learned with extended practice. In addition, most educators need to consider their communication skills in the context of working with colleagues and parents from diverse cultures. For this reason, Chapters 8, 9, and 10 outline those skills, provide many examples of their uses (and misuses), and offer opportunities to practice them. The assumption is that you will use these skills to implement the services that you learned about in other chapters.

The third component of collaboration includes *interaction processes*—that is, the steps that take an interaction from beginning to end. The most common interaction process is problem solving, and because many special education services are actually specialized forms of problem solving, that topic is addressed in Chapter 2 and referred to later in the chapters on teaming and consultation. Other processes include responding to conflict and resistance, topics addressed in Chapter 11. For all interaction processes, strong communication skills are essential.

The fourth component of collaboration is the set of *programs* or *services* in which collaborative activities occur. In this textbook, the services emphasized include teams (Chapter 3), consultation (Chapter 4), and co-teaching (Chapter 5). It is within these services that interaction processes to design and deliver student services occur.

The final component of collaboration is *context*, which refers to the overall environment in which collaboration occurs. Because people so often are critical in determining the climate for collaboration, special attention is given in this book to parents, paraprofessionals, and others (e.g., related services personnel and administrators) in Chapters 6 and 12. Pragmatic issues (Chapter 7) and issues related to collaboration, such as ethics (Chapter 12), complete this part of the framework.

As with any textbook, some topics cannot be adequately addressed. For example, although mention is made of peer collaboration, the emphasis here is on adult–adult interactions, and so student partnerships are not prioritized. Likewise, even though professionals often collaborate around designing and implementing academic and behavior interventions for students, those topics merit separate attention; we believe that attempting to address collaboration as well as instructional and behavioral strategies in one textbook does a disservice to both.

Summary

Collaboration is an interpersonal style that professionals may use in their interactions with colleagues, parents, and others. It can only exist voluntarily in situations in which individuals with parity have identified a mutual goal and are willing to share responsibility for key decisions, accountability for outcomes, and resources. Several characteristics of collaboration both contribute to its development and are potentially its outcomes: attitudes and beliefs supportive of a collaborative approach, mutual trust, and a sense of community. However, individuals who collaborate also may find that dilemmas occur related to the structural and professional isolation of schools, professional socialization, and practical matters concerning resources such as time. Collaboration in the realm of special services can be placed in a historical context. Further, it is a reflection of contemporary societal trends that are, in turn, being mirrored in schools through legislation and related reform efforts, including various forms of teaming and inclusive practices. Studying collaboration includes understanding your personal commitment, learning communication skills and interaction processes, creating programs and services in which collaborative approaches can be used, and recognizing context factors that foster or constrain collaboration.

Activities and Assignments

1. You probably have learned about the No Child Left Behind Act of 2001 (NCLB) in several courses. What provisions of this law might foster or impede collaboration? What is the rationale for your responses? How does the 2004 reauthorization of IDEA contribute to or detract from collaboration as promoted in NCLB?

2. Peruse recent issues of popular news magazines. What examples of societal collaboration are addressed? What universal themes can you identify related to the advantages and disadvantages of collaboration from these materials? How might current trends in collaboration in business, social services, and other disciplines affect school collaboration in the future?

3. Working with class members as teammates, explore the relationship between collaboration and outcomes for students by reading in the professional literature. What evidence of a relationship can you find? Why do researchers find it challenging to demonstrate the impact of collaboration on student outcomes?

4. How is collaboration being addressed in other university coursework you are taking? What collaborative activities (e.g., teaming, consultation) are most emphasized? If you have a colleague in a business program, compare your experiences, courses, and learning requirements on topics related to collaboration. How are they similar? How are they different?

5. Brainstorm a list with your classmates of all the different types of collaboration that you have witnessed or experienced in schools. Select one example and use it as the basis for analyzing the extent to which the defining characteristics of collaboration are present or could be established in each situation. Which characteristics can most easily be met? Which may pose significant barriers to developing effective collaborative relationships?

6. Discuss the issue of parity with a group of classroom teachers. To what extent do they perceive that they have equal status with special services providers? How could issues related to parity be addressed? Repeat your discussion of parity with

others who have roles similar to yours. How do their views about teachers' and special services providers' parity compare to those of the classroom teachers?

7. Suppose you are a new special education teacher in a school in which collaboration occurs informally among some teachers, but is not a highly valued part of the school's culture. Further, imagine that the school has received a mandate to move strongly toward inclusive practices. As a special educator, what do you believe your role is in accomplishing the dual goals of collaboration and inclusive practices? How might you use Figure 1.3 to analyze the steps that should be taken and to discuss them with your administrator?

8. If you have worked in a setting in which collaboration was valued and encouraged, write a summary of your experience. Use this as the basis for a discussion with others to generate specific examples of the characteristics of collaboration.

9. If collaboration was easy, it undoubtedly would be an integral part of every school initiative—but it is not. What makes collaboration difficult? Which of these barriers might be overcome by teachers and other professionals? Which by principals and other site administrators? Which by central office personnel? Are any of the barriers external to schools? How might these be overcome?

10. Complete an analysis of your preparation for school collaboration. On one sheet of paper, list courses, experiences, and activities you have had that have contributed to your professional socialization *for* working collaboratively. On another sheet, list the courses, experiences, and activities you have had that could *interfere* with a positive belief about collaboration. Write a reflective essay in which you assess your readiness for this crucial dimension of your professional responsibilities.

For Further Reading

Adkins, A., Awsumb, C., Noblit, G. W., & Richards, P. L. (1999). *Working together? Grounded perspectives on interagency collaboration.* Cresskill, NJ: Hampton Press.

Bennis, W., & Biederman, P. W. (1997). *Organizing genius: The secrets of creative collaboration.* Reading, MA: Addison-Wesley.

Burrello, L. C., Lashley, C., & Beatty, E. E. (2001). *Educating all students together: How school leaders create unified systems.* Thousand Oaks, CA: Corwin.

Chrispeels, J. H. (Ed.). (2004). *Learning to lead together: The promise and challenge of sharing leadership.* Thousand Oaks, CA: Corwin.

Congress, E. P., & Gonzalez, M. J. (2005). *Multicultural perspectives in working with families* (2nd ed.). New York: Springer.

Fishbaugh, M. S. E. (2000). *The collaboration guide for early career educators.* Baltimore: Brookes.

Friend, M., & Bursuck, W. (2006). *Including students with special needs: A practical guide for classroom teachers* (4th ed.). Boston: Allyn & Bacon.

Mattessich, P. W., Murray-Close, M., & Monsey, B. R. (2001). *Collaboration—What makes it work: A review of research literature on factors influencing successful collaboration* (2nd ed.). St. Paul, MN: Amherst H. Wilder Foundation.

Interpersonal Problem Solving

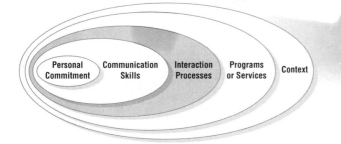

Connections

Chapter 2 presents interpersonal problem solving as the most commonly used interaction process through which professionals in education as well as other disciplines collaborate. It is a gateway to the remainder of this book since shared problem solving is at the heart of programs and services such as teaming (Chapter 3), consultation (Chapter 4), and co-teaching (Chapter 5). It also is a key context in which communication skills, the topic of Chapters 8, 9, and 10, are put to effective use. And, of course, problem solving is essential during difficult or awkward interactions, the focus for Chapter 11.

Learner Objectives

After reading this chapter you will be able to:

1. Identify three types of problems you may encounter in your professional role that would appropriately be addressed through interpersonal problem solving.
2. Distinguish between reactive and proactive approaches to problem solving.
3. Balance the potential value of interpersonal problem solving in terms of improved solutions with the possible costs of time and personnel resources.
4. Assess whether any specific professional problem you or your colleagues face is likely to be resolved through interpersonal problem solving.
5. State and carry out the steps in a systematic interpersonal problem-solving sequence with colleagues, other professionals, and parents or family members.

     6. Identify at least two strategies for facilitating each problem-solving step and note situations in which each might be useful.

Amanda is a freshman in high school. During the first grading period, she has been referred to the office a total of eight times for behavior issues; six of the referrals have been from her English class. Today, a meeting is being held to discuss this situation and to identify some proactive steps to head off what is developing into a chronic problem. Amanda's grandmother Ms. Palmer, her legal guardian, is present. Also attending are Ms. Ortiz, the English teacher; Mr. Burns, special educator; and Ms. Kobe, Amanda's counselor. The plan is to have this preliminary meeting prior to including Amanda in the discussion. After introductions and a brief discussion of Amanda's accomplishments thus far in high school, Ms. Kobe raises the issue of the behavior referrals. Ms. Ortiz expresses her dismay since she prides herself on understanding teenagers and seldom finds it necessary to resort to discipline referrals. As the conversation continues, Ms. Palmer notes how challenging the transition to high school has been for Amanda, particularly given the difficulty she has with reading. Mr. Burns suggests that they think carefully about when the discipline problems are occurring to see if they can discern a pattern—and they eventually conclude that Amanda might be disruptive in order to get out of difficult class assignments or other activities that are threatening to her. With this agreement, the problem-solving focus turns to generating ideas for helping Amanda to be successful in class while expressing her frustration or fear in more acceptable ways. After a discussion with Amanda, with an agreement between Mr. Burns and Ms. Ortiz to negotiate a behavior contract with her, and a follow-up phone call scheduled with Ms. Palmer, the meeting adjourns.

Introduction

Nearly all of the professional tasks and activities for which you are responsible can be conceptualized as some type of challenge or problem to be addressed. Many, many times each day you act essentially alone to solve problems or make decisions. You do this when you decide which intervention, therapeutic technique, or equipment would be best used with particular students. You also independently problem solve when you reallocate time in order to accommodate a disruption in your day's plan, when you design (and redesign) your schedule, and when you set priorities for supplies you need for the next school year. You also problem solve as you decide how to ask your administrator for a schedule change and how to approach parents who sometimes do not respond well to conversations focused on concerns related to their children.

Increasingly in school settings, though, you share responsibility for problem solving with others. This is referred to as *interpersonal* or *group problem solving*. Examples of interpersonal problem solving in special services are many: The team meetings you attend to determine the appropriate placement for students are interpersonal problem-solving activities, as are your planning sessions with specific colleagues to discuss how to adapt instruction to meet students' needs. These examples represent two very different contexts for interpersonal problem solving, one fairly broad and involving many people, the other quite specific and involving only two people. Even the other processes in which you are likely to engage with colleagues or parents (e.g., meeting as a committee, interviewing, conferencing) often are specialized applications of interpersonal problem solving. A single set of principles applies to the entire range of problem-solving activities you undertake with others, and that set of principles is the focus of this chapter.

Interpersonal problem solving is perhaps the most fundamental component of successful interactions. In fact, we are convinced that it is virtually impossible to collaborate with colleagues and parents without systematically and effectively employing an interpersonal problem-solving process, and the centrality of problem solving to contemporary society is illustrated by the attention it receives in a wide variety of professions, including business, health, psychology, and economics (e.g., Charney, 2004; DeJong & Berg, 2002; Marengo & Dosi, 2005; Norwood, 2003). However, a dilemma often occurs when educators problem solve: School professionals spend so much time problem solving by themselves that they sometimes presume that they already have the skills for problem solving with others. What is essential to realize is that group problem solving requires all the skills of problem solving alone as well as additional skills for going through this process with others (Chiu, 2000).

A Context for Interpersonal Problem Solving

Before turning to the steps in the interpersonal problem-solving process, it is important to examine concepts related to understanding problem characteristics in order to set the problem-solving context. Analyze these three interactions:

> **Speech/language therapist:** At our last meeting we discussed whether we should start working with Jason on using voice recognition software. Jason and his parents agree that this would help him immensely with his school assignments. Jason is eager to get started.
>
> **Inclusion facilitator:** Do we have the most current version of that software and a computer that Jason can have access to all day?
>
> **Teacher:** What do I need to learn if Jason is going to be using this software?
>
> **Principal:** Maybe we should make a list of what needs to be done and questions that we have.

> **Teacher 1:** I don't know how I'm going to get a schedule that I can live with this year. I'm supposed to get to three different classrooms for co-teaching, and I just don't see how to do it and still see the students as necessary in the resource room.
>
> **Teacher 2:** I know what you mean. The flexible services for kids are great, but I'm not sure I can handle what it does to *my* life!

Teacher 1: Let's start with the "givens." One of us has to be available to cover the English classes during first and second hour since so many students with IEPs are in those classes.

Teacher 2: And we promised that at least one of us would be free to meet with teachers during fourth-hour lunch.

Teacher 1: Let's block these things out on the master schedule.

Principal: We've taken many positive steps toward ensuring that our students are educated with their peers in general education classes whenever possible, but we've also decided that we're encountering some dilemmas and that we should make some refinements for next year.

General education teacher: For one thing, we really need to look at how much support classroom teachers are receiving. Some of the students have very challenging behaviors. Teachers would appreciate more opportunities to brainstorm ideas about supporting students without disrupting instruction. It would be even better if we could increase co-teaching time, but that would require more personnel.

Special education teacher: From the special education perspective, I'd like to see us discuss how to set priorities. Sometimes I feel like I'm being pulled in so many directions that I'm not accomplishing what is really necessary to support the students. My schedule was so full by last November that I was trying to see students during my lunch break.

Principal: That's a problem. You need your break. I'm also wondering how we could make better use of paraprofessionals and our grandparent and high school volunteers to provide more support in classrooms.

Although we will address in detail the topic of problem identification in the next section, it is clear that the situation addressed in the first interaction illustrates a straightforward, *well-defined problem:* identifying specific actions to help a student use assistive technology. The primary task is to list the actions and then ensure that they are initiated. Well-defined problems usually are fairly easily identified and understood. Difficulties in solving them often are the result of overlooking necessary solutions or encountering obstacles in implementing the solutions (e.g., the computer malfunctions). This type of problem generally can be readily understood by all involved and adequately addressed.

In the second interaction, the problem is somewhat more complex. The teachers have identified the problem situation as arranging their schedules, but no clear-cut single solution is apparent. Instead, they are working within a set of factors that have to be accommodated (e.g., the need to "cover" English classes and to have someone available during lunch). This is a *partially defined problem,* in which the goal is clear and some guidelines exist for addressing the goal, but the specific means for reaching it are varied. The problem could have multiple solutions, but the range is constrained by a set of external factors. Partially defined problems typically are not difficult to identify. Resolving them depends on the potential for successfully implementing any of several possible solutions.

The third interaction is the most complex. The problem is identified as a need to refine the programs and services in a school adhering to an inclusive belief system. What types of refinements are necessary to improve student learning? What are reasonable expectations for teachers and other staff for support? What resources are necessary to take the programs and services to the next level? How should decisions be made regarding the distribution of resources? The options for specifying and accomplishing the broad goal of increased inclusiveness are nearly infinite. This is an illustration of an *ill-defined problem*. It does not have clear parameters, nor is it easily resolved.

Although you undoubtedly address all three types of problems in your role as a professional educator, ill-defined problems probably occupy a significant portion of your time. Much of the complexity of collaborating to provide services to students is related to the number of ill-defined problems that must be addressed. The steps for problem solving outlined in the next section are valid for the first two types of problems, but they are especially critical for successfully addressing ill-defined ones.

Reactive and Proactive Problem Solving

Another dimension on which problem solving may vary is the urgency of the problem-solving activity. In *reactive problem solving*, you are faced with responding to a crisis or dilemma that requires attention and action in a relatively brief time frame. Some event occurs that focuses your attention on a matter to be resolved.

When professionals are faced with complex situations, collaborating with others in shared problem solving often can lead to effective solutions.

Examples of this type of situation might include the interactions you have with a parent concerning a sudden change in student behavior, a meeting between you and a teacher to adapt classroom materials to be more appropriate for a given student, and a conference among all the members of an intervention assistance team to generate strategies to enable a student with a significant disability to succeed in class. Much interpersonal problem solving in schools is reactive.

Conversely, in *proactive problem solving* an anticipated situation focuses your attention and triggers the problem-solving process before a crisis occurs. For example, in the first interaction described on page 29, proactive problem solving is illustrated: Members of a team are anticipating challenging areas for integrating Jason *before* dilemmas occur. Other illustrations of proactive problem solving include planning educational services for a student who has just transferred into the school from an out-of-state location, arranging the strategies for helping a student with autism transition from homeroom to his first-period class, and deciding how best to use staff time for the next school year given anticipated student enrollment and students' special needs.

Using a systematic approach for problem solving is beneficial in addressing both proactive and reactive problems. In fact, one benefit of following specific steps in problem solving is that less time may eventually be required for resolving reactive problems, so more proactive problem solving is possible.

Deciding Whether to Problem Solve

In addition to understanding the type of problem to be solved collaboratively and knowing whether the process will be reactive or proactive, you and your colleagues are faced with a crucial question prior to beginning problem solving: Is this a problem we should solve? Your immediate answer to this question might be "Of course—it's our job!" But that thinking is why special services personnel sometimes repeatedly discuss the same problem without progress. It is also one of the reasons why time is at such a premium for special services providers. The belief that any ill-defined problem, proactive or reactive, *must* be solved if it pertains to a student with special needs undoubtedly arises out of the professional socialization factors discussed in Chapter 1. Although laudable, it should be balanced by an analysis of the realities of the immediate situation.

Before even considering whether you should undertake problem solving with a colleague or group of colleagues, you should first consider the circumstances from the point of view of your own involvement. For example, you can reflect on whether the problem is one that you should even be involved in solving. If a student with a Section 504 plan is experiencing difficulties in class, you might provide limited assistance to the teacher. However, you also might need to clarify that you do not have time for a lengthy problem-solving process, given the needs of students with IEPs you are responsible for serving. Another consideration is whether a *collaborative* approach to problem solving is indicated. If you are an occupational therapist meeting with a group of teachers to develop fine-motor activities for students in inclusive classrooms, you are likely to provide technical assistance and use a somewhat directive style. This may be more efficient and effective than collaboratively problem solving.

After you consider your own role in the problem-solving situation, you can turn your attention to factors that affect problem solving with colleagues. These are questions to ask yourself as you encounter a problem that you and others are being asked to resolve:

1. Are the persons who have responsibility and resources for addressing the problem committed to resolving it?
2. What might happen if nothing is done to resolve the problem?
3. Are adequate time and resources available to resolve the problem?
4. Does the problem merit the effort and resources required to make significant change?

Combined, the answers to these questions can help you decide whether undertaking collaborative problem solving is warranted. In some cases, the information will lead you to an affirmative decision: Perhaps you are not familiar enough with the situation to make judgments about the impact of not addressing the problem. Or perhaps the individuals involved have expressed a strong commitment to tackle the problem. On the other hand, sometimes the answers to these questions lead you to a negative decision: Perhaps the people who would be key in addressing the problem do not have adequate time to devote to it. Or perhaps the problem—although affecting a student, a program, or some other aspect of the school setting—is beyond the control of the people interested in addressing it and therefore not a constructive use of staff time. The problem-solving situation described at the beginning of this chapter is one that meets the criteria for shared problem solving: The participants are committed to addressing the matter, not dealing with the problem is likely to lead to further discipline issues for Amanda, time and resources can be found, and overall, the problem seems to merit an intervention. If Amanda's behavior difficulties had been ascribed to a change in medication, the need for shared problem solving would have been diminished—a referral to her pediatrician would have been an immediate step to take. In Putting Ideas into Practice on page 34, other suggestions are outlined for what to do when interpersonal problem solving does not seem justified.

In addition to enabling you to assess the feasibility of problem solving, these preliminary questions also help you assess the possibility of collaborating to problem solve. The questions can alert you to participants' beliefs that there are probably many "right" solutions for this or any problem and that group problem solving and decision making are the preferred approaches for this situation. These are applications of the emergent characteristics of collaboration described in Chapter 1.

Because your judgment about whether to problem solve is based on preliminary information, throughout problem solving you should continually reassess the appropriateness of your decision. At any point in the process you may find

PUTTING IDEAS INTO PRACTICE

When Problem Solving Is Not the Best Approach

What should you do if a problem is not appropriate for you and your colleagues to address? The following are options that you could consider:

■ In some cases, the group members should try to reconceptualize the problem so that it becomes appropriate for them to address. For example, instead of focusing on the difficulty of implementing inclusive practices without additional staff members, a group might instead examine how to prioritize in-class services given the current resources.

■ Sometimes, changing some of the members of the problem-solving group is helpful. Perhaps the reason the problem was not considered appropriate was because of specific member perceptions. Often, it can be helpful to bring in someone who can view the situation with a "fresh eye"—that is, without extensive background knowledge that might be shaping others' opinions.

■ If an issue is significant, but not worth the time of a problem-solving team, perhaps one member should take responsibility for following up on the situation. The idea that Amanda, mentioned earlier in this chapter, has had a change in medication is an example of this type of situation. By having one person keep in touch with the parent as the medication is adjusted, time is saved but important information is available if needed by the team.

■ If a problem is not appropriate for a team, it might be because directive or supervisory action is needed, as opposed to a collaborative process. When this occurs, the problem should be referred to the principal, special education supervisor, or another administrator. Examples of problems in this arena sometimes include student schedules, teachers reluctant to work together in a classroom, and strong concerns expressed by a parent about a particular teacher.

■ If problem-solving team members are concerned about tabling a problem situation, a group member should keep records of such actions. That individual can then prompt the group to review such situations periodically. This might occur when a group of teachers meets as a grade-level or middle school team—in other words, when the formal record keeping of prereferral meetings is not typical.

■ Occasionally, a problem situation needs to be brought to the attention of a professional or group outside the problem-solving team. For example, if a student does not get adequate clothing at home, a church or social services group might be able to help.

that someone has lost commitment to solving the problem, that the problem is no longer within the control of the persons addressing it, or that the problem is no longer significant. If any of these situations occurs, you may want to reconsider your initial decision to address it.

Steps in Interpersonal Problem Solving

Once you and your colleagues have determined that you can and should address a given problem and that necessary conditions are in place for successful collaborative problem solving, you are ready to begin the problem-solving process. The steps for interpersonal problem solving have been described by many authors (e.g., Fishbaugh, 2000; Pugach & Johnson, 2002; Robson, 2002; Snell & Janney, 2000b), and although the steps seem straightforward, their complexity lies in skillful implementation (Erchul, 2003; Staw, 2004).

The steps and critical questions associated with each are outlined in Figure 2.1. Although this figure can seem daunting at first, if you look at it carefully as an organizer for understanding problem solving and review frequently the explanations of the steps you will find that it is a clear and accurate guide to the process of interpersonal problem solving. It clarifies how the process should be implemented, and it offers strategies for revisiting steps and correcting errors or misunderstandings that might occur. Each problem-solving step is explained in greater detail in the following sections.

Identifying the Problem

When special services providers are asked to list the steps for interpersonal problem solving, they nearly always correctly specify at least the first one: identifying the problem. However, in working with school professionals, we have learned that this step is far more easily recognized than implemented. Problem identification is difficult to accomplish, a point illustrated in A Basis in Research on page 37, and often is made even more so when the problem is ill-defined or the number of participants in interpersonal problem solving increases.

Not surprisingly, research supports the fact that problem identification is the most critical step in problem solving (Jayanthi & Friend, 1992; Nezu & D'Zurilla, 1981; Welch & Tulbert, 2000) and that the rest of the process can be successful only if the problem is accurately delineated (Brightman, 2002). We also find that phrasing problems as questions is a successful means of encouraging constructive problem identification. Phrasing problems as questions conveys to participants that "answers" are possible and lends a constructive tone to collaborative problem solving. Problems worded as statements are more likely to be seen as insurmountable. For example, instead of stating a problem as "Roger does not turn in his homework assignments," phrasing that emphasizes the negative, wording it as "How can we increase the rate at which Roger turns in his homework?" suggests that positive actions and outcomes will occur. This question-wording approach to stating problems is followed throughout this chapter.

Characteristics of Well-Identified Problems

When you identify problems, the issue may be as specific as addressing a student behavior problem (e.g., What strategies could be implemented to increase

Figure 2.1   Model for Interpersonal Problem Solving

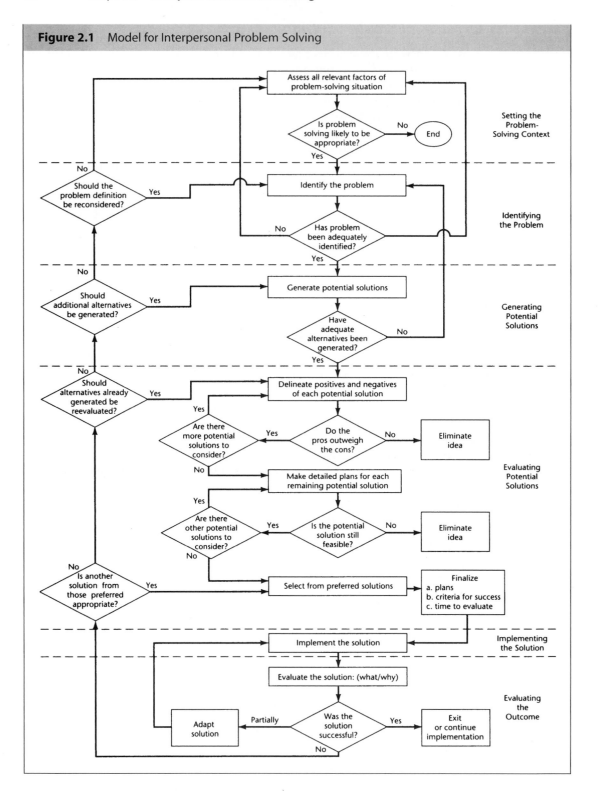

A BASIS IN RESEARCH

Understanding How Bias May Occur in Interpersonal Problem Solving

You might assume that if professionals follow a carefully prescribed problem-solving process that their description of the problem, analysis of its cause, selection of interventions, and judgment about intervention effectiveness would be fair and objective. A year-long study completed by Knotek (2003) suggests that this may not always be the case.

Knotek used a research method called *microethnography* in which he attended and participated in at least 20 meetings of prereferral teams in each of two elementary schools in a school district in which many students lived in poverty and approximately two-thirds of the students were African American. Examining transcripts of audiotapes of all the meetings, field notes taken during the meetings, notes from interviews, and other documents related to the problem solving on these teams, Knotek identified several themes that included these biases:

- When a general education teacher began team discussion with a generally negative perspective, often referring to student traits rather than specific skills (e.g., he just has a bad attitude), the team usually supported that view.

- Students who were referred for intervention because of behavior problems were inevitably referred for special education assessment. Knotek found that the team tended to confirm that what the general education teacher had done to support the student indeed had failed and that no other interventions would be successful.

- The learning or behavior problems of referred students who lived in poverty typically were attributed to their socioeconomic status, and alternative conceptualizations and interventions were very limited. Professionals sometimes mentioned having taught or known the students' parents or other family members, offering that knowledge as evidence of the inevitability of the students experiencing difficulty in school.

Knotek discussed his findings in terms of the social processes at work when groups problem solve. He noted that professionals may support a teacher's perception of a student because they have an interpersonal relationship with that teacher, and he described how high-status members in groups (e.g., principals and psychologists) can strongly influence the group's conversations and conclusions.

Source: Based on S. Knotek, "Bias in problem solving and the social process of student study teams: A qualitative investigation." *Journal of Special Education, 37* (2003): 2–15.

Jeff's appropriate play with other students on the playground?) or as broad as designing approaches for integrating students with disabilities (e.g., In what ways might we make our school more inclusive for all students, those with disabilities as well as those with other special needs?). Regardless of the scope of the problem, it should have the following set of characteristics.

An Identifiable Discrepancy Exists between Current and Desired Situations

In interpersonal problem solving, you should state the problem clearly enough so that the discrepancy between the current situation and the desired situation is apparent. For example, in a situation concerning a student's inappropriate classroom behavior, a description of the current conditions might focus on how often, for how long, and at what intensity the behavior is occurring. The desired situation might be the specification of appropriate behavior expectations for the classroom, using the same types of detail. In problem solving concerning a team's intent to plan a staff development program, the current situation might include information regarding the staff's knowledge about a topic of concern; the desired situation might be a description of the knowledge required for proficiency to be demonstrated.

Participants Share the Perception That the Problem Exists

For interpersonal problem solving to occur, all participants need to share recognition of a specific problem (Brightman, 2002). This is directly related to the concept of a mutual goal, which was presented as a defining characteristic of collaboration in Chapter 1. If a special education teacher is dissatisfied with the progress a student is making in a general education class, but the teacher in that class believes progress is adequate, the shared recognition of a discrepancy between the actual and the ideal is missing. Likewise, if a school social worker expresses concern about a student's self-concept, but the student's parents do not perceive a problem, the parents and social worker are unlikely to engage in interpersonal problem solving. Note that in both examples, a different problem might be mutually identified if the participants discuss further their initial perceptions. But unless this occurs, the problem-solving process should be terminated or the problem redefined to everyone's satisfaction.

Participants Agree on the Factors That Indicate the Discrepancy

Efforts to clarify the factors that define the gap between what is and what should be facilitate clear communication in problem solving. For example, analyze the problem of successfully including a student with a physical disability in a general education class. What is success? Without specifying how to define the current status of the student and the status after some intervention selected on the basis of interpersonal problem solving, there is no way to determine whether successful integration has been accomplished. In this example, success could be indicated by the student's improved attitude toward school, parents' and teachers' perceptions of student attitude, the extent to which other students interact with the student with a disability, or any number of additional measures. (You will read about the importance of specifically measuring the factors defining the gap in the later section, "Finalizing Implementation Plans.")

Problem Statements Invite Many Kinds of Solutions

The objective of problem identification is to describe in the clearest terms possible the discrepancy between the current and the ideal situations so participants can look for alternative strategies to move from the former to the latter. Therefore, you should avoid unnecessarily narrowing the problem statement (Hobbs & Westling, 1998; Reiter-Palmon & Ilies, 2004). To clarify this point, analyze this initial problem statement: How can we assist this student with learning disabilities to succeed in his math class? Although the problem is as yet incomplete, since the gap has not been specified and the factors defining the gap have not been outlined, it is appropriate because it does not attempt to suggest a single strategy that is needed to ensure success. But what if the problem had been stated in this way: How can we assist this student to learn his basic multiplication facts? The latter problem statement includes the assumption that success in math will occur if math facts are learned. If the goal of problem solving is to help a student succeed, it might be appropriate to provide a calculator and work on real-life problem-solving applications. The second problem statement might preclude this possibility from being discussed. The first problem statement is more likely to leave this option available, along with many other strategies that include the student, his peers, his teacher, other professionals, his family, and so on. The range of potential solutions is broadened because the problem statement is free of preferred strategies.

Suggestions for Identifying the Problem

The following strategies can help you and your colleagues identify problems in ways that foster creative and effective thinking during your interpersonal problem-solving efforts.

Think of Problem Identification as Having Both Divergent and Convergent Elements

Too often in schools, problem identification is thought of as primarily a convergent process—that is, one that focuses on rapidly narrowing the problem description. Although this may appear expedient, it is usually neither efficient nor constructive. Instead, we encourage you to think of the early phase of problem identification as divergent—that is, as a phase in which the goal is to explore all possible problem definitions so that none is overlooked.

One means of keeping early problem identification divergent is to challenge the assumptions that underlie initial problem statements. For example, this is a problem statement that you might encounter:

> How can we get Josh's parents, Mr. and Mrs. Keller, to participate in the behavior management program that Josh needs?

It has a number of assumptions, including the fact that Josh's parents should be involved in a behavior management program, that Josh truly needs the program, and that "we" should take responsibility for involving Mr. and Mrs. Keller. What would happen if you negated one or several of these assumptions? Perhaps the problem would be reconceptualized as one of these:

1. How can we get Josh's behavior management program to work at school?

2. How can we improve Josh's behavior at school?

3. How could Josh be helped to be more involved in controlling his behavior?

Once underlying assumptions have been challenged and alternative conceptualizations of the problem have been explored, participants in problem solving are more likely to be able to identify the problem's most essential characteristics and use them to formulate a revised problem statement. This reformulation of the problem is convergent. It emphasizes that all participants need to reach agreement on the problem prior to generating solutions for it. However, it is also important to recognize that challenging assumptions may or may not lead to a redefinition of a problem; the point is that it is a strategy for making problem identification deliberate for all participants in the problem-solving process.

Describe the Problem Precisely

The need for using concrete and specific language in verbal communication will be addressed in detail in Chapters 8, 9, and 10. Its importance in problem solving, especially during problem identification, cannot be overstated. For example, in problem solving about a student, you should strive to describe the observable behaviors or performance indicators that characterize the student's academic or social performance. Some teachers might call a student unmotivated. Your task during problem identification is to clarify what is meant by "unmotivated." Does this mean that the student is absent? Does it mean that assigned work is not returned to school? Does it imply that the student sleeps during lectures? Only by specifying the exact behaviors or performance indicators that comprise the meaning of "unmotivated" can the problem be identified clearly.

In addition to using concrete and specific language, when identifying a problem you will want to confirm that all participants share the same understanding of the particular words used. An example of a word that is often perceived differently by professionals is *inclusion*. For some special services providers, inclusion refers to integrating students with disabilities into general education classes primarily for social purposes. For others, it means having students attend classes in which they can complete the academic work. For yet others, inclusion means integrating students physically, instructionally, and socially, regardless of the disability. Imagine the difficulties that might result if a group of individuals were problem solving on this topic without establishing a shared meaning for the word! What other words might cause confusion in the schools where you work or will work?

Confirm Problems with Multiple Sources of Information

One of the dangers in interpersonal problem solving is that participants will rely on a single source of information to identify a problem. An important strategy for ensuring successful problem identification is the use of multiple sources. In problems related to students, this might entail completing an observation of the target student in several different school settings, reviewing student records, and interviewing parents and teachers. In problems related to programs, teams, or services, this might include confirming district policies, reviewing available data (e.g., needs assessment or a staff development activity evaluation), and interviewing key people to ascertain their perceptions.

Problems can be confirmed in many ways. Sometimes data already exist in the form of student records, district surveys, or state guidelines. In other cases, some type of data collection may be needed, whether formal or informal, quantitative or qualitative. The important point is to be certain that the problem identified is an accurate description of what is actually occurring.

Allow Adequate Time for Problem Identification

All of the strategies for accurately identifying problems require time. Successful problem identification relies on high-quality interactions between the participants in interpersonal problem solving and opportunities for reflection and analysis. Unfortunately, in many school settings the problem-solving context conveys the message that the problem identification step should be completed as quickly as possible so that the more important task of resolving the problem can begin. Such thinking overlooks one key point: Without adequate time, accurate problem identification is unlikely and problem resolution is improbable. In Chapter 7, you will learn more about prioritizing time use and making the best possible use of time for collaboration, including that for interpersonal problem solving.

Educators can learn many valuable lessons about interpersonal problem solving from their colleagues in the world of business.

Our recommendation is to begin systematically to increase the amount of time spent on identifying problems. In some situations, multiple sessions are preferred for this, especially when additional data need to be gathered. Although this approach may seem awkward and time consuming at first, the long-term benefit is far more efficient problem solving. For example, at a single meeting, a dilemma being experienced by a student could be outlined and team members asked to consider the situation and gather information for the next week's meeting. A student who had been described the week before would then be discussed in detail and the problem-solving process implemented.

One strategy for ensuring that adequate time is allowed for problem identification is to use a checklist for exploring various aspects of a problem. The checklist could include medical factors, instructional items, social areas, family or community factors, and so on.

Monitor the Problem-Solving Context

At the beginning of this chapter, we noted the importance of monitoring the problem-solving context. This is particularly critical during problem identification. The participants may not have had enough information initially to determine whether interpersonal problem solving was appropriate for a given situation; such information may emerge during this problem-solving step and lead to a different decision about the appropriateness of problem solving. Likewise, you should monitor to ensure that other participants remain committed to solving the problem once its parameters are set.

Generating Potential Solutions

After you have clearly identified the problem, you are faced with the sometimes daunting task of proposing alternative means for resolving it. The purpose of the second major step of problem solving is to stimulate the creation of the maximum number of potential solutions by the widest range of participants (VanGundy, 2005). This problem-solving step relies heavily on divergent thinking (Baker, 2005; Paulus & Brown, 2003; Pugach & Johnson, 2002; Raven, 2003).

Suggestions for Generating Potential Solutions

Studies of both creative processes and critical problem solving have contributed greatly to knowledge about how to generate potential solutions in interpersonal problem solving (Nunn & McMahan, 2000). The following are some solution-generating techniques designed to encourage divergent thinking.

Brainstorming

The most familiar strategy for generating potential solutions is *brainstorming*. In brainstorming, the participants in the problem-solving process call out solutions as they think of them, facilitating their own thinking by listening to the ideas generated by others. The rules typically given for brainstorming during interpersonal problem solving include these:

1. Accept all ideas that are offered without evaluating them.
2. Propose ideas freely, even if they seem improbable.
3. Have someone write down the ideas being generated.
4. "Play" with the ideas to generate even more ideas.

In addition, you may find it helpful to set a time limit for generating solutions; this focuses attention on the process but also acknowledges the time constraints of school-based problem solving.

The following example is an illustration of brainstorming in order to resolve a student problem:

A special education teacher described a dilemma to colleagues at a problem-solving meeting. He was responsible for supporting Jorge, a student with a mild learning disability but with significant problems with peer and adult social interactions. The student's behaviors included pushing other students, teasing and bullying, refusing to respond to requests by teachers and others, and often saying that any problem was someone else's fault. The special education teacher was concerned that other students were beginning to say they didn't like Jorge and they didn't want him in their groups. After the problem was identified as how to improve Jorge's social interactions in the classroom, the special education teacher and his colleagues generated these potential solutions:

1. Begin a formal social skills training program.
2. Teach the other students tolerance.
3. Involve the family in designing an intervention.
4. Videotape Jorge so he can see his behaviors.
5. Videotape the teacher to see whether her responses to the behaviors might be maintaining them.
6. Videotape the entire class to watch the students' interactions.
7. Transfer Jorge so he can get a "fresh start."
8. Transfer the teacher so Jorge can get a "fresh start."
9. Ask the counselor to schedule several sessions with the class on respectful interactions and understanding diversity.
10. Ask the principal to visit the class to convey to the students the seriousness of the matter.
11. Check the media center for a videotape on social interactions to use with the class.
12. Set up a classwide system that rewards respectful interactions.
13. Give bonuses to Jorge for appropriate social interactions.
14. Design some nonthreatening activities and arrange small student groups that include Jorge in order to help him practice social skills.
15. Have a class meeting to discuss the problem.
16. Hire a paraprofessional for the classroom.

17. Ask the district to provide an external consultant to observe the student and classroom and make recommendations.
18. Ask the district special education coordinator to observe the class.
19. Ask the district special education coordinator to teach the class for several days while the teachers work on a solution.
20. Look for a pattern based on the observations: Is Jorge experiencing more problems after weekends or holidays? Late in the day? During particular subjects (e.g., math) or activities (e.g., independent work time)?
21. Do an Internet search for websites on addressing social interactions problems and generate additional ideas from that search.

This example demonstrates why brainstorming can be such a powerful technique in problem solving. First, notice that playfulness was an integral part of the brainstorming. For example, no one seriously expects the student or the teacher to transfer for a fresh start (Ideas 7 and 8), and yet letting those ideas surface led to the idea of asking the counselor to come to the class to work with students, in essence a fresh start for the entire class.

Another brainstorming concept illustrated in this example is *chaining*, which is linking a series of ideas through a concept or other stimulus. Ideas 4, 5, and 6 form a chain about using videotaping to understand the teacher–student and student–student dynamics in the classroom. Items 17, 18, and 20 comprise a chain about classroom observation. In fact, the value of chaining in generating potential solutions is a primary reason why all ideas are accepted without evaluation: Each time you stop brainstorming to evaluate an idea, you decrease the likelihood that any participant will chain with the idea just presented.

Brainstorming is the preferred strategy for generating potential solutions in many problem-solving situations. You probably will find it helpful when you and the other participants know each other reasonably well and have comparable knowledge about the problem context. It is especially productive when the size of the problem-solving group is relatively small, and it often is used when the problem is not particularly emotion-laden.

Brainwriting

Another strategy for generating potential solutions is *brainwriting*. In brainwriting, participants individually write three or four potential solutions on a blank sheet of paper. They then place their lists in a pile on the table, from which they select someone else's list. The ideas on that list are the stimuli for them to generate additional solutions. This exchange of ideas continues until no new ideas are forthcoming. The complete set of ideas is then presented to the group with duplications eliminated. Figure 2.2 is an example of how brainwriting sheets might look.

Brainwriting is a productive option when open discussion of ideas may not be fruitful. For example, if you are problem solving about an emotionally charged issue, more ideas may be generated through this written process than through one involving verbal exchange. The same principle holds for topics that might

---

Figure 2.2   Example of Brainwriting Activity

Problem addressed by the school staff:

In what ways might we increase the involvement of parents and family members as instructional partners in our school?

ROUND ONE

Anna	**Jennifer**	**Travis**
1. Create a parent task force with lots of fanfare. 2. Set up a strong parent volunteer program with T-shirts, rewards, publicity.	1. Talk to J. Montgomery in Columbus Schools, where there is a high level of parent involvement.	1. Search Internet for ideas on parent involvement 2. Search Internet for formal programs or successful examples of parent involvement.

ROUND TWO

Travis (read Anna's list)	**Anna** (read Jennifer's list)	**Jennifer** (read Travis's list)
3. Get materials from state department of education on parent involvement. 4. Use our parent organization as a basis—meet with them? 5. Ask students how they would like their parents to be involved at school. 6. Be careful to work on ideas that will let lots of parents be involved, not just those who can come to school during the day.	2. Send a group of our staff to visit the Columbus program. 3. Pay a parent to lead this effort and contact other parents. 4. Survey parents to ask how they want to be instructional partners.	3. Ask parents how they could partner with us electronically. 4. Explore options such as volunteer-staffed homework hotlines or homework e-mail. 5. Open school so parents can access technology. 6. Hold parent invitational coffees to solicit input.

be considered sensitive—for example, if teachers are uncertain about their responsibilities for helping students who cannot read access learning. Another reason for choosing brainwriting is simply to change the procedure for generating alternative solutions to encourage a fresh perspective. Finally, brainwriting sometimes is preferred when the problem-solving group is so large that not everyone may have ample opportunity to speak if brainstorming is used.

Nominal Group Technique

A third strategy you may use to generate potential solutions combines aspects of brainstorming and brainwriting. In nominal group technique (NGT) (Fleming, 2000; Okhuysen, 2001), participants individually generate and write down as many potential solutions as they can. Then the ideas are shared by having one person state one idea, writing it so that all can see the idea. Then the next individual shares one idea. This process of persons sharing single ideas from their lists continues until all alternatives are presented. Individuals may "pass" at any time they are asked to share an idea and they do not have a new option to offer. The total list of ideas is then discussed by participants to identify the most important potential solutions and to begin the process of data reduction or idea combination. Each participant writes each prioritized solution on a separate card (as many as 10 ideas) and then rates each on a scale from very important (a ranking of 5) to unimportant (1). The facilitator gathers these cards and records all participants' votes for the ideas. If a clear pattern of preference for particular ideas emerges, the procedure is complete; if not, additional discussion is held and a second vote is taken.

Nominal group technique is valuable when many people need to participate in generating potential solutions and some means is needed to ensure their equal opportunity for participation. This might occur when participants traditionally have had unequal status or when some individuals tend to dominate the group.

Whether you choose to use brainstorming, brainwriting, nominal group technique, or other approaches for generating potential solutions, you should adhere to the rules outlined as part of brainstorming. Sometimes it is tempting to stop to evaluate each idea as it is expressed. But this derails the entire purpose of generating potential solutions; we have seen many problem-solving sessions in which participants never returned to this critical step once they began prematurely discussing an idea that had been offered. Worse, participants often seem to be unaware of the fact that they have derailed and of how this is limiting their problem-solving process. Remember, generating as many solutions as possible is the point of this problem-solving step.

Evaluating Potential Solutions

The list of potential solutions you generate serves as the raw material for making the specific decision about which solution to implement. In order to make an informed decision, each of the potential solutions should be evaluated. This involves two problem-solving steps: (1) delineating the positives and negatives of each potential solution and (2) outlining the tasks required to implement each.

Delineating the Positives and Negatives of Each Potential Solution

In this evaluative step, your task is to examine each potential solution from a balanced perspective. This entails listing the positive and negative aspects of each intervention or strategy. For example, in the brainstormed list of options for Jorge, the student experiencing social interaction problems, one idea was to videotape the student. Positive aspects of that solution might include these:

1. The very presence of the video equipment might improve Jorge's interactions because of his concern about being captured on tape acting in an inappropriate manner.

2. A videotape would provide objective evidence of the seriousness of the problem.

3. A videotape would enable teachers and others to demonstrate to the parents the nature of the problem, hopefully enlisting their support for a planned intervention.

Negative aspects of the intervention might include these:

1. Jorge, as well as other students, might be distracted in their schoolwork by the video equipment.

2. Student behavior might deteriorate as they "perform" for the camera.

3. District policies might prohibit the videotaping of any student without explicit parental permission. Obtaining permission for all the students might make the entire project too difficult to implement.

On the basis of these positive and negative aspects of videotaping, would you retain it as a potential solution? If your response is no, then you would eliminate it from the list. If your response is yes, then you would leave it on your list of options for further discussion later.

This step of weighing the advantages and drawbacks should be completed for all the items on the list of potential solutions, although for some the task will be brief. For example, another idea for addressing the student's problem was for the consultant to teach the class for several days. This was a preposterous idea that emerged from the playful part of brainstorming and then led to the generation of other possible solutions. Obviously, this unrealistic potential solution and others similar to it should be quickly discarded.

One way of formalizing this process of considering the opportunities and constraints of potential solutions is called Plus/Minus/Implications, or PMI. In a simple chart, each alternative is listed and three columns are used for the PMI. For example, Idea 9, asking the counselor to intervene with the class, might include these points:

- *Plus (positive results).* Removes the teacher from the immediate situation, permitting someone with a fresh perspective to get involved.
- *Minus (negative effects).* Counselor has many responsibilities and may have to miss sessions if a crisis occurs.
- *Implications (possible positive or negative outcomes of the action).* Potential increased class understanding of Jorge's behavior and so fewer complaints about it; possibility that Jorge would not gain any understanding from this indirect intervention.

Outlining Tasks for the Potential Solutions

By eliminating some of the potential solutions on the basis of their positive and negative aspects, you shorten considerably the list of potential interventions or strategies. But you probably still have several options, all of which seem possible. The second evaluation step, outlining the tasks that would be required to implement each of the remaining potential solutions, is the means through which these possibilities are further analyzed and narrowed.

Consider another idea from the brainstormed list. One of the potential solutions is to set up a classwide reward system for appropriate social interactions. What are the tasks that would have to be completed for this option to be implemented? You and your colleagues would have to discuss with the general education teacher what type of system might be consistent with classroom expectations already in place. You would need to specify what "appropriate social interactions" are and how they would be observed. Additionally, you would need to specify what the rewards would be and when they would be given. You might decide to discuss alerting parents/families that a system was being implemented, and so a letter of explanation might have to be generated. What other tasks would be required?

After considering the tasks associated with each of the possible solutions, you should decide whether each option still seems feasible. If not, you would discard the idea. If so, you would retain it as a likely solution, and you might select it for implementation.

Selecting the Solution

Following all of the steps described thus far should have led you to a list of several clearly articulated, carefully outlined potential solutions, all appropriate for resolving the problem. Now the task is to select one of these.

This selection can be based on several factors. One consideration may be intrusiveness. If an intervention or strategy will disrupt classroom routine or

When professionals have agreed on a solution, they should clarify who is responsible for implementation, what specific steps need to be taken, and when follow-up will occur.

require changes in staff assignments, it may become the second choice after one that fits into existing routines and staff responsibilities.

Feasibility is another factor that influences selection of solutions. A simple solution that requires no new resources typically is preferable to one that involves separate budget items or inordinate amounts of time. Similarly, a solution that necessitates coordinating multiple activities and people may be less feasible in a busy school setting than one that minimizes the number of implementers.

A third—and admittedly not very systematic—means for selecting among the potential solutions is individual preference. Although all the solutions may be feasible and none particularly intrusive, the people who have the most responsibility for implementing them may simply be more comfortable with one over the others. This consideration should not be ignored; the likelihood of a successful outcome is dependent to some extent on the commitment and attitude of those directly involved in implementation. That is, some teachers might prefer a contract written specifically for a student such as Jorge, while others might prefer a classwide intervention strategy.

As you and your colleagues select a solution, try to identify the basis on which this decision will be made. There are no "correct" criteria for making this judgment, but the criteria used should be clear to all participants.

Implementing the Solution

Now you have selected the solution to be implemented, and you have addressed challenges such as those outlined in the following Putting Ideas into Practice. Because you have done a great deal of planning throughout the problem-solving process, many details of implementation plans have already been identified. However, one more planning phase is required before actual implementation of the intervention or strategy.

Finalizing Implementation Plans

In preparation for implementation, your responsibility is to review with other participants the plans that were made during the evaluation step of problem solving. Finalizing these plans typically includes (1) reviewing and refining detailed plans for implementing the solutions, (2) determining the criteria by which success will be determined, and (3) scheduling a time to evaluate the outcome(s) of the applied solution.

Detailed Arrangements

The selected solution is more likely to be successful if you and your colleagues specify all necessary arrangements and assign all responsibilities. Some special services professionals find that listing responsibilities is helpful in accomplishing this. In the sample chart in Figure 2.3 (on page 51), the first column includes the task to be done, the second shows the person responsible, the third includes the target completion date, the fourth addresses the outcomes expected, and the fifth and final column contains space for writing comments.

PUTTING IDEAS INTO PRACTICE

Problem-Solving Practice

Problem solving in groups is often more easily discussed than implemented. Here are a few dilemmas that might occur and some suggestions for addressing them. If you have time, you could set up each of these dilemmas as a role-play.

■ At the very beginning of a problem-solving meeting, one teacher says, "We know what the problem is. Let's spend our time finding a way to solve it."

Among harried educators, this type of comment is not unusual. However, it can undermine problem-solving success. You might respond using strong communication skills, stating that you are not completely clear on everyone's perspective and that you would prefer that the group clarify the problem first.

■ As ideas are being generated, one participant makes a negative comment about each idea, pulling the conversation into arguments about the merit of each potential solution.

Creativity and chaining are unlikely to occur when brainstorming is interrupted by such discussion. If the problem is chronic, the problem-solving group might want to review its operating rules prior to the start of a meeting. Brainwriting could also be used as an alternative. A last-resort strategy is to say to the individual, "When we discuss each idea instead of getting a lot of ideas out together, it interferes with my thinking. I'd like to get a long list of ideas and then discuss whether each has value for this situation."

■ It is time to stop the meeting, but no one has agreed to take on responsibility for implementing the planned student intervention. People are packing up their belongings and moving toward the door.

Time problems can be especially acute for group problem solving. If a situation is complex, participants could plan to devote two sessions to the conversation. They might also use e-mail to complete the assignment of responsibilities after the meeting. However, if the issue is that everyone seemed reluctant to take on the responsibility of the selected intervention, they might need to assess why that is occurring. If the solution is too time consuming to be realistic or too complex to be easily put into place, perhaps another idea should be selected.

Criteria for Success

Yet another issue to clarify in the final planning for implementation is the selection of specific variables and criteria that will be used to determine whether the intervention or strategy has been successful. This is consonant with the definition of the desired situation discussed as part of problem identification. In interventions related to students, this could include specific levels of achievement

Figure 2.3 Problem-Solving Responsibility Chart

Student: _____   Date: _____

Problem summary: _____

Solution to be attempted: _____   Evaluation Date: _____

Results: _____

Action/Task	Person(s) Responsible	Target Completion Date	Expected Outcomes	Comments

on designated assessment instruments or a quantifiable improvement in attendance. In strategies that address staff problems, this may require the development of a needs assessment questionnaire or survey and clarification of what outcomes will signal success. The form presented in Figure 2.3 includes space for specifying criteria.

Scheduled Time for Evaluation of Outcomes

A final topic to address prior to implementation is a specific time for assessing the success of the solution (or the outcomes). Inattention to this issue is a mistake we repeatedly observe in interpersonal problem solving in schools. Well-intentioned interventions or strategies sometimes are abandoned because of failure to assess systematically whether they are having the desired impact, and the first step of assessment is arranging for a time to jointly discuss the solution and its effectiveness.

Carrying Out the Solution

After completing all of these steps, you are ready to implement the intervention or strategy. Quite simply, you *do* whatever it is you have planned—whether it is a student intervention concerning academic or social behavior, a staff development plan, a co-teaching unit, or an adaptation to the curriculum. The "what" of implementation is as varied as the problem situations you encounter. During implementation you rely on the commitment and expertise of those in your problem-solving setting.

Evaluating the Outcome

The evaluation time scheduled during final planning functions as "no-fault insurance" for interpersonal problem solving. During this step of the process, you should determine whether the established goal has been reached. You also determine whether those involved in the problem-solving process are satisfied with the impact of the intervention or strategy.

Depending on what you learn during this problem-solving step, you will plan different courses of action. If the intervention or strategy is meeting with success, it becomes an opportunity for congratulating each other on that success. In such a case, the decision to be made is whether to continue the intervention or strategy for another defined period of time or, if the problem has been resolved, to terminate it. A schoolwide behavior management system is an example of a "solution" that might be continued over a long period of time; a student reward system for completing assignments is one that you might choose to phase out.

If the implemented solution is only partially successful, your decisions focus on extending or adapting it. You and the other participants in the problem-solving process would analyze whether elements of the solution are unsatisfactory and should be modified or the current intervention needs to be continued for another period of time. In either of these situations, another date for feedback would be scheduled so that you can continue to monitor progress.

An unsuccessful outcome is a third possibility in interpersonal problem solving. Although this is much less likely if the steps in the process have been systematically followed, we recognize that you may need a set of strategies for addressing this frustrating situation.

The first action you and your colleagues should take when faced with an unsuccessful outcome is to analyze the reasons for the lack of success. You might examine the intervention or strategy itself to ascertain whether it was flawed, and consider whether the solution was implemented with integrity. You might also consider whether other ideas might have been more effective in solving the problem, whether the problem was accurately identified, and whether the problem-solving context was inappropriate. For example, perhaps you lacked certain information that was important for the success of the solution, or perhaps new information emerged during the problem-solving process that affected implementation. Additional possibilities might also account for the lack of success. In fact, your analysis should include a reexamination of each phase of the problem-solving process in a search for information that would explain what prevented the intervention or strategy from being successful. This procedure of tracking back through problem solving to determine where a breakdown may have occurred is clearly illustrated in Figure 2.1, presented earlier in this chapter. A list of questions to guide your analysis and the sequence you should follow for doing this are included in that model, beginning with the negative response to the question, Was the solution successful?

After you and your colleagues have identified the source of the breakdown, the next task is to return to the point of the interpersonal problem-solving process at which the difficulty occurred and complete the steps again, correcting it. This may be as simple as selecting another solution that was previously proposed and evaluated, or it may be as complex as returning to the very beginning of the problem-solving process to reanalyze the context and the presenting problem.

Putting the Problem-Solving Pieces Together

As you review the information you have learned about interpersonal problem solving, you may be thinking that the process seems cumbersome, that in your own experiences in schools no one seems to take such care in implementing each of the problem-solving steps. That often may be true, but here are some points to consider as you work to incorporate this technical information about problem solving into your own professional practice:

■ The care with which the problem-solving steps are implemented depends to a certain extent on the seriousness of the problem at hand. If a student with complex needs is being discussed, more explicit attention to each step may be warranted. If the problem at hand is well defined or partially defined, a somewhat less formal approach may still be successful.

■ Even if your colleagues are not accustomed to using a clear problem-solving procedure, you can use your knowledge to guide the process. For example, during problem identification you might comment, "It seems to me that we're assuming that Matthew does not want to come to school on time, and I'm not convinced that's a valid assumption." You are using the strategy of questioning assumptions, but doing so in a way that fits into the conversation in a natural manner. Can you generate ideas for how to work other problem-solving strategies into conversations as they often occur during school problem-solving meetings?

■ Interpersonal problem solving relies on collaboration, and it can be enhanced or constrained when participants are from different cultures. For instance, the differences among participants may lead to some tensions. These can result in spirited discussions and the need to clarify terms being used and strategies being suggested. For example, one teacher believes strongly that the student should either be expected to behave or be sent to the office for classroom infractions. Another sees that the behavior is the result of being overwhelmed by classroom demands and that providing structure and clarity is the true problem. Similarly, individuals with diverse backgrounds may think very differently about how to solve a problem. The result can be a longer list of potential solutions and a greater variety of ideas. Some individuals might believe that family involvement is essential for success, others may stress focusing on what can be accomplished at school with or without parent involvement, and yet others might see intervention as needing either a strong behavioral or humanistic focus.

■ Principals or other administrators who are participants in problem-solving sessions can play a key role in facilitating the process (Reiter-Palmon & Ilies, 2004; Rock, 2000). However, each person engaged in the process has a responsibility to help move the problem-solving process effectively through each step.

■ Be especially aware of the tendency in some school situations for meetings or conversations to be described as problem solving when in fact they are primarily interactions where one person is trying to convince another person that a particular predetermined solution is the right one. For instance, early in a meeting someone says, "We all agree that Jennifer is not working up to her potential, so don't you think we should let her know that she will have to take the consequences if she does not complete her work?" This type of comment suggests that one person has decided what the problem is without adequate discussion, that the same person has a favored way to address the problem, and that an expectation is being set that others will agree with the intervention. As a professional who understands problem solving, your role should be to speak up, to slow down the process, and to ensure that all participants have the opportunity to participate in both problem identification and the identification and selection of solutions.

Summary

Interpersonal or group problem solving is the central process used in collaborative activities, whether you are addressing well-defined, partially defined, or ill-defined problems. Prior to undertaking interpersonal problem solving, you should assess the problem-solving context. If interpersonal problem solving seems to be appropriate, then these steps are followed: Identify the problem; generate potential solutions; evaluate the potential solutions by outlining the pros and cons of each and then specifying the tasks that would have to be completed to accomplish each; select a solution from those preferred and finalize the implementation plan; implement the solution; and evaluate the outcome of the intervention or strategy. On the basis of the outcome, you may decide to continue with the implementation, make adaptations, or, if the outcome is unsuccessful, assess at which point the process may have broken down and return to that step in the interpersonal problem-solving process. Part of the success in problem solving is incorporating the concepts and strategies into the process as it naturally occurs in schools.

Activities and Assignments

1. How do individual and interpersonal problem solving differ? How might the barriers to collaboration that come from professional socialization (see Chapter 1) affect interpersonal problem solving?

2. With classmates, identify several problems that you find are common in your school. What types of problems are they? How appropriate do you think these problems are for the application of an interpersonal problem-solving process? Use the questions for analyzing the problem-solving context with these problems. How likely are the listed problems to be resolved through a shared process? What should you do if they cannot easily be resolved?

3. Why is it important to examine underlying assumptions during problem identification?

4. Use the professional problems you identified in Activity 2 to practice techniques for generating potential solutions. Write one problem statement (remember to frame it as a question) so that everyone in your group or class can read it. Then select and use one of the recommended techniques to generate potential solutions. Repeat this procedure, using different problem statements and different techniques.

5. Identify a problem you are addressing in your school. After generating a list of potential solutions, use the PMI strategy to analyze them. Which ideas generate more plus comments than minus comments? Do any of the implications you list influence your thinking on the solutions' feasibility? Once you have identified three solutions that seem workable, create a chart that includes all the tasks that would have to be completed to implement each of the remaining options.

6. Attend a problem-solving meeting, which could be either a pair of teachers doing instructional planning or a team meeting to discuss a student issue. Observe what occurs during the meeting. How clearly can you identify team members' use of the problem-solving steps? How often do members backtrack? Why? If you were asked to give participants feedback, what would you say?

7. In this chapter, feasibility and intrusiveness were included as criteria to consider in selecting a possible solution for a problem. What other criteria might participants in interpersonal problem solving apply in judging the potential of the solutions they have generated? How could you set these criteria as an explicit part of your solution?

8. Audiotape yourself engaged in problem solving with a colleague. As you review your tape, analyze how you ensure that you are proceeding from one step to the next. Have a classmate review your tape for the same purpose. Compare your analyses.

9. Consider the concepts that characterize collaboration that you learned in Chapter 1. Then think about the principles of interpersonal problem solving. How does the style of collaboration contribute to the process of interpersonal problem solving? Take each problem-solving step and analyze it using the defining and emergent characteristics of collaboration. How does this help you understand how these essential dimensions of school practice intersect?

For Further Reading

Hertzog, H. S. (2000, April). *When, how and who do I ask for help? Novices' perceptions of learning and assistance.* Paper presented at the annual meeting of the American Educational Research Association, New Orleans, LA. (ERIC Document Reproduction Service No. 446087).

Jayanthi, M., & Friend, M. (1992). Interpersonal problem solving: A selected literature review to guide practice. *Journal of Educational and Psychological Consultation, 3,* 147–152.

Nunn, G. D., & McMahan, K. R. (2000). "Ideal" problem solving using a collaborative effort for special needs and at-risk students [Electronic version]. *Education, 121,* 305–312.

Ochoa, T. A., & Robinson, J. M. (2005). Revisiting group consensus: Collaborative learning dynamics during a problem-based learning activity in education. *Teacher Education and Special Education, 28,* 10–20.

Robson, M. (2002). *Problem solving in groups* (3rd ed.). Burlington, VT: Gower.

Stambaugh, B. (2001). *Team troubleshooter: How to find and fix team problems.* Palo Alto, CA: Davies-Black.

CHAPTER 3

Teams

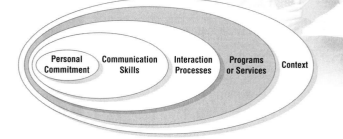

Personal Commitment — Communication Skills — Interaction Processes — Programs or Services — Context

Connections

Collaboration is critical to the success of a number of structures and applications in schools. Chapter 3 examines school teams as the first of several school activities and services that rely on collaboration and that are based on the process of problem solving. In Chapters 4 and 5 we offer comparable discussions of consultation and co-teaching as collaborative service delivery options, and in Chapter 7, staff development is explained as yet another opportunity for collaboration in order to achieve goals for students with disabilities and other special needs.

Learner Objectives

After reading this chapter you will be able to:

1. Define teams and outline their essential characteristics.
2. Enumerate the stages of team development and provide examples of team interactions during each stage.
3. Compare and contrast multidisciplinary, interdisciplinary, and transdisciplinary teams.
4. Outline three different purposes of student-centered teams and discuss their importance for special services providers.
5. Describe the relationship between teams and collaboration.
6. List strategies for promoting team effectiveness.
7. Discuss activities that contribute to the success of meetings.

Ms. Chamberlain is looking forward to the team meeting about to begin—an annual review for Nathan, a student on her caseload who is moving from elementary to middle school. Nathan's mother and father have indicated that they do not want Nathan to be placed into separate classes for his core academic instruction, but other team members are not sure that Nathan can succeed in the general education setting. As the meeting begins, Ms. Chamberlain makes sure that everyone has been introduced—Mr. Wayte, the principal; Ms. Stokes, the social worker; Mr. Sebastian, Nathan's fifth-grade teacher; and Ms. Springer, the middle school special education teacher who will be responsible for Nathan's IEP. Mr. Wayte and the others use recent achievement data to stress the strides in achievement that Nathan has made, and they comment on how they will miss him. Nathan's IEP goals are written based on the sixth-grade curriculum, and when a special education setting is recommended for English and math instruction and Nathan's parents decline, each team member is asked to address this topic. The key points made are listed in the electronic minutes being taken and projected on the wall. By the conclusion of the meeting, the team agrees that Nathan should begin the year in all general education core academic classes, but that a meeting will be held one month into the school year to evaluate this placement decision. The team finishes its work shortly thereafter and all members sign the IEP. With best wishes, the team adjourns. Ms. Chamberlain reflects on the meeting and feels a sense of loss at the conclusion of this team's work for this student.

Introduction

You were born into a social group—your family—and you have become increasingly involved in a wider and wider range of groups as you have become an adult and a professional. For example, you still are a member of a family group, and you may belong to a neighborhood or community group, staff group, sports group, recreational or fitness club, professional association, political party, or civic group. If you conduct an inventory of the groups to which you belong, you might be surprised to discover that your participation in these groups accounts for nearly all of your social activities. Although social scientists describe many different types of groups, they identify the three most important types relative to daily interaction as family, friendship, and work groups (Argyle, 1999; Ephross & Vassil, 2005). The focus of this chapter is on just one type of social group: work groups or teams.

Team approaches have become increasingly popular structures for addressing a wide range of school matters (e.g., Friend & Cook, 1990, 1997; Richardson, 2005). Teaming is the most frequently advocated structure for implementing school reform initiatives, as illustrated by continuing attention to site-based management teams, interdisciplinary and grade-level teaching teams, planning teams, professional development teams, school improvement teams, and so on. The activities in which such teams engage and the decisions they make are myriad. For example, they address school improvement planning, curriculum, student achievement goals, governance, professional development, and resource management. Changes have been made in school schedules, curriculum structure, budgeting priorities, staff development designs, and personnel roles and responsibilities through such teams (e.g., Darling-Hammond, 1999; Gable & Manning, 1999; Supovitz, 2002). The topics addressed in this text are appropriate for the full range of school teams, but in this chapter the focus is on teams that directly benefit students.

Teaming is quite familiar to most special educators. However, being a leader or a member of a team requires a detailed understanding of the characteristics and functioning of teams—topics that sometimes are part of special education professional preparation but often not part of professional preparation for general educators. This chapter, then, is designed to clarify key concepts related to teams and to emphasize their collaborative nature. By carefully studying teams, you will be better prepared to contribute to team effectiveness in your school.

Team Concepts

Team approaches were centerpieces in special education and related services for many years before federal and state laws mentioned them. Mental health teams served the needs of students with emotional disorders long before the schools were obligated to educate them (Elliott & Sheridan, 1992; Menninger, 1950). Similarly, a rich tradition exists of professional teams meeting to discuss and plan for students with mild to moderate disabilities (Armer & Thomas, 1978) and for students with moderate to severe disabilities (Gallivan-Fenlon, 1994; Hutchinson, 1978; Orelove & Sobsey, 1987). A team approach to assessment and decision making for students with disabilities has been mandated by federal law since the 1975 passage of P.L. 94-142, the Education for All Handicapped Children Act, and this continues today in the Individuals with Disabilities Education Improvement Act (IDEA-04).

A profusion of definitions for *teams* has been offered by authors in the various disciplines that rely on team structures, including business, health and medicine, psychology, and counseling (Baker, 2005; Gladding, 2003; Johnson & Johnson, 2002; Larivaara & Taanila, 2004; Wageman & Mannix, 2003). These definitions generally emphasize individuals from a variety of disciplines and experiences getting together in order to reach specific goals through shared problem solving. They also stress the importance of clear and direct communication, interdependence, coordination, and clear procedures as essential features of teams.

Additional conceptualizations of teams that emphasize service delivery have emerged in the literature that addresses education and services for students with disabilities and other special needs. For example, interactive teaming is described by Correa, Jones, Thomas, and Morsink (2005) as a mutual or reciprocal effort made by groups to provide a student with the best educational program possible. A strength of interactive teaming is its emphasis on effective, comprehensive, and cohesive services derived from the collaborative work, rather than individual efforts, of team members. Other authors have stressed the importance of strong interpersonal relationships and a sense of team cohesion, clarity of team goals, and clear team outcomes as being essential to teams (e.g., Bahr, Whitten, & Dieker, 1999; Fleming & Monda-Amaya, 2001; Gable & Manning, 1999). Some definitions specify that the purpose of special services teams is to make decisions about programs for children (Ormsbee, 2001); others have decision making as their purpose but also include the direct delivery of services (Ogletree, Bull, Drew, & Lunnen, 2001). If all these definitions of teams—from outside the field of education as well as within—are considered, the following working definition of teams can be extracted to serve as a framework for this chapter:

> An educational team is a set of interdependent individuals with unique skills and perspectives who interact directly to achieve their mutual goal of providing students with effective educational programs and services.

Characteristics of Teams

The preceding definition and discussion provide a foundation for understanding teams. This understanding can be clarified further by examining these characteristics integral to teams: (1) awareness of team membership, (2) regulation of interactions by shared norms, (3) interdependence of team members, (4) unique skills and perspectives of team members, and (5) the goal of shared service delivery. An alternative way of conceptualizing the characteristics of effective teams is summarized in the following Putting Ideas into Practice.

Awareness of Team Membership

Individuals cannot be part of a team unless they perceive themselves to be so. Extending this notion, team members also must be perceived by others as forming a team (Gold, 2005)—a situation that clearly existed in the case study presented at the beginning of this chapter. Although this characteristic of teams may seem almost too fundamental to mention, it is an issue in many schools. For example, a group of professionals in diverse roles is assigned to a staff development team to prepare colleagues for increased inclusive practice. The group functions effectively in their initial planning meetings, but then members express surprise that they are supposed to coordinate their efforts and otherwise function as a clearly delineated work group that provides ongoing staff development, and their actions (or lack thereof) reflect this confusion. Thus, just knowing that someone is a team member and that others are, too, is a critical first step of teaming.

This is not as straightforward as it may at first appear for teams involved with making program decisions and delivering services to students. Changes and lack of clarity regarding membership sometimes make awareness of team membership a complex matter. For example, the role of a paraprofessional may be extremely important to a team and that individual may be regarded as a member of a specific team. Yet schedule conflicts and limited work schedules may make it impossible for the paraprofessional to participate as an active and full member of the team, especially in meetings and decision making. In such situations the paraprofessional may not function as a team member despite the best intentions of the team. Another particular challenge—transient membership—occurs as

A Checklist for Effective Teamwork

Mature teams share characteristics that make them effective and efficient. Consider the teams on which you participate. To what extent can each of the following characteristics be found? What are examples of each concept? What specific actions might you take to help your team reach these important benchmarks?

_____ 1. Team members are committed to their work, valuing experimentation and the sharing of new ideas.

_____ 2. The team understands its goals and has a clear sense of purpose.

_____ 3. Team members are flexible in assuming roles that help the team accomplish its work, and they may occasionally take on each other's roles. For example, team members can assume both leader and follower roles, or they can function as a consensus builder, a question-asker, or a seeker of additional information.

_____ 4. Team members can recognize when they are being productive and should proceed versus when they are not being productive and should rethink their work.

_____ 5. The team uses a wide variety of problem-solving and decision-making strategies depending on the issue that it is addressing and the context in which it is occurring.

_____ 6. Team members can examine differences in their opinions openly and use those differences as a tool in their discussions. That is, tension is seen as an acceptable part of teaming.

_____ 7. Team members individually and the team collectively work to expand the zone of tolerance for the task, the people, and the process.

_____ 8. Team members appreciate the limits of the team as it exists within the context of the school or agency.

Source: Adapted from P. H. Ephross & T. V. Vassil, *Groups that work: Structure and process,* 2nd ed. (New York: Columbia University Press, 2005).

the caseloads or school assignments of professionals change or as students are transferred to new programs or classes. The dynamic nature of school teams requires members to take special care in monitoring team membership and clarifying changes to it (Downing, 1999).

Regulation of Interactions by Shared Norms

A team is an organized system of individuals whose behavior is regulated by a common set of norms or values (Heningsen, Heningsen, Cruz, & Morrill, 2003;

Johnson & Johnson, 2002; Sherif & Sherif, 1956). For example, teams may have both formal as well as unspoken but clear expectations for members about arriving on time, using lay language when parents are present, articulating and resolving conflict among members, and so on. In addition, regular and direct interaction among team members is central to the concept of a team (Correa et al., 2005; Salend, 2001). Shared norms regarding how interactions occur, what acceptable team member behavior is, and many other agreed-on norms facilitate effective team functioning (Chen & Rybak, 2004; Thousand & Villa, 2000).

When teams are first established, they need to devote considerable time to establishing these norms. This is sometimes a deliberate effort that results in written ground rules. More often, though, this process is less formal, even though it also may be quite deliberate. In these cases team members establish and learn norms through their successful and unsuccessful interactions with one another. When team membership changes frequently, an already-noted characteristic of many school teams, challenges may be encountered in maintaining team norms (Downing, 1999, 2002). In fact, as team membership changes, team norms likewise may change and all members will need to review and recommit to them.

Interdependence of Team Members

Members of teams are highly interdependent because their organizational roles are functionally interrelated (Ephross & Vassil, 2005; Johnson & Johnson, 2002); that is, an event that affects one member is likely to affect the rest of the team, and team actions will affect each individual member. For example, if one team member is called suddenly into a conference that conflicts with a team meeting, the remaining members may not be able to make important decisions because of that person's absence. Interdependence extends to the delivery of services as well (Hunt, Soto, Maier, Muller, & Goetz, 2002). Consider a situation in which a team develops an integrated service plan that calls for one person to supply a communication device and teach a student to use it. A second team member is to design class discussions in which the student can use the communication device to develop better language skills. If the first person is unable to secure the needed device, it will be most difficult for the second team member to proceed with the planned language instruction. The effectiveness of one team member has direct impact on the effectiveness of another, and perhaps of the entire team.

Unique Skills and Perspectives of Team Members

Concepts and definitions of teams as components of service delivery emphasize the unique and diverse skills and abilities of team members as central characteristics. For example, the entire premise of an IEP team is that each of the professionals participating—special and general education teacher, administrators, related services personnel, parents—brings unique and valuable perspectives that enhance planning (Clark, 2000; Johns, Crowley, & Guetzloe, 2002). A similar perspective is offered for teams that exist to support preschool children with disabilities (Hunt, Soto, Maier, Liborion, & Bae, 2004). Of particular importance is the perspective brought to a team by parents, a perspective that is essential for effective team outcomes (Valle & Aponte, 2002). Regardless of the purpose or size of a team, the unique skills, expertise, or perspectives of team members create a rich context for creating programs and services (Dettmer, Dyck, & Thurston, 2005; Taggar, 2001). How was this concept illustrated in the vignette about Nathan presented in the opening of this chapter?

Shared Goal of Effective Service Delivery

Having a mutual goal is an essential element of every team definition across the various disciplines. Contemporary concepts of teams in education and related services specify their service delivery focus as the overall goal shared by all members of the team. Whether the team's specific purpose is to study and plan a child's program or to deliver specific services or interventions directly, service delivery is fundamental. From this perspective, teams include those groups (often comprised of some members who will not be working with a student) that make decisions about a student's eligibility for services, as well as co-teaching teams or teacher–parent teams working to implement home and school behavior intervention programs. Maintaining the team's focus on the delivery of services is an important team function (Gable, Mostert, & Tonelson, 2004). This is particularly true when disagreements occur or when one or more team members is distracted from the central task.

Developmental Stages for Teams

Professionals who study teams generally agree that teams progress through developmental stages in their formation and operation (Correa et al., 2005; Ephross & Vassil, 2005). Teams have life cycles that progress from infancy to maturity regardless of their purposes or the tasks they must perform. Stages in the development of a team were described by Tuckman (1965) as *forming, storming, norming,* and *performing.* The notion of *adjourning* was later added (Tuckman & Jensen, 1977). The characteristics of teams at each of these stages are summarized in the next Putting Ideas into Practice.

Understanding the stages through which teams progress will help you appreciate how teams function. When a team initially comes together its members do not fully understand their task and they are not clear about how they will relate to each other and to the team leader. During the initial stage, *forming,* members tend to want clear instructions from others and they are polite in their efforts to learn about each other and their purpose for becoming a team. The *storming* stage demonstrates that a group can become a team by resolving issues of leadership, procedures, and purpose. During the storming stage members are more comfortable with one another and they communicate freely—which can lead to conflict. They may challenge the team's leadership and disagree with one another as they strive to gain a shared understanding of their task and how to approach it. Having weathered the storm, a team enters the *norming* stage, in which members begin to build trust as they redefine and establish

The Life Cycle of Teams

More than four decades ago, Tuckman (1965) identified four stages that teams go through as members learn about each other and learn to work together to accomplish their goals: forming, storming, norming, and performing. Figure 3.1 summarizes how teams might function during each of these stages. Most professionals who have studied teams agree that teams are most effective when members spend time discussing their function, member roles, and their procedures rather than addressing only the work at hand.

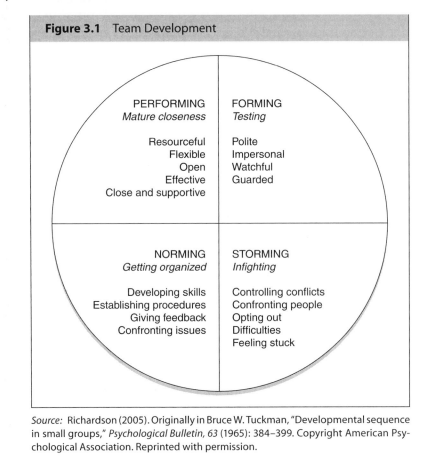

Figure 3.1   Team Development

PERFORMING
Mature closeness

Resourceful
Flexible
Open
Effective
Close and supportive

FORMING
Testing

Polite
Impersonal
Watchful
Guarded

NORMING
Getting organized

Developing skills
Establishing procedures
Giving feedback
Confronting issues

STORMING
Infighting

Controlling conflicts
Confronting people
Opting out
Difficulties
Feeling stuck

Source: Richardson (2005). Originally in Bruce W. Tuckman, "Developmental sequence in small groups," *Psychological Bulletin, 63* (1965): 384–399. Copyright American Psychological Association. Reprinted with permission.

role relationships and procedures for accomplishing their work and handling conflicts. Norming is necessary for teams to establish their patterns of functioning, which might have to do with record keeping, seating arrangements, communication patterns, and so on. What is most important at this stage is that a team culture develops and gives the team its unique identity. The *performing* stage occurs when a team's development levels off and the team can devote its primary efforts to accomplishing its goals. Finally, a team progresses to *adjourning* when its tasks are complete. For many special services teams, this latter stage may occur only when a school year ends or a student leaves the school.

Rationale for and Benefits of Teams

The primary rationale for a team approach to decision making and service delivery lies in its efficiency and potential for high-quality outcomes. If you accept the premise that educating students with special needs requires the participation of professionals with diverse and specialized skills, the challenge of coordinating the information and intervention efforts of the individual members of the group becomes clear. Having all the professionals meet to plan and discuss implementation of programs is far more time effective than any kind of individual reporting could be. Moreover, the process of group communication may lead to decisions and changes in perspectives that would not be possible in one-to-one communication. Implementing a coordinated and coherent program is more efficient and, happily, more effective when all the professionals involved are in communication with each other.

Given that teams are an application of collaboration, all the benefits and outcomes to be realized through collaboration (see Chapter 1) also are possible through teamwork. Specifically, all the emergent characteristics of collaboration could become outcomes of effective teaming. Team members can be expected to develop a high level of interpersonal trust and, thus, more respect for one another. As the trust grows so, too, does the sense of community among team members.

Team Models

Many models for effective teaming have been articulated (Howard et al., 2001; Lytle & Bordin, 2001; Thousand & Villa, 2000). In this section you'll learn about several models for student-centered teams that can be distinguished along two dimensions. The first distinguishing dimension is the team's configuration, or disciplinary working relationship, which can be identified as multidisciplinary, interdisciplinary, or transdisciplinary. The second dimension is the team's purpose or function. Three types of student-centered teams are considered along this dimension:

- Special education teams that make decisions about students' referral to, assessment for, and determination of eligibility for programs in special education
- Student-centered problem-solving teams that address issues related to students experiencing academic, behavioral, social, or emotional problems
- Service delivery teams of persons involved in the coordinated design, implementation, and evaluation of students' programs

Any given team may be classified on both dimensions simultaneously. For example, a service delivery team may be multidisciplinary, interdisciplinary, or transdisciplinary in its approach. A special education team or a problem-solving team could be similarly classified.

Disciplinary Relationships on Teams

The composition of student-centered teams varies according to the team's purposes and the student's needs (Salend, 2001). Team members may be direct service providers or support staff (Lytle & Bordin, 2001; Ohlund & Nelson, 2001); students also may be team members (Laurice, 2000). Direct service providers are parents and staff members who work directly with students on a regular basis. Support staff generally are professionals who provide indirect services such as teacher consultation, technical assistance, or staff development on a periodic basis. They may work directly with children or their families, but this is usually on a restricted or limited basis. Support staff members may include psychologists, occupational therapists, augmentative communication specialists, or other professionals whose services are not required on an intensive basis.

The nature of the working relationships among team members of different disciplines is essential for understanding teams. Three models have evolved over the years that occur along a continuum from little to great collaboration. These are (1) multidisciplinary, (2) interdisciplinary, and (3) transdisciplinary teams. The order in which these approaches developed in the field parallels their order on a collaboration continuum as you can see by reviewing the summary of them in Putting Ideas into Practice.

Multidisciplinary Teams

Although case-centered teams have a long history in special education and related fields, the passage of P.L. 94-142 in 1975 established as a federal requirement that multidisciplinary teams, including school professionals, parents, and sometimes the student, implement evaluation and placement procedures for students with disabilities. With this mandate and its reiteration in the IDEA-04, multidisciplinary assessment and group decision making regarding classification, placement, and the development of an individualized education program (IEP) became formal elements of special education procedures. The term *multidisciplinary* was applied to such teams to convey that a number of perspectives and disciplines were represented within them.

The rationale for multidisciplinary special education teams is that a group decision provides safeguards against individual errors in judgment and ensures greater adherence to the law's due process requirements. Research in behavioral sciences supports this use of teams to improve decision-making effectiveness and quality (Kroeger, Leibold, & Ryan, 1999; Valle & Aponte, 2002). Benefits include (1) a group offers a greater amount of knowledge and experience, (2) a greater number of possible approaches to resolve a problem exists within a group, (3) participation in decision making increases acceptance of the decision, and (4) problem solving in a group involves greater communication and understanding of the decision.

PUTTING IDEAS INTO PRACTICE

Three Models of Team Interaction

Team models may be distinguished by the nature of the working relationships among professionals from different disciplines—a notion that applies in the medical and health fields, as well as in education. As you review the following summary, think about how the goals, procedures, and outcomes for each type of team might differ. When might each team model be most appropriate?

Component	Multidisciplinary	Interdisciplinary	Transdisciplinary
Philosophy of team interaction	Members acknowledge importance of contributions from several disciplines; services remain independent.	Members share responsibility for services among disciplines; individuals are primarily responsible for specific disciplines.	Members commit to teach, learn, and work across disciplines in planning and providing integrated services.
Role of the family	Families typically meet with team members separately by discipline.	Families may meet with the team; individual team members report by discipline.	Families are members of the team and determine their own team roles.
Lines of communication	Members exchange information about independent work; may not see themselves as part of a team.	Teams meet regularly for case conferences and consultations.	Teams meet regularly for information sharing, learning across disciplines, consultation, and team building.
Assessment process	Members conduct assessments by discipline and in separate environments.	Members conduct assessments by discipline and share results.	Members participate in collaborative assessment, observing and recording across disciplines.
Service plan development	Members develop separate plans for intervention within their discipline.	Goals are developed by discipline and shared with the team to form a single service plan.	Staff and family members develop a plan together based on family concerns, resources, and priorities.
Service plan implementation	Members implement their plans separately by discipline.	Members implement the parts of the plan for which their discipline is responsible; coordinated services are an expectation.	Members share responsibility and accountability for how the plan is implemented by the team.

Source: Adapted from G. Woodruff & C. Hanson, *Project KAI,* 1987. 77B Warren Street, Brighton, MA 02135.

Multidisciplinary teams that make decisions about eligibility and programs may well realize these benefits, but such teams operate under some limitations as well. The professionals from different disciplines who make up the team maintain independence from one another as they perform their related duties. Representatives of each discipline contribute unique information and perspectives, but their efforts are not deliberately coordinated or integrated. For example, members of multidisciplinary teams individually provide specialized and discrete services directly to students whose complex needs require intervention from professionals representing different disciplines. In this model the professionals function independently, work toward their individual treatment goals, and do not consistently share or coordinate information. They communicate simply to exchange information about their independent work, and their model might best be viewed as a patchwork quilt in which different—sometimes contrasting— pieces (of information) are placed together, but not necessarily with a blended, unified result. As this description illustrates, true collaboration in a multidisciplinary team model often is minimal, if it occurs at all. An example might be when the team decides that a student's placement is the general education classroom and the special education teacher delivers services there, but at the same time the speech/language therapist, occupational therapist, and counselor—without coordination—pull the same student out of the classroom for those services.

Interdisciplinary Teams

Coordination of information and services is the primary goal shared by members of interdisciplinary teams (Shapiro & Sayers, 2003). In this model, as in

Individualized education program (IEP) teams are among the most important teams in schools, and they are most effective when they foster family and student participation.

the multidisciplinary model, professionals from different disciplines perform related, specialized functions independent of each other. However, they communicate more regularly than do members of multidisciplinary teams. Their ongoing sharing of information is instrumental in their efforts to develop and work toward a collective goal of service coordination. By doing this, they are more likely to develop and pursue interventions that support and complement one another. This helps to ensure that the services they provide students are not duplicated and that gaps do not occur. The coordination of services is such a central feature of interdisciplinary models that a specific role for managing such a team (sometimes called a service coordinator) may be established (Howard et al., 2001; Jung & Baird, 2003).

Transdisciplinary Teams

Transdisciplinary approaches to teaming are the most recent to have evolved in special education and related services, and they also are the most collaborative of all the team models. In these teams, professionals perform their related tasks interactively and, in a process known as *role release*, individual team members may share or blend their roles, at least in part, and one or two team members may be responsible for delivering all interventions to a student (Rogers, 2001). Other team members remain available to assist and advise the primary interventionists through consultation, training, and feedback. Members with different disciplinary expertise share their skills and engage in mutual training and staff development in order to make this possible.

Early intervention and preschool programs for young children often are implemented by transdisciplinary teams (Hunt et al., 2004). This is considered to be a holistic approach in which primary interventionists implement strategies common to their own disciplines as well as some that are derived from other disciplines. For example, a preschool teacher may implement specific language development interventions designed and modeled by the speech/language specialist. After receiving some training and technical assistance from the physical therapist, the teacher also may implement certain positioning routines. It is not uncommon for the teacher, who is a generalist in this situation, to feel insecure about her or his skills in the specialized language and physical therapy areas. The in-depth knowledge of the specialists is essential for designing interventions and assisting primary interventionists to implement them. However, the generalist orientation of the teacher actually may be best suited to providing services for the whole child.

Types of Student-Centered Teams

The second dimension in which teams can vary is their purpose or function. We refer to those teams that exist on behalf of students as *student-centered teams,* and they are the focus of this discussion. Three types of student-centered teams that differ in their primary purpose, their basis in law, and their accountability are described and illustrated here.

Special Education Teams

A special education team exists to make decisions about a student's referral, assessment, and eligibility for special education (Johns et al., 2002; Kroeger et al., 1999). This team may be called a child study team, school assessment team, planning and placement team, or multidisciplinary team. The specific composition, structure, and procedures of this type of team vary across states, but they must operate consistently with the requirements put forth in IDEA and highlighted in Putting Ideas into Practice. Members of these teams usually include a parent, a representative of the school district who is knowledgeable about special and general education services, a general education teacher (in many situations), a special education teacher, a psychologist, and other specialists whose expertise may be needed to evaluate the student and plan programs to meet the unique needs of the student. Whenever appropriate, the student with the disability also should be included. These teams gather and review information about referred students and determine if an individual assessment is needed. If an assessment is carried out, the team reviews the results and determines whether the student has a disability that interferes with his or her ability to progress in the general curriculum; whether the student requires special education and related services; what goals and, in some cases, objectives should be set to address the student's unique needs; and which setting is most appropriate for the student's education. If problems arise in implementing the student's program, the team reconvenes to consider strategies for resolving them. The team meeting you read about at the beginning of this chapter represented the work of this type of team.

The rationale for special education teams, including the presumed superiority of decisions made by these teams, was discussed earlier in this chapter. However, even though multidisciplinary special education teams were envisioned as having the potential to enhance school-based services to students with disabilities, early research demonstrated many problems with such teams. For example, team functioning was adversely affected by (1) use of nonsystematic approaches to collecting and analyzing diagnostic information, (2) minimal participation by parents or general educators on the teams, (3) use of a loosely constructed decision-making/planning process, (4) lack of interdisciplinary collaboration and trust, (5) territoriality, (6) ambiguous role definition and accountability, and (7) lack of experience and training for professionals to work together (Fenton, Yoshida, Maxwell, & Kaufman, 1979; Kaiser & Woodman, 1985; Pfeiffer, 1981).

As the field recognized the shortcomings of the multidisciplinary team concept, various analyses of their implementation were conducted and proposals for improving team functioning were advanced. Among the problems most frequently addressed was the lack of preparation in effective collaboration and team participation skills (Fleming & Monda-Amaya, 2001; Ormsbee & Haring, 2000). Fortunately, professional preparation programs, materials such as this textbook, and other resources listed at the end of this chapter have responded to this professional need.

PUTTING IDEAS INTO PRACTICE

IDEA-04 Guidelines for IEP Team Composition

IDEA-04 provides guidelines for the composition of multidisciplinary teams. A provision that had not been part of earlier versions of this law outlines conditions under which certain team members may be excused from the team meeting. What do you think the impact of excusing a team member might be?

Team Membership

The term *individualized education program team* or *IEP team* means a group of individuals composed of—
  (i) the parents of a child with a disability;
  (ii) not less than 1 regular education teacher of such child (if the child is, or may be, participating in the regular education environment);
  (iii) not less than 1 special education teacher, or where appropriate, not less than 1 special education provider of such child;
  (iv) a representative of the local educational agency who—
      (a) is qualified to provide, or supervise the provision of, specially designed instruction to meet the unique needs of children with disabilities;
      (b) is knowledgeable about the general education curriculum; and
      (c) is knowledgeable about the availability of resources of the local educational agency;
  (v) an individual who can interpret the instructional implications of evaluation results, who may be a member of the team described in clauses (ii) through (vi);
  (vi) at the discretion of the parent or the agency, other individuals who have knowledge or special expertise regarding the child, including related services personnel as appropriate; and
  (vii) whenever appropriate, the child with a disability.

Team Meeting Attendance

  (i) Attendance not necessary.—A member of the IEP Team shall not be required to attend an IEP meeting, in whole or in part, if the parent of a child with a disability and the local educational agency agree that the attendance of such member is not necessary because the member's area of the curriculum or related services is not being modified or discussed in the meeting.
  (ii) Excusal.—A member of the IEP Team may be excused from attending an IEP meeting, in whole or in part, when the meeting involves a modification to or discussion of the member's area of the curriculum or related services, if—
      (a) the parent and the local educational agency consent to the excusal; and
      (b) the member submits, in writing to the parent and the IEP Team, input into the development of the IEP prior to the meeting.

Source: Public Law 108-446, 20 USCS § 1414 (d) (B), (C).

Another serious barrier to effective special education teams, as noted by Pryzwansky and Rzepski (1983), may stem from the fact that they are mandatory. Pryzwansky and Rzepski suggest that this characteristic has led to a narrow definition of the team's purpose and functioning, preventing such teams from appropriately clarifying and expanding their conceptual base. Without a clearly understood foundation, teams lack the grounding on which to build a more integrated structure. The result is that many multidisciplinary teams serve mostly as gatekeepers of special education instead of teams that provide instructional program designs and support for all of the students they consider.

Student-Centered Problem-Solving Teams

One significant response to some of the practical barriers associated with special education teams was the development of building-level, problem-solving teams to assist teachers in accommodating students with behavioral or learning difficulties in their classrooms. These teams evolved, in part, to augment the formal referral and evaluation processes in special education. Often known as prereferral teams or prereferral intervention teams, they were meant to provide prereferral screening for special education services and immediate support for teachers trying to develop appropriate in-class interventions. Over the past several years, the focus for such teams has shifted to preventive problem solving, collegial support for responding to challenging student needs, and opportunities for professionals to problem solve about students—whether or not they have IEPs (Bangert & Cooch, 2001; Lane, Mahdavi, & Borthwick-Duffy, 2003; Logan, Hansen, & Neiminen, 2001). This shift is reflected in alternative names for prereferral teams—for example, intervention assistance teams (IATs), student support teams, instructional consultation teams, and student assistance teams.

Some student-centered teams in these categories have been formed specifically to address the unique needs of students. For example, teams may be created to address unique student behaviors (e.g., Yell, Rozalski, & Drasgow, 2001). Yet others exist for the purpose of providing ongoing support for students with significant needs. An example of the latter type of team is described in Putting Ideas into Practice.

Although evidence supports the effectiveness of intervention or prevention teams, limited comparative data have established the efficacy of specific team approaches (Rock & Zigmond, 2001; Welch, Brownell, & Sheridan, 1999). As you can see in the specific team descriptions that follow, variations in structures and implementation decisions may be necessary in different school ecologies, and schools must select appropriate criteria for discriminating and selecting among program structures.

Teacher Assistance Teams

Teacher assistance teams (TATs) served as one of the earliest examples of a prereferral intervention assistance model. As originally developed by Chalfant, Pysh, and Moultrie (1979), this teacher support system or peer problem-solving group consists of three elected teachers and the referring teacher. Parents are

PUTTING IDEAS INTO PRACTICE

Team Planning for Students with Significant Disabilities

Effective teaming is particularly important for meeting the needs of students with significant disabilities in inclusive schools. One approach that has been useful for students, parents, and school professionals is called the McGill Action Planning System (MAPS). Developed in Canada, MAPS is based on a set of questions focusing on strengths that parents, other family members, professionals, students, and peers answer in one or more meetings to ensure that the student has positive learning experiences. Here are the questions that guide this specialized team:

1. *What is this student's history?* This question is answered by family members so that others have a better understanding of the student.

2. *What is your dream for the child?* As participants answer this question, they are encouraged to think about what they want for the student and what they think the student wants. This is a question of "vision," not present-day realities.

3. *What is your nightmare?* Parents sometimes find this particularly hard to answer because it requires thinking of their child facing difficulties. But if participants can verbalize their nightmares and fears, they will have taken an important step in becoming committed to making sure this nightmare never occurs.

4. *Who is the student?* Everyone expresses in a few words what comes to their mind when they think of the student. Everyone takes a turn at the description; then, participants continue taking turns until no one has anything else to add. Family members then identify what they believe are three especially important descriptors.

5. *What are the student's gifts?* The individuals collaborating focus here on what they believe the student can do, instead of what the student cannot do.

6. *What are the student's needs?* The parents' answers to this question might vary considerably from those of the student's peers or teachers. When the list has been completed, the group then decides which needs are "top priority," or demand immediate attention.

7. *What would an ideal day at school be like for the student?* Some MAPS groups answer this question by outlining a typical school day for students without disabilities who are the student's age. The team might think about how the needs outlined before could be met at school. After that, the team would think about the kinds of help a student would need to truly achieve inclusion at school.

By answering these questions and periodically meeting to review them, team members can design, implement, and evaluate an inclusive education for students with significant needs. How might the MAPS team process be similar to or different from other team interactions in schools? In addition to students with significant disabilities, for whom might this type of teaming be effective?

Source: M. Friend & W.B. Bursuck, *Including students with special needs: A practical guide for classroom teachers,* 4th ed. (Boston: Allyn and Bacon, 2006). Originally adapted from Circle of Inclusion, *The MAPS process: Seven questions* (2002). Retrieved November 22, 2004, from www.circleofinclusion. org/english/guidelines/modulesix/a.html.

invited to become members and, when appropriate, specialists also are invited; the latter, however, are not regular members. The team provides teachers with the support needed to accommodate students with learning and behavior disorders in their classrooms. The referring teacher defines the problem, develops alternative interventions jointly with other TAT members, and then selects the preferred intervention. The TAT functions on the assumption that general education teachers have the knowledge and talent individually or jointly to resolve a great number of the problems they encounter in teaching students with learning and behavior problems. Teacher assistance teams reflect belief in the superiority of group decision making that underlies the multidisciplinary team structure, but they differ from these special education teams by not including specialists as team members unless a specialist's unique expertise is needed for a particular case. The TAT either provides direct assistance to the referring teacher or helps the teacher obtain follow-up from special education personnel. This model continues to have strong proponents (e.g., Epanchin & Friend, in press; Pugach & Johnson, 2002).

Intervention Assistance Teams

Another variation of a student-centered problem-solving team is the intervention assistance team (IAT). This team is premised on the belief that solving problems about students experiencing behavioral and learning problems should enlist all of the resources available at a school, including those of special education and related service staff (Burns, 1999; Whitten & Dieker, 1995). The IAT model uses procedures similar to those of the TAT in which the classroom teacher refers a student, team members gather additional information, and they all meet to consider the information as they engage in a team problem-solving process. The primary difference between IATs and TATs is that the IAT approach goes beyond the general education teachers and includes a special education teacher, a speech/language therapist, and often other specialists such as counselors, school psychologists, and social workers.

Intervention assistance teams have been found to be effective in meeting student needs and providing support to teachers (Burns, 1999; Whitten & Dieker, 1995), especially when administrative support for the process is strong. Other authors report that IATs can produce successful results, but that success certainly is not guaranteed (e.g., Rubinson, 2002).

Other Intervention Teams

Teacher assistance teams and intervention assistance teams are just two of many models being used in schools to assist general education teachers whose students are struggling academically or behaviorally. For example, instructional consultation teams (Bartels & Mortenson, 2002; Rosenfeld & Gravois, 1996) rely on a team of specialists dividing the responsibility for meeting individually with teachers in order to gather data and attempt to resolve student concerns without the necessity and potentially intimidating process of convening the entire team. In instances in which this consultative service is not sufficient, a

Many key principles for effective teaming and team collaboration are based in the research and practices of business, sports, medicine, and other fields outside education.

more traditional data-based team process is implemented. Similarly, prereferral intervention teams (Graden, Casey, & Bonstrom, 1985) use a multidisciplinary building-based team and combine teacher consultant and team formats in a six-stage process: (1) request for consultation, (2) consultation, (3) observation by the consultant, (4) conference to share information and decide whether to proceed to special education referral, (5) special education referral, and, as needed, (6) special education planning and placement.

Regardless of the specific approach, these student-centered teams are only effective to the extent that general education teachers perceive their value and seek from them support and ideas for addressing student concerns. When teachers perceive these teams negatively (e.g., Lane et al., 2003; Slonski-Fowler & Truscott, 2004) or when biases exist in their functioning (e.g., Knotek, 2003), serious problems may occur. This topic is addressed in A Basis in Research.

Service Delivery Teams

A number of team structures exist to plan and deliver education and related services to students. You may be familiar with examples such as teaching teams in middle school, grade-level teams in elementary school, and co-teaching teams at any level. These teams focus largely on planning for, implementing, and evaluating the ongoing, often daily, delivery of educational services to one or more students.

Co-Teaching Teams. In special education, co-teaching is an increasingly common service delivery arrangement in which special education teachers and general education teachers share planning and classroom instructional responsibilities in inclusive settings (Friend, 2007). In this model the general education and special education teachers engage in team planning and in jointly delivering instruction to a diverse group of students. This educational strategy is examined in depth in Chapter 5.

Middle School Teams. In many middle schools, interdisciplinary teams of teachers, each with an area of expertise in a core academic area, instruct the same group of students. This team model produces a wide range of benefits when there is strong team leadership, adequate planning time, and a commitment to the interdisciplinary team concept, demonstrated through team members' willingness to use planning time for team participation. Specifically, middle school teaching teams can increase the effectiveness of instruction, provide teachers with a much needed support system, help ensure that students' problems are recognized and solved, and improve students' work and attitudes.

Grade-Level Teams. A grade-level team structure is very similar to that of the middle school teaching team, even though it has not received wide attention in the professional literature. Grade-level or departmental teams are constructed around members with highly similar interests and expertise (i.e., the grade level or subject matter they teach). The nature of the decisions these groups make may focus on curriculum, division of labor for instructional preparation, schedule, budget, or other matters of group interest or concern. If a special educator can regularly attend such meetings to facilitate discussions about student needs, these teams can serve a function similar to that of prereferral teams.

Effectiveness of Teams

The effectiveness of a team can be evaluated in terms of its goal attainment because, as noted earlier, the team's purpose for existence is to achieve this goal.

A BASIS IN RESEARCH

General Education Teachers and Prereferral Teaming

Prereferral teams play a crucial role in addressing concerns of general education teachers regarding student academic achievement and behavior, and the effectiveness of these teams may have a profound influence on the effectiveness of special education referral procedures. Slonski-Fowler and Truscott (2004) decided to examine the perceptions of 12 experienced elementary teachers (kindergarten through grade 4) as they brought a total of 27 students to the prereferral intervention teams in their two suburban elementary schools. In this ethnographic study, the authors used interviews, observations at team meetings, and classroom observations, examining these data sets for patterns and themes. Eight of the teachers were strongly negative about the team process, and the researchers found three consistent themes among the teachers' perceptions that led to a withdrawal from the process:

■ Teachers sometimes perceived that their input was devalued or ignored by the team.

■ The intervention strategies suggested by team members tended to be limited and lacked clarity, and teachers believed it was just an exercise in documentation in preparation for referral for special education.

■ Teams demonstrated little accountability for strategy implementation or outcomes.

While acknowledging the limitations of this type of study—for example, lack of generalizability—Slonski-Fowler and Truscott concluded that many of the problems they found were related to collaboration: valuing team members' (i.e., general education teachers') input, effective communication among team members, and shared responsibility for the implementation of ideas and a sense of accountability for outcomes. What other collaboration factors do you think might have influenced these teams' functioning?

Source: Based on K. E. Slonski-Fowler & S. D. Truscott, "General education teachers' perceptions of the prereferral intervention team process," *Journal of Educational and Psychological Consultation, 15* (2004): 1–39.

That is, teams are only as effective as they are able to demonstrate that they are improving services and outcomes for students with disabilities and other special needs.

Another criterion for judging team effectiveness is output. Abelson and Woodman (1983) note that a team is effective when its productive output exceeds or meets the organization's standards of quality and quantity. In schools, teams are considered effective when their output meets the standards of their profession and the expectations of the various constituencies, including administrators, parents, and peers. The output might be the number of referrals to special education, the number of students on whose behalf problem solving occurs, or the number of evidence-based intervention strategies implemented in classrooms.

However, most teams' effectiveness also is judged on other factors. A model of business team effectiveness advanced by Nadler, Hackman, and Lawler (1979) suggests that the ultimate effectiveness of a team depends on (1) the level of effort team members devote to the team's task, (2) the level of knowledge and skills within the team, and (3) the strategies the team uses to accomplish its work. Further, these factors are affected by the design of the task, the composition of the team, and the appropriateness of the strategies used by the team. Additional criteria for judging team effectiveness are derived from the studies of multidisciplinary teams mentioned earlier. In combination, these factors and design elements are critical in developing effective teams, and we include them in the characteristics of effective teams described next.

The Team's Goals Are Clear

The goals of an effective team are clearly understood by all team members. Mutual goals represent the team's primary purposes, but each activity the team pursues to achieve its purposes will also have goals. Members of effective teams clearly understand both the central goals and the activity or process goals, and their actions as a team reflect this understanding.

Members' Needs Are Met

In effective teams, the personal needs of team members are satisfied more than frustrated by the group experience. The interpersonal needs of being included, respected, and valued can be met through active participation in a team. Conversely, teams in schools are not likely to be effective in achieving their goals if the team prevents individuals from meeting these interpersonal needs or attaining their individual professional goals. Satisfying members' needs, however, does not mean that individuals always "get their way." When members' needs differ, resistance and conflict may occur. These topics are addressed in Chapter 11.

Members Have Individual Accountability

Team members should clearly understand their roles as well as those of other members. Earlier, we identified role interdependence as a defining characteristic of teams because work teams are constructed with members who have complementary and interconnected parts to play. Each member has responsibility for something the group needs in order to function. The structure of an effective team provides for individual accountability that increases the tendency of team members to devote adequate effort to meeting their team responsibilities.

Group Processes Maintain the Team

The group processes used in effective teams serve to increase, or at least maintain, the team's capacity to work collaboratively on future endeavors. Specifically, these group processes ensure that leadership and participation are distributed throughout the team. Leadership skills, such as initiating discussion, setting standards, encouraging, summarizing, and gaining consensus, can be used by different members of the team. A team that wants to make maximum use of the diverse experience, expertise, and information of its members distributes leadership roles. Team members recognize that leadership is necessarily a shared responsibility and assume that role when necessary to support the functioning of the group.

Team Members Have Leadership Skills

A considerable literature documents the need for effective team leadership (Chen & Rybak, 2004; Johnson & Johnson, 2000). Most authorities agree that all team members need to have leadership skills, even when they are not assuming the formal role of team leader. Leadership skills are those that help the group function effectively and progress toward its goals. From that perspective it should be clear that a group member other than the designated leader may take an active role in facilitating the team's progress. By offering a summary of positions stated by others, asking clarifying questions, or simply helping to ensure that all team members have the opportunity to participate in discussion and decision making, a team member demonstrates leadership and helps the team progress.

Conducting Meetings

When we talk about teams with students or field-based colleagues, the discussion inevitably turns at some point to the burdens and challenges of meetings and then to strategies for ensuring successful team meetings. In this chapter we have presented background information on teams and discussed team characteristics as well as skills and strategies for developing effective teams. Knowing the purpose of teams, acquiring communication and interaction skills (Chapters 8–10), and understanding the team development process provide you with an important knowledge and skill base within which you can apply some key strategies for conducting meetings that will assist you in making your team successful.

Prior to the Meeting

Effective team meetings begin long before anyone gathers at a conference table. Often, the work done in preparation for the meeting determines to a great extent its outcomes.

Decide Whether a Meeting Is Needed

Sometimes meetings are held without a clear understanding of their need. In busy school settings, professionals occasionally get so caught up in the details of scheduling a meeting that they lose track of the specific reasons the meeting is being convened. Generally, you should avoid scheduling meetings about items that can be conveyed more easily or clearly in writing or on the telephone, such as schedules of events, procedures for ordering materials, and so on. Meetings are valuable when a need exists for a group or team to discuss a matter and reach a shared understanding of its elements. They are also useful when group advice or problem solving is needed or when it is not clear who is responsible for an issue that must be resolved. Clearly, meetings also are needed for student-centered decision making regarding such matters as program or intervention planning.

Decide the Purpose

Meetings may be held for information sharing, data gathering, problem solving, and decision making. Information sharing often occurs adequately outside of meetings by using e-mail or other written, one-way communication strategies. But groups may need to clarify the information and thus find that meetings provide helpful opportunities to ask clarifying questions and to gain a shared understanding of the information. The purpose of a data-gathering meeting is to obtain information from group members and to solicit feedback from them. This is particularly helpful when several members have different pieces of information all of which are integral to gaining a full understanding of the topic at hand. Problem-solving processes were discussed in Chapter 2, where their characteristics and strategies for their successful completion were delineated. Problem solving and decision making, particularly in regard to a student's program, require a meeting of a team of responsible persons.

Many meetings have more than one purpose, but usually one will be central. For example, when the primary purpose is problem solving, data gathering and information sharing will still occur and contribute to the effectiveness of the problem solving. Knowing the central purpose of a meeting helps determine who should be invited and what procedures and processes should be followed during the meeting.

Articulate Desired Outcomes

Expectations for the outcomes of a meeting will drive the behavior of team members. The desired outcomes should be explicitly stated so that all group members hold the same expectations and can work toward a common set of goals. Imagine a meeting in which one member believes the purpose is to explore common interests of members from two agencies while another believes the meeting has been called to agree to resource sharing between agencies. Suspicion is likely to develop as one shows exceptional interest in the resources of all participants. Imagine that same meeting if the purpose were articulated in advance: to examine the resources available within each agency for assisting the student's family to maintain a regular schedule of counseling and physical therapy.

Delineate a Realistic Agenda and Time Frame

Everyone attending a meeting should know what to expect at it. Distribution of an agenda lets participants know what to expect and what to do, bring, and

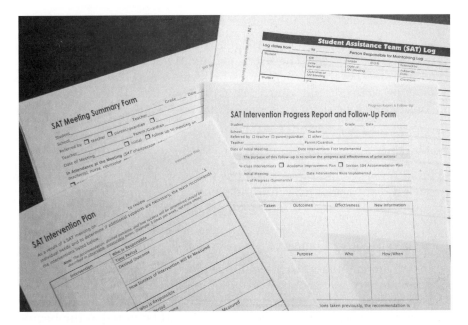

Effective teams have an agenda for their meetings and specific procedures to follow in order to encourage clear communication and to build a sense of purpose.

prepare. Although all school professionals are busy and may think that preparing an agenda is an unnecessary expenditure of time, it is time very well spent. It reduces confusion and greatly increases the likelihood that participants will come prepared. Agendas are most effective when they provide an explicit statement of the desired outcomes, participants' roles, the steps that will be followed during the meeting, the person responsible for individual items on the agenda, and the anticipated time allocation for each agenda item or step. Agreement on the importance of meeting agendas is so widespread that most word-processing programs and computer clip art packages include standard agenda templates.

Careful planning should ensure that the agenda is realistic in terms of potential outcomes and the time allotted for individual items. As a general rule of thumb, recognize that everything will take longer than one expects, especially if the team has not yet developed its norms and aligned itself with clearly articulated goals. As team members become comfortable with their roles and functions, they become more efficient and more time effective. The student assistance team at Wilson Middle School has worked together for a semester and has become accustomed to the team process and time management strategies. When they began their work in September, they could discuss only a single student during their one-hour meeting. After five months of team meetings, they are able to address at least two students in one session and to complete quick updates on one or two others.

Arrange the Setting

Several elements of room arrangement and atmosphere contribute to the success of your meetings. These factors can influence the psychological and physical comfort level of the participants. The location and physical characteristics of the meeting room should afford privacy and limited distractions. Other factors to consider include seating arrangements, temperature, and light and noise levels.

During the Meeting

In addition to careful preparation, the way in which the meeting itself is conducted is important for achieving planned outcomes. As you read about the following meeting elements, try to apply them to meetings you regularly attend.

Review Agenda and Timelines

After team members assemble, the facilitator should review the agenda and get team concurrence that the proposed sequence, time allocation, and member roles are appropriate. Of special importance is agreement on an ending time. If a team member has to depart early, it should be noted at the beginning of the meeting and the agenda order adjusted if needed. Other adjustments may be called for when the team examines the agenda. Teams should resist the desire to talk about team member schedules or team business early in the meeting. Because time is such a tremendously scarce commodity in schools, it is often the paramount concern as teams begin their meetings. Yet, if schedules become the first order of business they tend to become the primary topic of the meeting.

Participate Effectively

Different roles are significant to a team's success, and team members often rotate through the roles of facilitator, recorder, and timekeeper. For meetings to progress smoothly, members must know their roles and how to perform these roles. When teams are first forming, it is often useful to spend time learning the roles and the skills each entails. The topic of team member roles is explored in more detail in Putting Ideas into Practice.

The facilitator generally leads the meeting and takes responsibility for pre-meeting preparation and coordinating postmeeting follow-up. Designating a group member to serve as timekeeper, who signals the facilitator when scheduled time periods are ending, is a useful support for the facilitator, who can then concentrate on the quality and focus of the group work. The facilitator guides the team through its agenda by focusing energy on a common task, encouraging members to participate, remaining neutral, and suggesting alternative methods for reaching agreement or making a decision. Specific strategies that assist the facilitator include clearly defining the role, obtaining agreement on the purpose and process to be followed in the meeting, listening, supporting the recorder, and asking clarifying questions.

The recorder is the keeper of the group memory. Like the facilitator, this person remains neutral. The recorder captures the ideas and suggestions of

PUTTING IDEAS INTO PRACTICE

Roles for Team Members

Whether the team you are on has as its purpose helping general education teachers to solve problems related to student achievement or behavior, determining eligibility for special education or writing an IEP or an ISFP, or addressing special concerns about students with significant disabilities, its members assume various roles. Some of these roles are formal; that is, they are assigned in order to foster effective team functioning. Examples of formal roles include these:

- *Leader.* The person in this role is responsible for moving the team to accomplish its work, keeping the group focused, gathering any materials needs, and addressing problems in logistics or procedures.
- *Facilitator.* The facilitator helps to ensure that members follow ground rules (e.g., "Remember that we decided to have everyone quietly think for a minute before we make a final decision so that everyone has a chance to be sure they agree") and that everyone participates in decision making.
- *Recorder.* This individual is charged with keeping minutes of essential team decisions.
- *Timekeeper.* A timekeeper helps to ensure that all team agenda items are addressed in the allocated time. This individual often reminds team members of time matters (e.g., "We had agreed to spend 10 minutes discussing Thomas's behavior plan, and that time is up").

However, team members also make a valuable contribution when they assume informal roles that contribute to team effectiveness. Examples of the roles that teams sometimes need include these:

- *Coaches* make positive comments and help the team feel positive about its work.
- *Crusaders* identify the most important issues and make sure that the team stays focused on these, preventing the team from diverting its attention to other concerns.
- *Explorers* take a fresh look at situations, people, and interventions to generate new ideas.
- *Sculptors* help the group make decisions and move it from ideas to implementation.
- *Curators* clarify ideas of others, explaining information in a way that all team members can understand.
- *Conductors* help establish a logic for team conversations and the ideas they produce.
- *Scientists* focus on what is happening and can generate hypotheses that lead the team to look beyond obvious explanations.

Which formal and informal team member roles would you be most comfortable in assuming? Which of the informal roles do you think would be most important for prereferral teams? IEP teams? Other teams?

Sources: Adapted from NYS Governor's Office of Employee Relations, *Team roles and responsibilities* (2003), retrieved November 15, 2005, from www.goer.state.ny.us/train/onlinelearning/FTMS/200s1.html; and Teamtechnology, *Working out your team role* (2004), retrieved November 15, 2005, from www.team technology.co.uk/workingoutyourteamrole.htm.

group members without interpreting or evaluating them. When group members have trouble expressing themselves, it is tempting for the recorder to put words in their mouths, but effective recorders avoid that. Skills helpful in this role include the ability to listen for key words or concepts and record them verbatim. One cannot record all that is said, and so identifying the most salient points is critical. Usually, the recorder should prepare summary notes that the members may have following the meeting. One strategy for doing this is to have an established note-taking format and use it to record main points.

Group members are as important to team functioning as are the facilitator and recorder. Effective group members monitor and support the facilitator and recorder. They observe the facilitator to ensure that he or she remains neutral and does not try to influence the group. If the facilitator begins expressing opinions or disagreeing with the group members, the team members should call attention to it. A member of the Kennedy High School team might say, "Barb, I think that you may be steering the group toward a decision that James should have more time in the resource room." Similarly, a good group member monitors the recorder's writing. If the recorder misinterprets what a speaker has said, a group member catches it and suggests a change. Group members also need to employ effective interaction skills, listen to others, avoid being negative or defensive, and participate in the group discussion and decision making.

After the Meeting

Regardless of your role, you are likely to have responsibilities after a meeting. The group notes will indicate if you have a specific task or work assignment and the date at which it should be completed. All team members have responsibility for continuing their implementation of the educational plan, recording data, as well as supporting and coordinating with other members.

Collaboration and Teams

The first part of this chapter examined variations in school teams, distinguishing among many models for teaming based on a continuum of collaboration among members from different disciplines or perspectives. You learned that multidisciplinary teams have the least collaboration, interdisciplinary teams function with more, and transdisciplinary teams have the most collaboration of the three models. Thinking about collaboration is not limited to these team structures; it can be applied broadly to all types of teams.

The distinctions between the elements of a collaborative style and those of a team structure are not always completely clear, nor do they necessarily need to be. This is partly because the defining characteristics of a team are those that define the relationship among team members, just as the defining characteristics of collaboration are those that define the relationship among participants in any collaborative activity. Moreover, the defining characteristics of a team are very similar to those of collaboration because it is the elements of collaboration that distinguish a team from a loosely constructed work group or a committee.

Overall, all effective teams are characterized by strong collaborative relationships among members (Laframboise, Epanchin, Colucci, & Hocutt, 2004). Team members share parity, share a common goal, share responsibility for decision making, and share accountability for outcomes. Teams have common norms and shared beliefs and values, and team members trust one another. Collaboration's emergent characteristic of interdependence is a critical defining trait of a team. The relationship between teams and collaboration is simple: An effective team is a collaborative work group (McLaughlin, 2002). However, when some members dominate interactions or insist on pursuing only their own agenda, or when members defer to someone perceived as having the greatest power, a group referred to as a "team" is not functioning in a collaborative way, regardless of its label.

Summary

An educational team is a group of interdependent individuals with unique skills and perspectives who interact directly to achieve their mutual goal of providing students with effective educational programs and services. The defining characteristics of educational teams include awareness of team membership, shared norms, members with diverse skills and perspectives, a shared goal of effective service delivery, and interdependence. Teams have cycles and progress through stages as they mature. Models for teaming in schools can be distinguished along two dimensions. The first dimension is the working relationship among people from different disciplines, including multidisciplinary, interdisciplinary, and transdisciplinary team models. The second dimension is the purpose of the team. Three types of student-centered teams include (1) teams that make decisions about student referral, assessment, and eligibility for special education services; (2) problem-solving teams concerned with issues affecting students' academic, behavioral, social, or emotional problems at school; and (3) service delivery teams that provide direct services to students. Features of effective teams include clear goals, individual accountability, shared responsibility, functional group processes, and leadership. Careful attention should be given to planning and conducting team meetings so that they are well prepared, efficiently implemented, and effective in their outcomes. Teams, by definition, share many characteristics with collaboration. In fact, effective teams may be described as highly collaborative work groups.

Activities and Assignments

1. List the teams of which you are a member. Which of these teams are most effective? What are the characteristics of the effective and ineffective teams you have experienced?

2. Think about teams that exist outside the context of education. How are these teams (e.g., sports teams, surgical teams, emergency response teams) similar to and

different from the teams in schools? What could school teams learn by thinking about the characteristics and functioning of these other teams?

3. Think about the differences among multidisciplinary, interdisciplinary, and transdisciplinary teams. How might each type of team be the most effective in schools? Generate the profile of a student with a disability or other special needs with your classmates or find an already-prepared case study. What might each type of team accomplish on behalf of this student? What is the rationale for your responses?

4. The dynamics of a team meeting facilitate or impede its progress. Attend a team meeting and observe the roles taken and the behaviors and comments of team members. Prepare a description of member roles, and then outline behaviors that were helpful to the team's functioning and those that were not. What formal and informal roles did you observe team members assuming? If you were providing feedback to the team members, what would be the three most important points you would want to make?

5. Identify a team experience that you have had or observed that was not as successful as you would have liked it to be. Using the characteristics of collaboration presented in Chapter 1 and the issues raised in this chapter, analyze the situation and describe how factors related to collaboration may have contributed to the problems.

6. Interview a school professional who is responsible for arranging and conducting team meetings. What aspects of effective team meetings does this person mention? What are the dilemmas that this person identifies related to effective meetings? What role do you see that you should play in helping to ensure that team meetings are effective?

For Further Reading

Burn, S. M. (2004). *Groups: Theory and practice.* Belmont, CA: Wadsworth.

Fleming, J. L., & Monda-Amaya, L. E. (2001). Process variables critical for team effectiveness. *Remedial and Special Education, 22,* 158–171.

Friend, M., & Cook, L. (1997). Student-centered teams in schools: Still in search of an identity. *Journal of Educational and Psychological Consultation, 8,* 3–20.

Hunt, P., Soto, G., Maier, J., Liborion, N., & Bae, S. (2004). Collaborative teaming to support preschoolers with severe disabilities who are placed in general education early childhood programs [Electronic version]. *Topics in Early Childhood Special Education, 24,* 123–142.

Johnson, D. W., & Johnson, F. P. (2002). *Joining together: Group theory and group skills* (7th ed.). Boston: Allyn & Bacon.

Ogletree, B. T., Bull, J., Drew, R., & Lunnen, K. (2001). Team-based service delivery for students with disabilities: Practice options and guidelines for success. *Intervention in School and Clinic, 36,* 138–145.

Rubinson, F. (2002). Lessons learned from implementing problem-solving teams in urban high schools. *Journal of Educational and Psychological Consultation, 13,* 185–217.

CHAPTER 4

Consultation

Personal Commitment | Communication Skills | Interaction Processes | Programs or Services | Context

Connections

Similar to Chapter 3 on teaming and Chapter 5 on co-teaching, Chapter 4 explores a specific service delivery approach that emphasizes collaboration. This chapter uses the foundational information about collaboration contained in Chapter 1 to examine the definition and characteristics of consultation, approaches for implementing it in schools, and its relationship to collaboration. It also provides additional opportunities to apply the problem-solving process that was outlined in Chapter 2, and it relies on the communication skills you will learn in Chapters 8, 9, and 10. Consultation is appropriately used when students can be successful with indirect service, and it often is employed in work with parents and families as well as among professionals.

Learner Objectives

After reading this chapter you will be able to:

1. Define *consultation* and outline the characteristics of consulting relationships among professional educators and between educators and parents.
2. Articulate a rationale for the use of consultation in schools with diverse groups of learners.
3. Identify models of consultation that educators sometimes use, describe examples of each, and indicate when each might be instructionally appropriate.
4. Explain the relationship between consultation and collaboration.

5. Describe how collaboration can effectively serve consultants as an interpersonal style.

6. Outline several issues that currently affect consultation as a collaborative service delivery option in schools.

7. Recognize how consultation can be affected by the cultural perspectives of consultants and consultees.

Susan is an itinerant teacher of students who are deaf or hard of hearing. Because she visits an average of three schools each day, some of the services she offers are consultative. Today she has scheduled an appointment with Brandi Wilson, the fourth-grade teacher for Marshall, who has a moderate hearing loss. At the meeting, the educators first review the effectiveness of several classroom accommodations that Susan has suggested over the past month. Ms. Wilson comments that she is finding it difficult to remember to pair her words with visual cues when giving directions, but that she has assigned partners for all students in the classroom so that if Marshall or any other student does not understand directions, peer assistance is readily available. Ms. Wilson then explains a concern she has: Marshall is becoming more and more disruptive in class, at times refusing to work, sometimes grabbing materials away from other students, and occasionally hitting others. Susan asks several questions to understand better the behaviors and the context in which they are occurring, and she schedules an observation time for tomorrow. At that point, the meeting must conclude because Susan is due at another school.

Introduction

Professionals who work with students with special needs in schools have for many years recognized that one way to support them is indirectly, through consultation with their teachers. For example, in the 1960s school psychologists acknowledged that they were too few in number to meet directly with all the students who should access their services, and they recognized that this would always be the case. They therefore began shifting their role responsibilities to consult with general education teachers, who then implemented in their classrooms the ideas that were generated during a structured problem-solving process (Tractman, 1961). As noted in Chapter 1, as the idea of mainstreaming grew in the late 1960s and early 1970s, special education teachers also sometimes assumed consulting roles (McKenzie, 1972). Their purpose was to provide assistance to general education teachers whose class groups included students with disabilities. They seldom worked directly with the students, except to demonstrate a technique or strategy. They met with teachers to problem solve about needed classroom interventions and to troubleshoot with teachers when challenges arose.

With the emphasis in today's schools on inclusive practices and accountability for all students' learning, consultation continues to be a service delivery option used by special education teachers, school psychologists, speech/

language therapists, occupational therapists, early childhood educators, and other special services providers (e.g., Akin-Little, Little, & Delligatti, 2004; Amatea, Daniels, Bringman, & Vandiver, 2004; Denton, Hasbrouck, & Sekaquaptewa, 2003; Schmidt, 2003; Wesley & Buysse, 2004). For many of these professionals, consultation is just one type of support they are expected to provide; for others, consultation is their primary job responsibility.

Consultation Concepts

Because consultation has been used in schools for several decades, much has been written about it and many definitions have been offered for it. Some definitions have stressed that consultation is expertise offered by a counselor or psychologist to teachers to address student problems (Parker, 1975). Others have offered a more egalitarian view in which consultation occurs between any two professionals, one of whom has particular expertise to address the problem at hand (Caplan, 1970). Yet others have contributed the concepts that consultation is a voluntary and nonsupervisory interaction between individuals and that it is a specialized form of problem solving (Brown, Pryzwansky, & Schulte, 1995; Conoley & Conoley, 1992; Joshi, 2004).

From our perspective, key elements of these definitions as well as those proposed by many others (e.g., Brown, Pryzwansky, & Schulte, 2006; Dinkmeyer & Carlson, 2001; Donahue, Falk, & Provet, 2000; Schulte & Osborne, 2003; Sheridan & Cowan, 2004) contribute to a contemporary meaning for consultation. The definition of *consultation* can be summarized as follows:

> School consultation is a voluntary process in which one professional assists another to address a problem concerning a third party.

Further, the extensive research exploration of consultation documented in the professional literature demonstrates that this service delivery option has been clearly articulated, widely implemented, and carefully examined for its benefits and drawbacks. An example of this research is included in A Basis in Research on page 90.

Characteristics of Consultation

Of course, knowing a definition of consultation is only a beginning. In order to use consultation effectively, it also is essential to know more about its nature. The characteristics of school consultation have been extensively described in the literature for school psychology, counseling psychology, special education, and other special services (e.g., Brown et al., 2006; Dougherty, 2004; Kampwirth, 2006). The characteristics generally seen as most essential are discussed next.

Triadic and Indirect Relationship

Although consultation in other disciplines (e.g., law, business, and medicine) may occur between two individuals and not relate immediately to a third party,

---

A BASIS IN RESEARCH

Demonstrating the Effectiveness of Behavioral Consultation

Consultation has a long history of applications in education, and many professionals have studied specific aspects of it, including the extent to which consultees implement the strategies they identify when working with consultants (e.g., Sterling-Turner, Watson, & Moore, 2002), the perceptions of consultants and consultees regarding their roles and consultation effectiveness (e.g., Athanasiou, Geil, Hazel, & Copeland, 2002), and the characteristics of the communication that occurs during consultative interactions (e.g., Grissom, Erchul, & Sheridan, 2003). One area of particular interest is the use of behavioral consultation to address students' classroom behavior, and an example of research on this was completed by Wilkinson (2003).

Using a case study method, Wilkinson worked with a classroom teacher to address concerns related to Ana, a first-grade student who was frequently off task, who argued and fought with peers, and who refused to follow school rules. After Ana's teacher gathered data on her behavior for five sessions, she and the consultant developed a behavior contract that was presented to Ana as a game in which she could earn rewards such as stickers and classroom activities. Behaviors targeted included completing classroom assignments, interacting appropriately with peers and adults, and complying with teacher requests. Ana's teacher then implemented the contract while continuing to gather data on Ana's behavior. The intervention was successful in significantly reducing Ana's inappropriate behavior, and Ana's teacher rated both the intervention she and the consultant had designed and the consultant's effectiveness as highly effective.

Wilkinson concluded that his case study demonstrated that behavioral consultation can be used as a vehicle for positively affecting student behaviors and that it can be implemented so that it is acceptable to teachers. His work also illustrates that consultation about particular students might effectively be carried out by any number of professionals in a school—counselors, psychologists, or special education teachers.

Source: Based on L. A. Wilkinson, "Using behavioral consultation to reduce challenging behavior in the classroom" [Electronic version], *Preventing School Failure, 47* (2003): 100–105.

---

in schools it typically is triadic, involving three parties and with an indirect relationship between the consultant and the client. The consultant (special services provider) and the consultee (an individual teacher, parent, or administrator, or a group of professionals or parents) together design services that the consultee provides to the client (most often a student). The client is not a direct participant in the interaction but is the beneficiary of the process. For example, a psychologist who acts as a consultant may meet with a teacher to plan classroom-based positive behavior supports for a student, but since the psychologist does not interact with the student, his or her relationship with that student is indirect. Similarly, a consultant supporting students through the use of assistive technology might meet with a special education teacher, a general education teacher, and a parent to discuss the types of devices that might enhance students' participation in the classroom and the software that could be used to help them acquire critical academic skills. With the exception of observing and possibly modeling how to use a new piece of equipment, the consultant's interactions are entirely with the adults, but they occur for the benefit of the students.

Voluntariness

A consultee may be puzzled by a situation and seek the assistance of a consultant, or a consultant may notice some difficulty and offer insight to a consultee for remedying the problem. In each case, both the consultant and the consultee have the prerogative of entering or terminating the relationship at any time. This characteristic of voluntariness establishes the principle that consultation cannot be a coerced process (Brown et al., 2006; Dinkmeyer & Carlson, 2001). Both professionals agree to participate, and they each can withdraw when they choose. For example, Mr. Caldwell, a middle school social studies teacher, might ask Ms. Goldstein, a school counselor, to meet with him because he has concerns about Craig's sudden immature behavior in class, a problem that he thinks might be related to Craig's parents' recent divorce and family upheaval. Ms. Goldstein agrees to meet to problem solve about the issue, she also follows up two weeks later to see whether the strategies they planned were effective, and she raises the option of offering to Craig that he chat with her. Conversely, Ms. Goldstein might have heard about Craig's family situation and approached Mr. Caldwell and the rest of his team about it, and the team welcomed the conversation and was relieved to discuss and address the problem. It is important to note, however, that the nature of consultation may change when the consultant rather than the consultee initiates the process; this form of consultation sometimes might feel to the consultee as though it is not truly voluntary.

Expert and Directional Relationship

Most professionals who study consultation emphasize that consultants and consultees mutually influence each other and that consultants do not have authority over consultees. They also recommend that consultants be facilitative, empathic, and collegial (e.g., Gravois, 2002; Meyers, 2002; Walther-Thomas, Korinek, McLaughlin, & Williams, 2000). Regardless of its democratic nature, however, the consulting relationship exists only because it is perceived that the consultee, not the consultant, has a work-related problem. Thus, the primary reason for the interaction is the consultee's perception of a problem that cannot be solved without another's expertise. In fact, it is difficult to imagine why consultees would participate in consultation unless they were relatively certain a consultant had expert knowledge and could provide insight on the matters they had been unable to alleviate themselves. In schools, even when both the consultant and the consultee have a significant interest in the student, the assumption for consultation is still that the classroom teacher has primary daily teaching responsibility for the student and thus is the direct beneficiary of consulting assistance from a special service provider.

Problem-Solving Process with Steps or Stages

In Chapter 2 you learned that much collaboration in education centers on shared problem solving, and this point was illustrated in Chapter 3 as you learned about teaming. Consultation is yet another example of a specialized problem-solving process, one that gives particular attention to the beginning and end of the process. The number of steps in the consultation process varies according to the author outlining them, but they typically include (1) *entry,* the physical and psychological beginning of a series of interactions and the establishment of trust and respect; (2) *problem identification,* the establishment of a goal for the interaction; (3) *planning,* the decisions about how to reach the intended goal; (4) *intervention,* carrying out the planned interventions; (5) *evaluation,* the determination of intervention success; and (6) *exit,* the termination of the consulting relationship. Some evidence suggests that consultants do not follow these steps in a rigid manner; the specific sequence followed depends on the situation (Erchul & Martens, 1997). Thus, knowing the precise steps or stages is not as critical as recognizing that consultation is a process comprised of such steps.

The process of consulting might look like this: A school psychologist meets with a middle school team to discuss Ernie, an eighth-grader who is often absent, who is refusing to attempt assignments, and who is becoming disruptive in class. At that first meeting, the psychologist asks a few questions (e.g., In what areas does Ernie excel? How have Ernie's behaviors and patterns of learning changed since the beginning of the year?), but he mostly listens to the teachers discuss their frustrations. The group also jokes about its need for sweets and arranges for someone to stop at the local doughnut shop prior to the next session. At the second meeting, the psychologist and teachers more specifically identify the problem they will address, and they generate alternative solutions for it, weighing the pros and cons of each. The teachers agree to try several interventions for the next two weeks. After that time, the entire group meets (and another volunteer provides breakfast) to evaluate the effectiveness of the interventions. Some changes are made, and the psychologist clarifies that his role is essentially finished, but that he will check back with the group in a couple of weeks. The process, from entry to exit, has been carried out. If Ernie is a student receiving special education services through consultation, a series of problem-solving cycles would occur during the course of the school year. If the interventions for Ernie were not successful, the team might decide that he should be brought to the attention of the school's intervention team so that formal consideration of the need for possible special education might begin.

Shared but Differentiated Responsibilities and Accountability

Consultants and consultees do not share the same responsibility and accountability. If you are a consultant, your primary responsibility and areas of accountability are to ensure that the consulting process is appropriately followed and to offer specific and feasible assistance responsive to the consultee's needs (Kratochwill

Consultation may be used as a type of service delivery for students with IEPs, but it also has value for assisting teachers to address concerns related to students at risk of school failure.

& Pittman, 2002). Because consultants do not control consultees' decisions about whether to accept and implement specific strategies, ultimately they cannot be accountable for the success or failure of the consultation outcomes if they have appropriately carried out their part of the process, a topic addressed in Putting Ideas into Practice on page 94. On the other hand, if you are a consultee, you have the responsibility to participate in good faith in the consultation process and to seriously consider the assistance being offered (Heron & Harris, 2001). If you agree to use a strategy, you are responsible for doing so appropriately. This concept of *treatment integrity*—that is, the systematic implementation of strategies developed during the consultation process and carried out by a consultee—is essential (DiGennaro, Martens, & McIntyre, 2005; Sterling-Turner, Watson, & Moore, 2002). If consultees do not implement agreed-on interventions, the effectiveness of consultation cannot be assessed. Finally, a consultee's accountability includes gathering data and making judgments about if the problem has been resolved, or if another intervention is needed and desired.

The characteristics of consultation can be identified whether the professional in the consulting role is a school psychologist, a counselor, a speech/language therapist, or a special education teacher. If you look back at the vignette that opened this chapter, which of the characteristics can you find examples of as Susan's responsibilities were described? How might the characteristics apply in a slightly different way to a special educator who is assigned full-time to a single school? To other professionals?

PUTTING IDEAS INTO PRACTICE

Consultant Myths

Much has been written to help consultants refine their practice. One author, Allen Menlo, took the perspective that some of the beliefs that often guide professionals' practice might instead interfere with effective consultation. He suggested that consultants challenge and reverse their thinking on beliefs such as the following:

- *People tell the truth about themselves.* In fact, most people wish to present themselves in the best light, and so they may give a selective description of themselves or their actions. Consultants should keep in mind that when a consultee's recall of a situation does not match that of others it is not necessarily dishonest; it is most likely the consultee's actual perception, filtered by a need to appear skilled.

- *The best way to get a favor is to give a favor.* In fact, most people are glad to do a favor for others, but they may be uncomfortable receiving one. Think of a time when a friend had car trouble. You were probably pleased to be able to offer assistance in the form of a ride to work. But also think about a time when you had car trouble; you may have hesitated to ask for a ride because you did not want to inconvenience anyone. For consultants, the lesson is this: Sometimes it is better to enlist someone's participation by asking them to do so as a favor to you instead of offering them the favor of your expertise.

- *Each person's thoughts and feelings are unique.* In fact, educators are likely to share similar perspectives on many matters pertaining to working with students with disabilities, instructional strategies, and so on. If consultants want to establish a strong working relationship with a teacher or another consultee, sometimes it is beneficial to tap their own deepest thoughts about the situation. Those thoughts just may resonate with the consultee.

Source: Adapted from A. Menlo, "Consultant beliefs which make a significant difference in consultation," in C. L. Warger & L. Aldinger (Eds.), *Preparing special educators for teacher consultation* (Toledo, OH: Preservice Consultation Project, College of Education and Allied Professions, University of Toledo, 1986).

Rationale for and Benefits of Consultation

As with the other service delivery options discussed in this text, consultation is, first, a viable option for successfully educating students with disabilities or other special needs. Thus, when consultation is implemented, it should be designed to benefit students who have IEPs. For example, some students with IEPs are entitled to supports, but they do not need the amount or intensity of service offered through co-teaching or instruction in a separate setting, or they need it only in certain domains (Denton et al., 2003). In such cases, consultation may be an appropriate service, or part of a package of services. Consultation might also represent a transition strategy: If a student has made tremendous progress during elementary school, so much so that the student's eligibility for special services is marginal at best, the team might decide to send the student to middle school with consultative services instead of direct services. The consultation is provided as a means of helping the student move from elementary to middle school. In this case, it might also be a strategy for assisting the student and family to transition out of special education programs and services. Taking these various applications of consultation together, then, you can see that the overall rationale for consultation is that it comprises a low-intensity service that can be used to support students in the least restrictive environment.

Consultation, however, has many other benefits. For example, it can be a low-cost and efficient means by which students with special needs who do not have IEPs (e.g., at-risk learners) can receive focused attention by professional staff. That is, a special education teacher may have time to arrange three brief meetings with a classroom teacher who is concerned about a student, even though the special educator could not justify spending several class periods working with that student or being in that classroom.

In addition to providing a limited type of service to students at risk, consultation often plays a prevention role. If a general education teacher can work with a psychologist to assist a student who has serious behavior issues, as a team they may be able to prevent the problems from becoming so serious that consideration for special education is needed. Likewise, a speech/language therapist might assist a first-grade teacher to design language development lessons to help several of the students, thus eliminating the need for them to be referred for formal services. Students who are entitled to special education services should receive them, but consultation can prevent some students from ever needing such a high level of support.

Yet another benefit of consultation concerns professional development. When teachers seek assistance from consultants, one incidental outcome often is an increase in their knowledge and skills. For example, when Ms. Vogt asks Ms. Denton to observe DeWayne, a student with significant attentional problems, and to work with her to help him be more successful in the classroom, Ms. Denton introduces strategies for active student participation. Thus, Ms. Vogt learns how to implement "One Say, All Say"—that is, having all students repeat the answer given by one student. This technique benefits DeWayne, but it also helps other students to focus attention and participate in lessons. This professional development aspect of consultation can be enhanced when consultants specifically point out to consultees how to apply the ideas generated for one student to other students and situations.

When the benefits of consultation are considered along with its rationale, you can view consultation not only as a service delivery option for students with disabilities, but also as an alternative for meeting student needs and enhancing the strategies in consultees' repertoires by efficiently deploying the professional resources in a school. In fact, as mentioned in the opening to this chapter, one of the early justifications for using consultation occurred during the 1960s, when mental health services came to schools but there were not enough counselors and psychologists to serve all the students identified for assistance. Those professionals began working with teachers, who in turn provided services to students. This indirect approach was recommended again as behavioral approaches became popular in schools at the end of that decade (Tharp & Wetzel, 1969). Now, with students with IEPs in general education settings and many students who are at risk for failure commanding educators' attention, it is not surprising that the same strategy can be used effectively. For example, remember the example of Ernie and how the psychologist met with the middle school team? By doing this, all the teachers benefited from his expertise and they coordinated their intervention efforts. The psychologist's time investment was fairly limited, but the positive impact could be significant.

Consultation Models

Knowing the definition and characteristics of consultation along with the rationale for making it part of your school's service delivery options allows us to proceed to the next level of specificity—exploring models through which consultation may be practiced. Although there is little variation in the general consultation process, the practice of consultation is based on theoretical perspectives that have led to the development of several distinct consultation models (Behring, Cabello, Kushida, & Murguia, 2000; Kampwirth, 2005). These models prescribe consultants' orientation and the assumptions that undergird their interactions with consultees. They also dictate the types of interventions consultants are likely to use. Two models—behavioral consultation and clinical consultation—are particularly applicable to schools and are explored in detail in the following sections. Several other models exist, and these are summarized in Figure 4.1.

Behavioral Consultation

Tharp and Wetzel's (1969) text on using applied behavior analysis in naturalistic settings established *behavioral consultation* as a distinct model to guide the consulting process. These authors proposed that consultation was an efficient means of implementing behavioral interventions with large numbers of individuals. Educators took that message to heart, and since that time, the model has become the most frequently used type of consultation in schools (Luiselli & Diament, 2002), employed by special education teachers, school psychologists, occupational therapists, inclusion facilitators, and others.

Behavioral consultants rely on several assumptions to guide their practice (Luiselli, 2002). First, they themselves must have a thorough understanding of behavioral principles and practices and be able to apply them to their consultees. They also must ensure that consultees either have similar understanding or enough understanding of those principles to carry out behavioral interventions in a systematic way. Second, behavioral consultants presume that the consultee controls reinforcers that will be effective with the client or student; that is, teachers have rewards or consequences that will affect student actions. Third, consultants using this model believe that data collection is not only important but essential, and they stress data-based decision making.

Figure 4.1	Alternative Models of Consultation

In addition to behavioral and clinical consultation, the models most commonly implemented in schools, the following are examples of other consultation models:

■ *Mental health.* Based on Caplan's (1970) work, this consultation model addresses social and emotional problems, acknowledging that some issues are based in the client, some in the consultee's reaction to the client, some in the structure of a program, and some in the program's administration. Typical practitioners of this model are counselors or psychologists who have had specialized training in mental health consultation, and their emphasis is in helping consultees understand how their experiences shape their perceptions of clients (Knotek & Sandoval, 2003). Although this model can help special educators and other consultants understand why consultees may react to particular students in a negative manner, implementation of this model requires extensive professional training in therapeutic interventions that special educators generally have not had.

■ *Organizational.* Sometimes the appropriate level for intervention in consultation is the organization (Waclawski & Church, 2002). In this model, it is assumed that the leaders of an organization are the consultees (e.g., the principals in a school district) and that the clients are the employees (e.g., the teachers). Through needs assessment and other data gathering, self-analysis, and professional development, consultants using this model assist organizations to function more effectively and efficiently, often focusing on staff morale. Organizational consultation usually requires a lengthy timeline and a significant commitment of financial and personnel resources—factors that may limit its viability in many school districts.

■ *Education and training.* Although not always thought of as such, professional development can be considered a model for consultation (Gravois, 2002). Using large-group, small-group, demonstration, and other approaches, a consultant implementing this model would have as a goal improving the knowledge and skills of consultees (e.g., teachers) so that interventions for clients (e.g., students) will improve. Of course, this model presumes that principles of effective staff development are followed. That is, it suggests that training activities are supplemented with coaching and problem-solving sessions so that concepts can effectively be translated in practices that are sustained.

Procedures

Of all the consultation models described in the professional literature, behavioral consultation has the most clearly defined steps or stages, and those steps closely resemble both the general problem-solving process described in Chapter 2 as well as the consultation process outlined at the beginning of this chapter. These are the steps:

1. *Problem identification.* This step involves obtaining a description of the problem and determining how to gather information to confirm its existence and character.

2. *Problem analysis.* This step is closely related to the first. The consultant directs the consultee on how to gather detailed and objective information about the problem so that a strategy for addressing the student problem can be devised.

3. *Intervention.* At this step, the consultant and consultee plan a behavioral strategy to address the problem and positively affect the client, and they clarify each professional's responsibilities related to the intervention. For example, the teacher consultee might agree to provide a daily reward of 10 minutes of free computer time each day when the student has attempted all work without complaint during the class. The consultant might agree to write out the details of the agreement and to participate in introducing the plan to the student. During this step, the consultee carries out the plan with input as needed from the consultant.

4. *Evaluation.* Eventually, the final behavioral consultation step is reached. The consultant and consultee use the data the consultee has been collecting to determine whether the strategy has had the desired impact. Based on what they find, they either conclude the consultation, make changes in the strategy and continue, or begin again (Heron & Harris, 2001; Idol, Nevin, & Paolucci-Whitcomb, 2000; Kampwirth, 2005).

Although the fundamental problem-solving steps of behavioral consultation are very similar to the generic problem-solving steps that professionals carry out in team meetings, co-teaching planning, and informal interactions with colleagues, their uniqueness lies in their reliance on the principles of behaviorism—for example, describing problems in observable terms, using specific reinforcers applied to both the consultee and the client, using data to monitor progress, and employing a highly analytic approach to the entire process. Have you completed coursework in behavior management? If so, you undoubtedly have learned the principles of behaviorism that would make it possible for you to offer this type of consultation assistance. In what types of situations do you think this model would be most helpful?

Analysis of the Behavioral Model

The popularity of behavioral consultation for schools is undoubtedly due to its reliance on well-researched strategies that often result in successful outcomes (Duhon, 2005). Since behavioral consultants emphasize data collection, documentation of consultation's effectiveness can often be made. However, several issues and concerns may arise when behavioral consultation is used. For example, some consultees, including parents and classroom teachers, may object to seemingly coercive behavioral principles and thus may resist the use of this approach. Alternatively, they may lack the understanding of behavioral principles necessary to systematically carry out proposed interventions. For example, a parent might forget to consistently reward his child for completing homework, and if this happens, the plan for helping the student is unlikely to succeed.

In addition, behavioral consultants always must be aware of the ethical dilemma of using behavioral technology to change students' behavior to accommodate the preferences of teachers and parents, rather than assisting students in making self-identified changes that directly benefit them. That is, behavioral consultants need to stress building positive student behaviors such as asking for assistance when stumped on assignments or monitoring their own on-task behavior, rather than emphasizing compliance behavior such as sitting quietly in class.

To address some of the issues in traditional behavioral consultation, over the past several years a new variation of the model has emerged. In *conjoint behavioral consultation,* specialists, classroom teachers, and parents/families work closely together to design, implement, and evaluate interventions to improve student learning and behavior (Sheridan et al., 2004). By doing this, the key adults in a child's life can coordinate their efforts to assist the child. Research suggests that this model is perceived as being acceptable and effective by teachers and parents, and it is particularly valuable for increasing parent involvement in the child's education and building positive school–home relationships (Cowan & Sheridan, 2003; Elksnin & Elksnin, 2000).

Clinical Consultation

Clinical consultation is a diagnostic model that traditionally has been used by school and counseling psychologists, diagnosticians, speech/language specialists, and, to a lesser degree, by social workers and occupational and physical therapists. In addition, as educators work closely together to address the needs of students at risk in inclusive schools (LeCapitaine, 2000), special education teachers who provide services to students with IEPs in general education settings are using this model more and more. In clinical consultation, the consultant is concerned with accurately identifying or diagnosing a client's problem and prescribing strategies for resolving it (Kampwirth, 2005; Sanders, Mazzucchelli, & Studman, 2004). Clinical consultants' first consideration is that the source of the problem is in the client, not the consultee. For example, if a teacher asked a special education teacher for help in deciding how to respond to a student whose attention-getting behavior in the classroom was becoming a serious matter, the special educator would tend to assume that an intervention was needed for the student, not that the teacher's interactions with the student were rewarding the behavior. The consultant would try to help the classroom teacher see the problem clearly (perhaps the student behavior was a means of avoiding difficult assignments) and to design a strategy to change the student's behavior (perhaps by giving the student only a small part of the assignment at one time). If this approach was not successful, the consultant might look at the environment, the teacher's actions in the classroom, and so on.

However, in this model the consultant is not actually involved in the ongoing implementation of the intervention or the monitoring of it. The consultant presumes that the dilemma for the consultee is the identification of the specific problem, not the implementation of strategies to resolve it. In the previous example, the special educator who is the consultant would make suggestions about the intervention, but would not stay involved in the situation unless the teacher asked for a follow-up.

Procedure

The steps for clinical consultation are not as clearly prescribed as they are for behavioral consultation. Clinical consultants typically would meet with a consultee, either a parent or a teacher, to learn about a student's apparent problem, and they would assess the specific problem. In this model, that assessment might include observing the student, interviewing the student, or even directly administering some type of diagnostic instrument. Clinical consultants would then analyze the problem the teacher reported by considering the diagnostic information they had gathered, including the student's strengths and needs. Next, they would suggest interventions for the consultee to try. Although clinical consultants would not implement the intervention, at a later date they might follow up to determine whether the outcome was successful.

Analysis of the Clinical Model

Because consultant involvement generally is confined to the diagnostic and recommendation stages, clinical consultation may be preferred when consultants have limited time in which to offer assistance to consultees or when a complex problem needs clarification that can be offered by an expert diagnostician. The former situation might occur when a special educator is preparing to offer a general education teacher suggestions for interventions for a student who is at risk for failure. The latter might occur when a student who has an IEP has a sudden increase in disruptive or aggressive behavior or experiences unanticipated difficulties in meeting IEP goals and objectives. However, because this consultation model generally assumes that the problem exists primarily in the client, it is not particularly useful if the problem is one that involves the student, the teacher, the environment, and other factors in combination. Also, this model is premised on the consultee having the professional skills to act on the consultant's recommendations. If the consultee does not understand the consultant's conceptualization of the problem or does not have the skills to implement and monitor the intervention, the model has limited utility. How might this consultation model assist you—whether you might be the consultant or the consultee? What are its strengths and drawbacks?

Choosing and Using Consultation Models

As you were reading about behavioral and clinical consultation, you might have wondered whether consultation actually occurs in the distinct steps and following the theoretical perspective outlined, or whether you should just take ideas from these models as well as others and blend them into your own style. As with many concepts and procedures related to your profession, the answer is probably to use both approaches, thinking about consultation models but adapting them to your own experiences and job setting.

Much concern has been expressed about how consultants should be prepared and the content of their professional preparation, including the use of par-

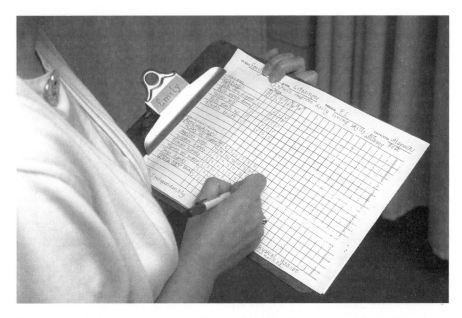

In most consultation models, data collection is an important step that provides a
basis for discussions about the causes of a student's classroom problems and possible
strategies for addressing them.

ticular models (Meyers, 2002). The advantage in learning about specific models
is that professionals in consulting roles then can make deliberate choices about
how to approach their work with other professionals. Without understanding
that consultation can be guided by models, professionals are likely to be unsure
how to proceed if the consultation approach they know is not effective. That is,
consultants who do not understand models may not have a strategy for changing
tactics when the situation calls for such an action.

At the same time, consultation is seldom as "pure" as the models described
in the preceding sections. All consultants tend to put their own signatures on
their work by incorporating their own personal styles, adapting procedures to
fit contextual variables, and relating their consulting to their other role responsibilities, whether direct service to students, staff development, co-teaching, or
others. This individualization of consultation models is certainly expected. The
only caution to raise is that individualizing should not have the effect of altering
the major assumptions and procedures of the various models. If it does, it will
undoubtedly compromise the likely effectiveness of the process.

Thus, a third option is emerging to guide consultants' practice. Some authors
(e.g., Erchul & Martens, 1997; Kampwirth, 2005) are proposing integrated models
of consultation that draw from multiple theoretical perspectives. The advantage
of this approach is that the best features of each of the traditional models can be
tapped, while at the same time the specific opportunities and constraints for consultative services that exist in school environments can be taken into account.

Consultation and Collaboration

The emphasis on relating collaboration and consultation in special education can be traced to the early 1970s, particularly in the fields of school and counseling psychology (e.g., Kurpius & Brubaker, 1976; Pryzwansky, 1974). The viewpoint was expressed that consultative interactions were more likely to be successful if they were facilitative and supportive rather than prescriptive (e.g., Parker, 1975). By the end of the 1970s, it was clear that for psychologists and counselors in schools, a collaborative or facilitative approach to consultation was generally recommended over other approaches.

Consultation as a role responsibility for special education teachers was rapidly evolving during the same time period (Friend, 1988). The Vermont Consulting Teacher Program (Christie, McKenzie, & Burdett, 1972), begun in the late 1960s, was setting a precedent for the systematic use of teacher consultation. It was implemented by highly trained consulting teachers who held specialist degrees and adjunct faculty appointments at the University of Vermont. As these consultants worked with, trained, and offered course credit to classroom teachers, their status as trainers and university faculty reinforced the notion of consultant as expert. Later, an additional issue arose in this model. Although in the original Vermont model the consultative relationship was voluntary, as this approach spread to other geographic areas the participation of teachers became less voluntary. Students with disabilities were mainstreamed and special education teachers or other special services providers were assigned to consult with general education teachers, often without any preparation for the consultant role.

The backlash that occurred should not have been surprising. Critics made it clear that it was inappropriate for special education to try to "fix" general education; general educators did not need special educators to serve as experts to tell them what to do with the students in their classrooms (Friend, 1988). Nor was it likely, in many instances, that special educators knew what to do in a general education classroom, since at that time most of them worked primarily in separate special education classrooms or resource rooms, with students coming to them and no in-class services being provided.

By the early 1980s, the special education teacher consultation literature was countering the criticism of special educators as questionable experts for general education settings by renewing an emphasis on collegial relationships (Evans, 1980; Friend, 1984). Collaborative approaches to consultation began to be advocated at this time (Idol, Nevin, & Paolucci-Whitcomb, 1994). This trend has continued and is also reflected in school and counseling psychology (Amatea et al., 2004; Kampwirth, 2005; Meyers, 2002), although some professionals believe that many teachers actually prefer a directive rather than a collaborative style to the consulting process (Erchul, Raven, & Ray, 2001).

The debate about the role of collaboration in the consultation process has continued in recent years. Some authors contend that collaboration is not a well-enough understood concept to consider its application to consultation (e.g., Schulte & Osborne, 2003). Some argue that interpersonal influence must be studied in order to understand the style consultants use in working with consultees (Erchul et al., 2001). Other authors (e.g., Gutkin, 1999) propose that the process of consultation can be implemented with variations along two dimensions: (1) coercive–collaborative and (2) directive–nondirective. Unlike most current thinking in the field and the perspective taken in this textbook, they suggest that directiveness is not the opposite of collaboration, and they offer that research is needed to examine consultation in light of this reconceptualization of the interpersonal aspect of it. For you as a practitioner of consultation, what is important to understand is that inquiry into the relationship between collaboration and consultation is far from complete and knowledge about how it affects consultant practice is likely to continue to emerge.

It should be noted that today, with the increased pressure for access to the general curriculum and the resulting increased enrollment of students with disabilities in general education classrooms, the concept of collaboration and the notion of consultation often are framed as a discussion of voluntariness. In some instances, a special services provider as well as a classroom teacher have responsibility for a student's education. This situation increases the likelihood that the teacher will initiate some consultation, but that the special educator may initiate even more. For example, if a student with autism is included in an intermediate classroom, an inclusion facilitator might request a weekly meeting to determine the student's progress and design interventions. The teacher may benefit from these meetings, but at the same time may feel unwanted pressure to participate in them, particularly during busy times of the school year. The teacher may not believe that the meetings are truly voluntary. Additional examples of teacher beliefs that sometimes challenge the consulting process are included in Putting Ideas into Practice on the next page.

Despite these historical and contemporary issues related to collaboration in consultation, by using our definitions the distinction between these two terms can be clearly articulated so that special services providers can base their practice on an understanding of each. Because collaboration is a style or an approach to interaction, it can be attached to the consultation process, just as it can be attached to problem solving, assessing, and co-teaching. Moreover, a consultant may choose to use a collaborative approach at some consultation stages and not others, just as the consultant may choose to use it with some consultees and not with others.

However, ascribing collaboration to the consultation process does not make it a unique model (Dougherty, 2004) in the sense of the models presented earlier. *Any* model of consultation can be implemented collaboratively. For example, behavioral consultation has clear, theoretically based principles that prescribe its practice. Whether or not behavioral consultation is carried out collaboratively is an issue that is distinct from the model itself. Behavioral consultation can be conducted collaboratively within a relationship characterized by parity, mutual goals, shared decision making, and all the additional characteristics of collaboration. However, behavioral consultation also may be conducted by someone who, using a directive style, retains much of the decision-making responsibility,

PUTTING IDEAS INTO PRACTICE

Teacher Beliefs That May Affect Consultation

Professionals who have consultation responsibilities may find that certain beliefs held by teachers influence those teachers' actions with students and also affect the outcomes of consultation. Positive teacher beliefs facilitate consultation. For example, teachers who believe that students can make good decisions, that all students can learn, and that no one can expect to be perfect are likely to embrace the ideas generated during consultation. On the other hand, as you read these problematic teacher beliefs, think about how you might recognize them during interactions with colleagues and how you might need to address them as a consultant in order to accomplish your goals for students.

■ *I must be capable of handling all students and all situations, or I am not a good teacher.* Teachers who hold this belief may approach consultation as an admission of failure, and they may be reluctant to fully participate in the process.

■ *My plans must succeed at all costs.* Teachers who hold this belief may find it difficult to make changes in the ways that they typically manage their classrooms or interact with students. Altering their practices may seem like too risky an option.

■ *I must control the classroom and all students so they do not control me. To be out of control is dangerous.* Certainly teachers need to be in control of their classrooms. However, teachers with this belief may not recognize the importance of addressing student behavior using positive means, and they may resort to negative consequences to address serious student academic and behavior problems. These teachers may be reluctant to reward students for what the teachers believe they should do intrinsically.

■ *Children are the product of their heredity and the larger environment, and they cannot be changed.* Teachers who hold this belief may be deliberately or inadvertently biased toward certain students. They may dismiss ideas for helping some students.

Source: Adapted from D. Dinkmeyer & J. Carlson, *Consultation: Creating school-based interventions,* 2nd ed. (Philadelphia: Brunner-Routledge, 2001), pp. 96–100.

prescribes interventions, and offers expert advice and explanations to consultees. This same analogy could be made for clinical and other models of consultation: Each could be implemented by a consultant who may or may not emphasize the use of a collaborative style of interaction.

The Consulting Relationship

As you observe and participate in consultative interactions you will notice that effective consultants deliberately select a style of interaction to suit the circumstances. Sometimes the nature of the consultation situation or the needs of the consultee require the consultant to use a directive style. For example, you may receive an isolated request from a colleague seeking assistance in interpreting a student's assessment results. Your caseload, available time, and knowledge of your colleague's other sources of professional support, among other considerations, may lead you simply to offer your expert opinion of the assessment results. Similarly, you may occasionally find in a collaborative, ongoing consultation relationship that a specific topic is more appropriately addressed directively.

Consider a consultation situation in which you and your colleague, Jane, have been working together collaboratively for several weeks to design and evaluate a systematic reward system for use with Henry, a student in her class. Increasing district demands, the inclusion of many students with disabilities, and a number of other events have created significant and competing demands for Jane. Henry, the student whom you share, is no longer responding satisfactorily to your jointly planned intervention and has begun to display again his problematic and disruptive behaviors. You and Jane both recognize that you have a problem that must be addressed, but Jane does not currently have the emotional, physical, or logistical resources to participate in any significant way in a collaborative problem-solving effort. Consequently, you may need to solve this pressing problem independently (e.g., by making an immediate adjustment in the implementation of the intervention with Henry). Alternatively, depending on the situation and your assessment of it, you may decide that neither a directive nor a collaborative approach is appropriate. If Henry's lack of progress appears to be only temporary and Jane's stress seems to be the most salient issue, you may determine that a nondirective, supportive, or empathic style is most appropriate.

If you develop an understanding of how collaboration and consultation can be distinguished from one another and how they work in tandem, it will guide you in your own practice and help you communicate clearly with your colleagues and others. This is particularly important since much of what has been written about consultation has been written for school and counseling psychologists, not for special education teachers or other special services providers. It is additionally significant because considerable confusion about essential concepts continues to flourish in the consultation literature (e.g., Correa, Jones, Thomas, & Morsink, 2005; Idol et al., 2000; Schulte & Osborne, 2003).

Issues in Consultation as Collaborative Service Delivery

The field of consultation has a rich history, and as it continues to evolve rapidly in the twenty-first century, it faces a number of significant issues. In addition to the various issues presented throughout this chapter and those summarized in Figure 4.2, the following are particular areas of concern for consultants.

Understanding of Consulting Relationships

Consultation is effective only if both parties are active participants. Consultants must strive to avoid being seen as academic and behavioral magicians; general

---

Figure 4.2   Current Issues in School Consultation

The field of school consultation is facing a wide variety of issues that will shape its future. In addition to the issues discussed in the text, the following represent other concerns for the field. Which ones might affect your practice? Which might be concerns among your school colleagues?

- The differences in consultation between professionals such as teachers and psychologists and consultation between professionals and parents/families

- The appropriate variations in practice for consultation when carried out by special education teachers versus specialists such as psychologists and counselors

- *Treatment integrity,* or the extent to which teachers receiving consultation assistance actually systematically carry out the agreed-on interventions

- The impact of special education teacher consultation on student achievement and behavior as compared to more direct interventions, particularly in the context of today's high academic standards and increased expectations for positive outcomes

- Accountability in consultation for both consultants and consultees

- The relative merits of the various models of consultation used in schools, and the potential to create integrated models that pull together the best aspects of each of the traditional models

- Parent/family involvement in and response to school-based consultation services, particularly for those from nondominant cultures

---

education teachers must contribute significant information about their classrooms and students for consultants to offer meaningful assistance. A dilemma occurs in some schools, however. Some consultants feel pressure to have solutions ready to dispense to consultees. In others, classroom teachers expect consultants to have answers and are disappointed when such on-the-spot advice does not improve the problem that led to the consultation in the first place. The challenge for schools that include consultation as a service option is to educate all participants about their roles in the process and to discourage professionals from making inaccurate assumptions about others' roles and responsibilities. For example, consultants should resist the urge to offer advice without an adequate understanding of the classroom environment and teacher expectations. However, classroom teachers must reciprocate with patience, recognizing that high-quality results are only likely with considerable effort. It is in this type of mutual understanding of the possibilities and constraints of consultation that skills for collaboration might most be necessary for all participants.

Time Allocation for Consultation

For special education teachers, psychologists, and others who have both consulting as well as direct service responsibilities, a dilemma often arises regarding the time available to consult. Understandably, time working directly with students is arranged first, and too often consulting becomes an informal, sometimes unstructured, and occasionally unsystematic add-on to professional schedules. Educators who consult should have time allocated in their schedules to do so. If consultation is seen as a luxury instead of as a necessity, the demands of direct instruction, testing, report preparation, and meetings may preclude its careful use. More information about the quandary of time in relationship to collaborative interactions is presented in Chapter 7.

Multiculturalism

Over the past several years, increased attention has been paid in consultation to issues that arise when a consultant is from one culture and the consultee, whether a teacher or the family, is from another culture (Henning-Stout & Meyers, 2000; Ingraham, 2003; Sue & Constantine, 2005). Concerns relate to language differences and the communication issues that may arise. They also pertain to consultants' appreciation of how their own culture may influence their practice. For example, a consultant whose own culture highly values independence and self-motivation may not understand why family members from another culture seem in no rush to foster self-determination for their adolescent child with an intellectual disability. In addition, consultants should ensure that they acquire and use appropriate cultural sensitivity in the development of the

When consultants work with families from cultures different from their own, they have a responsibility to be particularly sensitive to the impact of their words, communication patterns, and actions on family members and to adjust their actions to maximize consultation effectiveness.

interpersonal relationships, in the consultant's awareness of the consultee's receptivity to various interaction processes and communication styles, and in the appropriateness of various strategies and interventions consultants may suggest to consultees (e.g., Rogers, 2000).

Confidentiality

When consultants build trusting relationships with consultees and problem solve with them, information likely will be shared that should be held in confidence. For example, a teacher might mention that she is so frustrated with the acting-out behavior of a student that she finds herself negatively responding to nearly everything he does. This honest admission should not be shared with other colleagues. And although that might seem obvious, in the rush of completing many professional responsibilities and with the pressure that now comes with working in schools, many consultants need to be reminded that they are obligated to keep confidences, even relatively small ones, in order to preserve the benefits of this service delivery option and in order to convey respect for consultees. Ultimately, confidentiality is an ethical issue, one that merits serious and continued attention in schools.

When considered as a whole, consultation has an important niche in the array of services to students in schools. However, for it to be effective, consultants must select an approach carefully, monitor the impact of their suggestions on the student and consultee, and constantly evaluate the quality of their practice. Some consultants, such as psychologists, may find consultation a responsibility easily integrated into their jobs. For others, such as special education teachers, consultation may have to be mindfully nurtured to reach its potential.

Summary

Consultation is one of the activities that special services providers often associate with collaboration in schools. It is a voluntary process in which one professional assists another to address a problem concerning a third party, typically a student. The characteristics of consultation are that it is triadic and indirect as well as voluntary. It is also an expert and directional relationship, a problem-solving process, and a process that involves shared but differentiated responsibilities for decisions and accountability for outcomes. Consultation can have several different theoretical orientations, including behavioral and clinical models. Each model is based on specific assumptions, uses similar procedures explicated in varying degrees, and includes both advantages and disadvantages. Although consultants seldom use "pure" versions of consultation models, they provide a framework and alternatives for practice. Collaboration may be used within the consultation process, but consultation sometimes may be conducted with little collaboration. Currently, considerable confusion continues to exist, particularly in the special education literature, regarding how consultation and collaboration intersect. For consultation to be successful, a number of issues should be addressed: participants' understanding of the process and their roles and responsibilities in it; time allocations for consultation; participants' awareness of and responses to their cultural differences; and confidentiality.

Activities and Assignments

1. Either in your own school or in a school in which you are completing a field experience, identify individuals whose job responsibilities include consultation. What activities do they carry out within this role? How do the descriptions of their activities compare with the types of activities described in this chapter? What do you see as the benefits of working in a consulting role? The drawbacks?

2. Consultation has the characteristic of being voluntary. However, some special services providers consider consultation as an expected role responsibility with teachers who instruct students with special needs. How can you reconcile these seemingly contradictory notions?

3. What does it mean to say that consultation is expert and directional? What is the implication of this concept for working with general education teachers? What opportunities might it create? What barriers might it create in collegial relationships?

4. If you were offered a position that emphasized behavioral consultation, what specific skills of behaviorism do you perceive would be most important to have? How would these apply to your work with consultees? How do you think the current requirement in schools to complete a functional behavior analysis (FBA) and prepare a behavior intervention plan (BIP) for any students with serious behavior disorders is influencing this model of consultation?

5. If someone asked you to distinguish collaboration from consultation and define *collaborative consultation,* how would you respond? Why is collaborative consultation generally not considered a unique model of consultation?

6. Identify one consultation experience that you have had or observed that was not as successful as you would have liked it to be. Using the characteristics of collaboration presented in Chapter 1 and the issues raised in this chapter, analyze the situation and describe how these factors may have contributed to the problems encountered in the consultation.

7. As you have observed consultants working in schools, what have you noticed related to the issues mentioned in the chapter? To what extent do consultants seem sensitive to educating others about consulting relationships, time, multiculturalism, and confidentiality? Interview a teacher who recently has worked with a consultant. What was that professional's perceptions of the experience?

8. Consultation often is recommended as an approach for working with parents and families. What might the role of a special educator be in providing this type of service? For what types of situations or student problems might a special education teacher serve in this consulting capacity? What are the opportunities and risks of this application of consultation?

For Further Reading

Athanasiou, M. S., Geil, M., Hazel, C. E., & Copeland, E. P. (2002). A look inside school-based consultation: A qualitative study of the beliefs and practices of school psychologists and teachers [Electronic version]. *School Psychology Quarterly, 17,* 258–298.

Henning-Stout, M., & Meyers, J. (2000). Consultation and human diversity: First things first. *School Psychology Review, 29,* 419–420.

Kampwirth, T. J. (2006). *Collaborative consultation in the schools* (3rd ed.). Upper Saddle River, NJ: Merrill.

Kennedy, K. Y., Higgins, K., & Pierce, T. (2002). Collaborative partnerships among teachers of students who are gifted and have learning disabilities [Electronic version]. *Intervention in School and Clinic, 38,* 36–49.

Riley-Tillman, T. C., & Chafouleas, S. M. (2003). Using interventions that exist in the natural environment to increase treatment integrity and social influence in consultation. *Journal of Educational and Psychological Consultation, 14,* 139–156.

Wilkinson, L. A. (2003). Using behavioral consultation to reduce challenging behavior in the classroom. *Preventing School Failure, 47,* 100–105.

CHAPTER 5

Co-Teaching

| Personal Commitment | Communication Skills | Interaction Processes | Programs or Services | Context |

Connections

In Chapters 3 and 4 you learned about teaming and consultation as activities and services significantly enhanced by collaboration. In Chapter 5, we add a third example of collaboration in action—co-teaching. Co-teaching is a special form of teaming that is a unique blend of professional expertise in which a general educator and a special educator jointly instruct pupils in a single general education classroom. The requirements of the No Child Left Behind Act and the Individuals with Disabilities Education Act are fostering inclusive practices, and so these laws also are leading to increased attention to co-teaching. To introduce you to co-teaching, we outline basic concepts related to it, describe several specific ways for co-teachers to use this service delivery option while taking advantage of both professionals' skills, raise topics that co-teachers should discuss, and present some pragmatic issues that can affect the effectiveness of co-teaching. As with teaming and consultation, we also clarify how co-teaching relates to collaboration.

Learner Objectives

After reading this chapter you will be able to:

1. Define co-teaching and distinguish it from related concepts (for example, inclusion, team teaching).
2. Articulate a rationale for the use of co-teaching in schools with diverse groups of learners.

3. Identify six approaches for implementing co-teaching, describe examples of each, and indicate when each might be instructionally appropriate.

4. Explain the relationship between co-teaching and collaboration.

5. Describe professional concerns that educators implementing co-teaching may have to address.

6. Outline several administrative and pragmatic issues that can foster or constrain co-teaching.

7. Demonstrate a commitment to co-teaching by critically analyzing its application, explaining its appropriate use in public school settings, and planning lessons that incorporate it.

Terri and James have just begun their second year as a co-teaching partnership. They share instruction for two sections of language arts for eighth-graders. The first thing they discovered this year is that because they already know each other well, they lost no time with "getting to know you" interactions. They quickly outlined their classroom behavior expectations and procedures, discussed their priorities for the first several weeks of the semester, and laughed about the difference between this year and last.

When asked about co-teaching, Terri has this to say: "Working with James is a privilege. He knows so much about teaching literature and writing to middle school students, and his enthusiasm is contagious—for me and for the kids. Some of the students in this class who have IEPs already are writing more than they ever did before. And the students with IEPs develop so much confidence by being in classes with their peers. For some of them it's the first time they have really believed that they *can* succeed."

James adds, "I've learned so many strategies for helping students who struggle to read and who are afraid of writing. Terri has unbelievable patience with all kids, and she always seems to have a new idea for reaching them. I'm a much better teacher the rest of the day because of the work we do together. And our scores from last year—our shared sections were two of the four highest among all the eighth-grade classes in the district—show that we're effective in helping students to achieve."

Introduction

A number of factors continue to draw attention to collaboration among professional educators and its implementation on behalf of students with disabilities in general education settings. First, the decades-long effort by many professionals and parents to ensure that students with disabilities are educated with their typical peers in the least restrictive environment has not waned (Brownell & Walther-Thomas, 2002). However, the traditional views of inclusive philosophy have been strengthened through recent legislation. For example, the accountability movement codified in the No Child Left Behind Act has led to increasing recognition that students with disabilities are unlikely to gain equal access to the general curriculum if they are not receiving their education with their peers (Washburn-Moses, 2005). Second, professionals now acknowledge that most students with disabilities should be held to the same academic standards as other students; there simply is no reason for them to be excluded since most can, with appropriate supports and services, succeed (Spencer, 2005). Finally, the requirement in the 2004 reauthorization of the Individuals with Disabilities Education Act that all students be taught core academic subjects by teachers highly qualified in those academic areas has led to a rethinking of how to develop schedules and deploy staff so that all students receive the education to which they are entitled (Council for Exceptional Children, 2005).

The result of these trends is that more students with disabilities each year are spending more of their school day in general education (U.S. Department of Education, 2003). As this occurs, it is not surprising that general education teachers, special education teachers, speech/language specialists, and other service providers increasingly have turned to contemporary service delivery options that blend their expertise, offering specialized instruction within the general education classroom for some students and enhancing the learning of many students, including those with disabilities (Henderson, 2002). Perhaps the best known of these service delivery options is co-teaching, and it is being implemented to support many different groups of students, from those with learning, communication, and behavior disabilities, to those who have sensory impairments, to those with other significant special needs (e.g., Hunt, Soto, Maier, & Doering, 2003; McDonnell, Thorson, Disher, Mathot-Buckner, Mendel, & Ray, 2003; Stoessel & Miles, n.d.).

Co-Teaching Concepts

Although co-teaching is an increasingly common means for providing special education services in today's schools, the quality of what occurs in co-taught classes and the benefits for students—both those with and those without disabilities—vary considerably (Salend, Gordon, & Lopez-Vona, 2002). It is likely the result of its rapid growth that has led to lingering confusion about what co-teaching is and how it differs from other in-class services, as well as unevenness in its implementation. *Co-teaching*, as we discuss it here, is a service delivery option for providing special education or related services to students with disabilities or other special needs while they remain in their general education classes. Co-teaching occurs when two or more professionals jointly deliver substantive instruction to a diverse, blended group of students in a single physical space (Friend & Pope, 2005; Spencer, 2005).

Defining Characteristics of Co-Teaching

Teacher teams have used various structures for joint instructional efforts for many years, and at elementary, middle school, and high school levels (e.g., Crespin, 1971; Roth & Tobin, 2004; Trump, 1966; Warwick, 1971). Most of those teams, however, consisted of two general education teachers who pooled their class groups and their instructional efforts in a model generally called *team teaching*. Only for the past two decades has the use of teacher partnerships been seen as a mechanism for providing services to students with disabilities and other special needs in their general education classrooms (Bauwens, Hourcade, & Friend, 1989; Friend, Reising, & Cook, 1993; Murawski, 2005). The professional literature on co-teaching continues to emerge, including descriptions of the variations occurring in co-teaching practice and the challenges that accompanying this service option (Coltrane, 2003; Dieker & Murawski, 2003; Walsh & Jones, 2004). With increased emphasis on standards and accountability, also expanding is the research base on co-teaching (e.g., Mastropieri, Scruggs, Graetz, Norland, Gardizi, & McDuffie, 2005), a topic addressed in A Basis in Research. To truly understand co-teaching, however, an appropriate starting point is its defining characteristics, since these underscore co-teaching's uniqueness as a service delivery option.

Two or More Professionals

Co-teaching involves at least two appropriately credentialed professionals—two teachers (e.g., a general education teacher and a special education teacher who may be highly qualified only in special education or in special education and the academic content area); a teacher and a related services professional (e.g., a teacher and a speech/language therapist); or a teacher and another specialist (e.g., a teacher and a literacy coach). The importance of this defining characteristic comes from the notion that co-teachers are peers—they have equivalent credentials and employment status and thus can truly be partners in their instructional endeavors on behalf of students.

Notice that this characteristic of co-teaching excludes paraeducators, also called *paraprofessionals*. In general, paraeducators and other adults who might work in classrooms (e.g., volunteers) provide support rather than co-teaching; they typically have not had the professional preparation to co-teach nor is the instructional partnership of co-teaching an appropriate role expectation for them (French, 2001). (See Chapter 6 for a discussion of these relationships and other topics related to collaboration with paraprofessionals.) To underscore the differences in roles, classrooms in which paraeducators are delivering services sometimes are called *supported* or *assisted classrooms,* not *co-taught classrooms.* This distinction helps everyone involved to remember that, although paraprofessionals are valuable classroom personnel, they should not be asked to carry out the responsibilities of licensed or certificated staff, and it clarifies for general education teachers the nature of the services being provided. Of course, saying paraeducators generally should not co-teach does not in any way imply they do not have significant classroom responsibilities. They still work with individual students and groups, but under the direction of teachers or other specialists, and to reinforce instruction, not to routinely introduce it.

Joint Delivery of Instruction

In schools across the country, we have found a disturbing number of educators who call their arrangement "co-teaching" simply because it involves two educa-

A BASIS IN RESEARCH

Considering Practices versus Outcomes

Hundreds of articles have been written about co-teaching, and many of them describe programs, offer suggestions for improving instruction, or relate anecdotes about co-teachers' experiences. Although literature of this sort plays a valuable role, research on the practices of co-teaching and outcomes for students that result from co-teaching are essential. This research base for co-teaching is gradually emerging.

Most co-teaching research over the past several years has emphasized co-teaching practice. For example, Weiss and Lloyd (2002) studied the roles and responsibilities that general and special educators assume when they co-teach. They found that special educators take on a wide variety of roles, ranging from simply providing quiet support to students with disabilities to functioning as a true teaching partner. Similarly, Morocco and Aguilar (2002) found that in an urban middle school, although the general education teachers provided more initial instruction than special educators (which was to be expected), both educators assumed a wide variety of leading and supporting roles.

Far fewer studies have addressed directly the impact of co-teaching on outcomes for students with disabilities and their typical peers. One example was reported by Welch (2000). Focusing on two elementary classrooms in different schools and using curriculum-based assessment of word recognition and fluency, he found that all students made academic gains. Unanswered was the question of whether the gains made by students with disabilities would have been greater than, less than, or similar to those accomplished by offering instruction in a special education classroom.

Research on co-teaching is likely to evolve quickly as a result of the growing trend to educate students with disabilities in general education settings. What types of studies do you think are most needed? Why might such research be difficult to conduct? What type of data could you collect in your own classroom to evaluate both the practices and outcomes of co-teaching?

tors in a classroom at the same time. In some situations the classroom teacher typically conducts the same type of instruction as he or she would if teaching alone. That teacher may even express gratefulness for having in the classroom "an extra set of hands." The second teacher, usually a special educator or specialist, has the *de facto* role of instructional assistant for students with disabilities and possibly for some others with special needs. This individual hovers at the fringes of the class until the core instruction is delivered and then helps those who need it, or this educator pulls individual students or a small group aside to deliver instruction completely separate from that being provided to the rest of the class. Although such arrangements may occur occasionally in co-taught classes, particularly if a student (or students) in the class has significant disabilities, if these practices are routine, the arrangement should not be referred to as co-teaching. Instead, this situation is an inappropriate underuse of a qualified professional. It is a practice likely to stigmatize students at least as much as pullout strategies and to frustrate special services providers. It is also a situation in which any benefits derived from separate instruction are diminished by the increased noise and activity in the classroom. These considerations give rise to questions about why professionals consistently would use this arrangement for any length of time. A variation of this situation occurs when the educators decide to split teaching duties, each professional teaching on alternate days. Although not as obviously negative as the first example, it still represents a misunderstanding of what co-teaching is about.

In co-taught classes, each professional has an important contribution to make in coordinating and delivering substantive instruction (Murray, 2004). This does not mean that they always work with students in large groups, but it does mean that they share decision making about instruction and ensure that both have active roles in teaching (Austin, 2001; Gately & Gately, 2001). Specifically, the two professionals plan and use unique and high-involvement instructional strategies to engage all students in ways that are not possible when only one teacher is present. By doing so, they frequently can integrate specialized instruction into the general teaching/learning environment. The general education curriculum provides the instructional framework for the class, yet that curriculum is differentiated as necessary to foster student success and may be modified for students with the most significant needs (Fennick, 2001). Keep in mind that two qualified teachers or other professionals can arrange instruction in a number of creative ways to enhance learning options for all students, not just for those with disabilities. With two teachers delivering instruction and increasing the instructional options for students, all students can have more op-

When high school teachers co-teach, they often need to discuss how to integrate the specialized learning process knowledge and skills of the special educator with the content knowledge of the general educator.

portunities to participate actively in their learning and thus instructional intensity is increased. Successful co-teachers should review their practices to ensure that their instructional strategies do in fact lead to more engaged time and participation for all students in co-taught classes while meeting the individualized needs of students with identified disabilities.

Diverse Group of Students

Co-teachers provide instruction to a diverse, or blended, group of students that includes students with disabilities and other special needs as well as other learners who are not so identified (Hourcade & Bauwens, 2001). In fact, this dimension is one of the major advantages of co-teaching. Teachers initially may resist the perceived increase in student diversity that accompanies co-teaching, but as they implement more effective instructional interventions through their partnerships, they learn to value the arrangement. Co-teaching allows teachers to respond effectively to the varied needs of their students, lowers the teacher–student ratio, and expands the professional expertise that can be directed to those needs. The inclusion of one or several students who have IEPs sometimes increases the range of diversity in a classroom, but that change is accompanied by the addition of another teacher who brings an entire repertoire of instructional ideas to the classroom.

Co-teachers need to ensure that the diversity in the classroom does not inadvertently result in an inappropriate seating arrangement in the classroom. For example, some co-teachers try to seat students with special needs together, presumably so that they can more easily be helped with schoolwork. Other teachers seat students with disabilities on the fringes of the classroom so that when they are receiving assistance, other students are not distracted. Although both these strategies are well-intentioned, they may have the result of socially isolating students, often the very students who are most likely to need encouragement and instruction on social skills.

Shared Classroom Space

The definition of co-teaching notes that co-teachers operate in a single physical space or classroom. This is contrasted with earlier variations of teaching teams that commonly planned together, grouped students, but then taught them in separate classrooms (Geen, 1985; Trump, 1966). Although one teacher may occasionally take a small, heterogeneous group of students to a separate location for a specific instructional purpose and for a limited time period (for example, to the media center to complete web-based research for an assignment), co-teaching generally should be considered an instructional approach that occurs in a single physical environment. This definitional element helps to distinguish co-teaching from the practice of regrouping students for different kinds of pull-out programs. It also points out that the teacher relationship issues, discussed later in this chapter, are far more significant when a physical location is shared than when this does not occur.

Does co-teaching sound like an exciting but somewhat challenging service option for students with disabilities? In Putting Ideas into Practice you'll find some suggestions for getting a new co-teaching program off to a good start.

Rationale for Co-Teaching

Understanding the rationale for co-teaching provides a foundation on which professionals can ground the definition and consider co-teaching designs and structures for implementation in their schools. Co-teaching is first and foremost an approach for meeting the educational needs of students with diverse learning abilities (Cook & Friend, 1995; Wallace, Anderson, & Bartholomay, 2002). Thus, the driving force for creating co-teaching programs between general education teachers and special educators or related services personnel is the needs of students who have IEPs, and co-teaching should result in direct instructional and social benefits for these students. However, other students often also benefit significantly from this service approach, and this is a reasonable expectation for a co-teaching program (Dieker & Murawski, 2003; Hunt et al., 2003). For example, students who are academically gifted may have more opportunities in a co-taught class to complete alternative assignments and participate in enrichment activities (Gerber & Popp, 2000). Average students should receive more adult attention in co-taught classrooms and benefit from more teacher-led, small-group activities. Students at risk for learning failure often receive the extra instructional boost they need to make better academic progress.

A second part of the rationale for co-teaching concerns curricular access and instruction (Fisher & Frey, 2001; Morocco & Aguilar, 2002). We have stressed that the goal of co-teaching is to bring intense and individualized instruction to students in a general education setting while working as much as possible within the framework of the curriculum used there. As such, co-teaching should lead to a less fragmented and more contextualized education for students with disabilities as well as to greater instructional intensity and engaged time. For example, in elementary schools co-teaching may eliminate for some students the need to leave their classrooms, often during crucial instruction, to go to a special education setting for developmental or remedial work (Johnston, Tulbert, Sebastian, Devries, & Gompert, 2000). In middle schools and high schools, co-teaching enables students to learn curricular content from teachers who are specialists in those subjects while at the same time receiving the individualized support they need (Dieker, 2001; Morocco & Aguilar, 2002). Of course, an overriding consideration in co-teaching is that the students with disabilities who are to participate in the co-taught classroom should be those whose unique educational needs can be met through the general education curriculum with appropriate modifications and supports (Friend & Pope, 2005).

In addition to instructional benefits for diverse groups of students, co-teaching may have other positive effects. For example, in elementary schools it often reduces the stigma associated with students leaving their general educa-

PUTTING IDEAS INTO PRACTICE

Suggestions for New Co-Teaching Programs

Are you just beginning to implement co-teaching as part of your school's service delivery system? Here are a few suggestions for getting new programs off to the right start.

1. Co-teachers should enlist the assistance of their principal or another administrator to introduce the concept of co-teaching to the school staff. The message that should be conveyed is that although not everyone will co-teach every year and not everyone is expected to embrace co-teaching when it is a new option, as part of an inclusive service delivery system, most general education and special education teachers at some point will participate.

2. When paraprofessionals as well as professional staff members are going to go into classrooms, everyone involved should review the parameters of the paraprofessionals' roles and responsibilities. Further, the professional staff should communicate with each other and with paraprofessionals to clarify who has day-to-day responsibility for directing their work. Although it seems obvious, professionals must be aware that paraprofessionals should not be asked to function like teachers nor should special educators and other service providers function like paraprofessionals.

3. Co-teachers should be sure to develop the habit of using "we" language—"our students," "our classroom," "the lessons we planned." The words used will convey to both adults and students the belief that co-teaching is truly about partnership and parity in the instructional process.

4. New co-teaching programs inevitably need refinement. As part of a start-up plan, professionals should meet periodically to discuss program successes and problems. Everyone should anticipate that some changes may be needed after the first grading period or semester.

tion classrooms and going to a separate place to receive special instruction. In secondary settings, it increases the opportunities students have to take electives and consider themselves truly part of their class groups, since they may not have class periods allocated for special education services. Teachers also can use co-teaching as a vehicle for creating opportunities for positive social interactions between students with disabilities or other special needs and their nondisabled peers.

Finally, co-teachers often report that this service approach provides them with a sense of collegial support. Co-teachers are not expected to master all of each other's expertise, but they learn from each other in ways that enhance their own skills. For example, consider these observations from an algebra classroom: The special educator noted that she had to work very hard to master the concepts for the course, but that her partner was always ready to answer her questions. The general educator noted that he had learned that even a high school algebra class benefited when students used manipulatives and accessed learning visually, auditorily, and kinesthetically. Co-teachers also receive emotional support from someone with whom they share both classroom successes and challenges.

Co-Teaching Approaches

The instructional potential of co-teaching makes it imperative that those involved collaborate effectively in designing and delivering instructional interventions that will best meet the unique learning needs of the students. Co-teachers consider a large number of factors when deciding how to structure and deliver their instruction. Based on student needs, the ecology of the class, demands of the curriculum, teachers' comfort level and skills for teaching and co-teaching, co-teachers design many creative strategies to work together to meet students' diverse needs in a single classroom.

The following six co-teaching approaches depicted in Figure 5.1—(1) one teaching, one observing, (2) station teaching, (3) parallel teaching, (4) alternative teaching, (5) teaming, and (6) one teaching, one assisting—represent some of the options used most frequently in schools. To keep co-teaching relationships and instructional arrangements fresh and effective, teachers should consider trying several of the approaches, regularly changing their co-teaching methods and experimenting with variations on the basic information provided here.

One Teaching, One Observing

Co-teachers often find that they have options unavailable to other teachers for carefully observing their students in order to gain a sophisticated understanding of their academic and social functioning. When one professional teaches while the other observes, the first has primary responsibility for designing and delivering specific instruction to the entire group, whether that is a large-group lesson, individual assignments that the teacher is monitoring, cooperative groups, or any other teaching/learning arrangement. The second professional has the goal of systematically collecting data related to a single student, a small group of students, or the entire class for behaviors the professionals have previously agreed should be noted. For example, in the English class that Mr. St. James and Mrs. Goud co-teach, several students seem to be having difficulty getting started on individual assignments. The teachers agree to observe Michael, José, James, and Sarah to find out if the problem is comprehension (the students do not begin the task and are looking around to see what others are doing), or a matter of delay (by the time the students find their pens and get headings on their papers, they forget the instructions and ask to have them repeated).

One teaching, one observing requires little joint planning and, if arranged appropriately, provides opportunities for both educators. For example, special

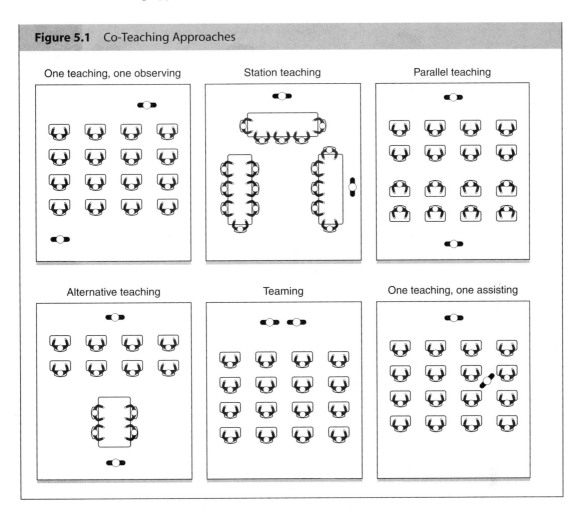

Figure 5.1 Co-Teaching Approaches

One teaching, one observing

Station teaching

Parallel teaching

Alternative teaching

Teaming

One teaching, one assisting

services professionals can focus attention on a student with significant needs to learn how to better provide important supplementary aids and services. General educators can scan the student group to learn more about the students' responses to instruction and possibly to gauge whether the behavior of a student perceived as having a problem really is different from that of other students. Early in the school year, both teachers can use this approach to deepen their shared understanding of students while learning about each other's teaching styles.

One teaching, one observing can have a serious drawback, however. If it is used indiscriminately or exclusively, it can result in one professional, most typically the special services provider, being relegated to the role of assistant. For this approach to be beneficial, the educators should exchange roles periodically. This strategy has two positive effects: First, it ensures that general education teachers have the opportunity to step back from the intensity of being the classroom manager to focus completely on what is occurring with students. Second, it clarifies for students that their class is led by two teachers with equivalent responsibility and authority.

To make observations most valuable, co-teachers should jointly decide on specific students and specific behaviors to analyze. For example, a pair of co-teachers may agree that they have serious concerns about Gary, a student who does not seem to be making much progress in reading and who seems to be expressing his frustration by refusing to work and occasionally bothering other students, taking their papers or pencils or calling them names. They decide to observe him at least three times each week across two weeks to tally what he does when given independent work. By completing these observations, the co-teachers can be better prepared for a meeting they have scheduled with the intervention assistance team.

In addition to making decisions about who to observe and for what purpose, co-teachers also should use a systematic method for recording their observations, whether they do so on class lists, seating charts, or more formal behavioral data forms such as those most special educators would have in their files. They also should be sure that both professionals have a copy of the information gathered. When co-teachers meet, they then can discuss the observations and make instructional decisions based on what they have learned.

Station Teaching

Station teaching is a co-teaching approach that actively involves both educators in instruction, and it enables them to make a clear division of labor. The co-teachers divide the instructional content and each takes responsibility for

Co-teachers develop many creative variations of the six basic co-teaching approaches in order to address their students' diverse needs.

planning and teaching part of it. In a classroom where station teaching is used, students move from one station to another according to a predetermined schedule. A third station may be used for students to complete independent work assignments, to participate in peer tutoring, or to work under supervision if a student teacher, paraeducator, or another adult is available in the classroom. For example, in a third-grade classroom, one group of students is reviewing the concept of cause and effect with one of the teachers. Another group is working with the other teacher on comprehension activities related to a story read the previous day. In the third group, students are working with partners to edit their writing assignments. During the 50-minute period of time for this instruction, each student participates in each of the groups. In a high school civics class during an 85-minute block, one teacher works with students using the textbook to review the structure of American government, one teacher discusses with students issues in an upcoming local election, and in the third group students work independently on web reports on their state's representatives and senators.

Although this approach requires that the teachers share responsibility for planning sufficiently to divide the instructional content, it has the advantage that each professional has separate responsibility for delivering instruction, and so it can be effective even when teachers have significantly different teaching styles or do not know each other well. In addition, students benefit from the lower teacher–pupil ratio, and students with disabilities may be integrated into each group rather than singled out. Further, because in this approach each teacher instructs all of the students, albeit in different groups, the equal status of both the students and the teachers can be maximized.

Two of the most common problems in using station teaching concern the amount of noise and movement in the classroom. Some teachers may be bothered by having two teachers talking at the same time, particularly if one of the educators has a loud or distinctive voice. Co-teachers also may worry that having students move around the room seems disruptive.

In addition to the above factors, co-teachers may need to think carefully about how to divide instruction so that the order in which curriculum is presented does not affect students' understanding. Material that is hierarchical cannot be presented using this approach. For example, in a social studies class, it would not work to have students in one group reading the chapter, students in a second group discussing the information, and students in the third group answering questions from the text; the group expected to write answers first, before reading or discussion, certainly would be at a disadvantage!

To effectively address concerns about station teaching, co-teachers can take several actions. If a student tends to have attention problems, that student might best be seated next to the teacher. With elementary and middle school students, co-teachers can make available sound-muffling headphones for students to use in the independent group when an individual assignment is given. They also can provide desk carrels to help reduce visual distractions. Rearranging the classroom slightly—for example, by having the teachers back-to-back—also may help reduce the distraction of both teachers' voices. If transitions are time consuming, instead of having students move from station to station, perhaps the teachers could move. Alternatively, the teachers could reward students for moving efficiently from station to station; experienced co-teachers report that transition can be kept to approximately 30 seconds. Of course, teachers also should ask for feedback from their teaching partners and periodically discuss topics such as these as part of their ongoing monitoring of their co-taught instruction. Co-teachers should also watch their time so that groups are prepared to move to the next station as scheduled.

Parallel Teaching

The primary purpose of parallel teaching is to lower the teacher–student ratio. In this type of co-teaching, the teachers jointly plan the instruction, but each delivers it to a heterogeneous group comprised of half of the students in the class. The teachers do not exchange groups as in station teaching. This approach requires both that the teachers coordinate their efforts so that all students receive essentially the same instruction and that grouping decisions are based on maintaining diversity within each group. For example, in Mr. Harris's and Ms. Brisky's history class, students are preparing for a unit exam. Mr. Harris has half of the students, including two students with learning disabilities. Ms. Brisky has the other half of the group, which includes a student with mild autism. The teachers are discussing key concepts that they highlighted during their planning period, and they are helping students go through a study guide. Their intent was to arrange the students so that each one had several opportunities to participate in discussion and to ask questions.

Parallel teaching often is appropriate for drill-and-practice activities, test reviews, topics needing a high level of student discussion, or projects needing close teacher supervision. It enables all students to participate more in instructional conversations and gives especially shy students a smaller audience. Parallel teaching can even be used for more creative teaching activities: Each co-teacher might take a particular point of view in presenting a topic or issue, orient students to that viewpoint, and then bring the students together later for large-group discussion. For example, as part of the history class, the co-teachers address current events. One time, Mr. Harris took the position that the United States was making a mistake in its actions regarding international trade and discussed this with half the students. Ms. Brisky adopted the opposite point of view with her group. When the students came together for large-group follow-up, the teachers were able to integrate information about understanding fact and opinion, the influence of the media on people's beliefs, and other related topics, as well as debate the issue at hand.

Note that this approach cannot be used for initial instruction unless both professionals are qualified to teach the material. Although seldom a serious concern in the primary grades, this can be a significant matter in secondary schools, and it is a topic co-teachers should directly discuss. In terms of pragmatic issues, noise and activity levels may need to be monitored, as in station teaching. Also, as in station teaching, teachers need to pace instruction similarly.

To co-teach using parallel teaching, teachers should begin by checking that they are both familiar with the content and comfortable teaching it. Especially in new co-teaching partnerships, teachers might want to use outlines, study guides, or notes to stay aware of the teaching expectations. Remember that if one group of students has significantly different instruction from the other, it will be difficult to make judgments about student mastery. Students also may complain that the disparity leads to unfairness during assessments. To address the issues of noise and distraction, elementary and middle school teachers may find that it works well to have the two student groups on the floor in opposite corners of the class with desks or tables used as a sight and sound barrier. Noise and distraction seldom are significant issues in secondary classrooms using this approach.

Alternative Teaching

In nearly every classroom, co-teachers sometimes decide to select a small group of students to receive instruction that is somehow different from that in which the large group is participating. For example, some students with special learning needs require adaptations in the form of preteaching. Students who benefit from preteaching might include those with attention problems, those who need reassurance about their knowledge or skills, and those for whom repetition is beneficial. Reteaching the instructional content is appropriate for students who did not understand the concepts taught, or for students who missed the instruction because of absence. Sometimes an alternative group is useful for conducting a skills assessment. One additional example concerns enrichment; students who already have mastered the concepts being taught might work in a small group to extend their learning. Thus, in alternative teaching, one teacher works with a small group of students while the other instructs the large group in some content or activity that the small group can afford to miss.

Alternative teaching is a strategy for providing highly intensive instruction within the general education classroom. Further, this approach can also be used to ensure that all students in a class receive opportunities to interact with a teacher in a small group. If one or two students have serious behavior disorders that cause classroom disruptions, sometimes having them work in a small group, one that includes positive class models, can help them and possibly alleviate classroom disruption.

The greatest risk in alternative teaching is that students with disabilities may be stigmatized by being grouped repeatedly for preteaching or reteaching, even if other students are rotated through the small instructional group. A variation of this approach, in which one teacher is located at a table and announces that students seeking assistance may come to the table, also can cause problems. Particularly with older groups, the student most likely to come to work with the teacher is the one who is capable of doing the task but who craves adult attention or seeks reassurance. The student who possibly would not join the teacher is the student with a disability who clearly needs assistance but is embarrassed to seek it in front of peers.

When co-teachers use alternative teaching, they first should be sure that each teacher sometimes takes responsibility for the small group. For example, sometimes reteaching is best accomplished by the general education teacher, not the special educator. In addition, co-teachers might keep a record of which students were assigned to which small groups so that they ensure all students participate and no student is stigmatized. Of course, the group composition and group membership should be fluid, with both factors varying depending on student need and planned small-group activity.

Teaming

In teaming, both teachers are responsible for planning. They also share the instruction of all students, whether that occurs in a large group, in monitoring students working independently, or in facilitating groups of students working on shared projects. For example, the teachers may lead a discussion by trading ideas with each other, or they may take on the roles of characters in a story as they act out a scene. One co-teacher may explain while the other demonstrates a concept or lab procedure; one may speak while the other models note taking on an overhead projector, and so on. Both teachers may circulate around the room as students work on dioramas that illustrate a piece of poetry, asking questions to stimulate student discussion or to check comprehension. Teachers may role-play, debate, simulate conflict, and model appropriate question asking or summarizing.

Co-teachers who team frequently report that it results in a synergy that enhances student participation and invigorates the professionals, sometimes even prompting them to try innovative techniques and activities that each professional would not have tried alone. They discuss how well it works when the teachers "click" and are able to have instructional conversations with each other and students. Some co-teachers consider teaming the most rewarding approach. This co-teaching approach also clearly communicates to students that both educators truly have equal status.

However, of the six co-teaching approaches, teaming requires the greatest level of mutual trust and commitment. If professionals are not comfortable working together in a classroom, attempting to team is likely to communicate that discomfort to students. Teaming also requires that the co-teachers mesh their teaching styles. If co-teachers are significantly different in their use of humor, their pacing, or their instructional format, the flow of the teaming often is not successful. Teachers may use different styles but they should take care to complement each other.

Novice co-teachers should not feel obligated to attempt teaming. Although some do and are successful, for many this approach is too fluid and relies too much on teacher compatibility and flexibility for use in a new relationship. Similarly, if a special educator is co-teaching with a teacher who seems uncomfortable with a shared classroom, perhaps experiencing some of the dilemmas described in Putting Ideas into Practice, this approach is probably not one to emphasize, at least at the outset. When teaming is implemented, co-teachers should check frequently to ensure that both are satisfied with their use of it.

PUTTING IDEAS INTO PRACTICE

Addressing Co-Teaching Dilemmas

Both novice and experienced co-teachers often have questions about the best ways to deal with dilemmas that occur during co-teaching. Here are a few common concerns and ideas for addressing them.

■ My co-teacher is responsible for students with emotional disabilities. He is frequently called away from our co-teaching to deal with a student problem. What should we do?

In some schools, general education teachers genuinely believe that they cannot address student issues and that the special educator is the only one equipped to respond to students with emotional disabilities. Although it is prudent to call for the special educator if a student is having a crisis, it is sometimes helpful to talk with participating teachers about what constitutes a crisis and to explicitly outline how noncrisis problems should be handled (e.g., ignoring, asking for administrator help).

■ I'm a special services provider. When I enter the classroom to co-teach, the general education teacher seems to think it is to release her for an extra preparation period. What should I do?

If a classroom teacher repeatedly leaves the room or withdraws from instruction (e.g., grades papers) during co-teaching, the special services provider should approach that person with words like these: "I'm concerned that I've miscommunicated what co-teaching is about. It's so important for both of us to be here, actively working with students, for it to be successful." If the teacher continues to leave, the special services provider should alert the teacher that a problem-solving session is needed and then enlist the assistance of a supervisor or administrator to resolve the matter.

■ As a special education teacher, I sometimes feel like I am being used in classrooms as a paraprofessional or helper, not a professional. How can I avoid this?

The best way to avoid this co-teaching problem is to discuss the issue openly with your co-teacher—earlier rather than later. If expectations have been clarified before co-teaching is initiated, this issue is less likely to occur. Also, if co-teachers use the six approaches outlined in this chapter, along with the many variations of them, both teachers can and should have an active role in instruction.

One Teaching, One Assisting

A final and relatively simple approach for co-teaching is to have one teacher teaching while the other supports the instructional process. That is, one teacher maintains the primary role for managing the classroom and leading instruction while the other walks around the room to assist students who need redirection or who have questions about their schoolwork. For example, as Ms. Ramirez explains to students the process for substituting variables in systems of equations,

Mr. Siler monitors all the students to be sure that they are correctly completing the examples on their papers. The teachers' goal is to be sure that all students, including those who have learning disabilities, are accurately solving the problems and to address any student confusion as soon as it is detected.

This approach to co-teaching requires little joint planning, and so it makes co-teaching possible even when shared planning time is scarce. It also gives a role to special services providers in situations in which they may not feel competent to lead instruction (for example, a special education teacher with an elementary education background and a K–12 special education license co-teaching in a high school geometry class for the first time).

However, one teaching, one assisting also is fraught with problems and should be used only occasionally. First, it sometimes becomes the sole or primary co-teaching approach in many classrooms, particularly when planning time in scarce. The classroom teacher probably takes the lead role, and the special services provider becomes an "assistant." Not only does this deny an active teaching role to the special educator but it also undermines that person's credibility, especially with older students. Second, a classroom in which one teacher continuously moves around the room during large-group instruction can be distracting to students. When professionals are walking around they can be a visual distraction, and when they whisper to individual students they may be an auditory distraction. Third, and most serious, this co-teaching approach includes the risk of encouraging students to become dependent learners. When one teacher is always available to help on student demand, students who crave adult attention but who should be capable of doing assigned work may develop a habit of saying "I can't" in order to get extra attention and assistance. Co-teachers need to be very alert to this possibility. If they have students needing adult attention, they should give it—but not at the cost of a student's independent learning skills.

Educators can take advantage of the positive aspects of one teaching, one assisting and avoid the negative aspects by limiting their use of this approach and by ensuring that when it is used, each teacher leads instruction and each teacher takes the role of assisting. Further, co-teachers should use this approach only when it will not distract students from their learning and when no other co-teaching approach seems appropriate for the instructional situation.

Understanding these six basic approaches for arranging teachers and students in a shared classroom is just a beginning. As you experiment with co-teaching and share ideas with classmates or colleagues, you will find that many variations of each approach exist and that approaches can be combined to even better address student needs. Most important, the co-teaching approaches demonstrate the importance of collaboration in co-teaching. In the next section, pragmatic and conceptual issues related to the professional relationships in co-teaching are presented to increase your readiness to implement this service delivery option.

Co-Teaching and Collaboration

We have identified co-teaching as a specific service delivery option that is based on collaboration. As you can see, however, it is not a synonym for collaboration.

We again clarify that co-teaching, like consultation or team decision making, is an activity that teachers may choose to engage in while using a collaborative style of interaction. Some would argue that collaboration is more critical to co-teaching than to applications like teaming and consultation since co-teaching involves an ongoing and intense relationship between two or more professionals engaged in this professional activity. We believe that co-teaching is optimized when a strong collaborative relationship exists, but we recognize that co-teaching also can exist, although in a significantly limited form, with nominal collaboration. In short, we agree with veteran co-teachers who tell us that in ideal situations, "Co-teaching is like a professional marriage."

The Co-Teaching Relationship

The most sophisticated types of co-teaching and the collaboration they require are not for everyone. The type of co-teaching and the level of collaboration in the relationship depend on the situation (Murray, 2004; Weiss & Lloyd, 2002). But it also depends on both the personal characteristics of the co-teachers and their skills in communication and collaboration (Appl, Troha, & Rowell, 2001; Caron & McLaughlin, 2002; Keefe, Moore, & Duff, 2004).

Many co-teaching issues are challenging—sometimes even threatening—to potential co-teachers. This collaborative structure requires a willingness to change teaching styles and preferences, work closely with another adult, share responsibility, and rely on another individual in order to perform tasks previously done alone. All of these factors can cause stress for the teachers. Yet what causes some teachers stress can be a source of excitement and motivation for others.

Specific skills and personal characteristics can be associated with successful co-teachers. The most essential requirement for a co-teacher is flexibility (Argüelles, Hughes, Shay, & Schumm, 2000). Commitment to co-teaching and to the co-teaching relationship also is needed (Allen-Malley & Bishop, 2000; Spencer, 2005). In addition, professionals generally concur that strong interpersonal communication skills—particularly problem-solving and decision-making skills—are essential for co-teachers (Gately & Gately, 2001; Keefe et al., 2004).

One other consideration for co-teachers is their broader background and culture. Just as stereotypes or other misunderstandings can undermine teacher–student and teacher–parent/family interactions, they also can affect co-teachers (Snell & Janney, 2000). For example, co-teachers may wish to learn a little about each other's own school experiences and how they affect their teaching styles and preferences. Similarly, co-teachers may find they need to discuss the basis for their beliefs about disabilities. Perhaps one teacher has a sibling with a disability and has been strongly affected by this experience. Perhaps the other teacher was raised in a culture in which disabilities are seen as a challenge given by God or as a punishment to parents for a wrongdoing. Such conversations lead co-teachers to a much deeper understanding of each other's perceptions of students, expectations for them, and instructional approaches. To enhance collaboration, co-teachers should reflect on their own characteristics, experiences, and expectations and express a willingness to share those reflections with their

---

Figure 5.2 Checking Your Readiness for Co-Teaching

My co-teacher and I have

_____ 1. Discussed our perceptions of how a classroom is shared, identifying both our similar beliefs and resolving differences in our understanding.

_____ 2. Reviewed the instructional needs of students with disabilities in the class and agreed on accommodations likely to be needed.

_____ 3. Identified how we will convey to students from the first day of co-teaching that the teachers are partners with equal classroom authority.

_____ 4. Conferred on day-to-day matters such as a location for the special services provider to put belongings, expectations for classroom routines, and a time to debrief about the first week of co-teaching.

_____ 5. Shared our perceptions on how classroom tasks can be shared.

_____ 6. Addressed what potential strengths and liabilities each of us brings to co-teaching.

---

co-teaching partners. The checklist in Figure 5.2 can provide a start for this type of discussion.

Maintaining Collaborative Relationships in Co-Teaching

Since effective co-teaching relies on teaching pairs having positive, collaborative working relationships, the skills discussed throughout this text, including those for effective communication and the resolution of disagreements introduced in chapters that follow, clearly are essential for co-teachers. In addition, though, numerous specific topics routinely require discussion by teaching partners. These topics are summarized on the following pages, and questions related to each are included in Figure 5.3. Using these questions as a guide for scheduled discussions, both prior to co-teaching and routinely throughout it, has proven useful to many co-teachers (Cook & Friend, 1995), clarifying roles and responsibilities and strengthening partnerships.

Philosophy and Beliefs

Understanding each other's general instructional beliefs, especially those that affect decisions about day-to-day teaching, is essential to a strong co-teaching relationship. In particular, teaching partners should explore the degree to which they agree on their expectations that all students learn the general curriculum, the right of all students to experience success and how that occurs, the teacher's role in student learning, and acceptable ways in which students can demonstrate what they have learned. However, co-teaching also requires discussion of more specific beliefs. For example, what does each teacher believe about the amount of noise and movement that is acceptable in a classroom? What types of behaviors are the co-teachers particularly bothered by? These day-to-day beliefs about classroom life are as important to discuss as the foundational beliefs each co-teacher brings to the situation.

Figure 5.3 Questions for Creating a Collaborative Working Relationship in Co-Teaching

Topic	Questions
Philosophy and beliefs	• What are our overriding philosophies about the roles of teachers and teaching and about students and learning? • How do our instructional beliefs affect our instructional practice?
Parity signals	• How will we convey to students and others (e.g., teachers, parents) that we are equals in the classroom? • How can we ensure a sense of parity in the planning and delivery of instruction?
Classroom routines	• What are the instructional routines for the classroom (e.g., how previous lessons are reviewed, what strategies are used to encourage student involvement)? • What are the organizational routines for the classroom (e.g., are students allowed to go to their lockers during class; what should students do if they complete independent work before classmates)?
Discipline	• What is acceptable and unacceptable student behavior? • Who is to intervene at what point in students' behavior? • What are the rewards and consequences used in the classroom?
Feedback	• What is the best way to give each other feedback? When? • How will we ensure that both positive and negative issues are raised?
Noise	• What noise level are we comfortable with in the classroom?
Pet peeves	• What aspects of teaching and classroom life does each of us feel strongly about? • How can we identify our pet peeves so as to avoid them?

Parity Signals

The nature of co-teaching requires that teaching partners have parity and recognize it. To that end, co-teachers find that determining in advance how they will ensure that students and others recognize their equal status helps them to build and maintain their relationship. Examples of parity signals include both teachers' names on the board or in the printed course schedule, both teachers' signatures on correspondence to parents, and desk or storage space for both in the classroom. It also includes shared participation in teaching, grading assignments, and assigning report card grades. Co-teachers should spend a few minutes generating ideas about how they can communicate to students and parents, as well as remind each other, that co-teaching is about true partnership.

Classroom Routines

All experienced teachers have preferred classroom routines. These include instructional routines (such as how students are expected to seek help and follow rules about formats for papers) and organizational routines (such as how students manage instructional materials and follow specific procedures at the beginning of the school day or class period). Teachers rarely are aware of how many routines they have established. When co-teachers make this discovery, they face the task of agreeing as to what routines they will employ in their shared classroom. It is not particularly important whose routines are adopted by the co-teachers, and in many instances the special educator defers to the preferences of the general educator, but both teachers should know what the routines are so that they can consistently communicate them to the students.

Discipline

What each teacher believes is acceptable behavior and what each views as appropriate teacher responses to unacceptable student behavior should be discussed and, if necessary, negotiated early in the co-teaching relationship. Because teachers tend to have stronger reactions to behavior transgressions than to academic difficulties, it is particularly important that co-teachers agree on how they will respond to students who violate classroom behavior expectations. For example, how critical is it to each teacher that students keep their heads up off their desks during instruction? May students wear hats in the classroom? Snack during instruction? In an elementary school, what are the consequences for saying something disrespectful to a peer or teacher?

Feedback

Knowing your own preferred way to receive feedback from a colleague is a significant first step in determining how you and a co-teacher will give each other feedback about your activities in a shared classroom. Some teachers prefer to hear their co-teachers' reaction to a co-taught lesson immediately after its completion. Others are more receptive if they have a break before debriefing. As important as *when* teachers give each other feedback is *how* they do so, a topic that will be addressed in detail in Chapter 9. Note that an assumption is made regarding this topic—namely, that co-teachers need to review and discuss their shared efforts periodically in order to maintain their professional relationship. Feedback should include not only highlighting those aspects of instruction that are especially successful and satisfying, but also planning alternatives to instructional dilemmas that occur.

Noise

Teachers sometimes differ as significantly in their tolerance for classroom noise as they do in preferences for discipline strategies or classroom routines. Noise includes teacher talk as well as student-generated noise. Since three of the six co-teaching approaches have noise levels as potential drawbacks, co-teachers should reflect on and acknowledge their tolerance for noise and talk with one another about it. As part of their feedback, they may decide either to modify specific co-teaching approaches to reduce noise or to develop signals to indicate that noise is approaching an unacceptable level.

Pet Peeves

All teachers have a few items that are especially important to them in their professional activities or, more likely, that bother them a great deal. Pet peeves are specific triggers that could put relationships in jeopardy. For some it may be interruptions during instruction; for others it may be the removal of supplies from their desks or failure to put materials away. Some co-teachers do not permit students to return to their lockers after they have come to class, and some are very particular in how grades are recorded in the grade book or on the computer. Pet peeves can be about student issues, classroom arrangements or materials, or adult issues. The critical task for co-teachers is to identify their own and their co-teacher's pet peeves, discuss these openly, respect their differences, and negotiate responses to them.

By carefully considering what co-teaching is and how it is enhanced through collaboration, co-teachers can select approaches that enable them to begin their partnership safely and nurture it until it encompasses a wide array of shared teaching activities that optimize student learning (Huber, 2005). By initially discussing and periodically reviewing topics that can influence co-teaching success,

Administrators play a key role in co-teaching success by clarifying expectations, arranging shared planning time and appropriate schedules, and assisting teachers in problem solving when dilemmas occur.

the teachers can strengthen their professional relationship and identify and resolve challenges or disagreements before they threaten classroom practice and student outcomes.

Administrative and Pragmatic Matters Related to Co-Teaching

This chapter has emphasized the key concepts related to co-teaching, the ways that co-teachers can arrange students and themselves to take full advantage of their differing expertise, and the types of topics and issues that co-teachers should discuss. However, for co-teaching to be more than an interesting option that professionals use when they like each other and when their schedules permit, strong administrative support also must be present (Lehr, 1999; Wilson, 2005). If co-teaching is to be a feasible service delivery option, it is necessary to ensure that teachers' schedules are coordinated and that teachers with particularly challenging groups of students are paired with a co-teacher. Administrators also facilitate problem solving when difficulties arise, and they reward co-teachers' efforts, even when they are not completely successful. As co-teaching programs mature, administrators clarify that it is a standard in the school that any teacher might be asked to co-teach, not just the individuals who initially volunteered. They also supervise situations in which one of the co-teaching participants is reluctant.

In addition to the direct support that administrators give to co-teachers, they can influence school and district policy on other matters that facilitate or hinder co-teaching efforts. These factors include the size of special educators caseloads, the distribution of students with special needs in classes throughout the school, the class size typical for general education settings, the expectation for in-class versus pullout (e.g., resource) services, the growing diversity of student needs, and special educators' assignments to one or more schools. Each of these factors is explained further in Figure 5.4, and several of them are discussed in more detail in Chapter 7.

Use of Planning Time

The most common example of a practical matter that arises in co-teaching is planning. Ideas for obtaining shared planning time for co-teaching are the same as those for all collaborative activities, a topic addressed in Chapter 7. Unique to co-teaching, however, is how shared planning time is used.

Think about what may happen to teachers when they meet during planning time. Often someone is late, caught in a conversation with a colleague on the way to the meeting. When together, professionals may find that they spend precious time chatting about school events and telling stories about student successes and challenges. Sometimes they struggle to find time for the instructional planning necessary for co-teaching. These are tips for co-teaching planning:

■ Always have an agenda for shared planning meetings. The agenda reminds educators of the many topics they need to discuss.

Figure 5.4 Logistical Issues That Affect Co-Teaching

Issue	Impact
Special educator caseload	With a reasonable caseload (for example, 20 or fewer students with learning or behavior needs), co-teaching can be feasible. If the special educator is responsible for too many students (for example, 30 or more), it may be nearly impossible to arrange co-teaching except on a very limited basis. Of course, feasibility related to caseloads depends on student needs.
Caseload distribution	If students on the special educator's caseload are clustered in classes (but not making up more than 33 percent of the class group), co-teaching is a reasonable expectation. If students are widely distributed (e.g., assigned by computer in secondary schools or placed two per class in a large elementary school), or the special educator is expected to co-teach in six or even more classes each day, difficulties arise.
General education class size	Co-taught classes should have approximately the same number of students as classes with one teacher. If several extra students are assigned because "after all, there are two teachers," the effectiveness of co-teaching likely will be diminished.
Priority for co-teaching	As a service delivery option, co-teaching occurs in lieu of other services students receive. If special educators are expected to provide resource or other pullout services to most or all of the students on their caseloads, co-teaching becomes a luxury that cannot be afforded because it is added on to those other services. In schools in which this dilemma occurs, educators often note that they cannot co-teach without additional staff being hired. Also, special educators may contend that in-class services can be offered only by paraprofessionals because teacher time must be spent delivering instruction in the special education setting.
Diversity of student needs	Some special educators have responsibility for one or several students who need a significant amount of pullout service while all the other students could be served in co-teaching. Unless special education staff members and other professionals collaborate to find a way to deliver the range of services needed by every student (e.g., by having a student receive instruction from another special educator in the school), co-teaching may be unnecessarily constrained.
Small schools	In small or rural school districts, special education teachers and other professional staff members may be itinerant, serving two, three, or even more schools, or in a single school they may serve students across many grade levels or subject areas. In such instances, co-teaching may be only a small part of their jobs, often in a single location where it can be justified based on student numbers and needs and sometimes supplemented with classroom support delivered by a paraprofessional.

■ Before the meeting, the general education teacher should prepare a brief overview of the curricular concepts to be addressed during the time the planning covers. For instance, what are the chapters, stories, concepts, and projects to be addressed?

■ After reviewing the curricular content, the co-teachers should decide how they will address the content using co-teaching approaches. They might find it most effective to use patterns in their co-teaching, especially if planning time is limited. For example, they might decide that every time a unit is introduced they will spend the first part of the lesson teaming and the second part of the lesson working with students in stations.

■ The next topic of conversation should be challenges for students. For example, is the reading level of the upcoming novel so high that an audiotaped version of it needs to be located? During this part of planning the co-teachers should brainstorm ideas for differentiating instruction.

■ The last topic of conversation for co-teachers concerns individual students. By placing this topic last on the agenda, co-teachers are more likely to accomplish the instructional planning that benefits all students, including those about whom additional conversation is needed, and they are more aware of the need to prioritize student conversations to situations or behaviors that are changing or presenting significant concerns.

■ After the meeting, the special educator has the responsibility of finding or making the significant accommodations discussed during planning. Although general education teachers should expect to make simple changes, such as re-arranging test items or enlarging print, special educators use their expertise of the learning process and individualization to produce audiotaped study guides, picture icons to supplement print information, structured notes to guide student reading, and other specialized adjustments.

This type of planning process maximizes the strengths of each teacher, provides an equitable division of labor, and focuses attention on both instruction and accommodation. If used consistently, it can help co-teachers be efficient and effective planners.

Summary

Co-teaching is an increasingly common approach to service delivery in inclusive schools, and it is one in which success relies on effective collaboration. Co-teaching occurs when two or more teachers deliver substantive instruction to a diverse and blended group of students in a single classroom. They do this to address a wide range of student needs, including specialized instruction, in general education settings. Successful co-teaching helps avoid the instructional fragmentation that can occur in more traditional services and the stigmatization that may occur when students leave classrooms. It also addresses the requirements that students with disabililities access the same curriculum as their peers and that all students are taught core academic content by teachers with highly qualified status in those content areas. In co-teaching, two teachers jointly decide how best to offer instruction using a range of approaches such as one teaching, one observing; station teaching; parallel teaching; alternative teaching; teaming; and one teaching, one assisting. Although co-teaching and collaboration are not synonyms, the former is greatly enhanced with the latter. To foster collaboration in co-teaching, co-teachers should discuss critical issues such as their philosophies and beliefs, parity signals, classroom routines, discipline, feedback, noise, and pet peeves. In order for co-teaching to become an integral part of the special education service delivery system, strong administrative support is needed. Without it, the use of co-teaching is likely to be limited to volunteers. Further, pragmatic matters related to caseloads and their distribution, class sizes, and other special and general educator responsibilities can foster or constrain co-teaching.

Activities and Assignments

1. Discuss co-teaching with classmates whose schools use it as a service delivery option, or talk with experienced educators about it. How does their understanding of what co-teaching is, how it should be implemented, and the issues that are part of it compare with the information presented in this book? How might you reconcile any differences? Write a reflective essay on your own perspectives of co-teaching as a role responsibility for your professional group (e.g., special education teacher, middle school math or science teacher, speech/language therapist).

2. Suppose that you are a new special educator at your school. You have been employed with the understanding that co-teaching is to be a significant part of your responsibilities. You introduce yourself to your co-teaching partners and believe that everything is working well. However, after the first week of school Ms. Hanson asks to meet with you. She explains that, although she likes you, she feels that your presence in the classroom is disruptive. She asks you to either take students out of the class or sit quietly during instruction, helping students once an assignment is given. How would you respond to Ms. Hanson? What types of solutions might be possible? What would you do if you believed the situation to be at an impasse?

3. Collaborate with a colleague to develop a series of lesson plans or a unit to be co-taught in a general education classroom. The plan should use at least three different co-teaching approaches and should specify clearly the unique needs of students and the roles of each teacher.

4. With several classmates or colleagues experienced in co-teaching, prepare a chart that compares one-teacher classrooms to two-teacher classrooms on as many elements as you can identify. For example, in a one-teacher classroom, lessons are taught from a single perspective, but in a two-teacher classroom teachers may share the same perspective, need to blend their perspectives, or decide to use differing

perspectives as part of instruction. What does this exercise tell you about aspects of co-teaching that might come easily for you? That might pose a difficulty for you?

5. You have been asked to prepare a webpage for your school that explains what co-teaching is, why it is a valuable service delivery option, and how it enhances students' education. Consider adding links to other information about co-teaching that you find by exploring this topic on the Internet. Remember that parents, community members, and others are likely to access the webpage you develop, and so you should present co-teaching in a manner easily understandable to others.

6. Suppose you are co-teaching and a problem related to your collaborative relationship arises. Either you are dissatisfied with how a discipline matter is being addressed, or your partner believes that your standards for students are too flexible. What skills would you need to air the issue and work to resolve it? How might the problem-solving process assist you in this situation? Role-play with a classmate how such an interaction might proceed.

7. Given what you have read about co-teaching, how would you go about deciding whether a co-teaching program was a success? What questions would you ask? To whom? How would you measure student success?

For Further Reading

Bahamonde, C., & Friend, M. (1999). Teaching English language learners: A proposal for effective service delivery through collaboration and co-teaching. *Journal of Educational and Psychological Consultation, 10*, 1–24.

Burrello, L., Friend, M., & Burrello, J. (Co-Producer with L. Burrello & J. Burrello). (2005). *The power of two: Including students through co-teaching*, 2nd ed. [videotape]. Bloomington, IN: Elephant Rock Productions.

Cook, L., & Friend, M. (1995). Co-teaching guidelines for creating effective practice. *Focus on Exceptional Children, 28*(3), 1–12.

Fishbaugh, M. S. E. (Ed.). (2000). *Collaboration guide for early career educators*. Baltimore: Brookes.

Magiera, K., Smith, C., Zigmond, N., & Gebaner, K. (2005). Benefits of co-teaching in secondary mathematics classes. *Teaching Exceptional Children, 37*(3), 20–24.

Villa, R. A., Thousand, J. S., & Nevin, A. I. (2004). *A guide to co-teaching: Practical tips for facilitating student learning*. Thousand Oaks, CA: Corwin.

Weiss, M. P., & Lloyd, J. (2003). Conditions for co-teaching: Lessons from a case study. *Teacher Education and Special Education, 26*, 27–41.

Wilson, G. L. (2005). This doesn't look familiar: A supervisor's guide for observing co-teachers. *Intervention in School and Clinic, 40*, 271–275.

CHAPTER 6

Paraeducators

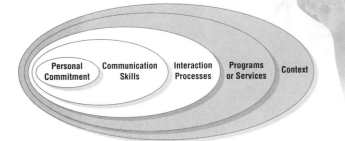

Connections

In Chapters 3, 4, and 5 you learned about services that rely heavily on collaboration between school professionals. This chapter also addresses a type of service, but one that is based on a slightly different type of working relationship, that of a teacher and a paraprofessional or paraeducator. In this chapter you will explore paraeducators' participation in the education of students with special needs and the nature of your interactions with them. You also will learn about several unique considerations for collaborating with paraeducators.

Learner Objectives

After reading this chapter you will be able to:

1. Describe how the roles and responsibilities of paraeducators in public schools have grown and changed over the past several decades.

2. Explain instructional and noninstructional responsibilities of paraeducators, and clarify activities that should and should not be assigned to paraeducators.

3. Identify strategies for effectively working with paraeducators as you assist them to understand the scope of their responsibilities, plan with them, maintain clear communication with them, and supervise their work with students.

4. Describe how collaboration pertains to the interactions between paraeducators and professionals.

5. Balance your professional obligation to value paraeducators as individuals who contribute to the education of students with special needs while recognizing their nonprofessional status and the parameters that are placed on the expectations that should be set for them.

Rebecca loves her job as a paraeducator—the work that she does with students in general education classes, the opportunity to learn from the wonderful teachers in whose classes she spends her days, and the interactions she has with Reneé, the special education teacher to whom she is assigned. This morning she will spend first block in a biology class as a notetaker for Justin. Second and third blocks will be in English 9, where she is responsible for implementing the behavior plan for Colette and Miguel. After lunch, she will be in the resource room to work with several students on instructional activities planned by Reneé. She knows that a few sophomores have a U.S. History project due in two weeks, and she is fairly certain she'll be helping students with finding resources, editing their writing, and organizing their references. Reneé and Rebecca are scheduled for their weekly meeting during the last 30 minutes of the day; this is a time for them to catch up on details about students, discuss any problems or concerns, and, for Rebecca, learn about her responsibilities for the upcoming week. The meeting cannot run over, though—Rebecca is taking classes in the evening toward teacher licensure and needs to leave school promptly at 3:15 PM so that she is not late to class.

Introduction

Whether you are a novice or an experienced special educator, you may find that not only do you need to interact effectively with general education teachers, administrators, other special services providers, as well as parents and families, but you also are assigned to work with one or more paraeducators. Consider these situations:

■ As a resource teacher in a local high school, your caseload has crept from the locally allowed 25 students to 32. Given student numbers and types of needs, administrators have decided that it is not necessary to employ another special education teacher, but they have notified you that they are seeking a paraeducator to assist you with your workload.

■ You work in an elementary school in a large, urban district. Your district has contracted with a private company to provide a paraeducator to support one of your students who has extraordinary needs for behavior supports. You have many questions about your role in providing information to this person, directing his work, and communicating about student progress and needs.

■ As a new special educator for students with autism, you are greeted on the first workday before school by your teaching assistant who explains that you have no reason to be anxious because she knows all the routines and can let you know how everything is supposed to happen. She proceeds to explain how the room is to be arranged, which general education teachers are willing to "allow" the students to visit their classrooms, and what activities to plan for the first day with students.

■ In your highly inclusive school, you are responsible as the special educator for guiding the work of three paraeducators who are assigned to work one-to-one with students with significant needs in general education classrooms. You also share a fourth paraeducator with the other special education teacher.

Have you encountered a situation similar to any of these? Do you know teachers who have? Collectively, these scenarios illustrate that the addition of a paraeducator to a school's special services staff can be a benefit to students and professionals, can be helpful yet somewhat problematic, or can be necessary but time consuming. In all instances, the use of paraeducators is a dimension of the adult–adult interactions in schools that has grown in importance and that requires careful consideration by the professionals responsible for working with them and directing their activities on a day-to-day basis.

Paraeducators in Public Schools

Paraeducators are individuals who provide instructional and other services to students and who are supervised by licensed professionals who are responsible for student outcomes (French, 2003). They may also be known as paraprofessionals, instructional assistants, classroom assistants, job coaches, therapy assistants, transition trainers, teacher aides, or teacher assistants. Paraeducators may work in remedial reading, English as a second language (ESL), and special education programs, but they may also serve, especially in large elementary schools, in a more general capacity to assist teachers in their classrooms, particularly in primary-grade classrooms when class sizes are large. Most paraeducators are women who have lived in their communities for a long time (Ashbaker & Morgan, 2001). In this chapter, the emphasis is on paraeducators who are employed for the purpose of assisting in the delivery of services to students who have disabilities.

Paraeducator Qualifications

The matter of paraeducator qualifications used to be simple: States and local school districts simply decided on the education and skills expected of these school personnel—whether a high school diploma, some type of specialized training, or a certain number of college credits. Recently, though, the expectations for paraeducator credentials have changed significantly. The qualifications required of paraeducators still can vary widely, but the No Child Left Behind Act of 2001 has established some parameters. Paraeducators who work in schools that receive Title I funds (that is, schools whose students have high levels of poverty)

In inclusive schools, paraeducators provide support to students, sometimes by grouping them with peers who are typical learners.

must have appropriate preparation for their roles—an associate's degree or the equivalent, or training such that they can pass a test demonstrating their skills for assisting in the areas of reading, writing, math, and school readiness. In many school districts, these requirements are being applied to all paraprofessionals who provide instruction, regardless of the specific schools in which they work.

However, these standards do not have to be met by paraeducators who do not have classroom instructional responsibilities. Examples of staff members in these roles include paraprofessionals whose jobs consist of increasing parent involvement in schools, providing personal care to students, acting as translators, working in the cafeteria or on a bus, or serving as a clerical assistant. As you might expect, though, many paraeducators have both instructional and noninstructional responsibilities, and these individuals are required to meet the higher standard of qualifications.

The Prevalence of Paraeducators

Because no uniform system exists for tracking paraeducators employed in public schools, estimates of their number vary widely, ranging from approximately 500,000 (French, 1999b; Pickett, 1996) to over 900,000 (Ashbaker & Morgan, 2001) or even more. What is clear is that the number of paraeducators is increasing and is likely to continue to do so. In fact, recent information from the *Occupational Outlook Handbook* of the U.S. Department of Labor Statistics indicates that the job of paraeducator will be, on average, one of the fastest growing occupations for the next several years (Ashbaker & Morgan, 2001). Further, of all the paraeducators in schools, approximately 80 percent work with special education and related services professionals and the students for whom they are responsible (Katisyannis, Hodge, & Lanford, 2000).

Many reasons have been given for the increasing use of paraeducators for special education (e.g., Giangreco, Edelman, Broer, & Doyle, 2001). The rising emphasis on early childhood programs has undoubtedly contributed (Killoran, Templeman, Peters, & Udell, 2001), as has the growth in programs to assist students to transition from school to work or community settings and the growing number of students and their families for whom English is not the first language (Chopra, Sandoval-Lucero, Aragon, Bernal, de Balderas, & Carroll, 2004). The increasing shortage of special education teachers (e.g., Daniels & McBride, 2001; Special Education News, 2000b) also is making paraeducators attractive employees to school administrators. The trend toward inclusive practices is an influence as well. When students with complex special needs are assigned to general education classrooms, their teachers report that paraeducator support is not just helpful but essential (French & Chopra, 1999; Giangreco, 2003; Marks, Schrader, & Levine, 1999). However, even for students with mild needs who typically are distributed among many classrooms in inclusive schools, paraeducators have become critical in supplementing the services of special educators who cannot themselves see every student every day (Doyle & Gurney, 2000; Hammeken, 2003).

Historically, paraeducators were expected to assume largely clerical duties (French, 1999a). They graded papers, took attendance, and collected lunch money, acting mostly to free teachers from routine tasks so they could spend more time instructing their students. Now, however, most paraeducators spend the majority of their time working with individual students or small groups of students (Doyle, 2002). They help students understand their assignments, listen to students read, provide physical support, and generally engage in a wide range of services that enable students to succeed, whether in inclusive classrooms or special education settings.

Until the passage of IDEA-97, few federal guidelines existed to inform school districts about the use of paraeducators for students with disabilities. The current federal law, IDEA-04, although still not detailed in its consideration of paraeducators, does specify that

> paraprofessionals and assistants who are appropriately trained and supervised, in accordance with State law, regulation, or written policy, in meeting the requirements of this part [may be] used to assist in the provision of special education and related services under this part to children with disabilities. (20 U.S.C. §1412 (a)(14)(B)(iii)

This brief statement clarifies several points: (1) paraeducators are legitimately employed to assist in the delivery of services to students; (2) paraeducators are not the primary service providers and must have supervision; and (3) paraeducators are entitled to training for their duties. Each of these key areas is addressed in the following sections, and further resources related to them are found in Putting Ideas into Practice on page 144.

PUTTING IDEAS INTO PRACTICE

Paraeducators on the Web

Are you looking for additional information about paraeducators? These websites contain a wealth of information:

www.cec.sped.org/ps/paraks.html

This Council for Exceptional Children webpage contains information about the knowledge and skills standards the organization recently set for paraeducators for students with special needs.

www.aft.org/psrp/index.html

This webpage of the American Federation of Teachers explains the types of paraeducators found in school settings. The site also includes a link to information pertaining to paraeducator certification.

www.nwrel.org/planning/paraeducator.html

On this webpage of the Northwest Regional Education Laboratory, you can access a report that provides guidance for school policymakers on professional development for paraeducators. The document offers an administrative perspective on issues related to ensuring that paraeducators are adequately prepared for their jobs.

www.nrcpara.org

The National Resource Center for Paraprofessionals contains a wealth of information about paraeducators, their responsibilities, and best practices for their use in public schools. The site includes links to many other useful resources.

http://ericec.org/osep/recon12/rc12cov.html

This 2003 issue of the web publication *Research Connections in Special Education,* offered by the U.S. Department of Education, summarizes the research base on the roles and responsibilities of paraeducators who work on behalf of students with disabilities.

remc7.k12.mi.us/remc/paraeducators.htm

This website was prepared by a special education coordinator as a resource for individuals working as paraeducators. The site includes many links to information about lesson planning, classroom management, multicultural resources, paraeducator roles and responsibilities, and professional materials (e.g., journals, laws).

Paraeducator Roles and Responsibilities

In special education and related services, paraeducators generally serve in one of two ways. First, some paraeducators are assigned as one-to-one assistants for students with extraordinary needs. These individuals typically spend most of the day with the particular student, whether in a general education or a special education classroom. Students who may need such intense support include those with autism, those with significant intellectual disabilities, and those with complex physical needs. For example, Robert, a paraeducator, may have the responsibility of meeting Josh, a student with multiple disabilities, when he arrives at school on the bus. Robert makes sure that Josh has his school supplies and changes Josh's diaper when needed. Josh participates in a general education art class, and Robert is responsible for getting Josh's art supplies and helping him to use them, attaching charcoal pencils and paintbrushes to the special adapted holder that Josh uses. Robert also accompanies Josh when he goes to his vocational exploratory each afternoon—job experiences that are designed to help Josh decide on the type of work he would like to do after he graduates from high school.

Second, some paraeducators support special education programs but are not assigned to specific students. For example, in a high school program for students with learning disabilities, a paraeducator may be available to read tests to students who need such service, assist students in organizing their assignments and materials, and take notes for a student in his history class. Rebecca, the paraeducator who you met at the beginning of this chapter, has this type of responsibility. In elementary schools, paraeducators working in this way may be assigned to a single grade level, or they may work across several grade levels based on the needs of students.

Although you might assume that the specific roles and responsibilities for paraeducators would be found in their job descriptions, you may find that most descriptions focus on the number of hours the individual is to work, the qualifications they must have for the job, and general expectations about working in schools (U.S. Department of Education, n.d.). Some school districts, particularly large ones, have clear and detailed job descriptions and may even distinguish among types of paraeducators (e.g., those addressing student behavior, those providing personal care, those assisting with instruction), but in many cases, you will not have specific guidelines to help you assign tasks to a paraeducator (Riggs & Mueller, 2001). Generally, paraeducator responsibilities can be divided into those that directly relate to instruction and those that are noninstructional.

Instructional Responsibilities

Whether working with an individual student or to support teachers and programs so that any number of students can be successful, the most common tasks for today's paraprofessionals in special education relate to instruction (Carroll, 2001). These tasks may include delivery of instruction, but they may also involve preparation for or follow-up to instruction.

Instructional Delivery

The number of examples of instructional delivery appropriate for paraeducators is almost infinite (Downing, Ryndak, & Clark, 2000). For example, for students with mild or moderate learning problems, paraprofessionals may read individually with them, review earlier instruction to ensure their understanding, or lead them through an assignment that other students are completing independently. Paraeducators also may read tests to students, help them find appropriate resources for an assigned project or paper, and assist them in keeping books, materials, and papers organized. To minimize the possibility of stigma from being singled out in the general education classroom you might see a paraeducator working with a small group of students that includes students with disabilities and typical learners. The paraeducator might also sometimes work individually with a range of students, always keeping the needs of students with disabilities as the priority.

For students with more significant needs, paraeducators sometimes deliver an alternative curriculum within the context of the general education classroom. For example, while some students add numbers, the paraeducator works with one student to identify the numbers. A paraeducator also might facilitate student participation in a class activity by ensuring that the student is following directions, simplifying multiple-step directions, or serving as a "partner" who helps the student in the activity. This individual may have the responsibility of observing a student's behavior and providing reinforcers to the student according to a plan prepared by the special education teachers. A paraeducator working with a student with significant needs often works with other students in a classroom, but is more likely than paraeducators for students with mild disabilities to need to be near the identified student to provide necessary physical, instructional, and social assistance.

Other Instructional Responsibilities

Like delivery-of-instruction responsibilities, the preparation and follow-up activities of paraeducators vary greatly. They may prepare flashcards for students, use a computer program to create a picture-based version of a story to be read, scan print material so that the student can "read" it using a computer, and adapt classroom materials (e.g., shorten, make larger, rearrange). After instruction, the paraeducator may grade student work, record information about student performance on particular tasks, and prepare routine correspondence for parents about a student's activities that day.

One issue should be raised regarding the instructional responsibilities of paraeducators. Despite all the anecdotal information about the instructional assistance paraeducators provide to students with special needs, studies that establish that student achievement improves as a result of interventions by paraeducators remain limited (Giangreco et al., 2001). A few isolated studies indicate that when paraeducators receive specific training to carry out interventions, students with whom they work benefit (e.g., Kotkin, 1995; Parsons & Reid, 1999), particularly very young children (French, 2003). In general, though, current practices on the instructional tasks paraeducators complete, the amount of time they spend in inclusive general education classes, the intensity of their contacts with students with disabilities, and the impact of their preparation for their responsibili-

Just as in other professions—including law—that employ a cadre of individuals to support professionals, educators work with paraeducators to maximize services for students.

ties are based largely on intuition and experience, not data-based knowledge. This situation should remind you of the importance of gathering your own data about paraeducators' work so that you create your own knowledge base on using them most effectively with the students for whom you are responsible.

Noninstructional Responsibilities

Even though instruction is usually a paraeducator's primary responsibility, many paraprofessionals also have noninstructional responsibilities (Doyle, 2002). These responsibilities may involve direct support for students, clerical work, or other activities that support students in an indirect way.

Direct Support for Students

Some students can receive instruction in public schools only because paraeducators provide for their personal care. This may involve feeding a student, moving the student from place to place, carrying out procedures such as catheterization, changing diapers, or assisting a student to use the toilet. Paraeducators who carry out these types of responsibilities often develop close relationships with their students, and they may even babysit for students on weekends and during holidays. Mary Ellen, for example, works as an one-to-one assistant for Lisa, an elementary student with autism. Mary Ellen is very knowledgeable concerning Lisa's personality and special needs, especially what to do if Lisa becomes upset because of a change in routine. Mary Ellen usually leaves school with Lisa on Wednesday afternoons, spending two or three hours with her at Lisa's home so that Lisa's mom can complete errands. If a paraeducator has this type of responsibility, usually clear plans need to be in place in case the paraeducator is absent.

Many paraeducators assist educators in student supervision. Some accompany students to recess, lunch, or assemblies to provide behavior support. Others assist in getting students safely off of buses and into the school building. Yet others are assigned a limited amount of lunchroom supervision, time-out monitoring, or playground duty. If a student is unable to self-ambulate, or if a student has serious behavior problems likely to be demonstrated during unstructured time such as occurs during passing periods, the paraeducator may accompany such a student from class to class for safety and efficiency.

Clerical Responsibilities

Special education, like all professions, includes a significant amount of paperwork. Paraeducators sometimes assist in getting this work completed. They may record scores on assessments onto a master record, update progress notes regarding student learning, or enter data on a behavior intervention plan. They also may assist in the day-to-day clerical work of teachers, duplicating materials for class, gathering money for field trips, or laminating materials that will be used several times. In addition, they may draft general correspondence being sent to all parents (about upcoming conferences, for example) and assist in obtaining information from or relaying information to outside agencies.

It may be tempting to assign a paraeducator many clerical responsibilities in order to free teacher time to work with students. However, you should keep in mind that paraeducators employed in special education, like teachers, have student instruction and support as a primary responsibility. In particular, they should not be asked to assist in the school office, to cover responsibilities for clerical assistants who are absent, or to carry out clerical chores during the time that they have been assigned to work with students because this detracts from the services to which students with IEPs are entitled.

Other Noninstructional Responsibilities

Paraeducators may have other responsibilities that facilitate student success and support the delivery of special education. For example, in schools where a significant number of students or family members are not native English speakers, some paraeducators can provide translation. Whether assisting a special education or general education teacher during a routine phone call, communicating with parents who come to school to meet with professionals, or clarifying technical terms during any interaction, translation may be an essential paraeducator responsibility. An indirect benefit may result as well: Family members may be more comfortable when a paraeducator who shares their culture and language is present, and better communication often results. Other positive results of paraeducators bringing their culture to their responsibilities—both instructional and noninstructional—is addressed in A Basis in Research.

A BASIS IN RESEARCH

Latino Paraeducators' Interactions with Latino Students

For all students from the minority cultures, but especially for students with special needs, learning is assisted when students can interact with adults who understand their language, culture, and communities. Monzó and Rueda (2000) interviewed 32 Latino paraeducators and observed them as they worked in classrooms in two large, inner-city, southern California elementary schools. They found that Latino paraeducators offered the following positive factors for Latino students:

1. *Demonstrating cariño.* The paraeducators used terms of endearment, touch, and softened facial expressions, particularly when correcting student behavior or academic work.

2. *Using a relaxed instructional style.* The paraeducators allowed students to chat with peers while they worked and to speak spontaneously during instruction. The relaxed style enabled paraeducators to learn about students' lives outside school.

3. *Accepting students' styles.* Latino paraeducators were tolerant of student misbehaviors and addressed them discreetly whenever possible. They were far more likely to talk with students about behaviors than to remove privileges.

4. *Incorporating student knowledge in instruction.* The paraeducators used their primary language to facilitate instruction. Likewise, they related concepts being taught in students' homes and communities. These approaches seemed to foster student participation.

5. *Employing wait time.* The paraeducators generally waited longer for student responses than would typically be expected. This often seemed to relate to understanding the language-processing problems of students for whom English is a second language.

6. *Sharing experiences.* Noninstructional interactions between paraeducators and students usually occurred in Spanish. The paraeducators indicated that this approach helped them to "connect" to the students.

Although these findings pertain to students at risk, not those with identified disabilities, they offer important insights into informal contributions that paraeducators can make in the instructional process. For example, if the general education teacher or special education teacher is not Latino, a Latino paraeducator may help to serve as a cultural liaison between student and professional. Likewise, because professionals, whether Latino or not, often are balancing the needs of many students and a wide range of setting factors, the paraeducators may be more able than the professionals to build a relationship with a reticent student.

Source: Adapted from Monzó, L. D., & Rueda, R. S. *Examining Latino paraeducators: Interactions with Latino students* (Washington, DC: ERIC Clearinghouse on Language and Linguistics, December 2000).

Paraeducators also can function as members of the instructional team. When they work with students on a daily basis, sometimes, more than any of the professionals on the team, they may have insights about student learning or behavior that can help shape decisions being made. Similarly, they may notice small problems students are encountering that others have missed (Darling-Hammond, 2001; Gursky, 2000). Of course, this responsibility requires their attendance at meetings to discuss students—sometimes a dilemma if those meetings typically are held after school hours, time outside most paraeducators' contracted work day.

Ethical Considerations

Because the use of paraeducators is not clearly prescribed in federal law and their roles continue to evolve in this era of higher student achievement standards, you may find that some of the roles we have described are common for paraeducators in your locale, while others are unusual or specifically prohibited. In addition, any of several ethical issues may arise concerning their work. Your responsibility is to make decisions concerning paraeducator assignments, keeping in mind local policies as well as factors such as these.

Paraeducators Supplement Instruction

Although paraeducators provide valuable instruction to students with special needs, it is clear that they are to supplement instruction that is delivered by professionals; they may not supplant it (French, 2003). Some authors even suggest that paraeducators provide an *indirect* service to students, not a *direct* service, since only professionals can offer the latter (Giangreco et al., 2001). This issue also affects accountability: Even if a paraeducator delivers a specific service to a student, the professional staff member, often the special educator, is ultimately accountable for the outcome of that service (Giangreco et al., 2001). For example, in Mr. Baker and Ms. Wright's co-taught classroom, three days each week Ms. Scott, the paraeducator, also is present. The three educators usually establish stations for these lessons. Mr. Baker and Ms. Wright provide instruction on specific skills while Ms. Scott either reviews skills taught earlier or rereads a story or set of poems the students are studying. This arrangement is appropriate; the professionals are delivering the initial instruction while the paraeducator supplements it through review.

Paraeducators themselves have raised issues related to instruction. They report that they feel a strong sense of ownership for and commitment to the students to whom they are assigned, but that they sometimes are asked to take responsibility for making instructional decisions they do not feel qualified to make (Marks et al., 1999; Riggs, 2001). For example, Downing and her colleagues (2000) interviewed paraeducators working with students with severe disabilities. The paraeducators reported that they were primarily responsible for making curricular adaptations and other decisions that could have a significant impact on students' education—decisions that they believed should be made by the teachers.

Giangreco and his colleagues (1997) add a sobering sociocultural perspective on this issue of paraeducators' work. They note that in too many situations paraeducators are becoming the de facto teachers for students with significant disabilities. They raise questions about the potential negative impact on the general education teachers and typical learners' perceptions when the group of staff members generally considered least powerful in schools provides most services for the students who are likely perceived as least powerful (that is, those with disabilities).

An unpleasant but realistic sidebar to this discussion of the ethical use of paraeducators concerns the occasional administrative rationale for employing them. In some locales, paraeducators are seen as an inexpensive alternative to hiring professional staff, particularly if the intent is to get "an extra set of hands" into inclusive classrooms. This approach reflects a gross underestimation of the skills of professional staff and their purpose in inclusive classrooms, and it is a highly questionable means of delivering student services.

Ultimately, a few matters related to what paraeducators instructionally should *not* do are clear: They should not design and deliver initial instruction without teacher supervision, they should not write students' education plans, and they should not make critical decisions concerning student education or safety (French, 1999a). Ultimately, they should not bear sole responsibility for any part of a student's education; rather, they should assist professionals in related tasks and carry out their work with ongoing and high-quality professional involvement. Can you think of any additional issues related to instruction that should be added to this list?

Parent Communication and Input

Another ethical issue can arise in the work of paraeducators. What are the topics and circumstances under which paraeducators should communicate with parents (Chopra & French, 2004)? This seemingly simple matter can become complex. Many special educators ask paraeducators to record in a notebook two or three highlights of the day for students with significant disabilities who cannot communicate what they have experienced at school. Others may request that paraeducators call parents to alert them that a form needing parent signature or an announcement of an upcoming school event is being sent home. However, if a discussion is needed about a behavior problem a student is experiencing or a concern related to a student's education, the teacher should be responsible for this communication. Complexity may arise when a paraeducator knows family members well. In such cases, a paraeducator may inadvertently or deliberately share information beyond the scope of what is appropriate. For example, Terry, a paraeducator, told Tony's mother that Tony had had a terrible day at school. She called the special education teacher, who was surprised at the mother's concern. The teacher's perception was that Tony's behavior was the result of a changed schedule because of a special program and not a cause for alarm.

The Problem of Proximity

One other issue can arise related to paraeducators and their work. When a team decides that part of a student's instruction can be provided by a paraeducator, parents and families are entitled to understand the qualifications of the individual delivering services and the scope of that person's responsibilities (Jacobson & Mulick, 2000; Mueller & Murphy, 2001; Werts, Harris, Tillery, & Roark, 2004). Often, professionals and parents alike are faced with an ethical dilemma: How much support from a paraeducator is optimal? Is more always better? What is the rationale that should be employed for deciding on the right blend of professional and paraeducator services?

Paraeducators report that they believe they are crucial for helping students succeed, and educators generally report that paraeducators are highly valuable staff members (e.g., American Federation of Teachers, 1999b). Sometimes, however, these laudable characteristics can lead to a dilemma. Particularly for those paraeducators assigned to a specific student in an inclusive setting, a risk exists that by remaining in close physical proximity to the student, negative outcomes can occur (Carroll, 2001). Among these are losing opportunities for the student to have typical social interactions with other students, inadvertently encouraging dependent instead of independent student behaviors, and unintentionally communicating to the general education teacher that he or she is not the primary teacher of the student (Canston-Theoharis & Malmgren, 2005). In addition,

Some paraprofessionals work with individual students, providing personal care, classroom and communication assistance, and support for moving from location to location within the school.

some concern also exists that assistants in close proximity may place students at greater risk for sexual abuse because the students do not learn appropriate social distance (Giangreco et al., 1997).

Generally, paraeducators should be taught that the goal of their work with an individual student is to gradually move away from directly and intrusively interacting with that student, except as absolutely needed (e.g., helping the student move from place to place). Although no one would want a student to miss needed supports, what also is important is that the student learn to interact with classmates in a natural way, to seek assistance from them without adult intervention, and to experience school in a way that adult mediation cannot replicate. If you are a special education teacher or a general education teacher, you may find it necessary to guide paraeducators in this responsibility, helping them to find the best balance between providing individual assistance and nurturing independence.

Working with Paraeducators

The first part of this chapter has addressed the scope of a paraeducator's roles and responsibilities. The essential complement to that discussion is one about your roles and responsibilities as a professional working with paraeducators (Ashbaker & Morgan, 2001; Calder & Grieve, 2004; French, 2004). You may find that you need to be competent and feel confident to address these five areas: training paraeducators, planning with paraeducators, effectively assigning specific responsibilities to paraeducators, communicating with paraeducators, and supervising these personnel. You also may learn that you have to think carefully about the subject of delegating responsibilities to paraeducators, which is the topic of Putting Ideas into Practice on the next page.

Training Paraeducators

Although federal law clearly states that paraeducators should be trained for the responsibilities they have in their jobs, the way in which this is accomplished varies by state and school district (Pardini, 2005). Some school districts offer general training to paraeducators through workshops or videotapes in order to prepare them to succeed on the required assessment of their skills. In other locales, completion of a community college program or a specific number of college credits is a condition of employment. However, the initial general training that paraeducators receive seldom can provide enough preparation for the specific roles and responsibilities they assume. This more specific training often is the result of efforts by the professional staff (Bernal & Aragon, 2004; Jolly & Evans, 2005). That is, professionals need to provide student-specific and context-based information in order for paraeducators to do their jobs effectively. As you can see from the topics presented in the sample needs assessment in Figure 6.1 on page 155, paraeducator training can include general knowledge about behavior, learning, and the law; specific knowledge about students' characteristics and needs; and knowledge and skills only indirectly related to students, such as working effectively with other adults.

PUTTING IDEAS INTO PRACTICE

Delegating Responsibilities to Paraprofessionals

Some special education teachers, general education teachers, and related services professionals (e.g., speech/language therapists) struggle with delegating responsibilities to paraeducators—that is, appropriately requiring them to carry out particular tasks or activities. Here are a few of the reasons why.

■ Paraeducators are paid too little to expect them to do many of the tasks that need attention.

■ I am a perfectionist and the paraeducator is unlikely to complete the task in the way that I want it done.

■ To do this activity, the paraeducator should be trained and there is no time for training in the schedule.

■ I am not confident about the quality of the work that the paraeducator does.

■ I can do it faster myself.

■ I don't want to be bossy.

How do you think each of these issues should be addressed, especially those that consider paraeducator skills and training?

Here are some reasons why delegation is so important.

■ Delegation makes the most of all the time available to provide services to students—that of both paraeducators and professionals.

■ Delegation creates teams in which everyone feels a sense of commitment.

■ Delegation challenges paraeducators to learn new skills and stretch their expertise.

■ Delgation empowers paraeducators.

■ Delegation means that you don't have to do everything yourself, permitting you to better manage all your responsibilities.

Source: Adapted from N. K. French, *Managing paraeducators in your school: How to hire, train, and supervise non-certified staff* (Thousand Oaks, CA: Sage, 2003), pp. 91–106.

You should discuss with your administrator and other special education team members how paraeducators in your school receive this focused training. If none is available, you might wish to use a needs assessment such as the one in Figure 6.1 to determine which topics are priorities. You might also wish to create a year-long plan for training all the paraeducators in your school (Lasater, Johnson, & Fitzgerald, 2000). As you work on this project, you should take into consideration the practical matter of finding brief periods of time during the school day during which this activity can occur. If you are in a school with several

Figure 6.1 Paraeducator Training Needs Assessment			

Directions: The information you provide in this survey will assist in developing relevant in-service opportunities for paraprofessionals. Using the scale, rate the importance of each of the following skills in your job situation. Put a star next to those on which you would like to receive training. Also, please provide general information about your job at the bottom of the form. Thank you!

	0 = No need	3 = Some need	5 = Great need			
1.	Rationale of integration of students with special needs/current issues of inclusion			0	3	5
2.	Background information on specific disabilities			0	3	5
3.	Background information about the special education process			0	3	5
4.	Information gathering about individual students			0	3	5
5.	Modification of materials			0	3	5
6.	Behavior management			0	3	5
7.	Observation and recording of behavior and academic progress			0	3	5
8.	Promoting social acceptance of children with disabilities			0	3	5
9.	Legal issues			0	3	5
10.	Learning styles			0	3	5
11.	Small-group instruction			0	3	5
12.	Techniques for dealing with adults in the school system			0	3	5
13.	Assistive technology			0	3	5
14.	Working with related service providers (occupational therapy, physical therapy, speech therapy)			0	3	5
15.	Communication			0	3	5

Type of assignment: inclusive class   special education   general education
Level: preschool   elementary   middle school   high school

Source: C. G. Riggs, "Ask the paraprofessionals," *Teaching Exceptional Children, 33*(3) (2001): 78–83. Copyright 2001 by the Council for Exceptional Children. Reprinted with permission.

special educators, one option is to share this effort with your special education and related services colleagues.

Planning with Paraeducators

Clearly, paraeducators are supposed to work under the direction of a special education teacher, general education teacher, or other professional. This implies that a need exists for professionals and paraeducators to meet so that plans can be discussed, dilemmas raised and resolved, and student progress monitored. However, the limited data available suggest that such interactions are the exception rather than the rule. In a study of the supervisory roles that resource teachers play in working with paraeducators in inclusive settings, French (2001) finds that more than 80 percent of the teachers reported that they had no written plan to guide paraeducators' work and that they prefer that paraeducators be able to just "go along" with whatever is occurring in the general education classroom. This degree of flexibility has the risk of slipping into unethical practice: How can IEP implementation be documented when no records are created for the part of IEPs that paraeducators implement? This is an especially important consideration given professionals' accountability for whatever tasks paraeducators complete.

Not surprisingly, the biggest reported obstacle to professional–paraeducator planning is time to meet (French, 2001). For example, in many school districts paraeducators have the same work hours as the school day for students, and so they are not available before or after school hours. Similarly, paraeducators typically are not paid on teacher workdays when students are not present or for preparation days prior to the start of the school year. Without an administrative commitment to professional–paraeducator planning, no simple solution to this problem exists. However, you can use some of the suggestions in Chapter 7 on finding time for collaboration to create opportunities for shared planning. In addition, you can be sure that the schedule you create for paraeducators working with you includes at least one planning period per week (Morgan & Ashbaker, 2001), a point illustrated in the chapter-opening story about Rebecca.

Assigning Responsibilities to Paraeducators

Perhaps the most important responsibility you have related to paraeducators is assigning particular tasks or responsibilities to them. Although it is not possible to consider all the possibilities, these are some points to keep in mind:

■ If you are working in an inclusive school, consider assigning paraeducators to work in general education classrooms where student needs are minimal and teacher support is not warranted. Examples might be science or social studies classes or lessons in which students use many manipulatives.

■ If the need for a second adult in a general education classroom pertains to a student who has a behavior intervention plan, consider training a paraeducator on the plan and assigning her to that classroom. Keep in mind, though, that if a student's behavior is unpredictable and problems are occurring with the plan, a teacher's presence may be necessary.

■ In some classrooms, general education teachers have a strong grasp of student needs and easily respond to them using differentiated instruction. What is needed is someone to help in implementing the instruction. This might be a situation in which a paraeducator can make a valuable contribution working under the direction of that teacher.

■ When paraeducators have received specific training to deliver remedial reading or math instruction, they may be assigned to this responsibility for part of the day (Granger & Greek, 2005). You should check local policies regarding the use of special education paraeducators for such instruction.

■ In some inclusive schools, paraeducators are assigned based on schedules rather than specific student and classroom needs. Although the difficulty of scheduling is clear (and addressed in Chapter 7), keep in mind that schedules alone should not dictate how paraeducators are assigned.

■ If paraeducators are working in special education classrooms, they often review specific skills with students while the special educator provides initial instruction with other students. This model is common both in resource classes as well as self-contained classes. The caution about paraeducators not offering ongoing initial instruction holds in the special education setting as well as in the general education setting.

■ Another common assignment for paraeducators working with students with significant needs is accompanying one or several students to related arts classes such as art, music, physical education, or computer lab. In such cases, you should be sure to clarify with the general education teachers and paraeducators any issues related to safety.

In general, the range of assignments for paraeducators is almost endless. You can obtain input on potential responsibilities for them by discussing ideas with your colleagues and administrators and even by seeking input from paraeducators. Of course, it is imperative that you monitor paraeducators' work to ensure that their time is well used on behalf of students and that their interactions with other professionals are appropriate.

Communicating with Paraeducators

Even if you have regularly scheduled planning periods with paraeducators, you still will need to use effective and efficient communication strategies to keep in touch with your paraeducator and to monitor their work and student progress (Calder & Grieve, 2004; French, 2000). Of course, the communication skills you will learn in Chapters 8, 9, and 10 are essential, as they are for all your professional interactions, but several other strategies also can be used. These are briefly described in Putting Ideas into Practice on the next page.

Communication entails more than interactions about instruction and student concerns, however. One initial form of communication is the paraeducator's job description. This is the instrument through which you can discuss with paraeducators the expectations of the job. You might want to check about the availability of a job description because—as noted earlier—not all school districts have them, and some that do have not updated them in many years (Riggs, 2001). You also should provide orientation at the beginning of the school year for paraeducators, including basic school policies and procedures on everything from parking to mailboxes to dress codes; your expectations for paraeducator interactions with students and other school staff; information about the school's philosophy (e.g., inclusive, problem-based learning); and steps to take if a problem arises either

PUTTING IDEAS INTO PRACTICE

Communicating with Your Paraeducator

In most schools, professionals and paraeducators have little, if any, time to formally meet, and they must become creative to maintain effective communication. Here are a few informal strategies for communicating about student academic and behavior programs with your paraeducator.

■ Create for each of you a planning agenda that is laminated and can be used repeatedly. For example, the agenda might include sections for instructional issues, assistive technology matters, student behaviors, and team concerns. You and your paraeducator note items as you become aware of them, using a water-based marker. When you do have time to meet, you have a ready agenda to ensure your time is used wisely. After the meeting, the agendas can be wiped clean and used again. This system also can be used for paraeducators and general education teachers.

■ Use a clipboard agenda. Hang or place a clipboard with a pad of paper in a location easily accessible to the paraeducator, special educator, and, as appropriate, the general education teacher, but away from the students (e.g., a teacher mailbox, in a special educator's office). Anyone lists agenda items on the paper, and when the meeting occurs, copies of the list are distributed and form the agenda.

■ E-mail communication can also help professionals keep in touch with paraeducators. If you establish a routine—say, spending 5 or 10 minutes each morning or afternoon providing e-mailed directions to your assistant—you can be certain that you are documenting the assigned work. If the paraeducator also e-mails with notes about implementing the directions, a detailed record exists and communication is assured.

■ If the paraeducator uses teacher's manuals or other materials in his or her work with students, you can use self-stick removable notes to provide directions and comments. Select one color to use for this purpose, and attach the note on the page where input is needed. The paraeducator could reply with notes in another color. Although this strategy is not shared planning, it can be an efficient and direct means of communication.

with a student or with a staff member. The more information that you formally communicate to paraeducators, the less they will have to learn incidentally and the less likely it is that miscommunication will occur (Gerlach, 2001).

Supervising Paraeducators

It has been implied throughout this chapter, but at this point it needs to be stated directly: Special education teachers, general education teachers, and other professionals have the responsibility of supervising paraeducators and the work they do with students (French, 2004). This may not be a formal responsibility; in many school districts, principals or special education supervisors are assigned the task of evaluating paraeducators. However, even when this is the case, those administrators rely heavily on input from the day-to-day supervision experiences of professionals in providing feedback to paraeducators.

What have you learned in your other coursework about supervising paraeducators? Approximately 88 percent of special education teachers report that they learned to work with paraeducators from real-life experience; they did not receive any instruction on this topic in their formal professional preparation programs (Conderman & Stephens, 2000; Pickett, 1999) even though teacher educators think the topic should receive significant attention (Katisyannis et al., 2000). Paraeducators report that teachers are not proficient in guiding their work (Special Education News, 2000a). Further, teachers sometimes indicate that they are reluctant to think of themselves as supervisors or to function in that capacity; they believe that it interferes with their working relationship with paraeducators (French, 1998). Whether you share these perceptions or not, in today's schools special educators should assume that they will have supervisory responsibilities related to paraeducators such as the following:

- Monitoring whether paraeducators are carrying out the specific tasks that have been assigned to them
- Providing feedback to paraeducators on their work with students, pointing out strategies or techniques they are using appropriately and redirecting them when the strategies they are using are not effective or are detrimental to the student
- Modeling effective ways to interact with students and instructional techniques to use with them
- Problem solving with general education teachers and paraeducators when disagreements arise about paraeducator roles in the general education setting
- Ensuring that paraeducators adhere to school policies
- Ensuring that paraeducators follow a code of ethics (such as that of the Council of Exceptional Children), particularly on matters such as confidentiality (Fleury, 2000), the topic of Putting Ideas into Practice on page 160
- Supporting paraeducators by answering their questions regarding students, classroom practices, legal issues, and other related topics
- Arranging for some type of public acknowledgment of the work that paraeducators do (e.g., an appreciation day, having students make cards, conveying positive parent comments)

The Matter of Conflict

One aspect of supervision that may be inevitable is conflict. Although you might think that conflict with paraeducators is rare, you should be prepared

PUTTING IDEAS INTO PRACTICE

Paraprofessionals and Confidentiality

One dilemma that can arise in working with paraeducators is confidentiality. Paraeducators are bound by the same rules for preserving confidentiality as teachers, but they may not be accustomed to attending to this crucial communication matter. These are guidelines to share with paraeducators regarding confidentiality:

- Never discuss information about a student in a public place (e.g., hallway, restaurant).
- Never discuss information about a student with the parents of another student.
- Never discuss information about a student with other students.
- Never discuss information about a student with staff members who are not considered directly involved in the delivery of services to that student.
- If you have a legitimate need to access confidential information about a student, obtain permission to do so and use the established district policy for accessing it.
- Do not create your own files on a student or a family.
- Review and adhere to any district or school policies regarding confidentiality, and ask your supervisor to answer any questions you may have.

Source: From M. B. Doyle, *The paraprofessionals' guide to the inclusive classroom: Working as a team* (2nd ed.) (Baltimore: Paul H. Brookes, 2002), pp. 77–83.

for the occasional situation in which it occurs. One common example concerns veteran paraeducators working with novice special educators. The paraeducator may inappropriately try to decide how the special education classroom may be run, how students should receive their services, how parents should be contacted, or how to enlist the assistance of parents in trying to direct your work.

Instances of conflict require that you use all the skills that you learn throughout this book. Your paraeducator truly may have valuable insights to share about students and their programs, but you ultimately are responsible for students' education. Your goals should be to listen carefully to paraeducator input, to consider it in your own planning and problem solving, and to make decisions based on that input as well as your own knowledge and skills.

Of course, unless you are the formally identified supervisor for paraeducators, if significant issues arise related to paraeducator performance, you should alert the appropriate administrator so that more formal procedures can be implemented if conflict occurs and persists. It also is important to keep in mind that addressing small conflicts is far easier than avoiding a problem that has the potential to become more serious.

Paraeducators and Collaboration

Perhaps you have been wondering if all the information in this chapter is supposed to give a particular message about collaboration and working with paraeducators. The primary intent is to articulate the fact that your relationship with paraeducators is perhaps at this time the least understood and most complex of all the professional relationships you will have in your job.

Is it possible to collaborate with a paraeducator? Of course! Remember that collaboration is a style, and you may use the style when interacting with a paraeducator just as you use it with other professionals and parents/families. What is less clear, however, is the extent to which collaboration with paraeducators is appropriate and how special education professionals can balance their preference for collaborative interactions with paraeducators with their responsibility to supervise them.

This is an area in which clear guidelines simply do not exist, and the available data are worrisome. Some professional literature suggests that teachers want to treat paraeducators just like other teachers, to ask them to take over a class, to be peers (French, 1998). Even some administrative literature suggests that this is acceptable practice (Daniels & McBride, 2001). At the same time, most paraeducators do not have professional credentials, they do not have a professional array of responsibilities in their jobs, and they do not make a professional salary. Taken together, these factors suggest that in some interactions, all the conditions for collaboration can be met, but in others, they cannot (Carroll, 2001; Hammeken, 2003). You might want to review the defining characteristics of collaboration in Chapter 1 and discuss with your classmates when they fit in interactions with paraeducators and when they do not.

Summary

With the increasing number of paraeducators employed to assist in the delivery of services to students with special needs, you are likely to be responsible for working with and guiding the activities of paraprofessionals. Although some paraeducators are used to assist teachers primarily with clerical tasks or other duties, most now spend the majority of their time completing instructional responsibilities and noninstructional responsibilities related to personal care and supervision. However assigned, the scope of a paraeducator's work should be clearly distinguished from that of individuals employed in a professionally licensed capacity. To work effectively with paraeducators, special education professionals need a wide range of skills. They often arrange for necessary training for their paraeducators, they should ensure that systematic planning meetings occur, they should assign paraeducator responsibilities based on student needs, they should foster clear day-to-day communication, and they should provide immediate if often informal supervision for these personnel. Collaboration between professionals and paraeducators is recommended, but it must be tempered with an understanding of the difference in status among the individuals participating and the context in which the interactions occur.

Activities and Assignments

1. How common is it in the school districts in your area to employ paraeducators? With your classmates, obtain job descriptions for paraeducators from several local school districts. How specific are they? How clearly would they guide your possible task of assigning tasks to the paraeducator? How have these roles and responsibilities been revised over the past several years to reflect the standards set by the No Child Left Behind Act of 2001?

2. Interview a general education teacher who works with a paraeducator about the instructional responsibilities the paraprofessional assumes. How do those responsibilities compare with the ones discussed in this chapter? If you were working with the teacher, how would you try to increase or decrease the paraeducator's responsibilities?

3. You read in this chapter several cautions about paraeducators spending too much time on clerical and other chores. How would you decide which clerical tasks are appropriate for a paraeducator and which are not? If you have the opportunity to interview a special educator, ask that professional about this matter and how it is addressed in local schools.

4. Suppose you accept a position to be a special education teacher in an inclusive middle school. Your students with mild to moderate learning and behavior disabilities are on two teams, but you are assigned a teaching assistant to ensure that all students receive appropriate services. What factors would you consider in deciding how to assign tasks to your paraeducator? How would you ensure that you retained appropriate accountability for the progress of students served primarily by the paraeducator?

5. A critical issue in today's schools is training for paraeducators. What does your local school district do to meet the requirements of the federal law regarding paraeducator training? If you were responsible for training paraeducators you supervised, how would you go about creating time in their schedules for training? Which topics might you prioritize for their training?

6. Although most paraeducators are wonderful, committed individuals who truly make a significant contribution to student success, problems also can occur. How would you respond to the following situations?

   ▪ The general education teacher mentions to you that your paraeducator, who is supposed to be in the classroom all morning, seems to disappear frequently for 15 to 20 minutes at a time.

   ▪ The paraeducator, who is nearly finished with a teaching credential, comments about today's lesson: "I just don't do much adapting on topics like that. I don't even see much point for him being there. The material being covered is just too hard for him. I'm thinking I'll start pulling him out."

■ A parent informs you that you are not providing appropriate services for his daughter. In discussing the parent's dissatisfaction, you learn that a paraeducator, who babysits for the student and is a member of the family's church, has told the parents that you do not give enough attention to the student and should be providing more direct service.

■ A general education teacher expresses a concern to you: The paraeducator seems to be doing too much to assist an assigned student, and the teacher believes the student should have more responsibility for beginning and completing assignments, turning them in, and behaving appropriately.

7. If you were asked to provide a one-hour staff development session to school staff members on the roles and responsibilities of paraeducators, what topics would you prioritize for inclusion? How would you address the topic of collaboration between professionals and paraeducators? What topics do you think would be of particular interest to general education teachers?

8. Imagine that it is the first day of school, and you have just met the newly hired paraeducator who is to assist you. What would you do to ensure that the paraeducator feels comfortable in his new job and school? That you and the paraeducator develop a strong and positive working relationship right from the beginning? That the paraeducator understands the scope of his responsibilities? Compare your responses to those of your classmates so that you can develop your own master checklist for getting started.

For Further Reading

Broer, S. M., Doyle, M. B., & Giangreco, M. F. (2005). Perspectives of students with intellectual disabilities about their experiences with paraprofessional support. *Exceptional Children, 71,* 415–430.

Council for Exceptional Children. (2004). *Parability: The CEC paraeducator standards workbook.* Arlington, VA: Author.

Giangreco, M. F., Edelman, S. W., Broder, S. M., & Doyle, M. B. (2001). Paraprofessional support of students with disabilities: Literature from the past decade. *Exceptional Children, 68,* 45–63.

Rueda, R., Monzó, L. D., & Higareda, I. (2004). Appropriating the sociocultural resources of Latino paraeducators for effective instruction with Latino students: Promise and problems [Electronic version]. *Urban Education, 39,* 52–90.

White, R. (2004). The recruitment of paraeducators into the special education profession: A review of progress, select evaluation outcomes, and new initiatives. *Remedial and Special Education, 25,* 214–218.

CHAPTER 7

Practical Matters

Connections

You have just finished reading several chapters that outline the types of programs and services that exist in collaborative schools. Usually, discussion of topics such as teaming, consultation, and co-teaching lead immediately to questions about feasibility: These are wonderful services, but they only work with planning time—how is it possible to get that time? What's a realistic schedule for a teacher who works in a school implementing these types of programs? What are the first steps in setting up services like these? How do my colleagues and I know if what we're doing is effective? How do I educate colleagues about collaborative services? How should my colleagues and I figure out who does what—what are the role responsibilities of everyone involved? This chapter will address questions such as these. It is an essential companion to the chapters you have already read as well as those ahead. Although you are unlikely to face all of the pragmatic issues raised in this chapter, you undoubtedly will have to address at least several of them.

Learner Objectives

After reading this chapter you will be able to:

1. Describe strategies for finding, prioritizing, and effectively using time for participation in collaborative activities.
2. Identify critical considerations for scheduling collaborative activities and coordinating them with other service delivery options in a school.

3. List issues related to the roles and responsibilities professionals may assume in collaborative schools and outline strategies for discussing these with colleagues.

4. Describe stages of program development and apply these when creating and sustaining collaborative programs and services.

5. Describe approaches for staff development that can educate professionals about collaborative and other program options.

6. Provide a rationale for addressing practical matters in schools fostering a collaborative culture.

Jordan rockets through the door of her office/classroom at 7:45 AM. She dumps her tote bag on her chair—which she probably won't sit in all day—and hangs up her coat. She ticks off in her head her before-school to-do list. She noticed that Ms. Gonzalez's car was in the teacher parking lot—and so she quickly stops by to see how the behavior plan they have devised for Destiny is working. She then briefly meets with two other teachers concerning specific student issues and chats with the social workers about getting shoes that fit for Austin, one of the students on her caseload. She picks up the project guidelines that the fifth-grade teachers have developed for the upcoming social studies unit, and she promises that she will provide some accommodations by Friday. At 8:15, Jordan collects her materials for an IEP meeting and heads for the conference room just as the parents enter. The meeting runs a little longer than anticipated, making Jordan late for co-teaching with the fourth-grade teacher. She apologizes, but senses the other teacher's frustration with the need to change their plans midstream.

Jordan's days usually fly by in this manner. She tells her roommate that she often feels like she has more to do than can possibly get done, no matter how efficient she is.

Introduction

Increasingly, school professionals find that collaboration is a significant component of their jobs (Dover, 2005). They teach with others, plan with others, meet with others, and share their specialized knowledge with others. Whether you are a teacher entering the field through an alternative route, a novice just completing your professional preparation, or an experienced educator, it is likely that you now have or soon will have responsibilities related to ensuring that collaborative initiatives in your school are successful—feasible for the adults and effective in producing outcomes for the students (Kaff, 2004). Whether you are developing a co-teaching program, coordinating the intervention assistance team, or working on a committee to integrate the services available to students, you are faced with several critical issues (Hobbs & Rose, 2000). First, you probably will need to work with your administrators to ensure that participants in any collaborative program have adequate shared planning time and that the time is used wisely. In addition, as you develop a collaborative program, you may have to coordinate it with existing programs and resolve scheduling problems, including those related to the number of adults working in a single classroom and the number of students placed there. Third, you may face the challenge of minimizing paperwork so that your time is spent directly working with colleagues and students, and you may have to address issues related to the roles and responsibilities of the participants in collaborative programs and services. In addition, you may have to place issues such as these in the context of a systematic program development process. Finally, you may be asked to explain a collaborative initiative by providing staff development for your colleagues. The purpose of this chapter is to assist you in succeeding at these rather formidable—but very real—tasks.

Time for Planning

School professionals repeatedly explain with dismay that collaboration is not possible without time for shared planning (Ellis et al., 2002; Hackman & Berry, 2000; Hobbs & Rose, 2000; Meister & Melnick, 2003), and that they seldom, if ever, have enough planning time to enable their collaborative efforts to reach their full potential. These concerns are not without some validity. Teachers in the United States spend more time in direct contact with their students and have significantly less time for planning in their schedules than teachers in most other industrialized countries (Darling-Hammond, 1999). In the current climate of school reform and accountability, no simple prescription exists for solving the problem of limited time, but there are some considerations you can take into account, and there are some suggestions for maximizing time use that others have found successful (DuFour, 1999; Ellis et al., 2002; Sharpe & Hawes, 2003).

We advocate allocating specific time in the school day for the collaborative interactions of professionals—whether those interactions concern students with disabilities or other school matters. However, before suggesting how to find time, we feel obligated to acknowledge some related issues. First, we have found that time alone is seldom the problem in fostering collaboration. Nearly all school professionals have a "relative yardstick" on the topic of time: No matter what their caseloads or other responsibilities, they find they need more time for collaboration. We hear nearly the same number of comments about time from special education teachers with caseloads of 8 students with high-incidence disabilities as those with caseloads of 28, and we hear similar concerns from those with weekly shared planning time as those with virtually no shared planning time. This similarity is due partly to a perception of time and partly to the priorities educators give to their various tasks that influence the time available for collaboration.

Second, experienced co-teachers have raised a time issue specific to that endeavor but applicable to all collaborative work. When time is available, it needs to be used to its fullest advantage. Because many educators still spend much of the day working in isolation, when they have the opportunity to interact with another adult outside the presence of students, they tend to want to chat about the day's events, vent concerns about school district and school issues, and so-cialize. Although such conversations serve a purpose, they need to be limited to ensure that time is available for collaboration. As you can easily understand, if chatting takes one-third of a planning session, it is difficult to justify a request for additional shared time.

Third, whether teachers are meeting to plan for co-teaching or to problem solve about meeting a student's needs in an upcoming unit of instruction, they should pay careful attention to the procedures they use for planning (Haw-baker, Balong, Buckwalter, & Runyon, 2001). It is helpful to think of planning as a three-part process. The general education teacher does the first part prior to the meeting by thinking about and outlining upcoming curricular content and typical related instructional activities. The second part of the planning occurs with both the general education teacher and the special services provider. They jointly review the curricular material, and if they are co-teaching, they decide how to arrange teachers and students in order to accomplish the learn-ing goals. They also make judgments about topics or activities that are likely to be easily understood by students with special needs as well as those likely to be challenging. The special educator carries out the third part of the planning process after the joint meeting. This professional is responsible for preparing any significantly adapted materials or alternative materials that will be needed by the students. This combination of shared planning and an appropriate divi-sion of the planning labor results in efficient and effective use of time, and it also can be applied to intervention assistance meetings, consultation, and other collaborative services.

Finally, many issues about time are problematic in new programs but dimin-ish as programs mature. It is true that time for intervention assistance team meetings, middle school team meetings, and other group interactions will need to be scheduled, but the time required for planning for co-teaching and in-formal problem solving decreases as professionals develop collaborative work relationships, learn specific interaction skills, and refine their time management skills. Eventually, many time needs, especially those related to planning in-class services, can be met partly through the use of quarterly or even summer meet-ings supplemented by brief planning meetings on an ongoing basis.

Options for Creating Shared Planning Time

The following three general ideas offer great promise for providing long-term solutions to creating planning time for individuals engaged in collaborative ser-vice delivery: scheduling early release/late arrival days, using substitute teach-ers, and employing instructional strategies that facilitate planning. These ideas also represent three very different points on a continuum of cost and need for community support.

Early Release/Late Arrival

In school districts across the country, there is increased recognition that schools are adult workplaces as well as places where children go to learn. With this recognition is the understanding that time needs to be allocated in the school day for adults to conduct the professional "business" needed for schools to be effective, including collaborating on behalf of students. One straightforward means of incorporating this time into the school schedule is the use of early release or late arrival days (Hackman & Berry, 2000).

In this approach, students arrive late or are dismissed early on a regular basis. The professionals use the time to meet, participate in professional development activities, confer with parents, and so on. In some schools, these shortened school days occur each week. In others, they happen once each month. A few districts restrict their use to once each grading period. Typically, the instructional time lost on these shortened days has been compensated for through an overall slightly longer instructional day. For example, in the Merryville School District, students leave school each Thursday at 1:50 PM. Teachers then have one hour for collaboration. However, each of the other school days is lengthened by fifteen minutes so that students are not losing instructional time. In the Hobart Community Schools, early release occurs once every month, with students leaving school at 1:00 PM. This gives teachers one and a half hours of time for collaboration. The school day is lengthened by just five minutes to accommodate this time for collaboration.

Small rural districts, large urban districts, suburban districts, and small-town districts are all using early release to create time for collaboration. For it to be successful, these guidelines should be kept in mind:

1. Community support must be developed. Since this approach has implications for parents who must arrange child care and for transportation in locales in which students ride buses, the members of the community must see a need for the time created because it also has a cost for them. Community members understandably will expect teachers to be accountable for this time as well.

2. The time created should be preserved for collaborative interactions. It should not be treated as extra preparation time during which teachers work in isolation, nor should it be used in its entirety for staff meetings or other administrative purposes.

3. Some flexibility should be kept in the time allocated for collaboration. For example, at one elementary school, all grade-level teams meet on the first week of the month during the late arrival time. The special education staff meets with each team for approximately 20 minutes to address concerns about students with IEPs and other students experiencing difficulty. All the teams have agreed that when the special educator arrives at the team meeting, other business is set aside and resumed later.

Use of Substitutes

Another common alternative for creating shared planning time is to employ substitute teachers to release professional staff members for collaboration. Many creative systems facilitate the maximum use of this type of resource. For ex-

Collaboration requires that teachers and other professionals find time to share planning, address program development and evaluation, resolve issues, and discuss student concerns.

ample, in one district, a permanent substitute is employed and is scheduled at each school one day every other week. If additional time is needed, a school administrator can request the time. In an elementary school in another district, a substitute is employed once each week. The special educators post a schedule of when they are available to meet with teachers. Teachers sign up to meet with the special educator, and the substitute moves from class to class, releasing general education teachers as needed. In a high school, two substitutes are employed once a month. One substitute releases special education staff; the other releases general education staff.

Although funding for substitute teachers can be problematic, this is a relatively low-cost option for creating shared planning time. In some school districts, substitutes are provided only for general education teachers; the time special educators allocate to planning is considered part of students' special education services. In other districts, special educators have made the argument that their time away from their other responsibilities also warrants a substitute. This is a matter for local negotiation. If funding is very restricted, you might be able to use creative strategies for obtaining substitutes. One district has provided a small financial incentive to qualified paraprofessionals who can then work in their schools one day a week as a substitute teacher instead of as a paraprofessional.

Your parent–teacher organization might be able to assist in funding substitutes, or a disability advocacy group might be willing to provide volunteer substitutes who meet employment requirements but who refuse a paycheck. Student groups from your local university might also serve as volunteer substitutes, as might recently retired teachers. Be aware that local policies may determine whether you can seek alternative funding sources for substitute teachers and whether volunteers can serve in this role. Of course, you are obligated to follow those policies.

These guidelines can facilitate the successful use of substitute teachers to create time for collaboration:

1. Substitutes working in these types of teacher-release programs have to be comfortable moving from class to class throughout the day. They should clearly understand that this is the expectation for the assignment.

2. Teachers sometimes worry that it takes more time to plan for a substitute teacher than the amount of release time this provides. One easy solution is for teachers to create notebooks of review activities as they deliver their instruction. When a substitute is in the classroom, he or she uses one of the review activities instead of attempting to continue the teacher's instructional program. This issue also can be minimized when the same substitute teacher is used, or if a skilled substitute teacher (e.g., a math educator) can provide supplemental or enrichment instruction during the time the teacher is out of the classroom.

3. Procedures for requesting and confirming the use of a substitute teacher should be established. For example, teachers may need to sign up for a substitute three days before the planning time occurs. They might also be expected to keep a log of the interactions that occur as a result of the availability of "sub" time.

4. In some areas of the country, the issue is not getting funding for substitute teachers; rather, it is finding individuals who are willing to substitute teach and who possess the skills for this job. If your school faces this dilemma, try to convince administrators to specify dates a favorite substitute will fill in for collaborating teachers in April or May for the following school year. By doing this, the substitute has a commitment for his or her time, and the staff benefits by knowing their students are in the hands of a competent individual.

Instructional Strategies That Facilitate Planning

One interesting approach to reduce the need for arranged planning time can be used when co-teaching is the selected collaborative activity. When release time is nonexistent, teachers can plan as part of instruction in a no-frills approach to creating time.

- In Ms. Mardell's English class, Ms. Lesson co-teaches three times each week. On these days, Ms. Mardell begins the class by explaining how each teacher will be working with students. This lets Ms. Lesson know how the class will operate and makes her feel more comfortable with co-teaching. It is not the same as having a shared planning time each week, but since Ms. Lesson co-teaches in five classrooms, that would not be possible anyway.
- Mr. Eliott uses a similar approach in his fourth-grade class. When Ms. Razmoski enters the room, he stops the instruction and asks the students to review what they have covered so far. He then has the class explain

what he had told them they would do when Ms. Razmoski arrived. This is sound instructional practice—the mid-lesson review helps students check their understanding and it also helps orient Ms. Razmoski.

In both these instructional arrangements, the general education teacher's planning is shared through student interactions.

When it comes to creating time for collaboration, we endorse the idea that working together is a legitimate professional responsibility for educators. We also suggest that time issues need to be raised with your administrator because that individual often can provide a tremendous amount of assistance in finding ways to make collaboration time available. We also understand that administrators and teachers are reluctant to leave their instructional responsibilities to plan when so much pressure is placed on them for raising student achievement. In some cases, the ideas like those just discussed are effective for addressing this essential practical matter; in others, more creative solutions must be found. Several of those other solutions for creating shared planning time ideas are included in the following Putting Ideas into Practice.

Scheduling and Coordinating Services

Any discussion of finding the time for collaborative planning and using it wisely leads to companion conversation about the matter of scheduling time for special education teachers and related services personnel and coordinating all the services offered through special education and other specialized school programs (e.g., reading or math remedial programs, enrichment programs). Finding feasible scheduling options and creating services that complement rather than compete with other programs often requires setting aside some assumptions about how students receive services and what professional responsibilities should be (Rieck & Wadsworth, 2000). It also requires taking into account the hectic schedules of professionals like Jordan, who you met at the beginning of this chapter.

Establishing Schedules in a Collaborative School

Although scheduling is an administrative matter, when professionals understand the issues related to it from a variety of perspectives, they can assist principals and assistant principals in finding the best solutions to arranging teachers and other professionals for the maximum benefit for students.

Scheduling Issues for Special Educators

Several scheduling issues arise when school professionals move to increased collaborative practice. Three scheduling issues common for special education staff will be addressed here: (1) scheduling teacher by teacher or collectively, (2) arranging co-teaching schedules on a daily or less-than-daily basis, and (3) creating flexibility in a special educator's daily schedule.

PUTTING IDEAS INTO PRACTICE

Finding Shared Planning Time

Finding time for collaboration is a challenge in today's schools. Here are several ways that principals and other administrators are making it possible for teachers to have shared planning time.

- Teachers working together are scheduled for a shared lunch and preparation period. By scheduling these times back-to-back, teachers have a 90-minute block of shared planning time.

- Teachers are paid once each month for two hours of planning outside the contract day. They are accountable for the time and submit a one-page summary of their planning decisions.

- Participants in co-teaching are given the option of meeting once or twice each month after school (sometimes with just others from their school, sometimes with co-teaching colleagues from several schools). They are not paid for these sessions, but the hours spent problem solving and planning are applied toward required continual professional development credit.

- Instead of using professional development days for large-group workshops, teachers use this time for two-hour release periods throughout the school year for collaborative activities, including shared planning.

- Teachers participating in co-teaching in one district are released for two hours of each districtwide staff development event. They use this time for shared planning.

- In an elementary school, students are dismissed 45 minutes early once each week so that teachers can jointly plan. The instructional time is added to the other school days.

- In a large school, fine and related arts staff (e.g., art, music, technology, media, and physical education) work with each other and with teachers to arrange schedules so that teachers receive a half day of collaboration time every two or three weeks.

- In an elementary school, grade-level teams are required to meet for 90 minutes each week to coordinate instruction. The special educator working at the grade level is released to attend at least 45 minutes of this time so that co-teaching needs can be addressed.

- In an alternative high school, classes are scheduled from 7:30 to 3:30. Even though the earliest classes are optional (e.g., tutoring, clubs), the school can meet minimum time requirements in 4.5 days. Teachers use the additional time to collaborate.

- As a supplement to face-to-face time, teachers are encouraged to use e-mail to communicate about co-teaching and to post lesson plans on a district website so that ideas can be shared and labor divided.

Individual versus Collective Scheduling

Some special education teachers, particularly at the elementary school level, arrange their schedules the way they used to arrange traditional special education services: by going from teacher to teacher, generally beginning with the least cooperative, and building a schedule based on when each teacher is willing to work together. Many special educators know firsthand the futility of this approach in a school that stresses collaboration, whether the scheduling issues surround co-teaching, teaming, or consultation. An alternative that can help is to schedule by grade level, or at the middle school level, to schedule by team. For example, Mr. Lowes is the special education teacher at Fielder Elementary. He alerts the third-grade team that he would like to meet with them once each week and requests that meeting for Thursdays. Since all grade-level teams meet twice each week, this request can be accommodated, and the teachers spend time at that meeting discussing the general problems and concerns that arise about students as well as planning upcoming units and needed adaptations. Mr. Lowes follows a similar pattern in each grade level in which he has students. In some high schools, special educators are disbanding their departments and assigning themselves to the academic departments. Thus, one special educator attends English department meetings, problem solves with those teachers, and does most of the English co-teaching. The special educators meet as a group only as needed.

Daily or Periodic Scheduling of Services

A second scheduling matter concerns co-teaching. Many special education teachers plan for co-teaching to be a daily service delivery option, but then they encounter difficulties meeting all the competing demands for their time. The schedule created by the special education staff of one junior high illustrates the dilemmas daily services can pose: The special education teachers were each spending four instructional periods every day rotating among eight different classrooms in order to provide services to all the students with IEPs. Neither the special education teachers nor the general education teachers sensed that students were getting individualized instruction. When resources and staff are readily available, daily co-teaching permits both teachers to have a higher sense of ownership in the co-taught class and assists in maintaining the continuity of instruction.

Other options can be more viable, however. For example, in the junior high just described, the program was modified so that co-teaching occurred every other day in each class for an entire class period. Thus, the teachers reduced from eight to four the number of classrooms in which they co-taught daily. In a high school, a special education teacher addressed the problem in this way: He identified two fourth-period classes in which co-teaching was appropriate, then he co-taught in each class twice each week, with the fifth day being left open for flexible scheduling. Keeping less-than-daily co-teaching as a program option is one specific strategy for reaching more students and increasing service intensity. It can be particularly viable at the secondary level. Of course, the extent to which this can occur depends on the nature and extent of students' needs and the requirements for services outlined in their IEPs.

Schedule Flexibility

A third scheduling issue for special education teachers concerns retaining some flexibility in the daily schedule. Many special educators have every minute of each day scheduled, and when an emergency meeting is called, a new student requires attention, or an assessment needs to be completed, some service has to be canceled, often to the understanding but annoyance of general education colleagues. Special educators should keep a bit of flexibility so that if they have to cancel a service, another option might be available. For example, in some schools, co-teaching occurs in paired classes as just described, but the fifth day is left open for meetings or as an alternative service delivery time. In elementary schools, some special educators schedule their lunch and preparation periods back-to-back so that they can flip-flop them as the need to meet with colleagues arises. Yet others keep two blocks of time (for a total of 45 minutes to one hour) reserved each week for flexible use. The time is used for student observation, additional consultation, team meetings, adaptations of instructional materials, or make-up sessions if a regularly scheduled in-class service has to be canceled during the week.

Many appropriate strategies exist for creating a professional schedule that both meets the needs of students and promotes professional collaboration. One sample teaching schedule is shown in Figure 7.1, but it must also be acknowledged that in schools that value collaboration as a strategy for meeting diverse student needs, professional schedules typically are periodically revised to reflect shifting priorities. They may change as often as once a month, but often change at least at the end of each grading period.

School Scheduling Issues

A second type of scheduling problem concerns the overall schedule on which the school operates. Although informal collaboration often occurs in spite of a difficult school schedule, if collaboration is a valued professional activity and an expectation for teachers and other staff members, the school schedule might need to be modified to make it feasible (Spencer, 2005).

One common scheduling matter in elementary schools concerns the time of day when language arts is taught. Most general education teachers prefer co-teaching during language arts instruction, but all the teachers may be teaching language arts at the same time, thus making it impossible to deliver services in a timely manner in every place it is needed. However, if teachers stagger the schedule for teaching language arts, in-class services are far more likely to be a feasible option. Alternatively, in some schools, grade-level teachers plan to offer core academics at the same time so that the special education teacher can move

Figure 7.1	Sample Teaching Schedule for Francine, a K–3 Special Educator				
Time	**Mon**	**Tues**	**Wed**	**Thurs**	**Fri**
8:15–8:40		Hall duty	Bus duty		
8:45–9:45	Math pullout (3rd)	Math pullout (3rd)	Math pullout (3rd)	Math pullout (3rd)	Math pullout (3rd)
9:55–10:55	Literacy (co-taught with Johnson—3rd)	Literacy (co-taught with Johnson—3rd)	Literacy (co-taught with Johnson—3rd)	Literacy (co-taught with Johnson—3rd)	Literacy pullout (3rd, as needed)
10:55–11:55	Literacy (co-taught with Lopez—3rd)	Literacy (co-taught with Lopez—3rd)	Literacy (co-taught with Lopez—3rd)	Literacy (co-taught with Lopez—3rd)	Literacy pullout (3rd, as needed)
12:00–12:30	Special ed. team meeting	Lunch	Lunch	Lunch	Lunch
12:30–12:55	Lunch	Planning and testing	Planning and testing	Planning and testing	Planning and testing
1:00–1:40	Math (co-taught with Salinas—K)	Math (co-taught with Salinas—K)	Math (co-taught with Salinas—K)	Math pullout (K, as needed)	Planning for co-teaching (rotated among teachers)
1:45–2:45	Literacy (co-taught with Edwards—1st)	Literacy (co-taught with Edwards—1st)	Literacy (co-taught with Edwards—1st)	Literacy pull-out (1st, as needed)	Literacy (co-taught with Edwards—1st)

among classrooms, or students can move across classrooms so as to be grouped for skills-based instruction.

Another scheduling matter for some elementary schools concerns art, music, physical education, media, and technology classes. In some schools, principals are working with central office administrators to arrange these classes simultaneously at one grade level. This creates an opportunity for team planning, and it allows for a special educator to meet with a grade-level team. In very large schools—for example, those with 8 to 12 sections in a single grade level—this scheduling strategy can at least allow for half the grade level to be released at one time.

At the high school level, scheduling issues often concern arranging shared preparation time for teachers and special educators. One strategy for doing so is to assign this time first, before other preparation times are established. This often disrupts traditional seniority-based scheduling approaches, but it does help teachers be successful in their collaborative efforts. As noted earlier, another high school option is to assign a special educator to each department. In addition to solving a scheduling problem, doing this has the advantage of ensuring that any general education teacher needs to contact only one person regarding a student concern, rather than try to figure out who the responsible special services person happens to be.

A final scheduling issue relates to block scheduling versus traditional class periods (Weller & McLeskey, 2000). Although the merits of longer or shorter instructional periods on student achievement probably will be subject to debate for some time to come, this aspect of scheduling also affects collaboration. For example, if co-teaching is a service delivery option, should special educators stay in one class for the entire 84 minutes of a block? Or would their time be better spent divided between two classes? Questions such as these should be carefully considered, and in many cases, more than a single solution should be implemented. For example, in ninth-grade English, it might be valuable for the two teachers to work together for the entire block; in twelfth-grade government, this intensity of service may not be justified.

Coordinating Services for Collaboration

Arranging a schedule that encourages collaboration is not sufficient in many cases. Another dimension of scheduling also important to consider concerns its impact on the schedules of other service providers in a school and the programs and services they are operating (Brownell & Walther-Thomas, 2002). This matter of service coordination becomes especially important in elementary and middle schools in which most, if not all, individualized services for students are delivered in the general education classroom.

Consider this list of individuals who could be going into a classroom to work with teachers and students:

- Special education teachers (could be several, depending on school size, student needs, and service delivery patterns)
- Speech/language therapists
- Counselors
- Social workers
- Psychologists
- Paraprofessionals (special education or from other programs)
- Title I math or reading teachers
- Paid tutors
- Parent volunteers
- Interns or student teachers
- Members of Future Teachers of America
- Bilingual educators

Would you want to be a general education teacher trying to coordinate the work of even half of these individuals coming to the classroom? One teacher we know was given just such a task. After one particularly grueling day, she told her principal to get everyone out, that she wanted just her classroom and her students by herself. She had had too much of a good thing.

Professionals delivering in-class services may need to coordinate their efforts and assist each other in meeting student needs. For example, if a speech/ language therapist is co-teaching in a first-grade classroom and one student in the class has a learning disability, the therapist may be able to meet that student's needs instead of the special educator going into the classroom. If a Title I reading specialist or a bilingual educator is spending an hour each day in a fourth-grade class, this specialist may be able to include students with IEPs who need reading instruction. In other words, care must be taken to prevent individual classrooms from being overrun by many service providers coming and going or otherwise disrupting instruction. This is especially true if the classroom already has a paraprofessional assigned to it because of either large class size or identified student needs. At the same time, high-quality services often can be delivered and personnel resources used more efficiently if the professionals are flexible in their approaches and in their willingness to share their responsibilities for service delivery with each other as appropriate. Of course, all these ideas can be viewed as applicable only if the needs of students with IEPs or other specialized services are being met and if local and state policies permit such sharing.

One other coordination issue should be raised. In some schools, collaboration is a priority, but its implementation relates only to core special education services. That is, although special education teachers co-teach, other service providers pull students out. The result can be fragmentation of instruction. Two

One practical matter for special education professionals is paperwork, and successful teachers must learn to complete it effectively but efficiently.

teachers may be in the room teaching math, but four students leave during that time for speech/language services. As they return, another three depart for bilingual instruction. The message to keep in mind is this: As more services are available, they have the potential to reach many students or to disrupt their education. Finding the best ways to coordinate services is a task that truly is worth the collaborative time it consumes.

Roles and Role Responsibilities

If schools were static places, addressing matters such as shared planning time and scheduling would be straightforward. But as you know, that is not at all the way schools operate. Students transfer to the school and from it—and sometimes back yet again, all in a single school year. Your teaching assistant finishes a licensure program and takes over for a colleague gone for the next semester on maternity leave. All the teachers in one grade level in an elementary school are directed to teach language arts at the same time, but you need to deliver services in three of those classrooms. Co-teaching is scheduled for civics, but that class period is when 10 students have been scheduled for the strategy instruction that you have just attended 40 hours of training to deliver. In addition, many professionals' days are much like Jordan's, as described in the chapter opening—a race from one task to another. And so, a chapter on the practical matters of collaborative schooling must at least mention the complexities of teacher roles and responsibilities.

School as a Professional Workplace

Only recently has attention been given to the fact that schools are not just locations where students learn—they also are adult workplaces where the context and conditions can have a significant impact on outcomes. The need to look at schools in this way is particularly important in the era of school reform and increased accountability and the professional pressure it has brought. Both general and special education teachers are concerned about the expectations being set for them and sometimes question their ability to meet all the demands on their time and skills (Billingsley, 2004a; DelSignore, 2003; Study of Personnel Needs in Special Education, 2001a, 2001b).

Concerns of Special Educators

A number of recent research efforts have examined the concerns that special educators have regarding their work conditions (Coleman, 2001; Mainzer, Deshler, Coleman, Kozleski, & Rodriguez-Walling, 2003), and several of these relate directly to the feasibility of collaboration. For example, one concern relates to caseload (e.g., Russ, Chiang, Rylance, & Bongers, 2001). Although some states set limits on the number of students with disabilities that any single special educator can be expected to serve, in others this is not the case. Caseload issues are further complicated when professionals deliver co-teaching services; they find it difficult to provide adequate services to students spread across multiple classrooms (Lamar-Dukes & Dukes, 2005).

Another special educator concern relates to paperwork (Study of Personnel Needs in Special Education, 2001a). Special educators report that the burden of paperwork takes time away from working directly with students and with colleagues and that it sometimes prompts them to leave their careers (Billingsley, 2004b). Although IDEA-04 includes provisions to reduce paperwork, including the possibility of writing only goals and not objectives for many students with disabilities, professionals still must work to ensure that they tackle this dimension of their jobs efficiently and effectively (Cook & Hall, 2004).

A third example of special educator concerns relates to role ambiguity and role overload. Special educators newly involved in collaborative service delivery programs may fear that their professional positions are gradually being eliminated. They also may experience doubts about their status. That is, they question whether or not they have valuable information to share with general education teachers. They have specific expertise, but they wonder how it applies to students in another context. A third type of role ambiguity relates specifically to concerns regarding co-teaching programs. Special services providers sometimes fear they will inadvertently be relegated to becoming glorified paraprofessionals. Finally, special services providers sometimes find that they struggle to balance their many competing job responsibilities, particularly when the scope of those responsibilities is not clear. Consider, for example, Ms. Hawkins. She provides co-teaching and pullout services to the 21 students on her caseload, but she also is expected to assist informally about 10 additional students who are considered at risk. How should she prioritize her time? What is her role in classrooms where the general education teacher is not interested in collaborating? One example of a study that has examined issues such as these is summarized in A Basis in Research on the next page.

Concerns of General Educators

General education teachers, too, may have concerns about roles and responsibilities related to collaboration. For example, they might fear that others will be coming into their classrooms to tell them what to do, and teachers used to working autonomously may resent this invasion of their turf. Other concerns include a conviction that many special services providers do not understand the limitations on teachers' time for implementing highly individualized interventions, and some classroom teachers fear that the dubious reward for participating in collaborative programs will be further requests to work with students with special needs. In this era of accountability, these professionals also may worry that they are held accountable for student outcomes even though a special educator also is working in the classroom by co-teaching and even though student needs may be significant.

General educators also may perceive that they do not receive adequate support for working with students with disabilities. Although these teachers report

A BASIS IN RESEARCH

Working as a Special Educator in a High School

Special education teachers have many roles and responsibilities in today's schools, and this variety is sometimes cited as a reason that special educators burn out and decide to leave the field. Wasburn-Moses notes that few studies have been completed that capture the specifics of the work conditions of high school special education teachers and therefore completed survey research to explore this topic. A total of 191 Michigan teachers for students with learning disabilities returned their surveys (a response rate of 50.5 percent); more than four-fifths of these were female and 60 percent held master's degrees. The average amount of experience was 16 years (with 14 of those spent teaching in special education). Here are a few of the study's findings.

- Teachers taught between three and four different classes each day in three different content areas; the most commonly taught class was some type of language arts (e.g., reading, English).

- Seventy-six percent of the classes taught were in separate settings (i.e., self-contained).

- Just 14 percent of courses taught were co-taught.

- The categories of job responsibilities most common to the teachers did not vary based on respondents' years of experience and degrees held. Those categories included

  - Teaching reading, writing, and other academic skills

  - Working with students through direct instruction, behavior management, or provision of accommodations

  - Working with others, including general education teacher, parents, and administrators

  - Paperwork

Although this study is limited because the teachers provided self-report data and all resided in Michigan, the results suggest that meeting the highly qualified teacher requirements of No Child Left Behind will be a challenge and that both teacher preparation programs and school service delivery models are likely to continue to face rapid change.

Source: Adapted from L. Wasburn-Moses, "Roles and responsibilities of secondary special education teachers in an age of reform," *Remedial and Special Education, 26* (2005): 151–158.

that they feel successful in their efforts (Study of Personnel Needs in Special Education, 2001b), they also note that they want special education teachers to provide background information on students, review lessons with teachers, make modifications, help in preparing assessments, work one-to-one with students, help with classroom management and behavior, and assist all students needing support

(Murray, 2004). That is, general education teachers expect their special education colleagues to address many of the tasks and activities integral to fostering success for students with disabilities who access the general education setting.

Role Management

In successful collaborative endeavors in schools, administrators pay careful attention to matters related to professional functioning, and they are proactive in ensuring that roles and responsibilities are clear, that dilemmas related to this dimension of collaboration are resolved when they are minor, and that ongoing program revision occurs so that all staff members can be effective—and feel comfortable and confident in their jobs (Sharpe & Hawes, 2003). Teachers note that this administrative support is an essential factor in determining whether they stay in a teaching career (Billingsley, 2004b). In addition, however, both special and general educators should reflect carefully on the demands of their jobs and have periodic conversations about role management. Only by raising concerns and using interpersonal problem-solving strategies are issues related to thriving in today's fast-paced and complex public schools likely to be satisfactorily resolved.

Program Development Tasks

All of the issues and concerns raised thus far in this chapter are parts of a whole. They are considerations that must be taken into account when planning or refining programs emphasizing collaboration (Roach, Salisbury, & McGregor, 2002). The next practical matter addressed here directly concerns how to go about planning, implementing, and maintaining programs.

Many authors have proposed models to facilitate the successful implementation of innovations in schools, including collaborative programs (e.g., Kruse, 1999; Sparks, 1999). The stages for program development depicted in Figure 7.2 incorporate key elements from these models and comprise the five-stage framework we recommend for school professionals. The stages apply both to new programs and to those being refined.

Stage 1: Establishing the Program and Its Goals

Much of what you accomplish in the initial stage of program development consists of communicating your preliminary plans while determining receptivity and commitment for the program. The critical components include clarifying intent, establishing a planning structure, and assessing needs and setting goals.

Clarify Intent

Once you have decided to undertake program development, fundamental questions are these: What is the purpose of this project? and What would this program look like in operation? Having a picture of what you want the program to

---

Figure 7.2 Stages for Program Development

Stage 1: Establishing the Program and Its Goals
- Clarify intent
- Establish a planning structure
- Assess needs and set goals

Stage 2: Planning for Implementation
- Identify and describe the ideal outcome
- Match the context and resources
- Design implementation strategies
- Specify component parts
- Establish timelines

Stage 3: Preparing for Implementation
- Create awareness

- Select implementers
- Make logistical arrangements
- Prepare personnel
- Design an evaluation plan

Stage 4: Implementing the Program
- Expand professional development activities
- Carry out program activities
- Evaluate the program

Stage 5: Maintaining the Program
- Refine the program
- Plan for ongoing support

---

accomplish enables you to better communicate about it and promotes necessary dialogue about topics such as program feasibility and resource allocation.

Clarifying your program's purpose also can help you identify the key stakeholders—those individuals or groups who will be most affected by your project. Stakeholders probably include at least one administrator and some of your colleagues, students, and their parents. You and these stakeholders need to reach a shared understanding of and agreement about program purpose. For example, if you are proposing to co-teach with a general education teacher, you, the principal, and the teacher all need to have the same understanding of what co-teaching involves. The principal could assume that you and the other teacher are dividing responsibility for the existing curriculum or taking turns leading in the classroom. The general education teacher may think the arrangement will result in reduced class size because you will divide the students and each teach some of them. You might be envisioning you and your colleague both teaching the whole group with one person presenting and the other supporting. These are three very different interpretations, and they demonstrate the importance of achieving shared understanding of program purpose.

Establish a Planning Structure

As you clarify the purpose of the program and begin the crucial task of building a base of relationships, forming a planning team and process is the next activity. This is particularly important if the program affects many people, since teams that include a representative group of stakeholders can ensure that diverse perspectives are considered and create a broad base of support. Recognize, too, that other types of diversity on a planning team are an asset. Thus, you should include veteran teachers, new teachers, teachers from different ethnic groups, and men and women. The team often is served well by having at least one skeptical member who will point out problems in the program and otherwise represent potential opposition to it.

Assess Needs and Set Goals

The final task in the initial program development stage is goal setting based on needs assessment. This task requires taking all the information gleaned during preliminary conversations and clearly articulating it. For example, consider the following project that the teachers at Coleman High School decided to develop.

> Ms. Linden and Mr. Kent both teach U.S. History, a graduation requirement. They use the district-adopted text, and students must pass a high-stakes test at the end of the course. Ms. Linden has five students who receive learning strategies assistance one period each day from Mr. Martin in the resource room. Mr. Kent has four students in his class who also receive these services. In addition, he has one student who was determined to be eligible for special education in middle school, but whose parents decided against these services, and one student on a Section 504 plan because of attention-deficit hyperactivity disorder. Ms. Linden and Mr. Kent each have an additional four to six students who consistently fail unit tests and have many learning problems, although they do not qualify for special education. Mr. Kent and Ms. Linden are proficient teachers with strong organizational and presentation skills who work diligently to reach their students. They are frustrated because they do not feel they are succeeding.

> Mr. Martin also is frustrated because he knows that the students from Mr. Kent's and Ms. Linden's classes are falling further behind even though they could learn most of the information with some additional adaptations. Mr. Martin believes that co-teaching is a preferable approach for serving these students as well as for assisting the high number of other students struggling in social studies. Although he would like to co-teach in every general education classroom, Mr. Martin has decided to begin with only Mr. Kent and Ms. Linden, treating their efforts as a pilot for possible later expansion. The course seems to be a good choice because of student needs and because of the testing requirement associated with it.

An analysis of this project and the initially identified goals are shown in Figure 7.3. The analysis illustrates a needs assessment and goal-setting process in a pilot activity involving a limited number of people. The same process also can be used to set goals for larger projects or programs.

Whether you are developing a program with limited or broad impact, goal setting should be derived from this question: What needs are we trying to address? At first glance this question may seem simplistic, but it is essential because it eventually guides the evaluation of the program. A team that emphasizes intervention assistance to general education teachers, for example, may address

Figure 7.3 Needs Analysis and Goals for a Pilot Co-Teaching Program

Kind of Program	General curriculum Curriculum access through co-teaching
Who Is Affected	Two U.S. History teachers Resource teacher Two sections of students in U.S. History Nine students with IEPs Eight to 12 at-risk students in general education
Current Situation	Students ■ Some unable to keep up ■ Some repeating material ■ Some tuning out and ditching classes Students with IEPs ■ Isolated from peers in resource service ■ Little access to class discussion Teachers ■ Frustrated by barriers to student learning ■ Unable to vary instruction for student needs
Evidence	Teacher observation of students' special education class Record of 6 to 8 students failing unit tests in each class
Goals	Improved student performance on unit tests Improved student pass rate on high-stakes test Increased teacher knowledge of ways to modify instruction to meet student needs Opportunities for enrichment activities Improved student attitudes toward social studies Improved student attendance Learning assistance for students with disabilities in general education classes Interest in co-teaching on the part of teachers in other classes

the need either to reduce referrals to special education, to increase general education teacher skills for responding to student learning and behavior problems, or to individualize services for all students. In other collaborative programs, needs addressed could include improved professional morale, increased skills, or expanded teacher empowerment. The clarification of needs helps you specify appropriate program goals, but these goals should be stated explicitly so that the expectations are unambiguous.

Stage 2: Planning for Implementation

The second stage of program development is to systematically plan a course of action to achieve program goals. This involves several tasks, including identifying and describing in detail the desired program outcomes, matching context and resources, designing implementation strategies derived from the program analysis, specifying program components, and establishing timelines.

Identify and Describe the Ideal Outcome

One strategy to describe the ideal outcome for the program you are developing is to determine who will benefit directly from the program and for whom the program is appropriate. For example, the program might include special education professionals serving students with IEPs in innovative ways and incidentally helping other students as well, with the outcome being an increase in the number of students receiving assistance. This type of outcome should be specific so that any legal or procedural issues can be addressed and so that realistic conversations about teacher and other resources can occur.

A second strategy for specifying ideal outcomes is to set the criteria for selecting initial participants. Because it often is advisable to start new programs on a small scale, this selection may determine the ultimate success or failure of the effort. Planning teams should select professionals who have the attitudes and skills to participate effectively, to work collaboratively, and to help disseminate information about the program to others. In programs that serve students, the question also concerns establishing entry and exit criteria. Many times, general professional judgment has been the primary criterion used for students' entry into and exit from programs. Although this approach may have some intuitive appeal, the necessity of establishing parameters that can be documented seems self-apparent. Which students should be assigned to co-taught classes? Which students are likely to receive appropriate educational benefit from consultation?

Match the Context and Resources

A new program cannot exist as an add-on to the already extensive responsibilities of school professionals. Establishing a new program or initiating a new project requires the careful assessment and allocation or reallocation of appropriate resources and may necessitate securing some outside resources. Many of the role requirements, time issues, and scheduling and coordination concerns already described in this chapter should be articulated during this part of program development. Decisions eventually should be reached based on what is possible balanced against what is ideal.

Design Implementation Strategies

After you analyze the context in which your program will operate, you can reconsider your program goal, making clearer decisions about feasible parameters for it. As you refine your program design and develop a plan for implementing it, you will be considering and selecting the implementation strategies that offer the most promise for success. By doing this, you should continually think about ways to build a sense of ownership and commitment among all planning participants.

Staying open to adapting your program implementation strategies can sometimes facilitate program development and implementation. For example, you might find that staff development related to inclusive practices is being offered through the local university and that your state is offering stipends to foster such practices. A group of team members might attend and bring their newly learned ideas back to the school. Or you might learn that your parent organization is willing to purchase materials that your planning team can use to create a new teaming structure using three-tiered interventions. By being willing to consider alternatives to the original plan, you may create opportunities for success.

Specify Component Parts

Another important element in the implementation plan is to specify the program's component parts. These might include the types of services or activities involved or the procedures needed to support the program. This specification provides guidance for carrying out the program and sets appropriate expectations for the individuals involved.

For example, in one local district a project to provide teachers with assistance in developing interventions for their students with learning or behavior difficulties was undertaken at five elementary school sites with the goal of eventually implementing the program districtwide. One of the first activities completed by the planning team was to clarify strategies to be used, including (1) individual assistance in developing techniques to improve student performance in classes, (2) assistance in implementing alternative classroom grouping arrangements such as cooperative learning and peer tutoring, (3) social worker and psychologist assistance for social skills training, (4) arrangement of in-service training for teachers as requested, and (5) development of supplemental materials for students. By creating this list, one of the most common sources of discomfort in new programs was eliminated: The intervention team members knew what they could and should do, and classroom teachers knew what services were available. In another district in which this was not done, the same questions are still occurring after two years of implementation: What exactly do I do when I work with a classroom teacher? So there's a team that is there to help me—what kind of help am I supposed to be getting and what do I have to do to get it?

Establish Timelines

A timeline for program implementation facilitates effective management and above all, communicates realistic expectations. Because overly ambitious timelines cause frustration and stress, they should be sufficiently generous to allow both for inevitable delays and adaptations and for demonstration of a program's success before expansion occurs.

Stage 3: Preparing for Implementation

Once an implementation plan is developed, a number of other preliminary tasks remain. By creating awareness, selecting implementers, making logistical arrangements, preparing personnel, and designing an evaluation plan, detailed preparation for implementation is accomplished.

Create Awareness

When individuals are first confronted with the possibility of changing their practices or roles, they are likely to have very self-oriented concerns: What is the new practice? What will it mean to me? Only after the concerns of a self-oriented nature are resolved do individuals progress to other concerns about managing the new practice (How do I implement it effectively?) or about its impact on students (How is this affecting students?) (Guskey & Peterson, 1996; Hall & George, 2000; Hall & Loucks, 1978).

This process of accepting change should guide preparation for implementation. That is, initial preparation should focus on increasing professionals' awareness and providing them with introductory information—for example, through staff meetings, grade-level meetings, or small-group briefings. You will learn more about conducting this and other types of staff development later in this chapter. In addition, information also can be shared in written form through school bulletins, faculty e-mails, the school website, fact sheets, and the like. Whatever approach is used, the emphasis should be on brevity, since staff members are not likely to want detailed procedures or skill development at this early point. You should be aware, too, that questions about roles and responsibilities, addressed in an earlier section of this chapter, may arise at this point.

Select Implementers

One early task—describing ideal outcomes—included a strategy to establish criteria for selecting participants. As you prepare to implement the program, you apply those criteria to identify the personnel and students to be involved. Generally, volunteers are preferred for initial implementation. However, there are some drawbacks to voluntary implementation, particularly if the program is meant to have an eventual schoolwide effect. The distinction between implementers and nonimplementers in a voluntary project may lead to divisions in staff and may create dissention. Awareness of this potential, emphasis on the emerging nature of new programs, and communication of selection criteria may help reduce this dilemma. The principal also should periodically clarify that after the initial phase of the project, many or all teachers may be expected to participate.

Make Logistical Arrangements

Securing needed resources and arranging for their use is part of preparing for implementation. Logistical arrangements may involve arranging for and scheduling the needed training for staff, determining room and other space assignments, selecting and ordering materials, scheduling services, and otherwise arranging program details.

One logistical arrangement that merits additional discussion here is to develop reporting forms and record-keeping procedures. When professionals become involved in programs that require them to interact with others, time accountability sometimes becomes an issue, and so procedures for time accounting should be created. A simple log to record team decisions or professionals' activities usually is sufficient, yet not burdensome on time.

Prepare Personnel

Preparing professionals and others for a new program has two parts. First, those who first received awareness information need to receive training in whatever knowledge or skills are essential for the program. In addition, if they are to help prepare others, they need to learn strategies for training others. Second, other staff members who eventually will participate should at this point begin to receive awareness information.

Design an Evaluation Plan

Determining whether a collaborative endeavor is successful depends on the assessment of many variables, both those addressing the program's outcomes and those considering the satisfaction of individuals affected by it. Any evaluation plan should, of course, be based on the goals set for the program as determined by the needs assessment. Topics for evaluation might include systematic assessment of student achievement, the number of referrals for other services, personnel satisfaction, and parent and student perceptions. Eventually, costs (time; financial resources; number of students served versus benefits for students, teachers, and parents) should be examined. In some cases, teachers' and other professionals' evaluation procedures will need to be modified to reflect the program's emphasis on collaboration. Standard evaluation practices should be used for evaluating a small-scale or a districtwide program.

Stage 4: Implementing the Program

Implementation is the point at which the results of careful planning begin to pay off; this section is relatively brief because its essence is carrying out all the items already discussed. However, several important tasks remain, including expanding professional development, addressing start-up problems, and following through on evaluation.

Expand Professional Development Activities

Professional development at this stage shifts to match the new level of participant concern, often including management issues. Those directly involved may need additional skills or advanced training in skills already introduced. In addition, considerable attention should be paid to assisting professionals to develop positive communication skills so that the collaborative aspects of the program flourish and interaction dilemmas are minimal.

Carry Out Program Activities

This is the task that is left to you. Whether you have planned a formal program that requires major changes in professionals' roles and responsibilities or you and a colleague or two are taking a first step toward sharing a program, the benefits of the detailed efforts you have taken to prepare will become apparent as you carry out your program. Be aware, though, that immediate changes may be needed: A serious schedule problem may suddenly become apparent, staff turnover during the summer may affect implementation in the fall, and so on. Matters such as these are not a cause for alarm; they are simply part of the very real and dynamic character of schools.

Evaluate the Program

During implementation, you should utilize the evaluation design that was developed earlier. Both formative and summative evaluation strategies should be undertaken. The formative evaluation can be coupled with progress-monitoring strategies for the project to assist you in obtaining valuable information during project implementation.

Stage 5: Maintaining the Program

Even well-designed programs are fragile during their early implementation and require nuturing, and when you are part of new program development, you should be sure that careful attention is paid to this stage.

Refine the Program

Reviewing evaluation data should assist you and the planning team in reviewing progress and identifying the program's problems and strengths. This review should lead to recommendations for program refinement and continuation, whether immediately, after a grading quarter, at the semester, or after a year. Of course, if data continually indicate that the program is not successful, termination also should be considered.

Plan for Ongoing Support

Assuming that program refinements can be designed and implemented successfully, the final task is to arrange ongoing program maintenance. Ideally, planning for maintenance was built into every stage of program development. It requires attention to all of the same issues reviewed throughout this chapter. Timelines, awareness, logistics, context assessment, and all of the other tasks need to be reconsidered and possibly reexecuted. Administrative support that facilitated development at earlier stages becomes particularly critical. Administrators or others with leadership skills and authority should take responsibility for troubleshooting and help obtain needed resources to ensure program continuation (Earley & Bubb, 2004; Hawley & Rollie, 2002). Without deliberate attention to maintenance, you may find that support for your program deteriorates over time.

Staff Development

A discussion of practical matters related to building school collaboration would not be complete without at least a brief mention of staff development, since it is through staff development that professionals usually become aware of initiatives such as collaborative programs and learn the skills to make them successful. Staff development is much more than single workshops or lectures by experts. It is results driven, standards based, school focused, job embedded, matched to desired professional practices, focused on specific pedagogy, and built on a core set of ideas and beliefs (Joyce & Showers, 2002). In twenty-first–century schools, professionals have more and more opportunities to design staff development for themselves and their colleagues and to view it as a continuous process instead of an event. The models and suggestions that follow should assist you in meeting these responsibilities.

Types of Staff Development

A wide variety of staff development approaches have been identified (Caffarella, 2002). Those outlined in the next sections are not entirely exclusive of one another, yet they represent a means for organizing principles and validated practices for this important professional responsibility. As you read about them, keep in mind that all staff development should be considered in light of what is known about adults as learners, a topic addressed in Putting Ideas into Practice.

Individually Guided Staff Development

In the individual approach, teachers choose and manage their own staff development. They first identify a learning need or interest, then set goals related to their need or interest, design a plan for meeting the goal, carry out the plan, and assess their learning. Individually guided staff development may be as simple as reading one or more journal articles or attending a professional conference. A significantly more elaborate example is found in teacher-designed and teacher-implemented professional projects, such as those supported by district or teacher incentive grants. One particularly rigorous example is the process of completing certification by the National Board for Professional Teaching Standards. This type of staff development is helpful when individuals have specific learning needs and can access the resources to address them.

Coaching

Teachers receive surprisingly little feedback on their teaching performance. In some school systems teachers are observed and given feedback by supervisors as infrequently as every three years if they have tenure and annually if they do not. In contrast with these practices, the overriding assumption of coaching is that reflection and analysis are the central processes in professional growth. Reflection is stimulated by receiving feedback from others and by observing others. Generally, coaching includes preobservation conferencing to determine the

PUTTING IDEAS INTO PRACTICE

Refining Your Skills as a Staff Developer

Effective staff developers modify their practices to take into account the characteristics of adult learners. Here are a few adult learner characteristics and some practices that are responsive to them. How might you use these ideas in the various types of staff development that you plan or lead?

Adults as Learners	Effective Practice
■ Adults have considerable experience, knowledge, and skills.	■ Tap participants' experience as a learning resource.
■ Adults seek learning experiences in order to address specific problems or life changes.	■ Provide learning experiences that give adults specific tools to cope with change.
■ Adults tend to prefer single-concept, single-theory workshops that focus on application.	■ Balance theory and application. Create learning opportunities so that new concepts can be integrated with existing concepts/practices.
■ Adults approach learning with a set of expectations.	■ Clarify leader's and participants' expectations at the beginning.
■ Adults need to be physically comfortable for effective learning.	■ Attend to adult needs with breaks, comfortable chairs, and adequate lighting and ventilation.
■ Adults have many commitments and demands on their time.	■ Provide learning experiences within an appropriate time frame. Begin and end on time.
■ Adults have established various ways to resist authority.	■ Provide for a balance of control between leader and participants.

focus and methods for observation, observation, analysis of observation data, and postobservation conferencing with decisions by the professional who was observed about planned changes. Coaching can be particularly useful when professionals are learning a new teaching strategy or implementing co-teaching for the first time.

Group Improvement Approaches

The primary difference between individually guided staff development and a group improvement approach is the focus of the staff development. The former is based on the needs of an *individual,* and the latter is focused on the needs of a *group.* The belief that staff development should enhance the abilities of administrators and teachers to think and solve problems directly related to their collective work is central to this approach (Peterson & Cosner, 2005; Walter, 2004). Examples of staff development that fall into this category are those addressing curriculum development projects and the activities of a school improvement team (Rowland & Patterson, 2004).

One other example of this type of staff development is a *learning community*. In this approach, a small group of teachers jointly address, over an extended period of time, a shared concern, exchanging information, studying the professional literature on the topic, and collectively building their knowledge and skills as they nurture a collaborative learning environment among themselves (Lieberman & Miller, 2002; Protheroe, 2004). For example, a middle school team of teachers might select differentiation as a topic for study. They might search for information on the Internet, read journals, meet once each month for the school year to discuss ideas, try strategies and share their successes and concerns, and eventually present a summary of their learning to other colleagues. A variation of this approach may occur on-line, with professionals from several schools addressing a shared topic, possibly on behalf of their colleagues (Charalambos, Michalinos, & Chamberlain, 2004).

Phases of activity for the improvement approach are (1) identification of and agreement on a problem by a group (such as a department, committee, grade-level team, or general faculty), (2) formulation of a response using problem-solving steps, (3) implementation of the plan or development of the product, and (4) assessment of the success of the response or program. The emphasis is on teachers' professional development and learning within the context of problem solving. This approach is gaining in popularity for addressing many of today's key educational concerns, including strategies to enhance literacy and mathematics, techniques of effective instruction for secondary teachers, and differentiation.

Training

A training approach is the one with which most teachers have the greatest familiarity. It generally is a large-group activity with the primary objectives being to promote awareness and provide initial information, change attitudes, or advance general knowledge and skills. The objectives usually are set by an expert who conducts the training or by those who arranged the event. The trainer must select the methods of delivery (e.g., lecture, simulation, role-playing, demonstration) that will produce the desired outcomes.

The training approach is cost effective because of the high participant-to-trainer ratio, and it may be the most efficient way for large numbers of teachers to become aware of new information or approaches. Joyce and Showers (2002) suggest that this is also a cost-effective way for groups of teachers to view demonstrations and have the opportunity for skill practice under the guidance of an objective observer.

In a training approach, phases of activity include (1) determination of the scope of the training (content, objectives, schedules); (2) conduct of the training, including modeling and demonstrating skills; (3) skill practice with feedback and discussion under simulated conditions; and (4) in-classroom assistance through observation and coaching to promote transfer of learning. This final activity phase is highly similar to the coaching approach described earlier because it makes use of similar procedures. Generally, this type of staff development is viewed as effective by teachers when it is relatively brief, includes practical ideas that teachers can immediately implement, and involves teachers in planning (Barnett, 2004).

As you think about these approaches, which has the greatest appeal to you as a learner? Which would you prefer to use when you have responsibility for providing others with staff development opportunities? No approach fits every kind of learning situation or every type of learner. Moreover, resource issues of time, cost, and personnel often restrict the kinds of staff development opportunities that are possible. We encourage you to keep this information on staff development in your thinking whenever you are engaged in program development activities so that you can suggest effective ways for ensuring that participants learn needed knowledge and skills. Of course, we also encourage you to learn more about effective staff development approaches if you are asked to lead such efforts; the sketch provided here is just an introduction to a complex topic with an extensive literature that supports it.

Participant Involvement

As you think about staff development, keep in mind how all participants will be involved. Based on more than three decades of research on staff development (e.g., Caffarella, 2002; Garmston & Wellman, 1992; Joyce & Showers, 2002; Sparks, 1986), the following suggestions should assist you in your efforts:

1. *Link staff development to the school culture.* The relationship among staff development, school culture, and innovation was discussed earlier in this chapter. Simple strategies such as conducting staff development programs in school settings may help to achieve this. But more significant efforts, such as ensuring that staff development is an integral aspect of existing schoolwide initiatives, are required to truly connect to school culture.

2. *Involve teachers in all aspects of the staff development program.* As pointed out in discussions of needs assessment and adult learners, teachers should participate in identifying their own learning needs and in planning to meet them. Teachers can be involved even further by engaging them as facilitators and coaches for one another, by having them try out new techniques and later sharing their results, and by asking their input in evaluating the overall staff development process.

3. *Combine effective training strategies with strategies derived from knowledge about adult learners.* Specific connections among demonstration, practice, and feedback are known to be effective for skill acquisition. Knowledge about adult learning and alternative approaches to staff development suggests that other elements also are necessary for effective staff development. For example, all staff development should allow for some level of self-directed learning activities with a breadth of opportunities. Opportunities and structures also must be provided that cause teachers to reflect on what they have learned, perhaps through structured discussions or journaling.

Design and Delivery

Regardless of the scope of your responsibilities for providing staff development to colleagues, you should keep in mind several core concepts for making it effective. These include (1) basing staff development on needs assessment data, (2) specifying objectives for the staff development, (3) selecting a format complementary to the objectives, and (4) making any presentations that are part of the staff development with careful attention to detail.

Needs Assessment

Whether completed individually or considered for a group or entire school staff, staff development should be based on a focused consideration of needs that is placed in the context of the immediate school environment. Several principles can guide this type of needs assessment:

1. Although it seems obvious, needs assessment should be linked clearly to the subsequent staff development program. Ideally, needs assessment should be designed to provide useful information that can advise the design and content for staff development efforts. If a clear link does not exist, participants may not see relevance and thus may minimize the importance of the activities in which they participate.

2. Teachers' perceptions about their needs and ways of meeting them should be a central concern of needs assessment. That is, in much the same way that teachers learn about the preferences and learning styles of their students, anyone leading staff development should learn about the preferences and styles of professionals.

3. Needs assessment should be an ongoing process. As teachers become more knowledgeable about a topic and more proficient in a skill, their awareness of their needs changes.

4. Valid, reliable, and comprehensive data are essential. Whenever possible, needs data should be collected from multiple sources using different methods of data collection (e.g., interviews, surveys, focus groups, and observation). This improves the validity and credibility of the results.

5. The information gathered in the needs assessment should be reported back to the participants and to others who may have a legitimate interest in it (e.g., parent organization, school board, and local university personnel).

When possible, needs assessment should be interactive. The process used should include opportunities for dialogue among those participating in it. In addition to obtaining data, interactive strategies serve to inform or instruct the participants of how data will be used and the intent of the questions or tasks.

Objectives

The needs assessment data you gather should help you decide the objectives for the staff development. You may wish to address one or more of these four types of staff development outcomes (Harris, 1989; Joyce & Showers, 1995; Sparks & Hirsch, 1997).

1. *Knowledge or awareness* concerns understanding educational practices, curriculum, concepts, academic content to be taught, educational theories, and legal or procedural requirements.

2. *Attitude change* concerns one's disposition toward oneself (confidence, role changes), others (colleagues, parents, students), academic content (math, English as a second language), or new requirements (teaming, paperwork, inclusion).

3. *Skill development* refers to the acquisition and refinement of discrete proficiencies and strategies.

4. *Adoption*—that is, embracing the innovation that is the basis for the staff development and consistently using it, including transferring the training to appropriate use in the learning environment.

Considering these types of outcomes helps clarify the intended results of select activities or a full staff development program. However, other elements also

Staff development can take many forms, but it is unlikely to be effective unless it is accompanied by coaching and other follow-up and accountability procedures for using the new ideas.

merit consideration: Is the training needed to help teachers refine or enhance existing practices? Or is it needed to introduce and develop something new that is not in their current repertoire? Answering these questions will help clarify the type, intensity, and duration of the training that may be required.

Formats

Once the objectives are determined, the next task is to select instructional strategies and formats to include as you design training components that will achieve the intended outcomes. This is particularly relevant when the staff development approach used is large-group training. For example, to increase knowledge or awareness, a lecture or mini-lecture (that is, a training approach) is straightforward and labor saving but has the disadvantage of leaving participants in a passive role. Listening teams in which small groups of participants are assigned particular topics to listen for and discuss later can address this problem. Likewise, a group from the audience may be asked to form a reaction panel that offers its perception of the information provided and facilitates participant discussion.

Another format that can be used in staff development is simulation. For example, co-teachers might place themselves in the situation of introducing each other to students and rehearse how they will accomplish this task to maintain parity. Team members might simulate an IEP meeting in which each professional receives a case study and directions on the perspective to be taken.

Various forms of discussion groups also can be effective means for delivering staff development. One variation of this format is a group buzz, which is a short discussion of a defined topic. Groups normally are comprised of three to five members who report back to a larger group when they have completed their buzz. Brainstorming, similar to the process described in Chapter 2, is a second variation of a group discussion. In this application group members suggest in rapid-fire order all the possible solutions or ideas that come to mind. Criticism and discussion are prohibited until a time limit is reached or ideas are no longer being offered.

Finally, the sequence of model, practice, and feedback is recommended for skill instruction (Joyce & Showers, 2002). Demonstration or modeling of the skill is used to present a clear example of the desired behavior. Practice under simulated circumstances follows demonstration. This may be accomplished through simulated teaching situations with other participants in the workshop or other training setting, or it may be done with small groups of children or a full classroom group. The more complex the skill, or the more it differs from other skills in the teacher's repertoire, the more practice it will require.

Presentation

Whether you are making a presentation in a self-contained workshop or as part of an ongoing professional development program, the attention you give to the design, preparation, and delivery of the session may well determine the success

PUTTING IDEAS INTO PRACTICE

Effective Presenting Techniques

Effective presenters use a wide variety of techniques to ensure that large-group staff development accomplishes it purposes. Here are a few strategies that can help make your instruction to colleagues successful.

■ *State specific objectives.* Objectives help focus participants' attention on the topics prioritized. Reviewing objectives at the conclusion of the session also helps them clarify their learning.

■ *Use periodic feedback.* If possible, use a pretest at the beginning of the session, check understanding during the session, and conclude a session with a posttest. This technique is effective even if the staff development presents information based on perception and opinions instead of specific knowledge and skills.

■ *Ask questions designed to elicit specific types of responses.* Using the information elsewhere in this text on question-asking strategies, use questions to check understanding, find out participants' opinions, and increase participant interest.

■ *Build a sense of learning community.* Staff development is enhanced when participants feel connected to one another and to the instructor. By providing opportunities for participants to work together, asking for their input, defusing confrontations, and seeing yourself as a learning facilitator rather than an information deliverer, this technique can be implemented.

Source: Adapted from S. S. Naquin & E. F. Holton, *Approaches to training and development* (3rd ed.) (Cambridge, MA: Perseus, 2003), pp. 183–194.

of the event. Conducting training is a complex process that requires practice and feedback to perfect, but a number of essentials will help you prepare and deliver presentations of any length. These are summarized in the Putting Ideas into Practice. As you can see in reviewing these ideas, the secrets of being a successful presenter often have to do with paying careful attention to detail, checking everything related to the presentation to be sure that any possible glitches can be avoided, and then being prepared to handle glitches that arise anyway!

Evaluation

Similar to program development, effectiveness should be judged based on data. Although professional perceptions about the effectiveness of staff development are valuable to know, strategies should be put in place to measure whether teachers learned new information and, more importantly, whether they implemented ideas in their practices. Ultimately, the effectiveness of staff development depends on whether it has a positive impact on student learning.

Summary

Whether you participate in collaborative activities involving just one or two colleagues or are involved in redesigning the entire service delivery structure for your school, practical matters related to collaboration will have to be addressed. One set of pragmatic issues concerns finding time for shared planning. Three common solutions for this dilemma are early release/late arrival days, the use of substitute teachers, and instructional strategies as a means of communicating about planning. A second set of pragmatic issues relates to scheduling and coordinating services. Matters to be addressed include establishing individual and school schedules and distributing personnel resources in order to meet all students' needs effectively and efficiently. Another practical matter concerns managing paperwork, and one other relates to the roles and responsibilities of both general and special educators. Practical matters often are addressed through a program development process. The five-stage process recommended includes establishing the program's purpose, planning for implementation, preparing for implementation, implementing the program, and maintaining the program. Finally, staff development, including model selection, participant involvement, and design and delivery, is frequently a significant component of fostering collaboration in schools.

Activities and Assignments

1. Using the list of options for finding time for shared planning—those in the text and those in Putting Ideas into Practice—create a questionnaire you can use to poll your colleagues about this important matter. Share the results with others. If possible, interview at least three principals about the feasibility of each option for your locale.

2. Duplicate copies of one of your weekly teaching/service schedules, or obtain a schedule from an educator in a collaborative school. With a small group, find ways to enhance the amount of time that could be available for collaborative activities. How might schedule changes affect the schedules of other professionals and programs? As an alternative, create what you would consider to be an ideal schedule for a special education professional.

3. If you currently are teaching or doing a field experience in a school in which special services providers go into classrooms on a regular basis, experiment with alternatives for increasing service efficiency. Begin by listing every individual (including paraprofessionals) who goes into classrooms. Obtain copies of their schedules and a list of the students in those classrooms. Then look for overlaps in services and ways to eliminate these. See if you can devise a plan for increasing the amount of time service providers spend in any particular classroom by blending their roles and eliminating duplication of services.

4. Interview the principal of a school with a strong culture of collaboration. Ask that person how pragmatic and logistical matters are addressed. Write a reflective essay summarizing your findings and relating them to effective collaboration in schools.

5. What have you heard about or experienced firsthand regarding special education paperwork? How effective do you think current federal efforts are to reduce paperwork in special education? With classmates, complete a web search and compile additional ideas for minimizing paperwork in your job.

6. What questions do you and your classmates have regarding roles and responsibilities of both special education and general education professionals in collaborative activities on behalf of students with special needs? Why do you think conversations to clarify roles would be important in collaborative schools? What topics do you think should be part of these conversations?

7. Based on your evaluation of a situation in your school or in a school with which you are familiar, describe a schoolwide program that emphasizes collaboration that you would like to see implemented. With a classmate or colleague, develop a plan for implementing the program.

8. Review the models of staff development presented in the chapter and answer these questions: Which model has the greatest appeal to you as a learner? Which would you prefer to use when you have responsibility for providing others with staff development opportunities? Consider your answers and identify principles or tenets common to your preferred models.

9. Design an awareness-level presentation for a one-hour workshop to teach the general education teachers in your school about the characteristics and types of instructional modifications needed by a particular group of students. Briefly explain how your presentation is based on the principles for effective staff development outlined in this chapter.

For Further Reading

Cook, L., & Hall, K. S. (2004). Making paperwork work for you and your students. In J. Burnette & C. Peters-Johnson (Eds.), *Thriving as a special educator: Balancing your practices and ideals* (pp. 49–61). Arlington, VA: Council for Exceptional Children.

Hackman, D. G., & Berry, J. E. (2000). Cracking the calendar. *Journal of Staff Development, 21*(3), 45–47.

Joyce, B. R., & Showers, B. (2002). *Student achievement through staff development* (3rd ed.). Alexandria, VA: Association for Supervision and Curriculum Development.

Kaff, M. S. (2004). Multitasking is multitaxing: Why special educators are leaving the field [Electronic version]. *Preventing School Failure, 48*(2), 10–17.

Lynn, L., & Sparks, D. (1999). Time: Squeeze, carve, apply, target, use, arrange, for adult learning [special issue]. *Journal of Staff Development, 20*(2), 1–73.

Meister, D. G., & Melnick, S. A. (2003). National new teacher study: Beginning teachers' concerns [Electronic version]. *Action in Teacher Education, 24*, 87–94.

Murray, C. (2004). Clarifying collaborative roles in urban high schools: General educators' perspectives. *Teaching Exceptional Children, 36*(5), 44–51.

Naquin, S. S., & Holton, E. F. (2003). *Approaches to training and development* (3rd ed.). Cambridge, MA: Perseus.

Interpersonal Communication

Connections

Regardless of the setting or structure, successful collaboration relies heavily on the effective interactions among those involved. Chapter 8 begins a discussion of the communication skills necessary for such interactions and provides a framework for understanding the specific skills presented in Chapters 9 and 10. Together, these three chapters examine and offer examples of the skills that are the foundation for engaging in interpersonal problem solving, as described in Chapter 2, and its use in consultation, teaming, and co-teaching. This chapter considers the nature of interpersonal communication and how it occurs. We identify skills that are prerequisites to successful interactions, consider factors that affect listening, examine the impact of nonverbal communication, and outline principles to guide your communication.

Learner Objectives

After reading this chapter you will be able to:

1. Identify the attributes and concepts of contemporary models of interpersonal communication.
2. Define *frame of reference* and apply it by describing a situation from different points of view.
3. Define *listening* as a skill and describe strategies to enhance the skill.
4. Identify and give examples of four types of nonverbal cues and describe how they affect communication.
5. Describe the principles of effective verbal and nonverbal communication.

Jennifer is thinking about the two very different meetings that she attended today—the inclusive practices committee meeting before school started and the math curriculum meeting at the end of the day. She reflects on how differently the two meetings were run and how the outcomes were affected. At the inclusive practices committee meeting, a monthly gathering of the building representatives responsible for changing service delivery practices and increasing differentiation, people arrived late because they know the sessions usually do not begin on time. The committee chair, Jeffrey, tried to focus the group on issues related to co-teaching, but much of the discussion consisted of committee members stating their opinions about co-teaching—who should participate, how much should occur, what should happen to add co-taught classes for next year. What Jennifer noticed most was that people did not listen to each other. At the end of the meeting, no decisions had been made and the air was filled with tensions related to varying opinions that hadn't been addressed; evidence of the dissatisfaction was evident as people conversed privately instead of participating in the group. In contrast, the meeting to make a decision on revising the math curriculum was a very satisfying way to end a busy school day. The agenda of the meeting—to summarize the dilemmas identified in algebra and geometry courses and brainstorm options for addressing them—was distributed in advance. Chris, the chair, briefly reviewed guidelines for the discussion before it began, and he ensured that each subcommittee had a member speak, writing down key ideas. As the conversation shifted to what to do, he did not dominate the interactions. By working to facilitate the session and drawing all members into the discussion, the group made several key decisions. Jennifer wishes that all the meetings she attends could be led by Chris.

Introduction

Communication is essential to both your personal and professional success. Here, we focus on its influence on your professional interactions and effectiveness. The skills of communication are critical in the performance of your instructional, administrative, planning, or other intervention responsibilities, as well as in your collaboration with colleagues and parents. Because of this, many professional preparation programs and school-based performance reviews include an assessment of communication skills and, increasingly, certification and licensure in education and related services professions require similar evidence of strong ability to communicate.

The Process of Communication

Human communication is a complex process that has been conceptualized in a variety of ways. Over the years models of communication have become more complex in an effort to illustrate the many factors that constitute and influence communication. In the sections that follow, you will learn about one model of the communication process, consider some of its conceptual elements, and clarify the definition of communication reflected in this book.

A Model of Communication

In the most general sense, human communication can be thought of as the means by which information is transmitted from one person to another. The earliest communication models focused on communication as a one-way event in which a *sender* delivers a message to a relatively passive *receiver* who decodes it. Subsequent models tried to capture the interactive nature of communication by representing the process as one in which information is exchanged between the sender who delivers a message and the receiver who decodes it and responds with feedback. More contemporary models have become increasingly sophisticated and attempt to represent more fully the complexity and subtlety of the communication process.

Adler, Rosenfeld, and Proctor (2004) describe one such model, which is presented in Figure 8.1. We concur with Adler and colleagues that no single schematic can adequately illustrate the complexity of this dynamic human process, but their visual representation provides an important foundation for examining concepts and principles of the communication process.

Concepts Reflected in the Communication Process

The model shown in Figure 8.1 provides a basis for discussing several central concepts that help explicate the communication process. Adler and colleagues (2004) identify four insights to be derived from the model, discussed next.

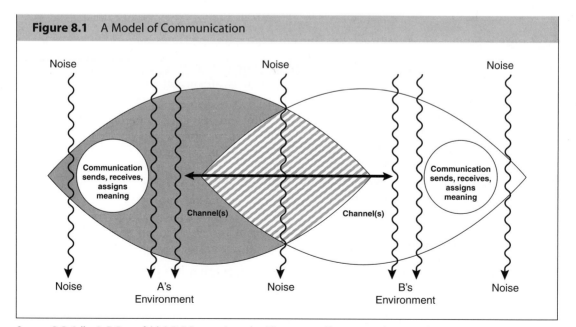

Figure 8.1 A Model of Communication

Source: R. B. Adler, L. B. Rosenfeld, & R. F. Proctor, *Interplay: The process of interpersonal communication* (New York: Oxford University Press, 2004), p. 7.

Simultaneous Sending and Receiving

In the contemporary model of communication there is recognition that both partners in a communicative interaction are simultaneously sending and receiving information, making it impossible to distinguish between a sender and a receiver. Thus, the traditional sender and receiver roles are replaced with the more descriptive term, *communicator.*

To illustrate the concept of simultaneous communication, try to discern who is sending and who is receiving information in these instances:

- A consultant is telling a teacher about a behavioral intervention that should be used with a student in his class.
- A teacher is asking a parent about her son's study space and schedule at home.
- A principal is informing a group of teachers of an innovative approach to schoolwide strategic planning.

It is tempting to see the consultant, teacher, and principal as senders of messages and the student, parent, and group of teachers as receivers. But imagine the teacher interrupting and advocating for another approach, the parent looking confused and guilty, and the group of teachers appearing bored while they grade papers and whisper to each other. Clearly, these intended receivers also are sending verbal and nonverbal messages to the speakers. Now, put yourself in this situation: Consider that when you speak you can hear yourself and judge if you are saying what you intended. If you decide that you have not been understood, you may elaborate or restate your message to clarify it. Simultaneous with your expressive communication, you are obtaining from your communication partner information that lets you know how your message is being received. A confused look, a frown, or a question may cause you to restate your message, whereas a smile, nod, or interested look may encourage you to continue speaking or to go on to a new topic.

Meanings in and among People

Messages, regardless of how carefully they are planned, have no meaning independent of the specific communication exchange in which they are expressed. The content of the communicative act, is the *message* (Trenholm, 2005). It is the totality of what is communicated—the words, noises, facial expressions, and stance of the communicator. Verbal messages are composed of printed or spoken words; nonverbal messages are conveyed by behaviors other than words (e.g., facial expressions, vocal noise, and gestures). Everything a communicator says or does is potentially part of the message, so long as someone receives and interprets the communication. The richness of the expressions and the ways in which the communicators interpret them give meaning to a message. As illustrated later in the discussion of frame of reference, the possibilities for misinterpretation of a message are tremendous and it is important for successful communicators to work to establish shared meanings.

Environment and Noise in Communication

Other elements important in understanding communication are environment and noise. Communicators exist in different *environments,* sometimes called *contexts.* These are the fields of experience that help the communicators derive meaning from each other's behavior. Environment refers to a physical location as well as one's personal experience and cultural background, or frame of reference, discussed later in this chapter. In the model shown in Figure 8.1 the environments of A and B overlap to demonstrate that the communicators share some common background or experiences that facilitate their ability to derive shared meaning from their communication. It is those areas of background or context where they differ that may interfere with their communication, such as significant differences in age, political orientation, cultural or ethnic background, or educational level.

Noise also can make communication difficult. It is anything that interferes with or distorts the ability of communicators to exchange messages. You are familiar with distracting sounds that may interfere with communication, such as public address system announcements, sirens, or loud talking in the hall. In addition, conditions such as physical discomfort, room temperature, an unpleasant odor, an inappropriate choice of words, a person's tendency to frown, or a person's physical appearance are other kinds of "noise" that interfere with the transmission of a message.

Communication through Channels

Channel refers to the medium through which messages are transmitted. Because nearly all messages in human communication are either seen or heard, the most frequently used channels are visual and auditory. However, all human senses may be involved in sending and receiving messages. The cologne someone wears or the firmness of a person's handshake also send messages through olfactory or tactile channels.

Information is shared through multiple channels. At any given point during interpersonal communication, several messages probably are being transmitted simultaneously over different channels. Sending a single message over multiple channels can strengthen or emphasize the message. You do this when you smile, nod, and touch someone's shoulder while giving that person a compliment. Alternatively, simultaneously sending discrepant messages through different channels complicates the communication. You do this when you smile while expressing disagreement with another's opinion. Discrepant messages constitute another common reason for miscommunication and should be guarded against.

The examples mentioned thus far are part of face-to-face interactions. Other channels for communication include electronic and written messages. Electronic communication through e-mail, voice mail, and even instant messaging is used with increasing frequency, especially by professionals in schools and similar settings, as is discussed in the following section on communication types. The channel you use as the primary one for communicating can affect

Unilateral communication through mediated channels is often necessary in schools. Although some people prefer this approach, it does not afford the opportunity for message clarification.

the way one receives, understands, and responds to a message. If you are sharing potentially upsetting information with a parent, consider the level of support you can give when communicating face to face, via e-mail, or through a voice mail message. The following factors may help you decide which channel to use in communications with colleagues, friends, or parents: length of time needed for feedback, amount of information conveyed, your control over how the message is composed, your control over the receiver's attention, your ability to assess the other's understanding, and the channel's effectiveness in conveying detailed messages (Adler & Elmhorst, 2002).

Communication Types

The communication process is best understood using the model and explanation just presented. Yet, an interesting categorization system presented by Schmuck and Runkel (1994) that reflects elements of older models remains valuable in understanding the types of communication that you are most accustomed to using in educational settings. This system classifies communication types as unilateral, directive, and transactional (see Figure 8.2).

Unilateral communication is intended to be one-way—a communicator provides information to another. No face-to-face interaction occurs; the recipient has no opportunity to query the communicator at the time the message is transmitted, nor can the communicator clarify or revise the original message.

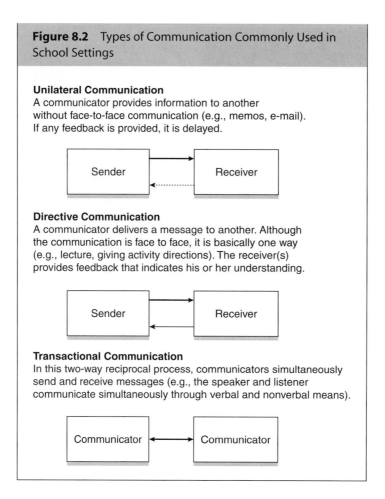

Figure 8.2 Types of Communication Commonly Used in School Settings

Unilateral Communication
A communicator provides information to another without face-to-face communication (e.g., memos, e-mail). If any feedback is provided, it is delayed.

Directive Communication
A communicator delivers a message to another. Although the communication is face to face, it is basically one way (e.g., lecture, giving activity directions). The receiver(s) provides feedback that indicates his or her understanding.

Transactional Communication
In this two-way reciprocal process, communicators simultaneously send and receive messages (e.g., the speaker and listener communicate simultaneously through verbal and nonverbal means).

Examples of unilateral communication include educational film or television, written messages, recorded lectures, and announcements over the school's public address system.

Some individuals prefer messages that are communicated unilaterally through mediated channels. In fact, evidence suggests that different mediated channels such as e-mail, fax, and voice mail have greater or lesser value depending on the communication intention and goal (Adler & Elmhorst, 2002; Nowak, Watt, & Walther, 2005). Under certain circumstances, such as a speaker's nervousness or another's hostility and inability to listen well, clear and unambiguous information without the opportunity for immediate discussion can be advantageous in managing the presentation of self-relevant information. Combined with the asynchronous dimension that can be introduced with a number of these approaches, mediated unilateral communication can be an important impression management tool (Lenhart, Madden, & Hitlin, 2005; O'Sullivan, 2000), sometimes better than face-to-face or other interactive modes.

Directive communication characterizes much of what occurs in schools. It occurs face to face when a speaker (usually an adult) communicates a message to another (generally a student), who indicates receipt and some level of comprehension of the message. This type of communication occurs as school professionals direct, explain, or lecture, and students listen, understand, and comply. The communication is complete when the student lets the adult know, or when the adult concludes, that the information has been understood. Because many adult–student interactions in schools consist largely of directive communication, instructional and special services professionals are likely to be quite accomplished at it and provide clear, meaningful directions, explanations, and lectures. Other professional situations in which you may experience directive communication are staff meetings and professional development activities conducted in lecture format. Despite the prevalence of directive communication in schools, it is in many ways incompatible with the effective interpersonal communication needed for collaborative interactions.

Transactional communication is the two-way, reciprocal interaction presented earlier in which communicators simultaneously send and receive messages while constantly exchanging information. Participants in this complex, reciprocal process mutually influence each other to create shared meanings. As noted earlier, contemporary models of interpersonal communication stress that participants simultaneously send and receive information throughout their interactions.

Interpersonal communication, the primary concern in this chapter, relies on a transactional approach. By adding this concept to those already presented, a more elaborated definition of communication can be offered:

> *Interpersonal communication* is a complex, reciprocal process through which participants create shared meanings as messages are transmitted continuously from one communicator to another via multiple communication channels.

This concept of transactional communication is a foundation for thinking about effective interpersonal communication. It is a basic premise in the model just presented and it can guide you in the entire range of your professional interactions. How might it help Jennifer, the teacher you met at the beginning of this chapter, to understand the differences in the meetings she has attended.

Prerequisites to Effective Interactions

Collaborative relationships require much more than just initiating interactions and hoping that the characteristics described in Chapter 1 fall into place. Effective interpersonal communication is essential for almost any kind of cooperation or collaboration (Bruzzo, 2004; Ulrich & Bauer, 2003), and there are some fundamental prerequisites to the needed communication skills. So, how do you assure your personal readiness to begin collaborating with a colleague? A starting point involves your self-awareness and your ability to understand others.

Frame of Reference

Every individual enters each life experience with a unique perspective. Your past experiences, acquired attitudes and beliefs, personal qualities, past and present feelings, and expectations for others affect what and how you observe and perceive, and ultimately how you respond and act. What you bring to a situation, independent of the situation itself, is called your *frame of reference.* It is your predisposition to respond in a particular manner to a particular situation. Earlier we indicated that frame of reference is a major part of what comprises the environment as depicted in Figure 8.1. Your frame of reference is a central influence in how you interpret messages or make meaning from the information others provide you.

Frame of Reference and Your Role

Your general professional socialization, discussed in Chapter 1, contributes to your frame of reference. At the same time, however, the specific discipline into which you were socialized (e.g., special education, school psychology, math, literacy, speech/language therapy) and through which you prepared for a particular professional role (e.g., classroom teacher, special educator, occupational therapist, speech/language therapist, school psychologist) also contributes elements to your frame of reference. This latter component may be considerably different from that of colleagues in other disciplines.

For example, general education teachers and special services providers may have pronounced differences in their perceived levels of responsibility for facilitating student learning. Consistent with their disciplinary preparation in general education, classroom teachers are likely to view their primary responsibilities as facilitating the progress of a *group* of students through a prescribed curriculum to meet established grade-level standards. Their professional studies emphasized curriculum and its scope and sequence, instructional methodology, techniques for group management, and strategies for delivering specific subject-matter content. Group instructional tasks, curriculum coverage, and assessment against established standards are prominent—appropriately so—in their frames of reference.

On the other hand, the professional preparation and socialization of special services providers probably emphasized individual variations in human development and learning, assessment of individual differences and learning needs, and intervention strategies to respond to unique needs of individual students. Not surprisingly, these professionals typically believe their primary responsibilities are to identify a student's current level of functioning and learning needs, then to design and deliver services tailored to meet those needs. Their professional background, a major component of frame of reference, leads them to focus on unique needs of *individual* students.

These differences in classroom teachers' and special services providers' frames of reference may have a profound impact on how they interact with one another. For you to collaborate successfully, you will no doubt find that awareness of these variations and sensitivity to their influences are essential, a topic addressed further in A Basis in Research.

A BASIS IN RESEARCH

Co-Teacher Frame of Reference, Relationship, and Program Quality

Research in single-teacher classrooms has long shown that teachers' beliefs influence their classroom practices and may have an effect on program quality. In a pilot study with 10 early childhood co-teacher pairs, McCormick, Noonan, Ogata, and Heck (2001) investigated the effects of co-teachers' perceptions and beliefs on their relationships with one another and on their subsequent behaviors and practices in co-teaching settings. They then examined the relationship of these practices to measures of quality in the co-teachers' programs using the Early Childhood Environment Rating Scale (ECERS), which provides an environmental quality score.* Previous research found that ECERS scores predict greater growth in childrens' intellectual, language, and social development; greater adult–child interaction; and more advanced communication skills and verbal intelligence. Further evaluation of program quality was based on observations assessing child engagement. The 20 participants completed the Co-teacher Relationship Scale (CRS) that explores how members of co-teaching pairs perceive their similarities with one another. The CRS measured participants' perceptions regarding the level of agreement in their values, philosophies, and beliefs, all elements of one's frame of reference. These included the degree to which they believed that they and their co-teachers were the same or different in their beliefs and approaches to teaching and personal/professional characteristics and style. These included such items as:

- Views regarding how to structure childrens' learning
- Beliefs about how children learn
- Views about how to adapt and individualize activities
- Beliefs about what curriculum for youngsters should be
- Views about parental involvement
- Views about how misbehavior should be managed

Those co-teachers who believed that they shared important instructionally related values and beliefs with their teaching partners achieved higher standards on the program quality indices. These findings suggest that co-teachers and other colleagues would be well advised to spend time learning about their own and each others' frames of reference in order to identify areas of shared beliefs and develop common understandings.

*The Early Childhood Environment Rating Scale (ECERS) is a well-researched measure used to assess "quality of socialization and communication environment" and "quality of space and material for learning experience." Because the two dimensions were so closely related, they were combined into a composite to represent an environmental quality score.

Although similar in some ways, substantial differences also can characterize the frames of reference held by the various disciplines that provide special services. Some of these differences reflect the diverse philosophical and theoretical orientations within these fields (e.g., a preference for psychoeducational versus behavioral approaches), some reflect variations in the nature of the special services provided (e.g., specialized instruction, therapy, or diagnostic evaluation), and still others relate to the specific knowledge bases of the disciplines. It is easy to understand how a speech/language therapist with responsibility for a student's articulation therapy might have a very different frame of reference from the adaptive physical education specialist. The former may work individually with students, diagnosing the speech disability, designing interventions to remediate it, and perhaps delivering services in a one-on-one situation. However, the adaptive physical education specialist may focus on assessing a student's general physical status and then design a program to maximize the strengths and reduce the deficits of the student. This specialist often will deliver individualized services for the particular student within the group of students served. Similarly, reading specialists are likely to have frames of reference that differ in significant ways from those of occupational and physical therapists, administrators who differ from special education teachers, and so on.

Frame of Reference in Multicultural Settings

Of equal or greater importance to your frame of reference is your cultural identity. It significantly contributes to the unique perspective, or worldview, you bring to every interaction. Culture is readily observable. It includes the artifacts, achievements, and symbols of a people. Culture also refers to many different elements that influence your sense of identity, including race, ethnicity, gender, age, occupation, geographic location, and religion (Banks & McGee-Banks, 2004; Halualani, Chitgopekar, Morrison, & Dodge, 2004; Kalyanpur & Harry, 1999).

Cultural identity is reflected in one's cultural orientation and worldview, and it has immense diversity. For example, Braithwaite (1997) describes orientations emanating from Navajo philosophy as focus on a sense of place, duality in life, and cultural identity. McCroskey, Fayer, Richmond, Sallinen, and Barraclough (1996) examined the degree to which cultural norms demonstrate a value for high or low immediacy in Australia, Finland, Puerto Rico, and the United States and how teacher immediacy relates to student achievement in those cultures. Others have posited that cultural orientations manifest themselves in such patterns as courtesy, respect, and tolerance for ambiguity (Cui, Van den Berg, & Jiang, 1998).

Culturally based value orientations are often described in terms of individualism versus collectivism. This is a continuum that represents the emphasis a culture places on individual goals, achievement, and fulfillment versus interdependence and emphasis on the well-being of the group as a whole (Lynch, 1998; Rothstein-Fisch & Trumbull, in press). Communication styles associated with both extremes of the continuum are outlined in Figure 8.3. Generally, the dominant culture of the United States is thought to reflect an individualistic orientation in which the uniqueness, self-realization, and self-expression of individuals are highly valued. However, about 70 percent of the world's cultures can be viewed as collectivistic (Trumbull, Rothstein-Fisch, Greenfield, & Quiroz, 2001). Collectivist cultures, such as most U.S. immigrant groups as well as African American, Native American, and Alaskan Native cultures, place value on meeting the needs of the group and are likely to be oriented toward the extended family and kinship-help patterns. No ethnic or other cultural group is only individualistic or collectivistic in its orientation, and not all members of a cultural group share the same values. These orientations are used to describe a continuum of values that may help distinguish key beliefs and patterns of groups and individuals. Here, this continuum serves as a framework for considering characteristics of cultural styles and patterns that are evident in cross-cultural communication.

Understanding one's own value orientations is a critical first step for thinking about cross-cultural communication. Next, it is important to consider how these orientations influence communication. Then it is helpful to examine how these match the orientations of others in the school and community. You will likely find you are more aligned with certain individuals than others—this is one indication of cultural similarities and differences. These are probably the same people with whom you believe you can work collaboratively. Your efforts to achieve cultural self-awareness will help you begin to develop culturally competent communication skills that will enhance your collaborative interactions with

Figure 8.3 Individualistic and Collectivistic Influences in Cross-Cultural Communication

Individualistic	Collectivistic
Low-context: Communication is explicit and direct; one "gets to the point."	*High-context:* Communication relies on context, past experience, and indirect cues.
Talk: Self-assertion is achieved through talk; talk is used to achieve comfort in groups.	*Silence:* Comfort may be derived from silence; silence is used communicatively and is valued.
Directness: Individuality and uniqueness are asserted, opinions are expressed to disagree, persuade, and avoid ambiguity.	*Indirectness:* Hints and subtle cues are used to maintain harmony, and ambiguity is tolerated to maintain harmony.
Uneven turn-taking: One party may dominate; both parties may introduce topics and speak at length about them.	*Balanced turn-taking:* Turns are distributed evenly; each party takes short turns and does not randomly shift topics.

Source: Based on R. Watkins, & J. Eatman, *An introduction to cross-cultural communication.* (Technical Report #14; chapter 2) [Electronic version] (Champaign-Urbana, IL: Culturally and Linguistically Appropriate Services for Early Childhood Research [CLAS] Institute, 2001).

colleagues and parents. The questions included in the chapter's Appendix, "A Cultural Self-Awareness Journey," can help you to reflect on this essential dimension of communication.

In our culturally pluralistic and self-conscious society, there is a temptation to try to avert the complexity of cultural differences by ascribing specific cultural values to groups of people who are of the same ethnicity, gender, or age. Do keep in mind that although members of these groups share similarities, considerable diversity exists within each of the groups, too.

We hope that these examples of variation in frames of reference help you focus on how your frame of reference—unique because of your personal, professional, and cultural history—is both similar to and different from those of others with whom you may want to collaborate. What is most important to understand is that no two people experience a single interaction in exactly the same way. Your responsibility is to be simultaneously aware of how you are influenced by your own and others' frames of reference and how others may react to yours.

Selective Perception

How often do you discuss a shared experience with a friend or colleague only to find later that you have quite different opinions about what transpired? Your understandings of what occurred may be so different that you even question if you were actually at the same meeting or if you participated in the same interaction. This is not uncommon. It is impossible for people to process and internalize everything that occurs around them. In any experience there is an infinite number of sounds, sights, smells, feelings, and tastes that compete for your attention. So you have to select which stimuli you will attend to or experience in the situation. This is an illustration of *perception,* a process for selecting, organizing, and interpreting all of the information available in a given situation. To be effective, these perceptual processes must be highly selective.

Everyone uses selective perception. They choose, either consciously or unconsciously, to focus on some pieces of information while largely ignoring others. This is often necessary in professional interactions because such communication is quite complex (Lustig & Koester, 2006). When more information is transmitted than can be assimilated, your frame of reference guides your selective perception, filtering out or obscuring some information and focusing your attention on other information. Generally, the biases in your frame of reference can enhance or inhibit your perception and thus your understanding of another's situation.

Consider the following exchange at a team meeting. Mr. Swanson, the tenth-grade English teacher, has come to a meeting of a child study team to discuss Lucia, a student in his class who has a learning disability. He reports,

> "Lucia is having an extremely hard time with our writing program. She can *tell* me all of her ideas in a very organized fashion, but she can't *write* them because her spelling is seriously deficient. Her written work is simply unacceptable. I'm an English teacher, not a spelling teacher! There's no way Lucia can succeed in my class. She really should be in a special education

class. I tried your peer-tutoring suggestion, and her papers are good, but it's probably because her tutor spells so well. Lucia just dictates her compositions. I have very high standards, and it wouldn't be fair to lower them for one student."

One team member at the meeting thinks, "Here we go again! It's another version of 'I can't stand having this kid in my class, and I won't adapt the assignment. Just get the kid out of my class.' I can't let this guy push Lucia out of his class. I'll have to stand firm on this."

Another team member says to herself, "It's always difficult for secondary teachers when they first start to include kids with learning disabilities. He's completed both his B.A. and M.A. in English literature and wants to teach English, not spelling. I could discuss accommodations with him. Maybe he'd see that Lucia is benefiting from the writing program and, as a result, she is making progress toward meeting her IEP goals. She's learning to structure her ideas and present them in a logical fashion. She's demonstrating strong composition skills that should be evaluated independent of her spelling."

In the example, both professionals picked up on information presented by Mr. Swanson, but they attended to different aspects of his report based on their individual roles and previous experiences. You can understand easily the thoughts of the two team members if you are aware of the different, strongly held biases of each: The first team member believes that classroom teachers do not care about students with disabilities and that they want to minimize their work. The second team member believes that all teachers want to teach well and feel that their teaching benefits their students. Both professionals identified and selectively perceived something in Mr. Swanson's statements that corresponded with critical elements in their own frames of reference.

The message for professionals who engage in collaborative activities is clear: Your own frame of reference may prevent you from understanding someone else's communication. You can become more aware of how you perceive others' communications and learn to consider multiple frames of reference by constantly challenging yourself to develop alternative explanations for others' statements. For example, what might a classroom teacher mean who says, "I'm not sure this student will ever learn how to divide!"? The teacher might be conveying general frustration at the student's difficulties, a statement of fact that the rest of the class is ready to learn a new skill while the student in question has not mastered the concept of division, or doubts about his or her own teaching abilities. Continuing to remind yourself to think divergently and consider alternative meanings will help you suspend judgment of others, critically examine your own perceptions, avoid drawing premature conclusions, and more accurately comprehend multiple elements of complex situations.

Communication Skills

Although the multiple dimensions of interpersonal communication processes are complex and occur simultaneously, our work with both novice and experienced educators has demonstrated the need to identify discrete skill categories and examine them individually. Precisely because of the complexity of interpersonal communication, effective skill acquisition requires the isolation and practice of distinct skills in much the same way that learning to speak a foreign language requires practice in vocabulary development, pronunciation, and phrase acquisition. Similarly, improving one's golf swing requires learning certain elements of the skill in isolation (e.g., addressing the ball, gauging the backswing, orienting the club face, and calibrating the follow-through). As with language learning or athletic development, mastery is achieved by acquiring and practicing discrete communication behaviors and then blending them into a smooth and effective process until you begin to integrate and use them together with other skills to facilitate the more complex interaction processes such as problem solving or conflict resolution.

Communication skills and strategies can be classified in many different ways (e.g., DeVito, 2005; Trenholm & Jensen, 2004). In this book, we treat verbal and nonverbal communication separately and organize our discussion of selected verbal strategies around the use of statements (Chapter 9) and the use of questions (Chapter 10). The remainder of this chapter examines listening skills, provides an overview of nonverbal communication factors, and considers principles and general suggestions for effective communication.

Listening

Listening is so critical an element of communication that we choose to present it separately rather than as part of a particular category of skills. It involves the simultaneous use of multiple skills, both verbal and nonverbal, some of which are prerequisite to the development of other skills and some of which result from skill development in other areas.

Listening is essential in all aspects of life. People listen for pleasure at concerts and movies, for learning in courses and meetings, and for understanding in day-to-day interactions with families and friends. You may best understand the importance of listening if you recall experiences of not being listened to—whether at a party, in a work setting, or at home. In all these settings, you may have participated in parallel conversations, much like the parallel play of children, in which individuals, either simultaneously or alternately, talk about the topic that most interests them without much regard for others. The speakers appear to have agreed to take turns speaking and acting as an audience for each other without responding in any meaningful way to what the other person communicates. If you have been part of such adult parallel play, you surely realize that dissatisfaction and feelings of being dismissed usually result.

Listening is the foundation for all relationships. In collaboration, listening is especially critical, a point that was demonstrated through Jennifer's meeting experiences, described in the chapter opening. It is a complex, difficult-to-measure process for attending to and accurately comprehending what another person is saying and then demonstrating that this has occurred (Brammer & MacDonald, 2003). It is a primary means for gaining information, but it is also a means of

A BASIS IN RESEARCH

Listening across Contexts

For many years, researchers have been exploring the science of listening. For example, they have examined whether men and women are similar in the way they approach listening tasks, and they have studied how specific situations such as those charged with emotion have an influence on listening skills.

One area of research that is particularly interesting for professional educators is the relationship between listening styles and contexts. Imhof (2004) asked teacher preparation candidates to complete a listening style profile for different situations (study, family, friend, work) and different listening goals. The listening profile had four dimensions:

1. *People-oriented style* in which concern for others lead to an emphasis on emotions and interests
2. *Action-oriented style* in which the primary concern is with a well-organized and succinct presentation of information
3. *Content-oriented style* in which the first focus is on the complexity of the information
4. *Time-oriented style* in which a goal is efficient communication within a time parameter.

Imhof found considerable variation in her results. First, she found that a people-oriented style was significantly more prevalent in listening situations related to friends, whereas an action-oriented style was more prevalent in an instructional context. In addition, she found that individuals were able to shift their listening profile based on context. Specifically, her results indicated that although shifting the content-oriented style and time-oriented style were unlikely, changing in the extent of using a people-oriented and action-oriented style was likely.

Imhof's results have implications for collaboration. They suggest that it is quite possible to shift the style of listening you use, and so you should be aware of these varying styles so that you can select from among them deliberately. Perhaps even more importantly, these results challenge you to recognize your own preferred listening profile and to recognize situations in which you should vary it.

Source: Based on M. Imhof, "Who are we as we listen? Individual listening profiles in varying contexts," *International Journal of Listening, 18* (2004): 36–45.

conveying interest in the messages of others. In A Basis in Research you can explore the complexity of listening as it relates to listening styles and context.

Rationale for Listening

A primary benefit of listening is that it helps establish rapport and build relationships (Seeley, 2005; Sunnafrank & Ramirez, 2004). This occurs in two ways:

First, when you listen, you show concern and a desire to understand the other person and the situation. By listening, you communicate both concern for the speaker as an individual and the intent to understand what that person has to say. Second, listening helps build rapport when it allows you to demonstrate accurate understanding. Attention, willingness to listen, and desire to understand are important elements in establishing rapport, but accurate understanding is required to build and maintain a relationship. When you demonstrate precise understanding of what the person has said, you are perceived as being both competent and a worthy collaborator.

Another major benefit of effective listening is that you obtain sufficient and accurate information necessary for participating in a collaborative activity. Too frequently, professionals assume they understand an inadequately articulated comment and begin acting on it as they perceive it. This is a dangerous practice for several reasons. First, it is quite improbable that anyone can accurately understand a situation that is not clearly described. Without accurate understanding, appropriate actions are rare. Second, a rapid-fire response may give others the impression that they are not competent. Perhaps you have had the following happen: People listened haphazardly as you described a problem, responded quickly, and left you thinking, "If it was so easy, why couldn't I think of an answer? I'm embarrassed to have thought it was such a problem!" This kind of situation does nothing to establish parity or rapport. Finally, and perhaps most threatening to the collaborative relationship, a rapid and inaccurate response to a person's comments suggests little concern for his or her perception of the issue and even less concern for the person as a significant individual.

Factors That Interfere with Effective Listening

Have you ever found that despite good intentions to listen carefully to what a colleague was describing, by the time the person finished giving a clear and precise description, you were not at all sure what had been said? This experience is common, and it illustrates how difficult it is to listen. In fact, although people spend about 50 percent of their communication time "listening" to others, their listening effectiveness is only about 25 percent (Boyd, 2001). Think back to those times when you recognized that you were not listening to someone else. Can you identify what interfered with your listening? DeVito (2004) describes several obstacles to effective listening that may be the culprits.

Daydreaming

When you listen, you are engaged in an inefficient process. You are capable of receiving information more rapidly through listening than an average speaker can convey, even a speaker who talks at an unusually high rate of speed. The result is that you have some spare time to think even while you listen. Unfortunately, you may use this time to mentally prepare a shopping list, plan a week's vacation, or think about a new instructional unit. You may find yourself suddenly daydreaming and discover that you have lost track of the speaker's message.

Sometimes communication is too slow or not sufficiently interesting to hold your attention. Daydreaming seriously hinders effective listening.

Rehearsing a Response

Perhaps while your colleague is talking you catch the drift of what is being said and proceed to work on framing what you will say when you have the opportunity to speak. Similarly, at a team meeting perhaps you anticipate that it will soon be your turn to report, and so you review your notes to prepare your comments and miss what someone else is saying.

Stumbling on "Hot" Words

To what words do you respond strongly? *Inclusion? Adequate yearly progress? Highly qualified? Accountability?* Sometimes when a speaker to whom you are listening uses a word that causes a visceral reaction, you may begin to think about the meaning of the word and its implications for you. This special category of daydreaming has the same impact: You temporarily halt effective listening while you cognitively address other matters.

Filtering Messages

Occasionally you may simply not want to listen to a particular message. For example, think about times you have attended a staff meeting on a topic about which you were already knowledgeable. Did you listen while the topic was announced and then tune out? If so, you were filtering the message. You might have done the same thing if you thought the information had little relevance to you. Finally, your frame of reference may cause you to filter messages. As noted earlier, your frame of reference may cause you to selectively attend to specific parts of a message and ignore others, thereby causing you to perceive the message inaccurately.

Being Distracted by Extraneous Details

Most people at one time or another find listening difficult because their attention is drawn to a detail that is extraneous to the message being conveyed. For example, have you ever spent so much time wondering where a colleague or parent got such an unusual haircut that you could not attend to what was being said? Perhaps you interacted with someone who had a minor speech impairment and you discovered it was especially difficult to attend to the words instead of the impediment. Any distractions—physical, verbal, gestural, environmental—may distract you and interfere with effective listening.

Suggestions for Improving Your Listening Skills

Because listening has a powerful metacognitive component, refining your listening skills requires addressing your ability to sustain attention and monitor your comprehension of the verbal message. And although there are no simple solutions for becoming a more effective listener, you can improve your skills by trying the strategies presented in Putting Ideas into Practice. The key to success, however, lies in deliberately monitoring your listening behavior and systematically using such strategies.

Nonverbal Communication

Much valuable information is transmitted without words. Skillful use of nonverbal behaviors is essential in communicating attitudes necessary for establishing and maintaining positive relationships (e.g., interest, acceptance, warmth) and powerful as a tool in clarifying, emphasizing, or obfuscating the meaning of verbal messages (Egan, 2001; Johnson, 2003).

Everyone is aware that body language and voice can influence communication, but the impact of nonverbal behaviors is greater than you may have suspected. In fact, the words used in your communication may convey far less information than do the nonverbal components. For example, nearly three decades ago Mehrabian (1980) reported that the full impact of an individual's spoken message could be broken down as follows: 7 percent verbal components, 38 percent vocal components (volume, pitch, rhythm) , and 55 percent facial expression.

People communicate nonverbally in several ways. Three primary classes of nonverbal cues are body movements, such as facial expression, eye contact, posture, and gestures; vocal cues, such as quality of voice and the pacing or flow of speech; and spatial relations, which include the physical distance between the participants. Minimal encouragers form a fourth class of nonverbal cues, even though they contain verbal components. Each of these categories of cues affects the nature of the communication between people. Two additional vocal behaviors—interruptions and the use of silence—also influence communication.

Body Movements

The phrase "one picture is worth a thousand words" shows recognition of the full impact of nonverbal communication. Without even using words, people can

PUTTING IDEAS INTO PRACTICE

Strategies for Improving Listening Skills

Good communicators are good listeners. Here are a few strategies to try when you want to hone your listening skills.

Mentally Prepare for Listening

- Clear your mind and deliberately shut out competing thoughts.
- Direct your attention to the speaker and do not engage in distractions such as e-mail, paperwork, or straightening papers on your desk.

Mentally Review the Information Being Given to You

- Identify main themes or key words.
- Practice mentally repeating these themes and adding additional ones as the speaker presents them.

Categorize the Information

- Develop a schema that helps to "map" the ideas (e.g., cluster case information according to behavior, academics, family).

Make Notes of Informational Details

- Use notes when a large amount of information is being shared.
- Explain the reason for note taking, explain what you will do with the notes, and obtain the speaker's permission.
- Jot down only important concepts and details.

Use a Signal as a Cue to Remember Ideas

- Use signals to help you remember a thought or concern that you want to share at the appropriate time (e.g., take note of a key word, bend your little finger down, turn your ring around).

Seek to Differentiate and Make Connections Between Inferences, Facts, and Opinions.

- Listen to what is *not* being said.
- Identify important facts or sequences omitted by the speaker.
- Attend to nonverbal behavior and tone of voice.

communicate a wide range of attitudes and feelings through *body movements*— gestures and facial expressions. Consider the influence of nonverbal communication in these examples:

- "I'm really interested in what's going on with Kim and Amir," the counselor said as she set her papers aside and sat down facing the teacher. She looked at the teacher and, leaning forward slightly in her chair, asked, "Do you have any insights that would help me understand their situation?" Without pause, she stated, "Please let me know what you think about their progress." She then sat quietly looking at the teacher, waiting for a response.

■ "I'm really interested in what's going on with Kim and Amir," the counselor said as she entered the room. She glanced at the teacher, then at the papers she was carrying, and sat down at her computer as she said, "Do you have any insights that would help me understand their situation?" Then, without pause, she glanced first at her watch, then at the teacher, and began reading and responding to e-mail as she said, "Please let me know what you think about their progress."

What did the counselor's body movements communicate to you? In the first example, they probably suggested that she was interested in the other person's information and ideas. In the second example, her nonverbal message probably contradicted her verbal message. What was the likely impact of her discrepant verbal and nonverbal communication on the teacher? In these examples, only a few movements and gestures were described. In the actual situation, one would observe many more nonverbal cues that contribute to the message. Eye contact, facial expression, and gestures, such as reaching out or touching someone's shoulder, also affect the meaning communicated.

Spatial Relations

Spatial relations refer to the physical distance you keep between yourself and another in an interaction. Hall (1966, 1981) describes four spatial zones that people seem to use in their interactions with others: (1) intimate distance, (2) personal distance, (3) social distance, and (4) public distance. These zones can be schematically represented by four concentric circles of personally defined space around each person (see Figure 8.4). The smallest circle represents the intimate distance and the largest, outermost circle represents public distance. Typically, the greater the distance between people in an interaction, the less their intimacy. Perhaps you have had experiences where you felt uncomfortable because the person with whom you were speaking stood too close to you. During interactions between colleagues who do not know each other well, the amount of space between them should be great enough to avoid such discomfort.

Another way of making judgments about appropriate personal space during interactions is the topic of conversation. Generally, when two colleagues discuss a problem that is very disturbing to one of them, the listener should be near enough to the speaker to indicate concern but not so close as to seem threatening or intrusive. On the other hand, if the speaker is distressed or sad, physical closeness and a touch on the shoulder might be exactly what the speaker needs.

Vocal Cues

Paralanguage—the vocal, rather than verbal, component of language—also communicates a great deal of information separate from the verbal content of the

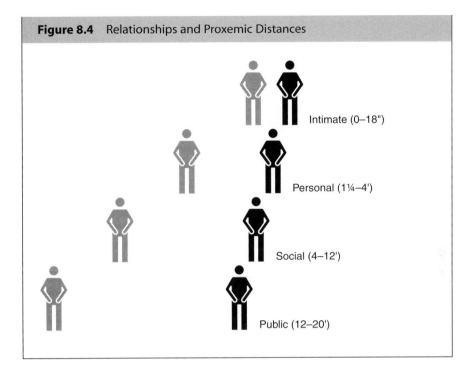

Figure 8.4 Relationships and Proxemic Distances

Intimate (0–18")

Personal (1¼–4')

Social (4–12')

Public (12–20')

message. Paralanguage includes voice tone, pitch, volume, speech rhythm, and pacing or tempo, as well as the use and timing of silence.

Many of the elements of paralanguage may reach extremes when the speaker is experiencing intense emotions. For example, pitch results from the tightness of one's vocal cords. When you are calm, depressed, or tired, your vocal cords are relaxed and your pitch is lower, whereas excitement or anxiety tends to make your pitch higher. The pace of speech may also indicate emotion; rapid speech can signal excitement and enthusiasm or nervousness and insecurity. Thus, you may observe that someone who is anxious or uncertain about a situation may speak very rapidly at a high pitch, whereas someone more confident and relaxed is likely to speak slowly at a lower pitch.

Minimal Encouragers

A category of skill that involves both nonverbal and verbal messages is called *minimal encouragers*. It includes words, phrases, silence, and other nonverbal cues designed to indicate that you are listening and understand what someone is expressing and to encourage the person to continue communicating. Common minimal encouragers include silence, head nods, quizzical facial expressions, hand gestures, other indications to keep talking, and spoken cues such as "Uh-huh," "Hmmm," "And," "So," and "Okay."

PUTTING IDEAS INTO PRACTICE

Observing and Attending to Nonverbal Communication

Nonverbal behaviors communicate far more than people expect. To maximize your communication skills, you need to understand and use nonverbal cues well. Here are some suggested practice activities.

Select and observe two different interpersonal interactions and see if you can identify examples of each type of nonverbal cue. The following list outlines the four types of nonverbal cues. Use the list as a guide for making notes about the speaker's body language and other nonverbal behaviors.

- Body movements (e.g., gestures and facial expressions)
- Vocal cues (e.g., voice tone, pitch, rhythm, volume, tempo)
- Spatial relations (e.g., intimate, personal, social, and public distance)
- Minimal encouragers (phrases, words, silence, and nonverbal behaviors that encourage others to continue talking)

Following the interaction, review your notes and describe the ways in which nonverbal cues influence (strengthen or detract from) the messages being conveyed. Does the degree of congruence between the verbal and nonverbal messages affect the communication? Consider what these behaviors may be communicating. Are they consistent with the words being used? Do they suggest a stronger or weaker interest than the words convey?

You use minimal encouragers to invite the person with whom you are interacting to continue sharing information with you. One of the most effective, but seriously underused, minimal encouragers is silence. As you become comfortable with allowing a few seconds of silence, you may find that it gives others time to gather their thoughts and then convey them to you. When you use silence, or when you nod or use one of the other encouragers, you also are allowing yourself time to phrase your next question or statement.

How aware are you of all these nonverbal components of communication—body movements, spatial relations, vocal cues, and minimal encouragers? Strategies for refining your skills in addressing them are included in Putting Ideas into Practice.

Developing Effective Communication Skills

In the two chapters that follow this one, you will learn many technical communication skills and have opportunities to practice them by completing activities and exercises. For this introduction to those skills, we stress the importance of understanding basic principles and the development of attitudes that facilitate the refinement of communication (Trenholm, 2005).

Principles for Effective Interpersonal Communication

In order to apply examples, rules, and suggestions for effective communication at the appropriate time and in the most effective manner, it is necessary to understand the principles that guide their use. Here are several essential universal principles for nonverbal and verbal communication.

Nonverbal Communication Principles

Nonverbal communication often is highly subjective. We noted that rapid speech may indicate enthusiasm or anxiety, but these are two distinctly different emotions. The physical distance between two individuals should be "near enough to" but "not so close as to"; what is appropriate for any particular interaction may be inappropriate for another. There simply are no specific prescriptions for "correct" body language. Instead, two critical concepts—congruence and individualism—may help you understand the meaning of your own nonverbal communication and that of others.

Congruence

Communication is composed of clusters of both verbal and nonverbal behaviors or cues that occur concurrently. When talking, an individual is communicating simultaneously through gestures, movements, facial expressions, posture, paralanguage, and words. As Rogers (1951) noted more than 50 years ago, believable behavior generally occurs in congruent clusters; that is, several behaviors occur simultaneously that have the same or highly similar meanings. Rogers attributed the characteristics of genuineness to congruence. Incongruence may unintentionally reveal feelings or attitudes one is hoping to conceal (e.g., the principal who chuckles while telling a staff member, "This is serious!"). This is illustrated in the following case description.

> The community liaison talked quietly with several parents while others freshened their coffee. When everyone returned to the seating area, he smiled and said, "If we're ready to continue I'd like to describe the role of the Community Liaison Office." He paused and, smiling slightly, looked around the room as people took their seats in the semicircle of chairs. "We are here to talk things over with you. Whenever you have questions or want more information about your child's program, we will be here to discuss your concerns and try to answer your questions." He paused, smiled slightly, and looked slowly around the room again. When he made eye contact with a group member, he maintained it long enough to give the member the opportunity to raise a question or offer a comment. "As parents, we all have concerns," he continued, moving a chair into the semicircle to sit between Diane Long and Jerome Jackson. Putting his hand on the arm of Diane's chair and looking at her, he

interrupted himself. "Diane, do you remember when my son started talking about getting a job and I ran checks on the business through the employee relations department at your office?" Smiling shyly and laughing, Diane said, "I sure do! That was one long week in our neighborhood." The community liaison laughed while still looking at Diane, then he leaned forward in his chair, put his elbows on his knees, and let his clasped hands fall between them. He glanced down for a silent second. Then, looking up, he said slowly, "Yes, as parents, we all have concerns about the decisions our children make and the challenges they must face. We know that we have to let go if we want our kids to grow into independent, productive adults. But it's hard—especially because we know their special needs." Quickening his pace slightly, he looked directly at each group member and said decidedly, "That's where the Community Liaison Office comes in. We have information about community opportunities, hazards, and supports; and we know your sons and daughters. Maybe most important," he continued while sitting up and smiling broadly, "we want to understand what you're experiencing. We've been there!"

This speaker's nonverbal cues strengthened his verbal message. His body movements or gestures (e.g., eye contact, touching Diane's chair, and smiling) and his vocal cues (e.g., speaking softly or decidedly, laughing, and changing

Nonverbal cues communicate powerful messages, especially when they are congruent with verbal communication.

verbal pace) were congruent with his verbal message. Together, his verbal and nonverbal strategies communicated sincere understanding and genuine interest in parents' concerns.

The speaker's use of space was also congruent with his verbal message. By physically joining the group and sitting among its members, he strengthened his verbal message that he was one of them. By leaning into the group while sharing his own feelings, he suggested that the group is a safe place to express intimate and personal feelings.

Individualism

The concept of individualism emphasizes the subjectivity involved in interpreting nonverbal communication. The meaning of a single nonverbal cue depends not only on the context in which it occurs but also on its specific meaning to the individual demonstrating the behavior and to the person observing it. For example, you may strive to maintain constant eye contact with a colleague to demonstrate your interest and attention. Your colleague, on the other hand, may feel uncomfortable and find your "interested" eye contact to be a penetrating stare that creates a feeling of being exposed or scrutinized too intensely. Similarly, you may observe a colleague sitting with his arms crossed and worry that he is not "open" to your ideas. In fact, he may be cold or searching for a comfortable position while seated in an armless chair!

To develop effective nonverbal skills you should identify your own patterns of nonverbal behavior that affect communication positively or negatively and learn to anticipate individual differences in how others react to your nonverbal behaviors. Several of the activities suggested at the end of the chapter can assist you in developing this understanding.

Verbal Communication Principles

In discussing the mutual influence that characterizes interpersonal communication, we stressed that the verbal and nonverbal messages you send greatly affect the types of responses you receive. In Chapters 9 and 10, we consider two primary verbal strategies—statements and questions—and examine how their use affects interpersonal communication. In this section of the chapter we take a look at two aspects of verbal communication that have significant impact on interaction—concreteness and neutrality—and also offer suggestions for enhancing the effectiveness of verbal communication.

Concreteness

You are more likely to understand verbal interactions if they involve the exchange of concrete, specific information. In fact, imprecise language is the cause of much miscommunication. Vague language may significantly obscure the message so that it may not be possible to determine what the sender intended. For example, if a teacher says he "handled" the problem, is it possible to determine what the teacher's actions were? If a colleague asks you for assistance with a student's disruptive behavior, do you know if the colleague wants you to help select strategies for her to use in class or if she wants you to intervene with the student? Do you even know the nature and extent of the student's "disruptive behavior" that is the source of her concern? The answer to each of these questions is "Of course not." In each of these interactions the language was far too vague to communicate effectively. The following examples illustrate how a vague statement or question may be made more concrete. The very different meanings conveyed in the concrete examples underscore the level of misunderstanding that occurs when communication is vague.

> *Statement:* I was concerned about her reaction.
>
> *Alternative A:* I felt somewhat angry and very rejected when she asked to have her son transferred to another class.
>
> *Alternative B:* I thought that she might turn her anger on her son when she got home.
>
> *Question:* Has Corretta improved in your class?
>
> *Alternative A:* Has Corretta's off-task behavior decreased in your science class?
>
> *Alternative B:* Has Corretta's participation and understanding improved in her literature assignments, now that we've provided her with books on tape to listen to prior to the class discussions?

As you review these examples using the information included in Figure 8.5, you can easily see how important concrete language is. Yet, listen to yourself and to your colleagues as you discuss students and school-related issues, and see how routinely your conversations proceed around vaguely described topics. As you listen, you probably will recognize that concreteness exists on a continuum from quite abstract to very specific. As you practice and develop proficiency in communicating clearly, you will learn to judge situationally the amount of concreteness needed for successful interactions.

Neutrality

Neutrality promotes the development of interpersonal trust because it conveys a nonjudgmental and accepting attitude. Although you often will be required to judge situations and evaluate ideas as you work with others, successful collaborators are people who communicate that they are nonjudgmental and nonevaluative about others. Consider the following alternatives:

> *Say:* I've noticed that you walk around the room while giving directions.
>
> *Rather than:* You pace around the room too much.
>
> *Or:* You shouldn't walk around the room so much.
>
> *Say:* I'm not sure I understand the selection of that activity for this lesson. Would you take a minute to help me see the connection?
>
> *Rather than:* Why would you have selected that activity? You couldn't have thought it would be effective with these students, could you?

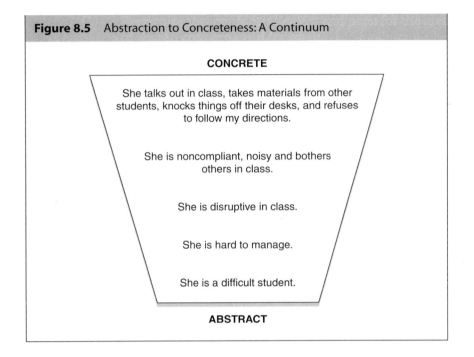

Figure 8.5   Abstraction to Concreteness: A Continuum

CONCRETE

She talks out in class, takes materials from other students, knocks things off their desks, and refuses to follow my directions.

She is noncompliant, noisy and bothers others in class.

She is disruptive in class.

She is hard to manage.

She is a difficult student.

ABSTRACT

Each example demonstrates how information can be communicated with or without neutrality. Notice, too, that positive evaluations and judgments can have undesirable effects on relationships similar to those with negative evaluations. If a colleague generally praises you and expresses positive evaluations of you as a person when discussing a shared project, you may come to expect it and feel criticized or uncertain when these evaluations are not offered. Evaluations of people can be avoided by focusing your comments on the activity rather than the person. Using concrete, specific language also helps to clarify the focus.

Say: Your calm, quiet voice helped me slow down and think about what I was saying.

Rather than: You're wonderful! Just your voice helps me think things through.

Suggestions for Improving Your Communication Skills

In addition to the communication principles given throughout this chapter, several additional suggestions may be helpful as you attempt to refine your own verbal and nonverbal skills.

Become a Student of Communication

Because communication is the smallest unit of concern in interactions and comprises the most basic set of skills needed in collaborative activities, you will want to learn more and become more skillful with communication skills as you participate in collaborative interactions. A note of caution is warranted, however. Like most people, you may conclude that you already have a high degree of communication skill, since you communicate regularly in your professional and personal life. As you read about the skills in this chapter and in Chapters 9 and 10, you may believe you have "had that course" or acquired the skills elsewhere. Keep these two points in mind: First, understanding or being aware of communication skills alone does not improve your communication. Only through self-reflection and continuing practice does improvement occur. Our students repeatedly share with us that focusing on and rehearsing skills is somewhat humbling; implementing the skills is much more difficult than simply recognizing them! Second, regardless of your knowledge or proficiency level after much practice, you will never fully master communication, since each new person, interaction, and situation will require you to practice and refine your skills further. We are reminded of this lesson regularly as we teach and learn from others.

Nurture and Communicate Openness

Perhaps the most pronounced theme that runs through our work on collaboration, and specifically this text, is the absolutely essential requirement for openness. *Openness* refers to a person's ability to suspend or eliminate judgment and evaluation of information and situations until he or she has explored adequately the various potential meanings and explanations. For example, when we discussed emergent characteristics of collaboration in Chapter 1, we noted that in order to collaborate, individuals should value joint decision making or at least be willing to experiment with it. In Chapter 2, we emphasized the importance of fully exploring problems to avoid formulating hasty and inaccurate problem statements. Hopefully, the importance of an attitude of openness became even more explicit earlier in this chapter, where we discussed the need for people to be aware of their frames of reference and those of others to minimize misunderstandings in communication and remove blocks to listening. Openness, in the context of verbal communication, is similar to the sense of acceptance associated with the neutrality principle, but the focus in that discussion was on eliminating judgments about people rather than deferring judgments about situations. In this context, the point is for you to set aside your biases and explore various aspects of a situation before attempting to decipher the message.

Keep Communication Meaningful

You will invest more in communication when you believe the information shared will be meaningful to you. It is unlikely that you will invest significantly in communication around topics or information that you have not sought or that you do not see as important. Specifically, unrequested suggestions and advice, although frequently shared, often have little meaning and may have an unintended negative impact. How would you react if, with no request from you, a colleague said to you over lunch, "I've watched you with José, and I think you might have more success if you used a concrete model of the task performance." The notion of providing a concrete model for this student may have great value, but such unsolicited advice is likely to seem intrusive. It may well make you feel defensive and hesitant to discuss the matter.

A second aspect that influences the meaningfulness of communication is the amount of information being communicated. Too much or too little information is not meaningful. Have you had the experience of asking a colleague or co-worker a simple question, such as, "How is the new student adjusting?" and you get a diatribe with more information than you ever wanted to know about the situation? You may have asked the question in passing or out of general interest and started a verbal landslide. You probably know a number of people who tend to give such lengthy responses. Do you try to avoid giving them an opening to speak? This, or simply "tuning out," is a common response to such highly talkative people. Conversely, have you ever found yourself providing too much information to others? As you begin observing your own communication, you may find that you sometimes obscure the meaning of what you are trying to communicate by doing this.

Alternatively, everyone experiences exchanges in which too little information is shared. You may have had experiences trying to communicate with someone who seems to expect you to be a mind reader. If so, you know how difficult it can be to ensure clear understanding when others withhold needed information.

As you work toward effective interpersonal communication, you should ensure that communication is meaningful by judging the amounts of information wanted by the people with whom you are interacting. When you are relying on information from others, you may find that when they give you too much or too little, your task is either to work to obtain more information or to focus and narrow the information they are supplying. Putting Ideas into Practice on page 230 summarizes additional information to assist you in making this principle part of your overall communication approach.

Use Silence Effectively

We noted earlier that silence and pauses are important nonverbal behaviors that are related to speech flow and pace or that may be used as minimal encouragers. However, beyond these uses, silence is an extremely powerful communication tool in its own right. You are undoubtedly familiar with the "deadly silence" used by parents and teachers to communicate disapproval or anger to children. You may have even used it or experienced it yourself in adult relationships. Surely, silence can be awkward or seem punishing in conversations, but very few people seem to understand how powerful it is in communicating interest, concern, and empathy, as well as respect to others. It also has another advantage and can be a very helpful strategy because it allows others to pause and think through what they are trying to communicate; this very often enhances the quality and meaning of their messages.

The definition of *silence* for our purposes is the absence of verbal noise or talk. But how long must there be no talk before a space in the talk can be

PUTTING IDEAS INTO PRACTICE

Planning for and Evaluating a Communication Event

Becoming a proficient communicator requires awareness of and attention to the factors that influence communication. As a student of communication striving to refine and enhance your communication skills, you will need to give advance thought to certain factors that will make your task easier or more difficult. In addition to the suggestions addressed in detail in the text, we suggest that when you have a team meeting or planning period with a colleague, you do the following:

■ Establish your communication goal. Identify ahead of time what information you want to try to share, obtain, or explore in this interaction.

■ Identify the most appropriate setting in which to accomplish this goal. Think about such things as privacy needs, convenience of location, and access to materials or resources that may be needed.

■ Consider the potential message-to-noise ratio. It is impossible to eliminate all noise or communcation interference, but you can and should work to minimize its effects on your interaction.

■ Evaluate the message and think about how the channel(s) to be used might affect the communication. Assess the amount of information to be conveyed, your desired control over how the message is composed, your desired control over the receiver's attention, your ability to assess the other's understanding, and how quickly you need feedback. These elements should help you determine which channel(s) is most appropriate for meeting your communication goal.

■ After the interaction, assess your success in attaining your communication goal. Write a summary of your colleague's primary points and concerns. Summarize your listening behaviors and decide which were most and least useful in accomplishing your listening goal.

considered silence? Goodman (1978, 1984) offers several concepts that help to clarify this. He suggests that the length of time between two speakers' verbal expressions varies within each conversation, and the amount of silent time that qualifies as a "silence response" is relative to each conversation's tempo and patterns of speech, two topics addressed earlier. For example, if two people exchange several comments and pause for about one and a half seconds after each speaker completes a thought and before another starts, then a pause of two or three seconds may be required for a silence response. On the other hand, if two people are talking but only allowing about a quarter of a second of verbal space between taking turns to talk, one second may constitute a silence response.

Silence and its impact are more easily understood when you consider the alternatives: interruptions, overtalk, and reduced verbal spacing. Interruptions occur when one speaker disrupts another's message in order to deliver his or her own. When someone is speaking and another interrupts, there is a period of overtalk in which both speakers are talking simultaneously until one relinquishes the conversation to the other. The final alternative, reduced verbal spacing, is related to silence and pauses but is also distinct from them. It refers to the pace of the turn taking in verbal interaction. It occurs when a new speaker begins talking during what is meant to be a brief pause in someone else's speech. In its most exaggerated form, one speaker appears to clip off the last word or two of the previous speaker's talk.

All of these alternatives to silence—interruptions, overtalk, and reduced verbal spacing—have similarities. Perhaps they occur because the person using them has a need to control the situation, to demonstrate knowledge, to try to reduce the speaker's rambling talk, or simply to be center stage. Whatever the reason, these responses are likely to have a negative impact on the conversation and relationship. They say, "Listen to me," "It's my turn," "What I have to say has more value than what you're saying." These responses certainly suggest to the other person that he or she is less competent, important, or interesting than the person taking control of the conversation. They are likely to produce frustration and sometimes anger as the person who is verbally "crowded" feels less and less understood and valued.

In your conversations, interviews, and professional discussions, try to develop a habit of protecting verbal space. It will give the other person the opportunity to finish talking and give you the opportunity to consider what the other has said and how you want to respond. In addition to avoiding verbal crowding, the silence response or verbal space conveys that you are interested in the other's comments and are taking the time to comprehend the message before responding.

A final point to consider is that the amount of silent space that creates the positive impact you desire varies with each conversational pair. Analogous to inadequate silence, unnaturally long periods of silence can convey disinterest or other negative messages. There are no precise rules about verbal spacing. Sometimes, in a fast-paced discussion, three seconds is a significant silence. At other times, particularly if the topic is emotional and one or more speakers are describing personal feelings, silences of several seconds or more than a minute may be appropriate nonverbal cues. Through experimentation you can learn to determine the desirable amounts of silence in each relationship and conversation within that relationship.

Adapt Your Communication to Match the Task and the Relationship

Professionals who are effective communicators tend to adapt their communication according to the task, the relationship, and the characteristics of the individuals involved. This includes choosing language that is clear and efficient, identifying the information content that is needed, and using verbal communication strategies that will best elicit the preferred responses. If you think about the individuals with whom you interact, you will probably include colleagues, administrators, parents, paraprofessionals, and professionals from other agencies.

Furthermore, you may differentiate ongoing and regular collegial relationships from more temporary and infrequent interactions, such as annual review meetings. The nature of the relationship and its level of development should influence your choice of the appropriate communication style. As you collaborate in established or developing relationships, one of your responsibilities is to use communication strategies that will best facilitate the collaborative activity. Because there are no simple rules or strategies for adapting your verbal communication, your ability to understand the principles and learn to use many of the skills included in this book can help you do this.

Summary

Effective communication is critical in all areas of life, and it is particularly essential to your success as a school professional. Three primary types of communication include unilateral, directive, and transactional. Unlike the first two, transactional communication emphasizes that participants in the communication process engage in continuous and simultaneous communication across multiple channels. This model is characterized by mutual influence as participants strive to develop shared meanings. Attributes common to this and most communication models include channel, message, communicators, and noise. It is also characterized by the concepts of simultaneous and multichannel communication.

In preparing for collaborative interactions, you should come to understand your own and others' frames of reference and how these have been shaped by past experiences, professional preparation, and cultural identity. Furthermore, you should remain vigilant in monitoring the possible effect your own frame of reference or that of others may have on your interactions.

Listening and nonverbal communication are fundamental to interpersonal communication. Listening is a complex process that can be impeded by various internal and external events. However, it can be improved by using metacognitive and other strategies. Nonverbal cues are powerful communication mechanisms that include body movements, vocal cues, spatial relations, and minimal encouragers. Principles of nonverbal and verbal communication provide guidance for successful interactions. Two significant concepts for understanding nonverbal communication are individualism and congruence. Principles of verbal communication emphasize concreteness and neutrality. Effective communication is characterized by openness, meaningfulness, effective use of silence, and an ability to adapt communication to meet the needs of the task and the relationship.

Activities and Assignments

1. As a way to practice considering alternative meanings and frames of reference, try to generate four distinctly different possible meanings for the following statements.

Get additional practice by doing the same for statements made by others in the course of conversations during the next few days.

> **Teacher:** I really don't know what to do to help her. I am not sure she should be in my class.
> **Parent:** He's been in special education for three years now. Isn't he caught up yet?
> **Occupational Therapist:** I haven't had any teaching courses or in-services about group instruction. How am I going to be able to provide Jill's program in the classroom?

2. Think about the characteristic behaviors of two or three individuals with whom you interact regularly. Knowing that behavior communicates, consider the characteristic behaviors of these people and describe some of the messages they communicate. How can you use this information to improve your communication with them?

3. Read the following vague statements or questions and imagine a situation in your professional setting where each could apply. Then write four alternative, more specific and concrete statements or questions for each.

> "How is his home life?"
> "She's really not invested in her work."
> "That parent is always upset."

4. No doubt you communicate with colleagues and/or parents using notes and e-mail or forms that have been created by you, colleagues, or the district. Collect a sample of teacher- or district-developed forms and share them with colleagues from other settings. Work with colleagues to identify ways in which the forms could be made more teacher or parent friendly. Modify the forms accordingly. Note that when this is done with classmates from other districts or settings, you are likely to get many new ideas and time-saving strategies than if you simply do this with colleagues in your own setting.

5. The power of silence or pauses in discussion can improve communication. Yet nearly everyone has to learn to allow and use silence in interactions. Challenge yourself to allow increasingly greater verbal space (pauses) in some conversations. Lengthen, ever so slightly, the verbal space that follows someone else's statements before you begin speaking. As you do this in different interactions, observe how it affects the pace and comfort of the conversation.

6. Visualize yourself in each of the following situations. For each situation, identify at least two barriers that could interfere with your listening (e.g., your own biases, ability to understand and remember, narrow range of appropriate responses, tendency to solve problems quickly, and so on). Then for each potential barrier, propose an appropriate remedy or strategy you might use to get around the obstacle.

   - A colleague with whom you collaborate demeans some of the students' cultural or religious beliefs in class, calling them foolish and irrelevant.
   - At a team meeting, your proposal for a new block scheduling plan—which you developed based on concerns expressed by the team and the quality of which you believed reflected the many hours you spent on it—is severely criticized and rejected by the team.

For Further Reading

Banbury, M. M., & Hebert, C. R. (1992). Do you see what I mean? Body language in classroom interactions. *Teaching Exceptional Children, 24*(2), 34–38.

Brownell, J. (2006). *Listening: Attitudes, principles and skills* (3rd ed.). Boston: Allyn & Bacon.

DeVito, J. A. (2006). *The interpersonal communication book* (10th ed.). Boston: Allyn & Bacon.

Griffith, D. A., & Harvey, M. G. (2001). Executive insights: An intercultural communication model for use in global organizational networks. *Journal of International Marketing, 9*(3), 87–104.

Hollingsworth, H. L. (2001). We need to talk, communication strategies for effective collaboration. *Teaching Exceptional Children, 33*(5), 4–8.

McKay, M., Davis, M., & Fanning, P. (1995). *Messages: The communication skills book* (2nd ed.). Oakland, CA: New Harbinger.

Schultz, K. (2003). *Listening: A framework for teaching across differences.* New York: Teachers College Press.

Appendix

A Cultural Self-Awareness Journey

Step 1: Your Cultural Roots and Heritage

1. When you think about your roots, what country(ies) other than the United States do you identify as a place of origin for you or your family?

2. Have you ever heard any stories about how your family or your ancestors came to the United States? Briefly, what was the story?

3. Are there any foods that you or someone else prepares that are traditional for your country(ies) of origin? What are they?

4. Are there any celebrations, ceremonies, rituals, or holidays that your family continues to celebrate that reflect your country(ies) of origin? What are they? How are they celebrated?

5. Do you or anyone in your family speak a language other than English because of your origins? If so, what language?

6. Can you think of one piece of advice that has been handed down through your family that reflects the values held by your ancestors in your country(ies) of origin? What was it?

Step 2: Your Cultural Values, Biases, and Behaviors

1. Have you ever heard anyone make a negative comment about your country(ies) of origin? If so, what was it?

2. As you were growing up, do you remember discovering that your family did anything differently from other families to which you were exposed because of your culture, religion, or ethnicity? Name something that you remember that was different.

3. Have you ever been with someone in a work situation who did something because of his or her culture, religion, or ethnicity that seemed unusual to you? What was it? Why did it seem unusual?

4. Have you ever felt shocked, upset, or appalled by something that you saw when you were traveling in another part of the world? If so, what was it? How did it make you feel? Pick some descriptive words to explain your feelings. In retrospect, how do you wish you would have reacted?

5. Have you ever done anything that you think was culturally inappropriate when you have been in another country or with someone from a different culture? In other words, have you ever done something that you think might have been upsetting or embarrassing to another person? What was it? What did you do to try to improve the situation?

6. If you could be from another culture or ethnic group, what culture would it be? Why?

7. What is one value from that culture or ethnic group that attracts you to it?

8. Is there anything about that culture or ethnic group that concerns or frightens you? What is it?

9. Name one concrete way in which you think your life would be different if you were from that culture or ethnic group.

Source: E. W. Lynch, "Developing cross-cultural competence," in E. W. Lynch & M. J. Hanson (Eds.), *Developing cross-cultural competence: A guide for working with young children and their families,* 2nd ed. (Baltimore: Brookes, 1998), pp. 87–89.

CHAPTER 9

Using Statements

Connections

Using the discussion of collaboration prerequisites and the basic structure for communication detailed in Chapter 8, this chapter outlines principles for making appropriate statements during interactions. Throughout the chapter these principles are applied, using situations for providing feedback as specific illustrations. As you consider the information presented, keep in mind how you might use it in a wide variety of collaborative efforts, including problem-solving meetings, conferences with parents, and consultation.

Learner Objectives

After reading this chapter you will be able to:

1. Identify the types of statements used to provide, seek, and clarify information.
2. Use descriptive and guiding statements to provide others with information.
3. Formulate indirect questions to seek information.
4. Use paraphrasing, reflection, summarizing, and checking to confirm information provided by another.
5. Define *interpersonal feedback* and list criteria for effective feedback.
6. Describe guidelines for effective interpersonal feedback.

Rory and James are discussing the past week of co-teaching. Rory is somewhat uncomfortable with the partnership, particularly because he senses that James, the general education teacher, is uncomfortable in addressing the needs of the five students with disabilities who are in the class. After some discussion of logistics, Rory comments to James, "I noticed that yesterday when Autumn [a student with a physical disability] asked you how to begin the biography assignment, you sent her immediately to me." James immediately interjected, "Yeah, I don't know what to expect of her so I thought it was better to just get her to you right away so you could do what she needed. Besides, so many of the kids were needing my attention that she was one that you should be responsible for anyway—you helping her let me get on with working with the other kids." Rory paused for a moment before stating, "You don't know what Autumn needs so you'd rather I assist her … and the other students in the room with disabilities." As James nodded, Rory continued, "I guess I have a somewhat different perspective of our class and the students." The conversation continues as the teachers work to clarify their views and find more integrated ways to instruct all their students.

Introduction

Statements are central elements of communication. Consider the message that each of these statements conveys:

- "Emil scored at the 4.6 grade level on reading comprehension."
- "You should ask José's parents to have his medication level checked."
- "You said that you're experiencing difficulty in accomplishing the language goals in the classroom."
- "I heard that they are trying to get a waiver from that testing requirement for the students with learning disabilities."
- "Veda seems overwhelmed by the academic demands."
- Bill slammed his book on the desk, yelled, "I won't!" and crossed his arms as he stared at you. You walked over and gently put one hand on his shoulder, looked him in the eyes, and quietly asked, "Why don't you want to go to recess?"
- "I'm curious about your thoughts on the situation."

Statements are an integral part of many types of communication. The material in this chapter will demonstrate that the way you structure, word, and deliver statements has a significant impact on the verbal responses you receive from others and on your relationship with the individuals with whom you are interacting. Certainly you use both questions and statements together in your interactions. But, as we noted in Chapter 8, our approach is to assist you in developing discrete skills. This requires treating statements and questions as though they occur separately so that later you can blend them into effective interactions.

Purposes of Statements

Statements generally have one of three purposes: to provide information, to obtain information, or to clarify information. Each of these purposes is described and illustrated in the following sections.

Statements That Provide Information

The most common function of statements is to provide information to others. You use statements when your primary purpose is to tell others something you think they want or need to know or to tell them what you want them to know. You may tell someone about a newly developed intervention strategy; you may explain how the changing composition of an interagency council will influence your program; or you may describe direct observations you made of instruction in a classroom or of a particular student's performance. You may also tell others about a situation or experience you have had, or perhaps give them advice about situations they face. Two primary types of statements have the overall purpose of providing information—*descriptive statements* that outline events or experiences without giving advice or making an evaluation and *guiding statements* that subtly or explicitly direct actions by evaluating or advising.

Descriptive Statements

Often, statements are used to provide a verbal account of a situation, behavior, opinion, or feeling. When such a verbal account is offered without evaluation or advice, it is descriptive. Descriptive statements can be used to relate both overt and covert information.

Describing Overt Information

The most straightforward form of descriptive statement is that which addresses *overt* content by providing a verbal account of an observable event, situation, or behavior. Such descriptive statements focus on facts. DeVito (2005) characterizes a factual statement as one that is made by an observer following an observation and is limited to what is observed. Facts can be directly verified because they are something that one can see, hear, or feel (Hayakawa, 1972). Thus, making descriptive statements of this sort requires identifying observable behaviors or permanent products, such as a student's written work, and describing them without making judgments about them. You probably already have skill in this area because providing precise and objective descriptions of behavior and work products is a basic component in the preprofessional training of most special services providers, although practice in this skill is usually aimed at describing student behavior.

Because the definition we have given for descriptive statements specifically excludes evaluating or advising, examples of evaluative and advisory statements are given to illustrate what descriptive statements are *not*. The following examples are provided solely to help you discriminate among descriptive, evaluative, and advisory statements. They are not meant to model effective means of delivering advice or evaluation, two topics addressed later in this chapter. Contrast the ways in which the same event can be described in the following statements:

Descriptive: When Maryanne left the room during the discussion, several team members looked at each other. You stopped speaking and asked the group, "Should I wait for Maryanne to return?"

Evaluative: You shouldn't have let Maryanne leave like that. It's rude for one of us to leave while we are trying to make a group decision.

Advisory: You need to get everyone's agreement on ground rules for participation before you have that team try to work together on problem solving again.

The first of the examples meets the criteria for descriptive statements and addresses overt events—the observable behaviors of Maryanne, the group leader (in this case, you), and the other group members. Those behaviors are described without evaluation or advice in the first example. The next statements do not meet the criteria for descriptive statements. The second is evaluative: "You shouldn't have" conveys judgment about another's behavior. The third statement is advisory: "You need to" suggests action.

Describing Covert Information

Descriptive statements are also used frequently in detailing *covert* events or conditions that are not observable, such as attitudes, perceptions, and feelings. When you discuss concerns and problems with colleagues or parents, they may well describe their feelings about a situation as well as the details of the situation. This often is described as *self-disclosure,* a communication about the *self* that is communicated to another person (Adler, Rosenfeld, & Proctor, 2004; Luft, 1984). This is information that is not directly observable and is sometimes referred to as part of one's private self. The nature of the self-disclosure and its usefulness in your collaborative problem solving is dependent on the speaker's depth of self-awareness as well as his or her openness and willingness to share that information with you. Strategies for you to use in expressing empathy and encouraging self disclosure are discussed in the next section.

Because covert material experienced by others cannot be observed directly, your perceptions of their covert experiences will involve some inference. An *inference* is a statement about the unknown that is based on something known or assumed. It is not limited to what was observed. Instead, it is more like a conclusion or assumption that is derived from reasoning about known evidence. You might infer that someone is angry after observing him throw a book across the room, raise his voice, and slam the door. This is a reasonable conclusion to draw based on your consideration of the behaviors displayed. There is nothing wrong with making inferential statements. In fact, they are often essential when talking about things that are most important to those involved. But keep in mind that they are just that—inferences, not facts. To illustrate the importance of this

Depending on the person's openness and trust in the relationship, she or he may express feelings of distress that are normally kept private.

distinction, consider that the previous example could be a description of some-one who, although thoroughly delighted by the antics of his new puppy, is using the strategy of disrupting and discouraging the puppy's behavior by responding immediately to undesirable behavior with loud noises.

We caution against using inferential statements before assessing known evidence carefully because fact-inference confusion can be problematic and interfere with clear communication. Problems inevitably occur when you confuse inferential statements with factual statements. To avoid this confusion, we encourage you to express a tentativeness when you make inferential statements. This communicates that you know you are making an assumption, even though it is based on your perception of the facts. It also indicates that you are aware that the inference you drew may be wrong and you are open to considering other explanations. This openness is equally important in listening, as we discussed in Chapter 8. The tentativeness we recommend can be likened to the responses we discuss later for confirming information (e.g., paraphasing, reflecting, summarizing, and checking).

Statements expressing covert information also can be classified as descriptive, evaluative, and advisory as is illustrated in the following examples:

Descriptive: I became so anxious when it was my turn to speak at the in-service workshop that my hands and the papers I held shook. I was sweating, my mouth was terribly dry, and I felt all tongue-tied. I thought the floor would fall out from under me.

Evaluative: I'm such a wretched speaker. I'm really not a good spokesperson. I *look* nervous and nobody can follow what I'm saying.

Advisory: I must avoid getting into situations where I'll have to talk in front of other people because they are so stressful for me. I should have Carlos represent us at meetings.

The covert topic in these examples is the speaker's feelings about public speaking. The descriptive statement includes neither evaluation nor advice, as it describes feelings (anxious, tongue-tied). This statement goes further in providing a concrete description of the feelings through describing observable behaviors (shaking hands, perspiration, dry mouth). The second statement is not descriptive because it contains evaluation ("I'm such a wretched speaker"; "I'm really not good"). Similarly, the third statement is not descriptive because it offers advice ("I must avoid"; "I should have") rather than description.

Although these statements were designed to illustrate the descriptive, evaluative, and advisory concepts, in your day-to-day interactions you are not likely to find such clear-cut examples. Instead, you generally will encounter statements similar to the next two examples. They each contain descriptive and nondescriptive components. Consider each carefully and see if you can identify their evaluative, advising, and descriptive elements. Consider, too, the levels of inference they imply.

- "I observed Timothy in his occupational therapy group and I was amazed! He was so devastated when he made a mistake that he marked all over his project in black marker and tore it up. He threw it at the wastebasket and put his head on the table. His behavior was outrageous."
- "I observed your group, and you shouldn't feel so bad about your lesson. You're a really good therapist and you do a great job with some very challenging students! Your presentation took only one minute, and you demonstrated all of the three movements we talked about."

The first example contains some descriptive phrases ("observed," "marked all over," "tore it," "threw it," "put his head on the table"). It also contains an evaluative phrase ("behavior was outrageous") and highly inferential reference ("so devastated"). It does not contain any advisory phrases. Similarly, the second example also includes descriptive and nondescriptive elements ("I observed," "Your presentation," "the three movements we talked about"). An evaluative phrase ("You're a really good therapist") and an advisory one ("You shouldn't feel so bad") also are present. The statement does not make inferences, but it includes nonspecific terms and would be improved by more concrete language.

As you begin to attend more closely to the statements you and others make during your interactions, you undoubtedly will find that purely descriptive statements are rare. And although it is often difficult to describe something without evaluating or advising, you can improve your skills in this area by monitoring your own statements. As you will see later in this chapter and in the next, skill in using descriptive statements contributes greatly to effective interactions. By conveying

---

PUTTING IDEAS INTO PRACTICE

Tips for Sharing Information

Knowledge or information is power. When you provide others with accurate, objective, and useful information, you are empowering them. Once empowered with information and the knowledge and skills to use it, people are increasingly able to take control over their professional and personal lives and to take action to get what they want and need to succeed (DeVito, 2006a; Turnbull & Turnbull, 2001). As teachers and service providers, your tendency may be to explain regularly and provide copious information that may not be received as useful or relevant to colleagues or parents. Here are some tips to help you practice useful strategies and avoid others.

- Determine what information is needed or requested.
- Offer objective, accurate descriptions or explanations.
- Identify and focus on main points.
- Ensure that the information is relevant to the person receiving it.
- Avoid the use of jargon and clarify those terms that cannot be avoided.
- Minimize the use of evaluation and advice unless it is requested.
- Do not offer interpretations of behaviors or try to be a mind reader.

---

information without judging or advising, purely descriptive statements minimize the likelihood of offending the receiver. Such statements promote clear and honest communication without causing listeners to become defensive. Some additional tips for providing information effectively are highlighted in Putting Ideas into Practice.

Guiding Statements

Some statements provide information in order to guide action. *Guiding statements* urge others to act, feel, or think in a certain way. Two categories of guiding statements are those that explain and those that advise.

Statements that provide information in an instructive way and rely on reasoning, an understanding of cause-and-effect relationships, or logic are *explanations*. They translate ideas and interpret information. Use of these statements nearly always means that the person offering the explanation has greater expertise or knowledge than the one receiving it. Explanations can be appreciated, particularly when someone requests them—such as when you ask a colleague to explain a new service delivery policy to you or when you ask another specialist to help you interpret student performance data. You will find that statements of this type are particularly valuable when you are asked to share your knowledge to clarify a point, elaborate an idea, or answer a question. The use of explanations is also an effective strategy for developing the shared meanings that are so important in effective communication.

Although the ability to give clear explanations is considered an essential competency for teachers, it generally is classified as an instructional rather than interpersonal skill (Johnson & Roellke, 1999; McCaleb, 1987). As an instructional skill, explaining typically involves clearly presenting material and using examples. Some frameworks also include use of advance organizers, demonstrations, paraphrasing, or review of salient points as components of effective explaining. The skills of defining concepts, answering questions, and giving corrective feedback also are considered part of explaining in instruction.

As a school professional, you are familiar with explanations and aware of their value in your professional interactions. Our caution here, however, is that because you are likely to be proficient in giving explanations, you may tend to overuse them. We suggest that you strive to employ them infrequently with colleagues because they tend to represent directive communication more than the two-way transactional communication described in Chapter 8. Explanations are most appropriate when someone provides others with information they have explicitly requested. When uninvited, explanations may have all of the undesirable effects of unsolicited advice.

Advice is a category of information-providing statements intended to guide action by suggesting, hinting, or even commanding that someone take specific actions or accept certain beliefs. *Suggestions* are statements of "gentle advice" offered as possibilities for consideration; they communicate clearly that they are tentative and subject to the evaluation of their recipient. For example, when a colleague suggests to you, "One option might be to consider some of the new materials we just received," he or she is giving you a hint or a tip. Your colleague is simply offering one of potentially many sets of information for your evaluation and is acknowledging that in your role as decision maker you may accept or reject it.

Advice also may be offered as a direct *command* that insists on compliance or cooperation. In many interactions, commands may seem overly directive, such as when someone says, "You will certainly have to change that" or "You need to get some hands-on training." Commands are often received badly. They may remind their recipients of someone's inappropriate exercise of authority over them or of years of parental directives. They often imply that the speaker has greater power than those to whom the command is issued. When any of these things happen, commands are likely to cause resistance and become less effective than other efforts to guide behavior.

However, commands are not always negative, and they do not necessarily imply that the recipient is less powerful or inferior to the speaker. Sometimes they are time-savers, such as when the participants agree that one party has greater expertise than the others in a given area. When such agreement is present it can eliminate the air of arrogance that some people perceive is associated with commands. This situation is illustrated in the following statement made by a physical education teacher, who is telling a special education teacher how to adapt a classroom game so a particular student can participate. In this example, a series of commands may well be the most efficient approach to guiding the action of a colleague.

"First, point to the target and say, 'Throw it there.' Then wait 10 seconds to see if Victor responds. If not, physically prompt him to throw the beanbag."

Like explanations, whether offered as a suggestion or a command, advice is unlikely to be helpful and may well be detrimental to relationships if given to someone who has not requested or otherwise demonstrated an openness to it. Unfortunately, advice is a frequently overused response when people are trying to assist others in problem solving. This should not be difficult to understand in the context of the professional socialization factors we discussed in the first chapter. School professionals are likely to be competent, independent problem solvers, and they may quickly take on the role of designing and presenting solutions as advice when they begin working with others. However, unsolicited advice is often perceived as intrusive and even arrogant. Aphorist Mason Cooley is attributed with saying, "Advice is more agreeable in the mouth than in the ear." Although advice may seem appropriate and helpful when you are formulating it, recipients of this unrequested information are likely to feel defensive and misunderstood. For these reasons, we encourage professionals in collaborative situations to wait until asked before giving advice to other adults.

The communication strategies professionals use in classrooms are generally directive and involve explanations, directions, or even lectures. More interactive strategies are needed for effective communication with adults.

Statements That Seek Information

A second function of the statements you use is to seek or solicit information from others. This function may be accomplished through the use of inflection, commands, and indirect questions. *Inflection,* an element of paralanguage discussed in Chapter 8, is any change in the tone or pitch of one's voice. To illustrate the use of inflection to seek information, imagine these statements spoken with a querying tone of voice that may sound almost like a question.

"The books are no longer available."

"There are no substitute readers."

Commands and *indirect questions* also may be used to request information in conversation. Statements like the following request information without using direct questions. You may notice that the tone changes across these examples. The first, a command, is demanding and does not invite interaction or discussion. The second and third are indirect questions and are more invitational.

"Give us the results of the assessment by Tuesday."

"I wonder what would happen if you scheduled reading earlier."

"I'm quite interested in learning more about that."

Using statements to seek information is an appealing alternative to excessive question asking, as discussed in the next chapter. You can alternate or integrate information-seeking statements with questions to avoid creating an atmosphere of interrogation. Using general statements similar to the preceding examples is particularly valuable when initially exploring an issue.

Information-seeking statements offer a viable alternative to serial questions, but they cannot substitute entirely for questions. Indirect questions and inflection express one's interest and invite others to continue talking, but they often are vague and may not adequately communicate your wish for a response. They seem to be most effective in initiating discussions. As discussions progress and require greater focus, you may find yourself using more focused information-seeking statements, such as commands (e.g., "Tell me which of the students was late") to obtain specific information. To ensure that commands used in such situations are not too demanding in tone, they can be embedded in a series of information-seeking strategies or be softened with a querying inflection. After you have used inflection, commands, and indirect questions to initiate discussions and invite others to share their thoughts and ideas, you will find that you need specific information to understand a situation. At that point, carefully worded and strategic questions become the preferable strategy. Asking questions is addressed in detail in Chapter 10.

Statements That Confirm or Clarify Information

Statements often are used to confirm or clarify information that has already been provided. When used in this way, they may be addressing simultaneously

PUTTING IDEAS INTO PRACTICE

Clarifying and Confirming Information Using Statements

Sometimes people use statements to confirm or clarify information. When used this way, statements are a powerful means of demonstrating that you are listening to others and that you want to understand them.

- *Paraphrasing:* Restate what another has said, using many of the same words.
- *Reflecting:* Restate what another has said but use additional descriptive words to try to capture the affective message as well.
- *Summarizing:* Restate concisely several main points from a preceding or ongoing discussion.
- *Checking:* Restate and often ask for confirmation that the restatement is accurate and that the persons involved have similar perceptions of what has occurred.

the combined purposes of providing information and seeking information. Frequently, statements designed to confirm or clarify are restatements of already available information offered to ensure that participants are developing the common meanings and shared understanding essential for effective communication. Typical ways of clarifying statements are through paraphrasing, reflecting, summarizing, and checking, which are explained next and in Putting Ideas into Practice.

Paraphrasing

In paraphrasing, you restate in your own words what you think another person has just said. Paraphrasing focuses on relatively small units of information that were discussed by just one other individual, and it involves little or no inference. Consider the following example in which a teacher and principal are discussing how to handle a problematic situation that includes the parents of a student with disabilities.

> **Teacher:**   I'm not sure I should meet alone with his parents. We seem to be in conflict all the time.
>
> **Principal:**   You have ongoing conflict with these parents (inflection indicates the tentative nature of this response and suggests a querying attitude).
>
> **Teacher:**   Well, not "ongoing." Actually, it was just once—at our meeting last month. They were furious at me when I told them what his grades were. The father got red in the face, hit the table a couple of times, and left really angry. He won't return any of my phone calls.
>
> **Principal:**   It was only one event, but it's still unresolved and you think they—especially the father—are still angry with you.

Teacher: Yes, but I did get to talk to the mother on the phone. She apologized and explained that her husband has been working two shifts, is really tired, and has been getting angry easily. He also feels guilty because he can't help with homework while he works so much. The mother says he wants to meet with me to see how we can help their son—I'm just not sure.

Principal: Even though the parents seem to have gotten over their anger and say they want to respond constructively, you're still not certain you should meet with them.

Teacher: Yes. It may be calm now, but I've given two tests since our last meeting. He failed both of them. His father's having problems with his temper.

Principal: His father may get angry again if you tell him about the test grades.

Can you see how this example demonstrates how paraphrasing functions to influence the relationship? By accurately restating the main points in the teacher's statements, the principal demonstrated attention to and accurate understanding of what the teacher was relating and thus conveyed interest in the problem as well as in the teacher as a person.

The principal's paraphrasing also helped to clarify the information provided. If any of the principal's restatements had been incorrect, the teacher would have been able to rephrase or modify them. Because the principal's paraphrases were succinct and captured the essence of the teacher's comments, they also helped to focus the discussion and encourage the teacher to examine the situation more closely. This strategy maintained the teacher as the central figure and helped the principal and the teacher establish a shared understanding of the situation. These effects on the relationship may become clearer if you contrast that example with the following alternative:

Teacher: I'm not sure I should meet alone with his parents. We had a falling-out last month.

Principal: I agree. We don't need conflict between parents and staff. Let's have the counselor meet with them instead.

The principal may appear to be supporting the teacher, but such a quick response reveals the principal's tendency to solve problems independently and suggests both lack of concern for the teacher and her perception of the problem as well as lack of respect for the teacher's own resources. Perhaps more important, by contrasting the two examples and their resolutions, you can see how the principal's quick solution or advice in the second example neither solved the problem nor demonstrated respect for the teacher as an independent professional capable of solving a problem with some support.

These examples illustrate how paraphrasing might work and how it compares to a faster, independent problem-solving response from the principal. In reality the teacher probably would be less than satisfied with either of these interactions. Although the first example demonstrated parphrasing responses, it did not end with any sense of resolution. As with the other skills, we are presenting this out of context. For the teacher to have a satisfactory resolution in this situation, paraphrasing would need to be combined with a wide range of other communication skills and the interpersonal problem-solving process described in Chapter 2 would most likely be needed. The importance of planned instruction for paraphrasing and other communication skills is highlighted in A Basis in Research.

Reflecting

Reflection, a clarifying statement more complex than paraphrasing, was popularized by psychologist Carl Rogers (1951) almost 60 years ago. It focuses on circumscribed information provided by a single individual, but it also includes references on the part of the speaker. In reflection, you describe what another person has said and try to capture the affective meaning of the message. Because you cannot observe another's feelings, you examine the verbal and nonverbal information provided in both the overt and covert aspects of the communication and infer what this information communicates about the emotional meaning. Reflection is a way of making explicit the information that is being conveyed implicitly during interaction. It demonstrates that you understand another's feelings, as the following conversation illustrates. Imagine that the previous example of the teacher and principal discussing an angry father ends like this.

> **Teacher:**   Yes. It may be calm now, but I've given two tests since our last meeting (heavy sigh). He failed both of them (laughs and looks away). His father's having problems with his temper.
>
> **Principal:**   His father may get angry again if you tell him about the test grades. From your laughter I get the sense that you're anxious about this.
>
> **Teacher:**   Yes, I met another angry father alone last year. He was really a bully and he actually pushed me. I know he was *trying* to scare me, and he was successful. I'm afraid to meet alone with people like that. Can you meet with us?
>
> **Principal:**   His father may get angry again and possibly even pose a physical threat. It sounds as if you'll feel safer if someone could meet with you and the parents. I'm quite sure I'm available, but if not, can we reschedule the meeting?

In this example, the principal, in her own words, restated the teacher's messages and reflected the teacher's feelings, thus conveying her understanding of the situation from the teacher's point of view. This response is often integral in building relationships and in promoting a sense of trust because it conveys that the speaker's ideas and feelings are understood and valued. In this way the principal has validated, not diminished, the teacher's experience.

These illustrations of reflection are presented out of context and can only suggest how reflection functions. In fact, our examples may unintentionally suggest that reflection is a simple type of verbal statement. Although the wording may be simple, accurately perceiving and reflecting someone's verbal and nonverbal messages is an extremely complex endeavor.

A BASIS IN RESEARCH

Teaching Communication Skills

Throughout this book, communication skills have been emphasized as essential tools for collaboration. There is an intuitive logic to this emphasis—that is, building effective professional relationships would clearly seem to require clear and consistent interaction—but research supports it as well. Bulach (2003) investigated whether providing direct instruction and related practice on communication skills to professionals learning to be school administrators would have an impact on their sense of openness and trust (factors noted in Chapter 1 as being emergent characteristics of collaboration). A total of 17 graduate students participated in an eight-week course with a behaviorally based curriculum to teach both verbal and nonverbal communication skills as well as conflict resolution skills and those for distributing power. Prior to beginning the course and again at the end of it, the students completed a valid and reliable survey designed to measure openness and trust.

Although the results obtained by Bulach were not statistically significant, a fact not surprising given the small number of participants in his study and the relatively short period of time over which it occurred, the students' responses moved in a positive direction on all but one aspect of openness and trust, and the one negative change (on the factor of character) was minimal (.01 on a 5-point scale). Students' reactions to the course were quite positive (4.7 on a 5-point scale for overall quality of the course), and they indicated that the course was valuable in terms of their professional preparation. The materials rated most highly in the course were those on interpersonal communication.

Bulach concluded that larger scale studies on this type of professional preparation are needed, and he encouraged other universities to incorporate it in their programs. His message might be expanded to suggest that such coursework should be shared by diverse groups of professionals, including teachers, administrators, related services personnel, and others.

Source: Based on C. R. Bulach, "The impact of human relations training on levels of openness and trust," *Research for Educational Reform, 8*(4) (2003): 43–57.

When you reflect accurately, you convey understanding of another person's thoughts, feelings, and experiences; in other words, you *empathize*. Understanding accompanied by congruent nonverbal behavior that conveys an intent to help someone deal with a problem is referred to as *empathic listening* (Gamble & Gamble, 2005; Rogers & Farson, 1981; Trenholm & Jensen, 2004). When you convey empathy through reflection and supportive nonverbal behaviors, you help establish trust in your relationship with others. Reflection has other advantages as well. When you hear your own messages reflected it may give you the opportunity to consider complex thoughts a little longer and may allow you to have a better understanding of your own experiences. However, as with learning most new skills, there are pitfalls to be avoided, which are discussed in Putting Ideas into Practice.

It is important to recognize that reflection does not go very far beyond the speaker's overt messages. Its intention is not to explain anything new to the speaker. Reflection is thus distinguished from interpretation, which does go beyond the information the speaker has presented. *Interpretation* attempts to explain the speaker's experience in terms of a theory or a level of understanding beyond what the speaker knows. As Goodman (1978) points out, interpretation is usually an attempt to show an understanding of the speaker that is better than the speaker's self-understanding. Consider this alternative response to the teacher's concern about meeting with an angry parent.

> **Principal:**   You're afraid the father will be angry and violent. This is a lot like your conflict with many of the male teachers. You seem to be easily threatened by men.

This example is exagerated to emphasize the potentially intrusive nature of this type of response and to support our contention that interpretation should be used very little, if at all, between school professionals in work settings. Interpretation may be very appropriate in more help-oriented or therapist–client relationships, but interpretation as described here goes beyond the scope of what is appropriate between colleagues.

Summarizing

Summarizing consists of one or more statements that restate, in concise form, several preceding statements made by the individuals involved in the interaction. It is a means of ensuring that all involved individuals understand what has been said, and it functions in much the same way as a summary section at the end of a lengthy piece of expository text. Summarizing differs from paraphrasing in at least two significant ways. When you paraphrase, you are simply restating what one other person has just said. Paraphrasing is relatively immediate and it is a response to a discrete, self-contained piece of information. On the other hand, summarizing is not as immediate and it is a response to several pieces of information, often presented by more than one participant. The following examples of summarizing heard at team meetings illustrate this point:

> "Let's see if we agree on the major points. Mrs. Cardenas, you've said you're concerned about Tom's disruptive and off-task behavior in your math class. Mr. O'Reilly said Tom's behavior is appropriate but wants him to have an extra period of art since he does so well in that class. And, Tom, you want to drop the math class until next semester because you feel like you're too far behind to ever catch up. Does anyone want to correct anything or add comments?"

It seems we've considered all the main issues. Cathy, you've described your efforts to implement peer tutoring, self-instructional materials, and

PUTTING IDEAS INTO PRACTICE

Avoiding Pitfalls in Practicing Empathic Listening

Empathy is an important element in developing trust in a relationship. By listening carefully and reflecting accurately the other's words, feelings, thoughts, and situations, you express empathy and a desire to help. Empathic responses are helpful to the speaker in that they encourage an authentic exploration of the problem or situation that has been presented. Yet it is not uncommon for those in the helping professions to undermine their own efforts at expressing empathy, even though they have the best of intentions. This is especially true as they are beginning to learn the skills of empathic listening.

Inexperienced communicators may invalidate another's experience through misguided efforts to provide encouragement and lessen the person's despair. Mancillas (2005) suggests that responses such as the following invalidate the speaker's experience and should be avoided:

1. *Finding the silver lining.* Statements such as "At least you've still got a job" or "At least the child wasn't seriously hurt" rarely allow the speaker to feel truly understood. The statement detracts from understanding how the speaker experienced the situation.

2. *Being overly optimistic.* Although seemingly supportive, some statements may interfere with the speaker's willingness to reveal his true concerns by trivializing the situation through identification of a relatively small positive aspect. "How fantastic for you! Now you have extra time for collaborating with the English teachers" is less likely to console a speaker than to invalidate his distress about having the math teacher refuse to co-teach with him.

3. *Offering blind reassurance.* It is appropriate to offer the speaker hope that a situation may be improved, but to offer assurances that "everything will improve" is dangerous because it cannot be guaranteed.

4. *Engaging in mind reading.* Although motivated by the desire to encourage or support the speaker, "mind-reading" comments invalidate the speaker's experience and interfere with efforts at deeper understanding. Such comments include "I know just how you feel," "Your strength is inspiring," and "I understand what that's like."

Source: Based on A. Mancillas, "Empathic invalidations," *Counseling Today* (October 2005): 9, 19.

computer-based activities in the classroom. Despite all the planning you and the grade-level team have done, Yanina still requires too much assistance to work independently in your classroom. And Hank, you've seen Yanina work semi-independently with the computer when you sit near her, and you'd like to try to provide some in-class assistance. Have I missed anything?"

Summarizing is very helpful in confirming information and ensuring that participants have a shared understanding of the discussion.

Checking

Checking—the clarifying or confirming function of communication—sometimes is referred to as *perception checking* or *checking for accuracy.* All of these referents have the same purpose as we have described for clarifying. We mention checking here and again in Chapter 10 because this function so frequently is addressed through combining a statement and a question. In fact, if paraphrasing, reflecting, and summarizing are to be maximally effective, they themselves will be checked, or followed up with a question, to ensure agreement and accuracy. The final questions in the two preceding examples of summarizing are illustrations of checking.

Giving Verbal Feedback

In Chapter 8 we described the communication process as one in which communicators simultaneously send and receive messages as they interact, and so it is not possible to communicate without feedback. In the strictest sense, all transactional communication—whether verbal statements, questions, or nonverbal messages—is feedback. This kind of feedback is often not intentional, but it provides important information and often leads to changes in behaviors of the participants. In this chapter our focus is on intentional verbal feedback as a skill that should be purposefully developed and used by school professionals.

Although you will use statements throughout your interactions, one specific situation in which they will be relied on extensively is when you provide verbal feedback to others. And since effectively giving feedback is an essential but often poorly applied communication skill, the ideas in this section should provide opportunities to practice both your general skill for making statements and their specific application in giving feedback. Most simply, *feedback* is providing others with information about their behaviors or performance. It can be given for many different purposes, including the following:

1. Providing objective information about observed behaviors of others or observed conditions

2. Providing information about the impressions or feelings that these behaviors or conditions cause

3. Clarifying what the observed behaviors or conditions might mean or signify to the individual involved

Characteristics of Effective Interpersonal Feedback

To collaborate successfully with others, you will need to be adept at giving effective feedback. You also will want to learn to solicit and accept feedback from others as a means of securing valuable information about your own communication behaviors and about your collaborative relationships. This is true whether your collaboration is aimed at helping each other develop and refine the skills presented in this text or targeted at work-related activities.

Feedback has a clear set of characteristics. It should be (1) descriptive, (2) specific, (3) directed toward changeable behaviors and situations, (4) concise, and (5) checked for clarity. Any effective feedback statement includes all of these characteristics.

Descriptive Feedback Rather than Evaluative or Advisory

An individual is more likely to listen when someone simply describes what has been observed. As noted earlier, descriptive information is nonthreatening and nonjudgmental. The implication of this for feedback is depicted in the following example:

Say: "You told them to sit quietly and line up. Some students went to the door and others went to sit in their seats."

Rather than: "You confuse the students with your directions."

Or: "You shouldn't give two contradictory directions at the same time."

Or: "Have you tried giving one direction at a time?"

When you describe a personal observation, the other individual is free to use the information or not, as he or she sees fit. On the other hand, evaluative or advisory feedback conveys that the other person should take action or change. This is likely to cause the person to feel defensive and criticized rather than willing to make a change.

As you may have surmised, avoiding judgmental statements requires the elimination of both negative and positive comments. The following statements might easily be seen as evaluative and are likely to be threatening to the person hearing them:

"You weren't effective with that activity."

"Your activity sequence doesn't seem to work."

Equally important, however, is the fact that positive comments also convey a judgment. For example:

"You did good work when you . . ."

"You do such a good job with . . ."

Individuals who make positive judgments are likely also to make negative ones. The person receiving the feedback is justified in assuming that those who give praise or compliments also make critical evaluations, whether they are stated openly or not.

Specific Feedback Rather than General

Descriptions of specific behaviors are more easily understood than are general comments. "You lost it when he got out of his seat again" communicates much less than "When he got out of his seat that last time, you responded very quickly and raised your voice as you told him to sit down. As emphasized in Chapter 8, specific and concrete language helps ensure clear communication.

Feedback Directed toward Changeable Behaviors or Situations

In order for feedback to be useful, it needs to be directed at something the receiver can control or do something about. Feedback directed toward an attribute or situation the receiver cannot control generally is pointless and likely to interfere with effective communication. Physical traits, such as height, age, and sex, and situational factors, such as the size of the room and the administrator's leadership style, are not behaviors that an individual can change. Telling someone that his age and physical appearance make it hard to talk to him could be more detrimental than helpful. On the other hand, information such as "You were busy filing papers when I was talking to you" or "I notice that you usually look at the desk when I'm talking" is information that may be acted on if one chooses. You only increase others' frustration when you remind them of some attribute that cannot be changed.

Concise Feedback

Concise feedback is easier to understand than feedback that contains extraneous detail or information. When first learning to give feedback, you may feel obligated to give very detailed information or to make many statements. Keep in mind that more is not necessarily better with feedback; too much information or too much verbiage, irrelevant information, and redundancy detract from the main message. For example, compare the following two feedback statements. Which is more likely to help a teacher understand the colleague's confusion?

"In terms of your language, I mean the words you used, you kept mentioning complex and technical words that I hadn't ever heard. The vocabulary was too specialized for me. I didn't know what all your vocabulary meant so I kept missing your main points. Everything has to be explained well or I get really frustrated and close out everything you say. Then I can't help the kids in their work."

"When you used technical terms I got lost. It would help me if you would define your terms and make your point again."

Feedback Checked to Ensure Clear Communication

Perceptions of any event usually vary among individuals. Several people may participate in the same situation and yet experience it differently. Similarly, when you give feedback, the receiver may not receive the information the way it was intended. Although most of our examples of characteristics of effective feedback have focused on statements, questions often are needed to check for accuracy. An effective method for checking others' understanding of the feedback you have given is to ask them to paraphrase your feedback to see if it corresponds to what you intended. For example, you might say,

"I'm concerned about whether I'm communicating clearly. Would you summarize what you've understood me to say?"

Frequently when receiving feedback, the person will spontaneously confirm or appear to understand the feedback with a general comment, such as "Yes, I did do that" or "That's right." In this situation it may still be advisable to check for understanding. This checking might be done by rephrasing or questioning as shown here:

Rephrasing: "So, it's correct to say that you were reinforcing that behavior?"

Questioning: "You said, 'That's right.' Which particular observations were correct?"

You also may want to check the accuracy of your observations that are the subject of your feedback, particularly if you are uncertain about what you observed. In checking for accuracy you might ask if the receiver agrees with your description of the observation. Two examples follow:

"It seemed to me that you were asking James questions more frequently than you were the others. Would you agree with that?"

"Does it seem accurate to you that you asked James more questions than you asked the others?"

Guidelines for Giving Effective Feedback

We have discussed and provided examples of the characteristics of effective feedback statements. Regardless of how well worded the feedback is, it will have little value if its delivery is not effective. Four guidelines for providing feedback are extremely important. Feedback should be (1) solicited, (2) direct, (3) culturally sensitive, and (4) well timed.

Before you read about these guidelines, refer back to the interaction between Rory and James described in the beginning of the chapter. How effective was the feedback provided? How well were these guidelines followed?

Solicited Feedback Rather than Imposed

Feedback, like advice and explanations, is most effective when someone has requested it. An individual who requests feedback is more likely to use it than one on whom feedback is imposed. Unsolicited feedback may make the receiver feel defensive and assume a "And you're telling me this because . . . ?" attitude. When you first begin to work collaboratively with a colleague, you should not assume that person actually wants feedback. One way to avoid ineffective interactions is to wait for your colleague to provide an opportunity for you to give feedback. Then you need merely to confirm the request. The most direct way of ensuring that your colleague wants the feedback you believe he has requested is to respond to his apparent request with a question, such as, "Are you asking for my feedback?" or "Is that something you want to know more about?" The following excerpt illustrates this:

> *Statement:* "I don't know why Jimmy doesn't follow directions. Do you think I'm not giving them clearly? How can I be more successful with him?"

Unsolicited feedback is often unwelcome and therefore not very helpful.

Response: "It sounds like you'd like to examine how you give directions. Would it be helpful if I shared my observations on that?"

Frequently your colleague will not ask for feedback and you will face the prerequisite task of finding a way to be invited to provide it. Depending on the openness and attitude of that colleague, you may emphasize different aspects of the situation and use different communication skills to set the stage for giving feedback. In Chapter 4 we provided guidelines for ensuring that you and your co-teacher give each other feedback. Some of those should be useful in any collaborative relationship.

Direct Feedback Rather than Indirect

Feedback is most effective when it is given directly to the person who can use it by the person who has made some observation. For example, instead of asking the principal to tell your co-teacher about ineffective teaching behavior, generally you should tell him or her personally. Similarly, although many school professionals write notes to communicate with other adults, notes also may decrease the effectiveness of feedback. Indirect feedback is more easily misinterpreted than is feedback given directly to the person involved. This is due in part to the lack of transactional communication in notes. The giver cannot check the feedback for accuracy, and the receiver cannot adequately clarify it.

Culturally Sensitive Feedback

In Chapter 8 cultural influences on communication were outlined. Collectivistic cultures were described as highly contextual, comfortable with silence, often indirect, and characteristically balanced in turn taking. Based on that distinction some strategies are useful in all situations in which you give feedback but may make giving and receiving feedback more comfortable in cross-cultural situations.

We suggest that you begin a session or conversation by creating a welcoming environment with salutations and inquiries about the individual's well-being. Demonstration of interest in and respect for the other is an important element of the relationship. Ensure that the other person has time for the interaction and will be able to participate in discussing and responding to the feedback.

In presenting the observations, include many contextual examples and descriptions. Use the same communication skills you would in any feedback meeting, but deliberately insert pauses and short periods of silence to allow the other to speak, clarify, or question. We also suggest that you consider incorporating reflection to provide the other with feedback about subtle cues and behaviors observed. This will help avoid any misperceptions of or impressions based on cultural components.

Well-Timed Feedback

The immediacy of feedback is a subject of considerable attention in the research on learning, particularly in reference to learning new skills. Corrective feedback is most beneficial to learners when it is given immediately following the relevant event or behavior. This is not always possible or appropriate for interpersonal feedback, partly because it is not necessarily meant to be corrective or instructional in nature. But several guidelines can help you determine the appropriate timing for feedback.

You should always ask yourself, "Is now the best time to give feedback?" If your colleague is extremely busy or rushed, the feedback may seem like an irritating intrusion. Or if some event has left your colleague upset and confused, immediate feedback may be seen as unduly demanding or even critical. Our recommendation is to provide feedback as soon as appropriate, not only so that it is recent but also so that it demonstrates your sensitivity to your colleague's receptiveness.

When you find you must delay giving feedback, you should use recent examples in your feedback statement. Your receiving colleague is more likely to understand and benefit from recent examples than from those that are more distant and possibly forgotten. The more time that passes between the event and the feedback, the less vivid the event will be in your colleague's memory.

In general, when giving feedback to others, ask yourself these questions.

- Will this person understand me?
- Will this person be able to accept my feedback?
- Will this person be able to use the information?

The most significant consideration is that feedback be constructive to the recipient. What you are about to say should be helpful and appreciated by this person. These considerations, along with use of the other characteristics and strategies we have presented, should maximize the effectiveness of the feedback you give to others.

Summary

Statements are the primary verbal means of providing information to others. Information may be overt or covert, and inferences are involved in communicating covert information. Statements that describe events or experiences and those that attempt to guide action are the most frequent forms of statements that provide information. A second purpose of statements is to seek information, often through commands or indirect questions. Confirming or clarifying information is the final purpose of statements and frequently is achieved through paraphrasing, reflecting, summarizing, or checking.

A communication skill that relies largely on statements—giving interpersonal feedback—illustrates several principles of communication. Characteristics of effective feedback include that it is descriptive, specific, directed toward changeable behaviors and situations, concise, and checked for clarity. In addition, for feedback to be maximally effective, it should be solicited, direct, culturally sensitive, and well timed.

Activities and Assignments

1. Think of a problem with a student one of your colleagues has mentioned. Imagine an interaction in which you try to assist your colleague to solve the problem. Write down 8 to 10 statements you would probably make, then classify the purpose and format of each. Do you use certain types of statements more than others? What is the primary purpose of most of the statements you wrote? Is this what you believe is the best approach to helping someone solve a problem? If you find you are not using an appropriate range, review your responses to these questions and construct different types of statements.

2. Explain to a colleague or a parent that you are trying to improve your verbal communication skills, and ask permission to tape-record an interaction with him or her. Review your tape and classify each statement according to its purpose and format. Consider which statements could be improved and write improved versions. Discuss your tape and written responses with a classmate or colleague.

3. We have stressed that advice and feedback are not likely to have much impact unless the person receiving this information has requested it or is at least open to receiving it. Meet with a colleague or classmate and discuss ways to assess someone's openness to hearing feedback or advice. Then reflect on ways in which you might get an individual to "invite" your feedback.

4. Record a television drama and practice paraphrasing, reflecting, and summarizing the conversations. Invite a classmate to join you, and compare notes. You also can use this same recording to practice giving feedback.

5. Inferential statements often are necessary, but they are problematic when you act as if the inferences are facts. It is important to be able to distinguish between the two. Review each of the following statements and consider the extent to which each involves inference or fact. After you complete your assessment, discuss the results with a colleague. How can you be absolutely certain if a statement is factual?

    "His smile conveyed his sense of pride in his accomplishment."
    "He was five minutes late but came in the back door so we wouldn't realize it."
    "She finished her poetry piece after 20 minutes, turned it in, and began her homework."
    "The girls' scores on the test are, on average, 8 percent higher than that of the boys."
    "Boys are just as smart as girls."
    "His mother is ill-mannered and hostile toward authority figures."

6. Critique each of the following examples to determine if they include the characteristics for effective feedback. Revise statements as necessary to include all characteristics.

    "After you smiled and said, 'Okay,' Juan looked very relieved. Then when you nodded for him to join the group, a big smile covered his face. Is that what you observed too?"

"You dealt with James better today. He's advanced a lot in math and you seem to be tolerating his antics better."

"You've really managed to get Sandy to behave in class. You should be very proud of yourself for what you've accomplished!"

7. Keep an observation log for a week and record two or three examples of ways in which you observe colleagues giving professional information to one another. For each observation, describe ways in which statements were used to provide, seek, or clarify information. Identify and describe both good and bad examples.

For Further Reading

Brammer, L. M., & MacDonald, G. (2003). *The helping relationship: Process and skills* (8th ed.). Boston: Allyn & Bacon.

Cochran, J. L., & Cochran, N. H. (2006). *The heart of counseling: A guide to developing therapeutic relationships.* Belmont, CA: Wadsworth.

DeVito, J. A. (2006). *Human communication: The basic course* (10th ed.). Boston: Allyn & Bacon.

Egan, G. (2006). *Essentials of skilled helping: Managing problems, developing opportunities.* Belmont, CA: Wadsworth.

Mancillas, A. (2005, October). Empathic invalidations. *Counseling Today,* pp. 9, 19.

Okun, B. (2002). *Effective helping: Interviewing and counseling techniques* (6th ed.). Pacific Grove, CA: Brooks/Cole.

Verderber, R. F., & Verderber, S. K. (2005). *Communicate!* (11th ed.). Belmont, CA: Wadsworth.

CHAPTER 10

Asking Questions

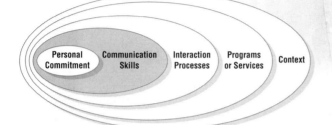

Connections

In many ways Chapter 10 is analogous to Chapter 9. It focuses on a specific type of verbal communication skill—asking questions—and relates it to communication information presented in earlier chapters. Strategies for enhancing your skill in asking questions are presented, and interviewing is outlined as a common context in which question-asking skills are used. As with statements, the skill of asking questions effectively forms a set of tools that can foster your collaborative work.

Learner Objectives

After reading this chapter you will be able to:

1. Describe the major purposes of questions.
2. Distinguish among different formats of questions, including open/closed, direct/indirect, and single/multiple formats.
3. Analyze questions and modify them as needed to increase their degree of concreteness.
4. Describe strategies that facilitate effective question asking.
5. Delineate the purpose of interviews.
6. Outline activities that increase the effectiveness of interviews.

Graham is a little anxious as he begins his interaction with Ms. Martinez, Shawn's mother. After introductions and a conversation about the significant gains in reading that Shawn has made this year, Graham begins to address the matter of behavior. He describes Shawn as a very active student who seems to talk out frequently and who sometimes reacts physically before he thinks through his actions. He says to Ms. Martinez, "My observations of Shawn have made me curious about how he acts at home. When Shawn is in a situation where he is supposed to be quiet—like in the doctor's office or at church—how does he behave?" Ms. Martinez describes behaviors similar to those noticed at school, and then Graham asks, "What do you find is effective in reacting to Shawn's behavior?" As the discussion continues and Ms. Martinez discusses her strategies for responding to Shawn's behavior, Graham decides to move to a different topic to gain additional information. He begins by saying, "Ms. Martinez, what you're describing is similar to what we've been seeing with Shawn at school, and your strategies are helpful for understanding Shawn better. One thing that interests me is that you mentioned that he really enjoys fishing; I didn't know that, and perhaps fishing could give us ideas for how to encourage school behavior. Where does he go fishing?" Ms. Martinez becomes animated as she describes the weekend fishing trips that Shawn takes with his father and uncle.

Introduction

Considered "the most popular piece of language" (Goodman & Esterly, 1990), questions are a primary means of verbally soliciting information during interactions, including collaborative ones. They are crucial at the outset of interpersonal problem solving when they are used to elicit pertinent information, and they continue to be essential throughout the process for clarifying information and sharing ideas and understandings. Skillful use of questions can mean the difference between an interaction that is successful and one fraught with misperceptions and miscommunication.

Because questions are used in casual conversation and informal collaborative interactions as well as in more formal situations such as meetings and interviews, mastering the skill of asking well-phrased, appropriate questions should be a priority. This is especially true for teachers who may have to learn to modify existing behaviors because many of the question-asking techniques they learned during their professional preparation are focused on querying students for instructional purposes—a communication situation that differs significantly from interacting collaboratively with other professionals and parents.

As with any verbal communication, the way a person phrases a question will greatly affect the quality of response received. Therefore, prior to asking a question, you should decide what type of response you are seeking and what type of question would best elicit that information; then you can phrase your questions accordingly. At the same time, you should strive to clarify your questions and also embed them within your interaction processes such as problem solving, negotiation, or interviews. In this chapter we focus on the interviewing process as one common question-asking context.

Purposes of Questions

As you learned in Chapter 8, virtually all of your communication with others both provides information to them and enables you to gather information from them. When you look more closely at how questions are used in interactions, you will find that they can be categorized as having one of three primary intentions or purposes: (1) to seek information, (2) to provide information, and (3) to clarify or confirm information. These intentions parallel those for statements addressed in Chapter 9. Because these purposes have been described in detail, in that chapter, they are treated here only briefly.

Questions That Seek Information

The most straightforward function of questions is to query others for information. You often ask querying questions when your primary purpose is to seek information about a topic on which you do not have sufficient experience or knowledge. You might ask whether a student's program is effective, what steps need to be taken to arrange a new service for a student, or when the next team meeting will be. All of these questions have information seeking as their foundation, as do these examples.

- What are your professional development goals for this school year?
- Which instructional strategies have you used with him?
- What led the parents to involve an independent evaluator?
- How do you think her feelings will influence her decision?

Seeking information may be the central purpose in many of your question-asking efforts, but success in actually obtaining the information you want is not always as straightforward. In fact, some of your efforts to gain specific information through questioning may be unsuccessful or frustrating. Throughout this chapter we suggest ways to make your questioning efforts more effective, but some particularly helpful guiding principles that may help you understand your information needs and design appropriate questions are summarized in Putting Ideas into Practice on page 264.

Questions That Provide Information

Another function of some of the questions you ask may be to provide information to the persons with whom you are interacting (Johnson & Johnson, 2006; Trenholm & Jensen, 2004). As with statements, this often is accomplished by making evaluations or by attempting to guide the action of others by giving suggestions or advice. Evaluative questions, although seemingly constructed to query and spoken with a questioning inflection, typically convey far more information than they elicit. For example, think about the impact of these questions.

"What about the resistance you are going to get from the other teachers?"

"Whatever would make you think that such an intervention would work with a kid like Shannon?"

PUTTING IDEAS INTO PRACTICE

Questioning Yourself

Reflection and introspection are important activities for the good communicator. Understanding your own motivations and opinions and how they influence your communication is important to your success. Try questioning yourself to assess if your personal perspective or frame of reference may interfere with the success of your communication. Consider the following questions:

- What are my feelings about the situation?
- What is my opinion?
- What assumptions am I making about the person or situation?

Questioning yourself is also useful for planning the questions you will ask others.

- What is the goal of this interaction?
- How much do I really understand about the situation?
- What information do I need?
- How will the person respond to different approaches I could use to get the information we need?
- What will I do with this information?

"What do you think would happen if you actually followed through on our agreement and asked Maria's parents to take her for a psychological assessment?"

"You still haven't talked to his parents, have you?"

"Why would you even want to attempt that type of intervention?"

Questions that evaluate the behavior, actions, or thinking of another have limited value in interactions. Did you find yourself feeling defensive in response to some of the questions just presented? If so, your reaction is a common one to questions that imply you have not done or thought enough about a situation.

Some of the questions you ask may convey an even stronger message than those just illustrated. Such questions are actually direct commands or advice with a querying format attached as an apparent afterthought. Like statements that are meant to guide others, these questions are used to direct or advise a person to take an action or to respond to a situation in a prescribed manner. For example, consider these questions.

"You'll take care of the book orders, won't you?"

"Why don't you try giving him only one task at a time?"

As with questions that evaluate, you should rarely use questions that advise. They, too, may be perceived as negative by respondents. For one thing, advisory

Communication is not always clear. Questions are useful tools for clarifying or confirming what is meant.

questions are sometimes viewed as dishonest. If the speaker has advice to give, why disguise it as a question? The exception to this situation is when a question format is used to convey a tentative suggestion or gentle piece of advice, such as "Would parent conferencing or a meeting with the school counselor help in any way?" A second negative aspect of an advisory question is that it tends to put others "on the spot" because it usually implies that there is only one right answer to give—and that right answer has been predetermined by the person asking the question. Generally, if your purpose is to convey information, you should do so with statements, not with questions.

Questions That Clarify or Confirm Information

Sometimes people ask clarifying questions to confirm information that they already have obtained but may not fully understand. For example:

"Do I understand you correctly that Mohammed has missed three classes this week?"

"Are you saying that you favor the tutoring option over the after-school program?"

"What indications led you to believe that his parents are aware of the problem?"

As you strive to develop the shared meaning that is so important in interpersonal communication, questions that clarify information through confirmation constitute an extremely valuable strategy. They allow you to check your perception of the information being shared with your colleague's perception of that same information. Clarifying questions may serve the same purpose as paraphrasing or reflecting. In fact, they often are used in conjunction with these types of statements. After paraphrasing information provided by a colleague, you may check your mutual understanding with a brief confirming question such as, "Did I describe your situation correctly?" or "Have I summarized your position correctly?"

Characteristics of Questions

In addition to understanding the purposes of questions, your skill in using questions relies on your ability to recognize and strategically make use of their various characteristics. Considering aspects of format and the degree of concreteness will help you phrase your questions effectively and efficiently.

Question Format

An essential characteristic of questions is their *format,* the way in which words are used and sequenced to create the question. Although format is not usually a critical dimension of the statements someone makes during interactions, it is very important for the information-seeking purpose of questions. You may receive widely varying responses to questions based simply on how you word them (Brammer & MacDonald, 2003).

Direct/Indirect

Most questions use a *direct* format. That is, the question is phrased as an interrogative and, if written, would end in a question mark. All of the examples in the previous section were direct questions.

An alternative question-asking format is the *indirect* question. In this format, it is not completely clear that anyone is being queried, since the question is phrased as a statement, not as a question (Hackett & Martin, 1993; Snow, Zurcher, & Sjoberg, 1982). This topic was mentioned in Chapter 9 (see "Statements That Seek Information"). Perhaps you have used indirect questions similar to these. Compare them to the direct questions that follow them.

Indirect: "I wonder what would happen if we included Jorge in the community-based training program."

Direct: "What would happen if we included Jorge in the community-based training program?"

Indirect: "I would like to know if it would work out to ask Amy's parents to talk to the other parents about accessing support groups."

Direct: "What would be the effect of asking Amy's parents to talk to the other parents about accessing support groups?"

Asking indirect questions may be appropriate when you are unsure whether a direct question would offend another person. Notice that by using the first-person singular pronoun ("I wonder"; "I would like to know"), the implied responsibility for the idea contained in the question stays with the question asker; the person answering the question need not assume ownership for the idea expressed. In contrast, when you ask direct questions, you turn responsibility for the response to the other person. Thus, in awkward or uncomfortable situations, or in other cases in which you want to be certain you are not imposing a potentially unwanted idea, an indirect format may be preferable. Figure 10.1 includes additional examples of indirect question starters.

However, an indirect question format also carries a risk. Your question could be perceived by the other person as rhetorical; if this occurs you may not receive a response. You should then rephrase the question to be direct if you judge that a response is required.

Open/Closed

An *open question* is defined as one for which an infinite range of responses is possible (Bloor, Frankland, Thomas, & Robson, 2001; Johnson, 2006). For example, if you ask a colleague, "How did things go today?" you cannot predict the nature of the response you will receive. Other examples of open questions are as follows:

"What kinds of behaviors are you considering to be disruptive?"

"How could I assist you with Mario?"

Figure 10.1 Indirect Question Starters

Asking indirect questions is often challenging for school professionals because in your role as teacher, administrator, or special services provider, you are accustomed to asking direct questions. It may take some practice to change to this question style. Below is a menu of "starters" that should help you to generate indirect questions.

"I'm wondering how you responded to ..."

"I'm getting the feeling that ..."

"I wonder whether ..."

"I can't remember how ..."

"It would be helpful if we knew ..."

"I'd like to know ..."

"I don't understand what ..."

Sometimes you want to encourage others to continue speaking or to obtain their perception of an event or situation without imposing any limits to their responses. In such instances an open question is the best choice.

In contrast, a *closed question* is one in which the range of responses is limited either explicitly or implicitly (Gamble & Gamble, 2005; Johnson, 2006). First, you may explicitly limit the range by specifying the response options in the questions, as in the following examples:

"Would you prefer to have me observe during math, reading, or science?"

"Is Nirukshi older or younger than the others in his group?"

"Does Jennifer have no friends, just one friend, or several friends on the team?"

A second way in which you may limit response options is by making them implicit in the wording of the question. Analyze these examples.

"May I observe during the reading period today?"

"How old is Nirukshi?"

"How many friends does Jennifer have on the team?"

In the first example, the implicit limit on the response is yes or no. In the second, the limit is set because there is only one correct answer. In the third, the limit is established by the assumption that there is a finite number of students on the team with whom Jennifer may have friendships.

One basis for deciding whether to use open or closed questions should be whether you are seeking an elaborated response or a simple one. Closed questions may be used to limit the scope of the conversation or confirm information. However, sometimes you will find that even though you ask a closed question, you receive an elaborated response, such as when the question "Has Lupita's time management improved?" launches a five-minute description of her latest rash of missed classes and incomplete work. Conversely, even an open question such as "What does Paul say about school when he's at home?" may elicit only the very narrow answer "Nothing." Your choice of open or closed question format nevertheless establishes general parameters for the type of response you hope to receive.

Another consideration in choosing between open and closed formats is the nature of your relationship with the person from whom you are seeking information. Sometimes your concern about building a relationship will be as great as or greater than your need for specific information. In these cases, you may decide to ask open questions that allow your colleague to offer freely any information he or she wishes to share. When open questions are used, the person is less likely to infer that certain correct answers or precise responses are needed. Questioning only with closed questions may cause the person being queried to feel that he or she is being tested, since the range of appropriate responses is limited. Such a situation may cause the person to become defensive and less forthcoming.

Figure 10.2	Examples of Open/Closed and Direct/Indirect Question Formats	

	Open	**Closed**
Direct	What is your opinion of Fred's performance in math?	What was Fred's score on the math section of the test?
Indirect	I'm interested in knowing more about Fred's performance in math.	It would be helpful if you would tell us Fred's score on the math section of the test.

Note too that you can combine the open/closed characteristic of questions with the direct/indirect dimension in order to create even more options for asking questions. This idea is illustrated in Figure 10.2.

Single/Multiple

Another element of how you format your questions concerns the number of questions you ask at one time (Hargie, Saunders, & Dickson, 1994; Ivey & Ivey, 2003). In general, *single* questions are preferable to *multiple* questions. Which of these question-asking examples is likely to result in the most constructive interchange?

"When you think about the changes we've been making for Erminia over the past couple of weeks, which ones seem most responsible for the improvement in her behavior?"

"What do you think of the changes we've made for Erminia over the past couple of weeks? Do you agree that they're really improving her behavior? Which ones do you think have been most effective?"

In the first example, one well-phrased question is asked and the other person has the option of sharing ideas and perceptions. In the second example, three questions are asked and the respondent is likely left wondering which one to answer.

Multiple questions occur for several reasons. First, perhaps you have the habit of beginning to talk even while you are still mentally phrasing your question. This could cause you to need several tries to arrive finally at the question you intended. Another cause of multiple questions relates to specificity. You may first ask a vague question, then realize that it will not elicit the specific information you intended, and so you then try again and perhaps again. A third reason multiple questions occur is that individuals may conversationally rush past the person with whom they are speaking. That is, they ask at one time an entire series of questions they wish to have answered. Examples of these types of multiple questions follow.

■ *Thinking and talking at the same time.* "Is Shiva mastering her math facts? How about her problem solving? Is she turning in her math homework? Overall, how successful is Shiva in her math class?"

- *Moving from vague to focused questions.* "How is Changnam doing? How has he adjusted to his vocational program? What issues are still coming up in having Changnam work with his job coach?"
- *Asking a series of related questions at one time.* "What are the highest needs the parents listed on the community services questionnaire? What resources do we have available for meeting their needs? When can we meet to begin planning the partnership program for next year?"

Regardless of the reason for multiple questions, when you use them you leave your interaction partner unsure how to respond. That person may wonder which question you really meant to have addressed. Or the person may simply answer the single question that was best remembered, often the first or last question asked. Alternatively, you may put him or her in the position of being suspicious or defensive, since multiple questions sometimes convey the impression that you are "fishing" for information.

Our simple and firm recommendation is to avoid asking multiple questions. If you have several questions, carefully phrase each one, ask the questions in a logical sequence, and permit the other person time to respond after each one. If you find that you tend to ask multiple questions on a regular basis, monitor this behavior and learn to pause for a few seconds before asking a question in order to phrase it effectively. The other advantage of increasing your use of pauses is that it provides space for the other person to process the information and better answer the question.

A barrage of direct closed questions may create a sense of being interrogated rather than one of collaboration.

Degree of Concreteness

Just as statements can be phrased with varying levels of specificity or concreteness, so too can questions. At times you will want to pose very general questions, such as when you are initiating relationships or just beginning to explore situations. Most often, however, you should ask questions that elicit more specific and concrete information. We refer to the latter as *focused* questions.

A focused question delimits the topic sufficiently so that the respondent can clearly identify the specific type of information requested. With few exceptions, once you have established a relationship and gathered contextual information, you should be able to increase your use of focused questions in your problem-solving interactions (Alessandra & Hunsaker, 1993). Possibly the most convincing evidence of this comes from one type of experience most special services providers have had. Surely you remember a time when you asked a question such as "How is Katie doing?" because you specifically wanted to know about Katie's reaction to the intervention you had spent hours designing. If so, you may have found that your vague or unfocused question resulted in an accounting of Katie's overall progress, her upcoming surgery, the progress she was making in other areas, and so on. A more focused question, such as "How is Katie progressing in the language program we designed?" would have been more likely to elicit the information you wanted.

Focused questions play a critical role in clear communication. When questions are too vague they encourage respondents to provide abstract, nonspecific answers, a dilemma discussed in Putting Ideas into Practice on page 272. In these cases you may have to interpret someone's abstract response or, at the very least, ask additional questions in order to refocus attention on the information you seek. Occasionally, a vague question may lead the respondent in a direction that pulls the entire interaction off a constructive course. Focused questions, on the other hand, help guide the course of the interaction and direct attention to specific, concrete information, a fact illustrated in the chapter opening by Graham's questions to Ms. Martinez about Shawn.

Making questions more focused in order to obtain specific and concrete information can be achieved primarily in two ways. First, by considering carefully the purpose of your question, determining the type of information you wish to access, and then selecting the most appropriate format, you greatly improve your ability to gather specific, concrete information. Second, particular wording or phrasing considerations can also help you further focus your question. These focusing techniques, described in the following presentation of presupposition and prefatory statements, can be used whether the question is open, closed, single, direct, or indirect.

Presupposition

Presupposition refers to specific question content that conveys to respondents an expectation of what they should know and thus helps focus the question.

PUTTING IDEAS INTO PRACTICE

Generalities Require Closer Examination

Sometimes questions elicit very general responses rather than the specifics that are needed. Generalities communicate little. "I really value that" or "He's doing absolutely great work" may communicate that someone is pleased, but it is unclear what aspects of the event are valued, great, or otherwise pleasing. Sometimes overly precise words (e.g., *always, every time*) are used carelessly and have the effect of a generality. To understand the message, it is necessary to examine the situation further with such responses as "What elements do you value most?" or "What aspects of the work do you think he did well?" The following words and phrases are a few of those that signal the need for further clarification.

all	every	more	all the time	usually
never	always	soon	worse	rarely
more or less	nearly	once in a while	they say	sometimes
almost	about	better	a bit	worry
could be	sort of like	nice	soon	concern

Presupposition can vary from little to great, depending on question construction. The following questions contain a high level of presupposition:

"What is your greatest concern about having Erin in your classroom?"

"What behavior management system are you using with Evan?"

In the first question, the presupposition is that the respondent has concerns and that these are prioritized. In the second, the presupposition is that the respondent is using a behavior management system with the student. In contrast, the following questions have little presupposition:

"Do you know whether Pat is returning?"

"How did you do that?"

Presupposition is a potent tool for focusing interactions. Especially when used in an open question, it is a means of embedding in the question a particular topic that you want targeted in the response. It thus enables you to query in a way that maximizes the likelihood you will receive elaborated, accurate information that is concrete and specific. For example, consider the following versions of the same basic question that you might ask parents about their satisfaction with their child's current educational program.

"Are you satisfied with your child's program this year?"

"Are you satisfied with the progress your child has made in her program this year?"

"What aspects of your child's program have you been most satisfied with this year?" [after parents' response] "What aspects have caused you the most concern?"

Little presupposition is contained in the first version of the question. If you use this question format, the parents probably will give a yes or no answer and they might not explain their specific reactions to the program. The second variation includes a greater degree of presupposition by making the assumption that the student has made progress, but since the question is closed, you may receive a response similar to what you received with the first question. The third set of questions contains a high level of presupposition. They assume that the parents have identified program strengths and weaknesses and that some of these are more important than others. Further, since their format is open, highly presuppositional questions are likely to enable the parents to discuss in more detail their response to the program.

Another benefit to presupposition is that it often conveys that you value another person's perception of and interest in a situation. Communicating such valuing may help strengthen your relationship.

Prefatory Statements

Careful phrasing is the heart of effective question asking, but sometimes you precede your question with a carefully structured statement to establish the context (Wolf, 1979). Several types of statements you might use during an interaction to respond to others (e.g., those that describe or guide) were presented in Chapter 8. Here, we are concerned with statements you may use when you want to ask a question but must first "set it up," a technique used by Graham as he interacted with Ms. Martinez in the chapter opening. You are establishing parameters for the question and the response, sometimes by raising possible answers, sometimes by reminding the other person of previously discussed issues, and sometimes by cueing your interaction partner that you are going to change the subject. The statements you use to accomplish this are called *prefatory statements*.

Each of the following questions is preceded by a prefatory statement. What purpose does each accomplish?

"We've considered an immediate program change for Harbajan as well as several interventions that might eliminate the need for the change. At this point, what strategy do you think would be best for him?"

"Yesterday you mentioned that the adaptation to Maria's communication board was not working. I wanted to get back to you about that. What seems to be the problem?"

"We've been talking about finding ways for teachers to be released to attend team meetings. I am also concerned about the scheduling difficulties of arranging for the occupational therapist to be here. What are our options for adjusting the OT's schedule to match the rest of the team's?"

In the first two examples, the prefatory statement focuses the respondent's attention on specific aspects of the topic the person asking the question wants addressed. In the final example, the prefatory statement signals the person about a change in topic ("I am also concerned"). The result in all these cases is that the respondent may be more prepared to participate in the interaction.

In addition to these general prefatory statements, two specific types may sometimes be appropriate during your interactions: the exemplar and the continuum. In an *exemplar,* you phrase a prefatory statement that provides examples of the types of answers that you might be seeking. For example, in the following segment of the interaction, an administrator set up options in her prefatory statement.

> "We've agreed that we'd like to have a series of meetings with teachers to clarify how the general education setting could be more supportive of students with special needs. There are quite a few options for doing this. We could use the upcoming staff development day or ask the superintendent for an extra day at the beginning of the next school year. Another option would be to discuss this at the staff meeting. I'm sure there are others. What ways do you think would be best for holding these meetings?"

The examples of alternatives for conducting the meetings help the others think about options. And yet, the phrasing of the question conveys that the administrator has not already selected a specific option.

The other type of prefatory statement, the *continuum,* is similar to the exemplar but is used when feasible responses tend to fall along a range. For example, you might use a continuum prefatory statement to raise options for reward or punishment systems to employ with a student, to describe potential levels of staff involvement in decision making on a special services team, or to raise programming options that are progressively more restrictive. The following example illustrates a continuum prefatory statement.

> "Through the years, Juan's teachers have used a wide variety of behavior management techniques with him. Some have preferred to rely almost totally on a system of rewards, others have used a combination of rewards and punishers, and still others have found that punishers alone are most effective. What type of behavior management system have you found most appropriate for Juan?"

In general, the statements with which you preface your questions become integral to them. You can use prefatory statements to raise issues you believe should be noted but that are not being discussed. You also may implicitly give the person you are interacting with permission to address a sensitive or awkward topic by mentioning it.

Suggestions for Effectively Asking Questions

In addition to the principles and examples for constructing effective questions that are given throughout this chapter, these specific suggestions may help you further refine your question-asking skills.

Use Pauses Effectively

A key to being a skilled questioner is pausing (Adler et al, 2004; Brammer & MacDonald, 2003). Two particular uses of pauses can improve the effectiveness of your question asking. The first involves pausing for a moment before you ask a question. You use these pauses to ensure that your question is phrased to convey exactly the message you intend. Second, you should pause after asking a question to allow the person you are questioning time to think about, phrase, and deliver a reply.

We meet many school professionals who find that pausing is an initially frustrating technique, but once they master it they find it very powerful. Perhaps you know that you have a tendency to keep talking if someone does not respond immediately to a question you have asked. Do you follow it with another question? Do you propose a response for the person? Both these habits seriously interfere with one of the primary purposes of asking questions—to obtain information from the respondent. Adding pauses to your repertoire of communication skills can only increase your effectiveness.

Monitor Question-Asking Interactions

Another strategy for becoming a successful question asker is to monitor your understanding of the relationship between how a question is asked and the type of response obtained. If you begin consciously to observe others asking questions, you will increase your own skill in discriminating appropriate from inappropriate questions. Another variation of this strategy, of course, is monitoring your own question-asking skill. How often do you use a closed question when your intent is to obtain an open response? In what situations do you tend to resort to vague instead of focused questions? How aware are you of how your questions are affecting others?

You will sometimes have successful interactions in your collaborative activities even though the quality of your questions is mediocre. However, this may create other problems. For example, some people want to interact and tend to respond in great detail even to closed questions. They may do so by taking their cue about the type of response desired from the way a question is asked. Thus, in some situations you may need to be especially careful that your questions are accurate, well phrased, and designed to elicit the type of information you seek. Otherwise, the information you receive may be simply a reflection of what you unintentionally conveyed that you wished to hear.

Attend to the Cultural Context

As illustrated in Chapter 8 and Chapter 9, the individualism/collectivism continuum is a useful framework for observing and responding to communication patterns in cross-cultural contexts. By the very nature of their work, busy educational professionals who operate on tight schedules are likely to adopt communication patterns that are characteristic of individualistic cultures. This may result in communication challenges with families or colleagues who hold more collectivistic orientations. We suggest that you work to bridge these cultural differences by using high-context strategies when asking questions. The suggestions that follow are appropriate for any interaction, as they tend to make the person comfortable and thus are apt to enhance your relationship. However, we point them out here because they are especially responsive to persons with collectivistic orientations.

Using high-context strategies would suggest that you employ a conversational tone, using "small talk" when appropriate. When you are ready to ask a question, ask permission with, "May I ask you a question?" It is best to rely more on indirect questions initially and accept the ambiguity in responses. This will encourage the person to talk more openly about past and current experiences. When you are ready to increase the focus in your questions, use prefatory statements and presupposition. Be patient and attend to the relationship at least as carefully as your need for information. Putting Ideas into Practice presents some additional ideas to make questioning nonthreatening and to promote participation.

Make Questions Meaningful

Too many or too few questions during an interaction can seriously limit communication clarity (Stewart & Cash, 2006). Have you ever participated in a question-asking situation that sounded like this?

Counselor: Did you try that strategy we discussed?

Teacher: Yes.

Counselor: Did it work?

Teacher: Yes.

Counselor: Are you satisfied with how things are going now?

Teacher: Not really.

Counselor: Why? Is it still her behavior?

Teacher: Yes.

In this exchange you may get the sense that the two are playing the old game of Twenty Questions. It is unlikely that either participant will find this exchange meaningful. The counselor is not getting progress information and the teacher is not gaining any information that might help with the student. Often, combining prefatory statements and different question formats will improve this type of interaction. Before reading further, take a few minutes to try to rephrase the counselor's questions using this strategy.

At the other end of the continuum, asking too few questions while seeking information is just as inappropriate. Consider this exchange.

Psychologist: Tell me what you're concerned about with Miguel.

Teacher: He has a poor attitude toward school.

Psychologist: Clarify that for me.

Teacher: He is often late, he seldom completes assignments, and he doesn't respond to rewards.

Psychologist: And you've tried the contract system we discussed.

PUTTING IDEAS INTO PRACTICE

Making Questions Nonthreatening

Whether in team meetings, parent interviews or conferences, or meetings with one individual, seeking information through asking questions can cause those being questioned to become uncomfortable or to feel threatened. You surely can recall times when you were asked questions for which you may not have felt prepared or for which you did not have a ready answer. Perhaps you were asked an unanticipated question by an instructor, a parent, or an administrator that you did not know how to answer. These experiences likely caused you surprise, panic, or embarrassment and they probably led you to be a less active participant in the interaction. These are some actions you can take when asking questions, especially in small groups, to make questioning nonthreatening and promote participation.

1. *Begin by asking a question without directing it to a particular person.* When meeting with parents, for example, ask a question openly so that either may answer, rather than asking, "Mrs. Sumner, how many times each week does Sabine fail to complete her homework?"

2. *Pause and wait for one of the participants to develop and offer an answer.* Like many others, you may become anxious when there is not an immediate answer to a question you ask. Although it may seem like a painfully long wait, pausing and allowing participants time to think about how they wish to answer goes a long way toward getting useful information and setting a facilitating climate.

3. *If no one responds after the pause, look for cues that someone may want to be involved and direct the question to him. It may also help to rephrase the question.* You might say, for example, "Mr. Sumner, it looks as if you have some thoughts on this. I'm interested in knowing if there is anything you'd like to say about Sabine not finishing her homework."

4. *Construct questions that incorporate the characteristics most likely to be viewed as inviting participation. Single, direct, and open questions are most appropriate for this purpose.* Depending on your assessment of the relationship and the others' readiness for direct questions, you might ask a direct question that is a bit more focused than the indirect question above, such as "Mrs. Sumner, what are the activities that compete with Sabine's efforts to get her homework done?"

These strategies may not result immediately in the specific information you want, but they are examples of techniques that can help you create a nonthreatening climate that is needed for effective communication.

Teacher: Yes. Miguel lost interest.

Psychologist: That should have worked. Tell me what happened.

With no questions but many commands and other statements, the interaction becomes directive and its sense of parity and mutual participation are seriously undermined. Furthermore, you can see that this kind of interest does not encourage emergent characteristics in a collaborative relationship. Trust and respect are not nurtured using this approach to interactions.

By paying careful attention to the information you need and by carefully constructing questions to elicit that information, you are most likely to ask meaningful questions that accomplish their communication purpose and contribute to your collaborative relationship.

Conducting Interviews

When we discuss the topic of question asking with students and field-based professionals, they frequently assume that questions are used primarily in an interviewing process. We hope that this chapter has illustrated the tremendous range of uses for questions and that you see their value in problem solving and its various contexts (e.g., consultation, co-teaching). Interviewing also provides an opportunity for you to focus your attention on your question-asking skills, and we address it here for that purpose.

An *interview* is an interactive process with multiple purposes. In school-based professional interactions, a primary purpose is for one party to obtain information from the other. Interviews can be thought of as occurring in steps or stages (Gamble & Gamble, 2005). First, you prepare for an interview by generating appropriate questions and arranging the setting so that it is as comfortable as possible. Second, you introduce the interview by stating its purpose and ensuring that the persons being interviewed are comfortable. Next, you ask the substantive questions of concern, and then you close the interview by reviewing the information collected, checking its accuracy, and stating the actions, if any, to be taken later. Finally, after the interview, you carry out those responsibilities you agreed to during the interview. The success of an interview requires knowledge about the context and process of interviews and skillful use of various verbal statements, as well as skillful question asking. To use interviews successfully as a specialized process in your collaborative activities, you should consider these suggestions. An example of obtaining valuable information through interviewing is included in A Basis in Research.

Prior to the Interview

Have you ever attempted to interview a teacher about a student's progress while standing in the classroom doorway so that the teacher can keep an eye on his class? Perhaps the teacher was repeatedly distracted by student behavior. You were probably interrupted several times as students sought the teacher's assistance. And both you and the teacher may have been uncomfortable because you did not have a place to put your notes and materials. If so, it is likely that neither of you was particularly satisfied with the outcome of the interview.

The goal of your activities prior to an interview should be to create an interaction situation that will be conducive to effective communication. To accomplish

A BASIS IN RESEARCH

Parents' Perceptions of School Involvement and Communication

The strongly positive impact of parent involvement in their children's education has long been recognized, but relatively few studies have explored the nature of that involvement and the role that various communication strategies play in it. Barge and Loges (2003), as part of a larger study examining parent, teacher, and student perceptions of parent involvement, used qualitative methodology to obtain parents' views on their involvement and communication activities. A total of 80 middle school parents (78 percent female; 55 percent African American, 36 percent Caucasian, 7 percent Hispanic) participated in nine focus groups led by trained facilitators. Among the many findings that contribute to understanding parents' perspectives were these:

■ Parents reported that monitoring their children's academic progress was their most important involvement strategy. Often they accomplished this by communicating with their children or accessing other information such as grade cards and posted information, not necessarily by discussing achievement with the teacher.

■ Parents perceived that their children would receive better treatment at school if teachers believed parents were involved.

■ Parents believed that establishing a personal relationship with teachers would lead to open communication and more shared information about their children.

■ Initiating contact with teachers early in the semester and participating in parent–teacher conferences were noted by parents as strategies they used to foster a positive relationship with teachers.

■ Parents voiced a desire for teachers to change their communication patterns with parents—for example, calling them to report excellent work.

■ Parents reported that they believed that developing a community support system (e.g., community agencies, extracurricular programs, parent organizations) also was an important form of involvement. Through such a network, they noted, their children were more likely to accomplish positive school outcomes.

This research provides a glimpse into the thinking of one group of middle school parents, but it suggests that honestly asking parents about their preferences for communication and responding to them could improve communication between school personnel and parents. As you consider the parents' perspectives, how do you think they might have been similar to or different from those of teachers?

Source: Based on J. K. Barge & W. E. Loges, "Parent, student, and teacher perceptions of parental involvement," *Journal of Applied Communication Research, 31* (2003): 140–163.

Interviews should be well planned and conducted in a comfortable setting that affords privacy.

this, you should arrange an appropriate setting for the interview, prepare yourself for the interview, and assist the interviewee to prepare.

Arranging the Setting

The physical characteristics of the interview setting can have a significant impact on the psychological comfort of the person being interviewed and thus on the quality of the information that is shared. There is a wide range of factors to think about if the setting is to be optimum. Consider the privacy and relative quiet of the space selected, appropriate adult furniture, freedom from clutter and other distractions, comfortable lighting and temperature, as well as setting neutrality (e.g., a conference room instead of your office). The items collectively address privacy, comfort, and equality of status. Although you may not be able to produce all of these conditions in your school setting, you should strive to maximize these three overall setting characteristics.

Preparing Yourself

You will obtain more information in a more efficient manner if you prepare yourself carefully for the interview (Ivey & Ivey, 2003). This requires two distinct tasks. First, prepare the questions you plan to ask (Clayton et al., 2003). For an informal interview, this may be a matter of jotting a few notes or simply gathering your thoughts prior to the interaction. For more formal interviews, you may choose to write out the questions to be used and the order in which they will

Funnel Approaches to Sequencing Questions

The sequence of the questions one asks may be as important to the quality of the communication as the specific question format. If you are trying to decide between using closed or open questions to obtain information from a colleague or parent, you will no doubt weigh the advantages and disadvantages of each. But consider, too, the advantages of two different approaches to how you sequence them.

As the name suggests, the *funnel* approach to questioning begins with broad, open questions and proceeds to the more narrow and limiting closed questions. This often is useful when the topic is sensitive, the person being questioned is uneasy or insecure about the questions, or the person is highly invested in the topic and has much to share before focusing on specifics. The funnel approach is particularly appropriate when you are questioning a teacher or a parent about a situation that that person brought to you for your assistance. Often, the problem, or the person's perception of it, is so complex that it should be explored broadly before it can be accurately focused and identified.

An *inverted funnel* approach begins with closed questions and proceeds to more open ones. The objective is to use very focused questions in the beginning to get the respondent to recall issues and facts about the topic of concern. The inverted funnel approach may help the respondent think about elements of the situation that he might not otherwise consider. It may raise his consciousness and get him into the right mind-set. Proponents of this approach report that it motivates the person gradually to speak more freely about a topic than other approaches do. Both ways of sequencing questions are useful. You will learn the advantages of each as you practice implementing them in a variety of situations.

be asked. Planning the nature and sequence of questions you intend to ask will greatly enhance the outcomes of the interview. Second, anticipate how your interviewee may react to the questions. Consider the topic from that person's perspective. Is it sensitive or emotion laden? Might the person be confused by your questions? What areas might need clarification? How will you respond to the interviewee's reactions? Based on your assessment of the potential reaction of the interviewee, you might want to revise the questions or rethink the scope of material to be addressed in this particular session. Several considerations for reorganizing and modifying questions are offered in our upcoming discussion of the body of the interview, and one technique for sequencing questions, funneling, is the topic of Putting Ideas into Practice.

Assisting Others to Prepare

Too often, interviews are unsuccessful because the person being interviewed was surprised by certain questions and became suspicious of the interviewer's motives, or the interviewee was simply unprepared to address the topic the interviewer had planned. When you function in the role of interviewer, you can avoid these problems by sharing information in advance with the person you will interview. Specifically, you should let the person know ahead of time that you wish to conduct an interview or discussion in order to collect information relative to a specific topic. This seems like an obvious and necessary courtesy when considering parents or perhaps administrators, but it is frequently overlooked when the person is a colleague with an office or classroom down the hall. In addition, you should clarify with the other person the purpose and topic for the interview. With a close colleague, a general comment about the topic may be sufficient. With parents, others outside the immediate school setting, and sometimes colleagues, it may be beneficial to provide a specific set of questions you plan to ask, a list of the topics, or a summary of the information that may be discussed.

During the Interview

Once you are seated face to face with the person you are interviewing, what should you do to ensure that the interview accomplishes your goals? Answering that question involves separately examining each of the three phases of an interview: (1) the introduction, (2) the body, and (3) the close.

The Introduction

The purpose of the introduction to any interview is to establish the ground rules for it and to put both the interviewee and yourself at ease. The introduction includes completing the following tasks:

1. Spend a short period of time chatting to establish a relaxed atmosphere.
2. State the purpose of the interview and clarify the confidentiality issues (e.g., is the information to be shared with anyone else? Under what conditions?).
3. Indicate how much time should be needed for the interview. This assists you and the other person to keep to a schedule as needed.
4. Thank the other person for her time and cooperation.
5. If you plan to take notes or record the interview, explain what you plan to do and, particularly with recording, obtain permission. Because tapes have to be reviewed—a time-consuming task—you may find that notes are often a more expedient recording option. However, you may also have to learn to be comfortable with the additional time it takes to jot notes while interacting with another person.

The Body

The substantive part of the interview commences once the introduction has been completed. During this stage, you will rely heavily on the skills discussed in this chapter and Chapter 9 for seeking and gathering information. In addition, the following interviewing suggestions (Brinkley, 1989) may be helpful:

1. *Carefully order your questions and statements.* Usually, ordering means focusing on low-inference information that is overt early in the interview and minimizing or leaving until later the high-inference observations and discussion of content that is covert. For example, you probably should ask a colleague early during the interview about events that have happened in the classroom setting, delaying discussion about the affective components until later.

2. *Cluster your questions and statements by topic.* Clustering assists the logical flow of information during the interview. For example, you probably will benefit from grouping together all discussion pertaining to a student's academic functioning and likewise clustering discussion about social skills.

3. *Use silence and minimal encouragers.* The more you talk during an interview, the less likely it is that you will achieve the purpose of the interview.

4. *Monitor your time.* Once time limits have been established, try to adhere to them, even if it means scheduling an additional interview session. This is a matter of courtesy. Colleagues, parents, and others have other obligations, and you should be sensitive to their needs to finish an interview within the established time frame.

The Close

Closing an interview should provide an opportunity to summarize what has occurred during the rest of the interview and to conclude the interview in a manner that leaves a sense of closure for all participants. Here are some suggestions for closing your interviews.

1. *Review the major topics.* Highlight all perspectives discussed so that your summary is an accurate description of the interview. Your efforts to ensure accuracy will be aided by the material on summarizing in Chapter 8. As stressed there and elsewhere, checking with the interviewee on the accuracy of your understanding is an important part of this step.

2. *Outline any plans made during the interview.* This is an opportunity to clarify who has agreed to do what after the interview is concluded. You may find that it is useful to write this information so that no confusion occurs later.

3. *Set a time to follow up on any actions you have planned.* Follow-up can occur in subsequent face-to-face interactions, by electronic means, or through correspondence.

4. *Ask if any additional topics should be addressed.* If the other person introduces a new topic and time is becoming an issue, you may decide to schedule an additional interview. You should clearly convey to the interviewee that the only reason for delaying discussion is the time factor. If you are perceived as avoiding the topic, the positive atmosphere of the interaction may be compromised.

5. *Indicate what you will do with the information you have gathered.* This should be a repeat and clarification of your introductory comments on confidentiality.

If you have taken notes, you might offer to duplicate them for the other person. Clarify again whether the information should be shared with others.

6. *Express appreciation for the person's time and participation.*

After the Interview

How much follow-up occurs after an interview depends on its original purpose. Of course, if you agreed to provide materials, complete a task, or contact another resource person during the interview, you will fulfill these responsibilities according to the timeline you established in the closing. If you agreed to share the notes or audiotape of the interview with the other person, you should do so as soon as possible.

The most critical element for you to follow through on after an interview is honoring the confidentiality agreement you made with the interviewee. Unless you have clarified with the interviewee that the information conveyed will be shared with others, you should make every effort to protect the confidentiality of the information, even if it seems innocuous. For example, sometimes special services providers share with other teachers the success that a particular teacher is having with an instructional technique. Although that seems harmless and perhaps flattering, it could cause problems. The teacher who has been used as an example may wonder why the other techniques she is using are not being praised, she may be annoyed at being used as an example, and other teachers may feel some resentment because of the attention to the teacher. The point is this: Assume that information shared during an interview is confidential. If you are not sure about the information, check with the other person before repeating it so that you do not violate a confidence and thus damage the quality of your work relationship.

Final Thoughts on Interviewing

Our examination of techniques for interviewing describes the process as it should occur in ideal conditions. Admittedly, you may find that you have to interview parents or colleagues when insufficient time is allocated, no private space is available, or your respondent is uncooperative or uncommunicative, as discussed in Putting Ideas into Practice. In such situations, our advice is to assess the situation and adjust your expectations for what you will be able to accomplish during the interaction. Once you have recognized the challenges of this interview and revised your goals, you will want to consider the extent to which you attempt to follow all the recommendations we have offered. For example, if you are interviewing a parent who becomes angry, it may be nonproductive to summarize points and propose follow-up strategies. Instead, you should quickly adjust the goal to be one of listening and demonstrating understanding of the parent's feelings and perceptions. An alternative would be to spend time listening carefully to the parent and use your skills in paraphrasing, reflecting, and checking. You can telephone the parent at a later time and propose a follow-up to the meeting. Similarly, if only 10 minutes are available for an interview, you probably should make the judgment to dispense with introductory visiting and comments (except

Quick Tips for Handling Uncooperative Communicators

Regardless of how well developed your communication skills are, you will encounter colleagues and parents whose communication styles are challenging and require concerted efforts on your part. Here are a few examples of uncooperative communicators and some suggestions for responding to them.

1. The **passive communicator** seems to participate not at all, reveals no expression, and does not contribute anything. *Pause and use brief silent spaces to allow time for her to process what is being discussed and say something. Ask her questions. Use facial expressions to indicate that you are waiting for a response or seeking agreement.*

2. The **overly expressive communicator** has an excited or enthusiastic response to everything. Even when what you are saying seems inconsequential, this person has extremely intense reactions. *You might take some satisfaction from having such an impact; some people do not respond at all. You might also find this is disconcerting and that such intensity interferes with your communication. If this is the case, try slowing the pace of your speech and speaking more quietly. Often a communication partner will modify his speech to more closely match yours. Alternatively, tell him, "You seem excited about all of this. Help me understand the two items about which you are most enthusiastic."*

3. The **overly talkative communicator** seems to talk incessantly and often about things quite unrelated to your intended topic. *Listen and try to determine why the person is so talkative. Reasons may include nervousness, other emotional states, being rushed, being typically talkative, or characteristically lacking clear focus. Emotional states require you to listen and reflect. Being rushed may require rescheduling. With the simply unfocused and talkative communicator you will need to reflect and summarize relevant elements and use redirection statements such as, "Getting back to your concerns about Mike's reading, tell me a bit more about . . . ."*

4. The **pseudo-communicator** seems to be interacting, but his responses are static—they never vary and always seem to be noncommittal restatements of what you have said, providing you with no real sense of his position. *Ask for a response. For example you might say, "Do you agree?" or "What part of what I said seems most plausible to you?"*

5. The **preoccupied communicator** may claim to be a multitasker; she is doing other things while you are talking. *If you feel that the person is not attending and what you are saying requires her concentration, ask for it. You could say, "This is really important and I need your attention." Or if the person is unable to give full attention at this time, you might offer to reschedule, and say, "This topic really needs both of us to concentrate on it. Should we reschedule for a time when you have less to do?"*

6. The **distracted communicator** looks all around the room, at others, but rarely at you. *Recall past interactions with this person—is this a common behavior? Is he easily distractible? If so, consider changing your positions so that you are facing the others in the room and he is facing you and the wall behind you. This way he will have fewer visual distractions. If he still is not making eye contact, try to maintain a direct gaze at him while varying your communication style to ask more questions that will engage him.*

purpose). Being able to assess situations such as interviews and adapt your goals, skills, and techniques indicate a high degree of interactive competence.

Summary

Asking questions is the primary means through which you seek information during collaborative activities. Three key characteristics of questions are purpose (to seek, clarify, or provide information), format (open/closed, single/multiple, direct/indirect), and concreteness. Questions often are surrounded by statements or words that are not directly part of the query but serve to clarify or facilitate it. One example is the prefatory statement, including the exemplar and the continuum. Suggestions for asking questions effectively include using pauses (silence) well, monitoring question-asking interactions, attending to the cultural context, and ensuring that the questions are meaningful. The process of interviewing is a common context for using questions. Care should be taken prior to, during, and after interviews to ensure that appropriate information is sought, clarified, and acted on.

Activities and Assignments

1. For a day or two, pay attention to the types of questions you use in your interactions. How do the questions you ask students differ from those you ask colleagues, friends, or family members? Find examples of when your questions absolutely missed the mark. That is, identify questions to which you received irrelevant or useless information. Make a list of some of the ineffective questions and how you did or would rephrase them to get the information you wanted. Consider the context and setting as well as the phrasing and sequencing of your questions.

2. Listen to a professional interviewer on radio or television. Analyze the questions the person asks according to the information outlined in this chapter. How would you rate the quality of the interviewer's question-asking skills? To what extent do interviewers use single or multiple questions, direct or indirect? What examples of indirect questions were found? (The value of this exercise derives from studying the interviewer, not the interviewee, because of the differences in responses that are likely to occur between interviews in media and those in day-to-day situations.)

3. Question asking is a sophisticated skill that requires attention and considerable practice, but attending to all its characteristics simultaneously while you are interacting with someone can cause frustration and make it difficult for you to carry on the conversation. To reduce the frustration and make the task more valuable, select one or two of the characteristics of questions and practice asking questions that focus on those characteristics. Once you master those, select another, and then another until attending to the way in which you phrase questions becomes an automatic part of your communication. Ask a classmate to assist you in assessing your question-asking skill.

4. People often have patterns they use in asking questions. However, it is important to use questions with different formats to achieve different communication goals. This activity is designed to ensure that you have practice with two question-asking patterns, including the one you would be least likely to select on your own. Pair up with a classmate and practice interviewing, with each of you taking two turns as interviewer. Use the funnel approach in one interview and the inverted funnel in the other. After both of you have interviewed the other two times, discuss the experience. Was one format more comfortable for the interviewer? How did the interviewee feel about each format? Which format provided the most useful information? Which format would likely enhance your relationship and willingness to talk again later?

5. With permission from other participants, tape-record yourself during a collaborative activity in your school setting. Write down each question that was asked, highlighting those that you asked. Classify each of your questions according to its purpose and identify its characteristics. A variation of this activity is to ask the other participants to listen to the tape with you and then discuss your questions and explain why they elicited particular responses. Afterward, exchange tapes with a classmate and repeat the analysis. Compare your results and resolve any discrepancies.

6. Recall an interview in which you were present but were not the facilitator. To what extent were the tasks and activities for interviewing carried out? What recommendations would you now make to the person who facilitated that interview?

7. Observe a colleague or one of your own instructors and listen for the use of yes–no questions, such as: "Does that make sense?" "Do you understand?" For every time they ask such a question, construct a question of your own that would better assess the understanding of the individual or class. Compile a list of the closed, dichotomous questions and the alternatives that you constructed and discuss the list with a classmate.

For Further Reading

Black, S. (2005). Rethinking parent conferences. *American School Board Journal, 192*(10), 46–48.

Cormier, B., Cormier, L. S., & Cormier, W. H. (2003). *Interviewing strategies for helpers: Fundamental skills and cognitive behavioral interventions* (5th ed.). Monterey, CA: Brooks/Cole.

Million, J. (2005). Getting teachers set for parent conferences. *Education Digest, 70*(8), 54–56.

Palmer, B. B. (2003). *Interpersonal skills for helping professionals: An interactive online guide for students.* Boston: Allyn & Bacon.

Sandoval, J. (2003). Constructing conceptual change in consultee-centered consultation. *Journal of Educational and Psychological Consultation, 14*(3/4), 251–261.

Schaeffer, N. C., & Preser, S. (2003). The science of asking questions. *Annual Review of Sociology, 29*(1), 65–88.

Stewart, C. J., & Cash, W. B. (2006). *Interviewing principles and practices* (11th ed.). New York: McGraw-Hill.

CHAPTER 11

Difficult Interactions

Connections

As you have studied the topics addressed throughout this textbook, you have learned both the specific skills for effective communication (Chapters 8, 9, and 10) as well as the processes in which that communication occurs (for example, Chapter 2). In this chapter you have the opportunity to blend all your knowledge about collaboration and skills for operationalizing it because this chapter—about difficult interactions—explores the situations in which you most need them. When you find yourself interacting with an angry parent or a colleague who does not seem to share your priorities for working with students, you have a critical opportunity to demonstrate your expertise as a collaborator.

Learner Objectives

After reading this chapter you will be able to:

1. Define conflict and resistance.
2. Appreciate the benefits that can occur when conflict and resistance are addressed in a respectful and constructive manner.
3. Explain why conflict and resistance should be expected by special services professionals in today's schools.
4. Describe three major causes of conflict.
5. Explain the five response styles professionals typically use during interactions in which conflict occurs.

6. Outline the principles of negotiation as a strategy for addressing conflict.

7. Describe the causes of resistance.

8. Recognize indicators of resistance.

9. Outline persuasion strategies that can be used to respond to resistance.

The school day has ended and Jasmine is ready for a quiet hour as she sorts papers from today's lessons and prepares for tomorrow. Just as she enters her room, the intercom crackles to life and the clerk asks her to come to the office for a brief meeting with Gordon's parents, Dr. and Mrs. Huber, and principal Mr. DeVey. Sighing because she suspects a problem, Jasmine heads for the conference room. Mrs. Huber begins by noting that she is still displeased with the accommodations being made for Gordon in his English and World History classes, commenting that before this meeting is over she would like one scheduled for later this week on that topic. She then states that she has learned that her request for hallway railings for Gordon has not been acted on, and she wants to know why. Mr. DeVey explains that the physical therapist completed a detailed evaluation of Gordon's balance skills and found that they are in the typical range and that a letter was sent detailing this information and a voice mail message was left asking the Hubers to call the school to discuss this matter. Dr. Huber reacts with anger. Raising his voice, he begins talking about how school personnel do not understand his son, and that this is another example of trying to cut corners in providing for him. Jasmine wants to help move this conversation to a more productive arena, but she senses that will not be possible. When the Hubers threaten a due process over this matter, the principal ends the meeting and indicates that a follow-up will occur soon with the director of special education in attendance.

Introduction

Have you ever experienced a situation similar to the one with Dr. and Mrs. Huber? Although few interactions with others at schools have this air of tension, you should be prepared for those that do. Here are a few other examples of situations that may be difficult or awkward to address.

- You call the technology coordinator to ask for a copy of a new program to be put on your computer. The coordinator explains that you are welcome to have a copy, but that the district's policy is that you must first attend a one-hour after-school workshop on its use. You reply that you are very adept at using the computer and undoubtedly can figure out how to operate the program without having to take the workshop. The technology coordinator is sympathetic, but says that the program will be installed only after you attend the after-school session.

- The parents of a student refuse to give permission for an assessment, despite the student's failing grades. You are a member of the special services team that agrees the student should be considered for possible eligibility for special education services.

- You are meeting with your teaching assistant (TA) to discuss how to use the newly installed software to adapt instruction for a student with a mild cognitive disability with whom the assistant works in a general education setting. The assistant agrees with everything you say, but asks few questions. Two days later, the classroom teacher asks when you are going to meet with the TA because it's a shame to have all that software going unused in the classroom.

- You arrange a twice-monthly series of meetings with your co-teacher to plan, wishing for more but grateful for these opportunities. The first meeting goes well, but at the last minute before the next meeting, the other teacher cancels. Over the next four meeting times, she either does this or arrives very late three times. You decide that for some reason your co-teacher does not want to plan with you.

Some incidents such as these are relatively trivial and mostly annoying, and you may be able to easily resolve them (e.g., by attending the workshop on the software). Others concern the fundamental decisions made about students' educational needs (e.g., planning for co-teaching). The first two scenarios as well as the one that opened this chapter are examples of conflict. The latter two are examples of resistance. In this chapter you will learn more about both of these difficult interactions and how to respond to them. Both conflict and resistance are natural occurrences in collaboration, but depending on your response to them, they can either enhance collaboration or impede it.

Understanding Conflict

Conflict has been defined by numerous authors (e.g., Barsky, 2000; Littlejohn & Domenici, 2001; Melamed & Reiman, 2000), and their definitions have tended to vary based on the theoretical perspective of the author. For example, some view conflict as a situation that occurs when one party perceives that his or her status is no longer equitable to that of another party; that is, it is viewed as a matter of perceived power inequity within a relationship. Others see it as the result of attributions that some individuals assign to others, as when teachers consider parents "uninterested" or when school staff members perceive some of their colleagues as "inflexible." For our discussion, we provide this definition of conflict:

> *Conflict* is a struggle that occurs when individuals, interdependent with others, perceive that those others are interfering with their goal attainment.

You can apply this definition to the scenario that opened the chapter. What might have been the needs of the parents and the principal? What was the perceived interference?

Traditionally, school professionals have been uncomfortable addressing conflict. In fact, Barsky (2000) notes that when compared to other professions such as business, law, and psychology, education has not evolved a systematic means of considering conflict as part of the work environment nor developed models for resolving it. Educators were particularly successful at avoiding conflict when school culture emphasized isolation, as was true until the past two decades. Now, however, it is unlikely that conflict can be avoided. The same approach that Tjosvold (1987) uses to analyze why conflict is inevitable in business settings can be applied to traditional schools to explain why this is so. First, each individual in traditional schools had clearly delineated tasks to accomplish and did these without relying to any great extent on others. As we discussed in Chapter 1, this picture accurately described special services providers, too. In today's schools, this isolation and delineation of individuals' tasks is outdated. Increasingly, staff members are expected to work together, and they are therefore more likely to experience conflict just because they are in closer proximity (Cornille, Pestle, & Vanwy, 1999; Masters & Albright, 2002). An example of this happens on teams: When professionals from several disciplines with different frames of reference are making decisions about student needs, they are likely to differ occasionally about desired outcomes (Fleming & Monda-Amaya, 2001).

Second, the traditional value system of schools tended to downplay emotions and keep school somewhat impersonal. Emerging trends, however, support all workplaces—including schools—being nurturing environments (Harlos, 2001) that give voice to teachers' preferences and opinions. As more needs are expressed, conflict is likely to emerge, since meeting some individuals' needs can interfere with meeting the needs of others. For example, this may occur as professionals request smaller caseloads in order to implement innovative programs.

A third reason conflict is increasingly common in schools is that leadership approaches have changed (Kosmoski & Pollack, 2000). In traditional schools, principals were considered effective when they were strongly directive in school decision making. Now, however, participatory management approaches are preferred (Gooden, 2005; Protheroe, 2005). The resulting increased staff involvement in decision making also increases the opportunities for conflicts. For example, when school professionals are meeting to decide the focus for staff development for the next school year, conflict may occur. Similarly, when a grade-level team is deciding how to address curriculum goals, disagreements are to be expected.

Because you are likely to experience at least some conflict in your professional role, you should also understand how it can be beneficial (e.g., Masters & Albright, 2002). By itself, conflict is neither good nor bad. You determine whether it will have positive or negative outcomes. Consider these potentially positive results from conflict.

1. Decisions made after addressing a conflict often are of high quality because of the intense effort invested in discussing perspectives and generating alternatives.
2. Professionals implementing decisions emerging from conflict are likely to have a strong sense of ownership for the decisions and for the commitment to carry them out.

3. Conflict typically causes professionals to sharpen their thinking about their points of view so that they can clearly communicate them. The result is a more carefully reasoned discussion that often includes a wider range of ideas and options.

4. Often, professionals who successfully manage conflict develop more open, trusting relationships with one another. This facilitates their subsequent interactions.

5. Practice in effectively communicating during conflict can make it easier to address future conflict situations.

Notice that we are not saying that interactions with conflict are simple or enjoyable; in fact, they are complex and often stressful (Attanucci, 2004; Kosmoski & Pollack, 2001). But conflict does not have to be viewed as exclusively negative. If you look at it as an opportunity, it will be one. Expanding your understanding of why conflict occurs and how it can be managed will help you view it this way.

Causes of Conflict

Think about your school or a school with which you are familiar. What types of conflicts have occurred there? Who has been involved in these conflicts? When you review these professional conflicts, you might identify different reasons why they occurred. We categorize these as related to interests, rights, and power (Masters & Albright, 2002).

When a school's culture is collaborative, conflict is viewed as a normal occurrence that provides opportunities for professional growth and better outcomes for students.

Conflict between Individuals with Different Goals

One major cause of conflict occurs when two individuals want different outcomes but must settle for the same outcome (Brooks, 2001; Christie & Jassi, 2002). For example, in a suburban school district, team members and parents disagree about the mission of a proposed program to include students with moderate disabilities. Some school professionals believe that few students will be able to be integrated because they cannot meet academic and social expectations, especially given the mandates of the No Child Left Behind Act and the pressures it places on teachers to ensure that students reach specific academic standards. Others believe that the program's primary goal should be making any modifications that are needed in order to include all students for most of each school day. Some parents are not in favor of inclusion at all; they prefer the current service delivery system with limited mainstreaming. Others want their children with typical peers all day.

Each of the groups in this example wants a different outcome concerning the inclusive program; they have different goals. However, when a decision is made about the program, all the groups must abide by those guidelines. Although students may spend varying amounts of the day in general education settings, how staff is deployed and schedules developed will rely on the mission statement set. Other common examples of conflict between individuals with different goals include disagreements between parents and school professionals about the amount of service a student will receive and disagreements among professionals about how special education services should be arranged in their school. Another example concerns the roles for special educators when they are in general education classes: Are they there to teach all students as appropriate or to provide support just for those with disabilities? What additional examples of conflicts occurring for this reason have you observed in your professional role?

Conflict between Individuals with the Same Goals

The second major cause of conflict occurs when professionals all have the same goal, but not all of them can access it (e.g., DeVoe, 1999). The master school schedule offers an example of this cause of conflict. In a local high school, the master schedule is created by first blocking in the academic courses, then the vocational and special subjects, and finally the special education classes. However, with more students with disabilities enrolled in core academic classes, the special education teachers encounter problems arranging services. They request that the scheduling of special education classes occur immediately after the academic classes and before others. The special subject teachers argue that far more students are affected by art, music, and physical education classes and that those classes should thus have a higher priority. The teachers of the honors classes ask that other classes be arranged so that students who attend classes at the local university in the afternoons are not penalized.

In this example, the various parties have the same goal: receiving priority treatment in the scheduling process. However, when one group is given priority, the others cannot have it. One group is likely to be dissatisfied with the resolution of this conflict. You have probably witnessed or participated in many similar conflicts, such as when only two individuals can go to a professional conference and several requested to attend, when a position in a preferred school opened and several individuals requested a transfer, and so on. Scarce resources often result in competing goal conflicts (Morris & Su, 1999).

Conflict about Power

In some cases, conflict is not about goals at all. Instead, it may be about each person's perceived sense of power (Cheldelin, Druckman, & Fast, 2003; Deutsch, 2002). If a principal, for instance, mandates that certain professionals are to be members of the school's intervention assistance team, conflict may result. It is not a matter of whether the educators want to participate or want to assist students—it is the fact that they were told to accept this responsibility instead of being given a choice. Another example sometimes occurs in co-teaching. One teacher may contradict the other during instruction or change the directions given, and these difficult interactions may result in conflict. A careful analysis shows, though, that the reason for these issues is one teacher's perception of needing to establish power and status in the classroom. What are other examples of conflicts about power that occur in schools?

Conflict within Individuals

One additional cause of conflict is an internal discrepancy that you perceive within your own goals. We mention this cause of conflict for completeness, but this is an intrapersonal dilemma that does not necessarily affect others, although it can pose a very serious job stressor for special educators (Miller, Brownell, & Smith, 1999). For example, suppose you are responsible for scheduling a student for 60 minutes a week of direct services complemented by systematic consultation with his teacher. You know that you should not schedule the student for three such 60-minute periods each week, but you also believe strongly that by doing so you could deliver higher-quality services that would better meet his needs. You delay finalizing your schedule for several days while you worry about the appropriate ethical decision to make. Internal causes of conflict such as these are extremely common in schools where professionals are changing their roles and where expectations for their services are evolving rapidly.

Intrapersonal conflict may cause unclear communication that negatively affects professional interactions. As you discuss the student with the teacher, for example, you may inadvertently convey the message that you believe the student should receive more intense direct services. If you do this while communicating that indirect services are the most appropriate approach, the teacher may wonder which message is accurate. If this same student is discussed at a team meeting, your internal conflict could even lead to interpersonal conflict. Although you agreed in a previous meeting that the team's recommendation for service was appropriate, you may vacillate in your opinion about the service's appropriateness and experience unanticipated disagreements with the teacher.

The Influence of Organizational Variables

Understanding the causes of conflict provides a framework for identifying and managing it; however, other factors interact with these causes to affect the frequency and intensity of conflicts in your school setting. One factor particularly important for school professionals concerns organizational variables.

School Administration and Organization

The conflict you encounter is influenced significantly by the organization and administration of your school (Achinstein, 2002; Gooden, 2005; Kosmoski & Pollack, 2000). For example, your principal's leadership style affects conflict. If the principal tends to use a laissez-faire style, you and your colleagues may find yourselves in conflict with one another for scarce resources. Without leadership to set guidelines on the distribution of resources, you may disagree with their allocation and compete with one another for them.

Another cause of conflict in schools is lack of clarity in procedures (Isenhart & Spangle, 2000). For example, some professionals believe that permission to attend a staff development conference is to be given by the principal. Others know that the director of special education is responsible for paying the registration fees, and so they believe that the director must give permission. Various staff members contact these two individuals. In the confusion, more people initially receive approval to attend than funds exist to support. Some professionals express anger when they are later told that they cannot attend, and they question how attendees were selected from those who applied to attend.

Communication Patterns

Another critical organizational variable that affects conflict is the pattern of communication among the individuals in various parts of the organization (Jehn, 2000). Many different types of dysfunctional communication can create conflict situations. One type occurs when similar information is not available to all individuals. For example, the school psychologists and social workers are informed that the procedures for conducting multidisciplinary team meetings are changing, but the special education teachers do not receive this notice. At a subsequent team meeting, the special education teachers challenge the change in procedures initiated by the social worker and question whether the change is mandatory or optional. Because the communication was dysfunctional, a conflict was caused.

Another dysfunctional communication pattern that affects the likelihood of conflict occurs when information is conveyed differently by the individuals who communicate with the same staff members (Kruk, 1997). You experience this when you attend a meeting with all the other members of your discipline and learn a new piece of information about how to write IEPs. A week later, you attend a meeting for all special services providers, and a different set of instructions is given on the same topic. Shortly after these meetings, several staff members experience conflict about the correct procedure for IEPs. Their differences are attributable to the conflicting information they received about the change.

Conflict Response Styles

The next component in learning to understand and respond to conflict concerns the style you are likely to use when participating in a conflict interaction. Figure 11.1 visually represents common conflict response styles. Notice that the styles vary along two dimensions: the importance of the relationship and the importance of the outcome. Avoidance has the least amount of both these characteristics, collaboration has the greatest amount of each, and compromise has roughly equal, moderate amounts of both types of concern (Shell, 2001). You can assess your style using the Conflict Management Style Survey included in the appendix at the end of this chapter.

Most people have a preferred style for responding to conflict (Jensen-Campbell, Gleason, Adams, & Malcolm, 2003; Kelker, 2000; Rudawsky & Lundgren, 1999). As each style is explained on the following pages, keep in mind that no style is entirely positive or negative. Depending on the situations in which a style is used, it has both merits and drawbacks.

Competitive Style

Some individuals address conflict using a competitive style, which is sometimes associated with the use of power, as people who use it might attempt to over-

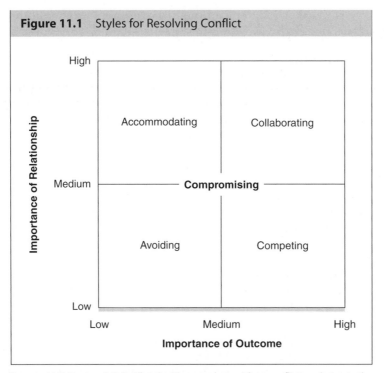

Figure 11.1   Styles for Resolving Conflict

Source: M. F. Masters & R. R. Albright, *The complete guide to conflict resolution in the workplace* (New York: American Management Association, 2002).

power others. Their goal tends to be winning, regardless of the potential negative repercussions of their strategy.

A competitive conflict management style might be desirable when ethical issues are at stake or when you are certain that you are right. Occasionally, you may use this style when a decision must be made for which you alone have responsibility. The disadvantages of this style relate to its inappropriate use: If you frequently compete during conflict, others may stop interacting with you in a meaningful way. Too much use of a competitive style can seriously damage collaborative relationships. Also, few issues in schools have an absolute "right" solution; most are a matter of interpretation. If you often compete because you know you are right, you may be perceived by others as rigid and directive.

Avoidance Style

Individuals who prefer avoidance usually try to ignore the discrepancy between their own goals and those of others. They deal with conflict by turning away from it. If you have ever participated in a meeting in which an issue needed to be brought to the surface but everyone appeared to have tacitly agreed not to discuss it, you were experiencing avoidance. Notice that in this situation the conflict is not being resolved and may continue to trouble the group.

In some instances, avoidance is advisable. If a conflict is extremely serious and emotion laden, temporary avoidance may enable the individuals involved to think about their positions and participate more constructively. Similarly, if there is not enough time to adequately address a conflict or if the issue is relatively inconsequential, avoidance may be the preferred strategy. However, using avoidance may create difficulties in your collaborative relationships. For example, if you and a colleague disagree on a teaching technique, avoiding discussion of the topic can exacerbate the conflict. Avoidance is a seductive strategy because it gives the appearance that all is well; its hidden danger is that a situation may become more difficult or awkward by inaction.

Accommodative Style

Individuals who use an accommodative style set aside their own needs in order to ensure that others' needs are met. Their characteristic response to conflict is to give in. Occasionally, special services providers use this style because they believe it may help to initiate or preserve positive relationships with colleagues, particularly in service options such as co-teaching.

An accommodative style can be beneficial when the issue is relatively unimportant or when you cannot alter the situation. Accommodating has a distinct advantage in that it brings conflict to a quick close, enabling you to turn your attention to other issues. The drawbacks of accommodating include the risk of feeling as though others are taking advantage of you, the potential that the issue is one for which you have the best answer and yet you do not insist that it be selected, and the possible devaluing of your ideas when you quickly accommodate on an important matter. Generally, accommodating can be especially appropriate for professionals who need to overcome the tendency to try to win every disagreement; it is often inappropriate for those who feel powerless in their professional relationships.

Compromising Style

Many school professionals use a compromising style in responding to conflict. They give up some of their ideas related to an issue and insist that others do the same. They keep some of their ideas and go along with some of the ideas others have proposed. The result typically is an outcome that may not exactly meet everyone's needs, but is acceptable to all.

Because compromising is a style whose strength is expedience, it is often appropriate when limited time is available to manage a conflict. It is also useful when the issue at hand is not especially problematic and when two competitive individuals have a conflict. Although compromise seems like an ideal style since it infers that part of each individual's goal is achieved, it, too, has drawbacks. For example, sometimes typically competitive professionals who decide to compromise feel that they have partly "lost" and so may be somewhat dissatisfied. As a result, additional conflict may occur later. The compromised resolution of an issue can be a bit like the agreement reached for a seaside vacation planned by two friends, one of whom wanted to go to the East Coast while the other wanted to go to the West Coast: They ended up in Kansas, and neither person was happy.

Collaborative Style

Collaboration in the context of responding to conflict is consistent with the conceptual foundation laid earlier in this text, and it is recommended as the most satisfying approach to resolving conflict (Masters & Albright, 2002). Use of a collaborative style requires commitment to the defining elements we described, as well as to the emergent characteristics of collaboration. It often includes developing a completely new alternative to resolve the conflict situation. For example, a collaborative response to the vacation example might be for the friends to decide that the vacation was not the issue at all. Since both were looking for a relaxing experience near water, they could decide to spend a week in a lakeside retreat only 50 miles from their hometown.

Although collaboration has many positive aspects, in conflict situations it cannot always be achieved: It is time consuming, it requires that certain defining elements be in place, and it can be undertaken only as professionals learn about and come to trust one another. Thus, collaboration is sometimes not even an option for addressing conflict.

By learning to monitor the style you use to respond to conflict in your professional interactions, you will grow in your knowledge about how you handle such situations. Further, by knowing what causes conflict, understanding conflict response styles, and learning specific strategies such as those described next, you will be more successful in managing difficult interactions.

Resolving Conflict through Negotiation

Negotiation is a conflict management technique that has a long history of success in business settings (Cloke & Goldsmith, 2000; Coleman & Lim, 2001; Putnam, 2004) that can also help you resolve school conflict. Negotiation can be used in many types of conflict, as illustrated in this example of a principal and a special education teacher deciding on materials needed in a new classroom.

Principal: What are your needs for materials for your room?

Teacher: I've reviewed the records of my students and looked through the catalogues. I have a list here of the materials I need to begin the program, but I would like to be able to request an additional $500 for instructional supplies once I have the opportunity to work with the students. Also, I have concerns about equipment. I would like to have three computers in the classroom.

Principal: (looking at the list and her notes) I'd like to be able to provide all these items, but it's just not possible within the budget. How about if I managed to get funding for the top 20 prioritized items on this list and agreed that we would discuss additional resources next year?

Teacher: That's a problem. I'm concerned that in a new classroom I'll need more than the items with the highest priority. And the computer issue is important to me.

Principal: Perhaps we can resolve that one. You already have one computer. There are three loaner computers in the learning center. We could locate one in your classroom; the only time you would have to share it would be when the others are in use. That shouldn't happen too often. Then you would have two computers, and you could use one of the laptops as a third.

Teacher: That's fine. But what about the other items?

Principal: I simply can't promise you the amount of money you are requesting for materials and supplies. What would be a reasonable solution?

Teacher: What if you furnished the initial materials and I prepared a request for the parent–teacher organization to assist in supplying additional materials I might need later in the year, especially computer software?

Principal: I can do that. I would want to work with you on the proposal though.

Teacher: Great! Then we've agreed you'll fund the initial list of needed supplies, I'll borrow the computer, and we'll approach the PTO about additional needs.

The key to successful negotiation, whether it is formal or informal, is to keep in mind that the object of the interaction is not for one person to win while the other loses. In their extensive work on this topic, Ury and his colleagues (Fisher,

Ury, & Patton, 1997; Ury, 1991; Ury, Brett, & Goldberg, 1988) have derived these principles for successful negotiation:

1. Focus on issues, not people, whenever you experience conflict. Instead of saying, "You don't understand how changing the intervention will affect the entire class," you might say, "The strategy we're discussing now is problematic because it has the potential to negatively affect classroom routine." The former makes the disagreement an adversarial situation based on people; the latter acknowledges disagreement but anchors it on the proposed intervention instead of on the person who proposed it.

2. To the greatest extent possible, keep the conflict focused on issues that have the potential to be agreed on. This reminds you as well as the others that you have a common ground from which to work to manage the conflict. For example, it is often more constructive to suggest specific accommodations for a student (e.g., oral responding, extended time for testing) than to discuss a colleague's disagreement with the school's commitment to provide nearly all students with full access to the general curriculum. The former can be addressed; in most cases, the latter cannot.

3. Reduce the emotional component of the conflict. If the issue in conflict has raised strong emotional responses, you may find that it is not possible to proceed and temporary avoidance is needed. However, you can also sometimes defuse emotions by responding positively to others' negative comments, not responding to comments that might cause you to become angry, and by acknowledging others' feelings (Jordan & Troth, 2004).

4. We would be remiss if we did not include a final strategy: the option for you to adapt to the issue or, if possible, to exit the situation. At some point it becomes self-defeating to continue to try to address a conflict if the other person does not view the matter as an issue or if you cannot influence the conflict situation. Resolving the matter within yourself so that you no longer fret about it may be the most viable option. If that is not possible and the issue is critical, you may choose to leave the situation or even the school setting. For example, a student with a moderate cognitive disability is moving to first grade. The first-year special education teacher believes strongly that the child should spend most of the day with nondisabled peers. The first-grade teachers are adamant that they do not know how to meet the child's needs. The principal does not want to anger the first-grade teachers, and so she is tending to agree with their point of view unless the district is willing to provide a one-to-one assistant for the student. The parent is not strongly advocating for any arrangement but does like the idea of the assistant. In spite of repeated efforts using superb communication skills and in light of so many factors constraining placement in a typical classroom, including the fact that no assistant will be assigned, the special educator might decide that she should simply keep quiet about her beliefs. If this pattern of making decisions about children is common, she may decide that she would prefer to work in another school or another district.

PUTTING IDEAS INTO PRACTICE

Effective Negotiation

In addition to understanding the principles on which successful negotiation is based, you can use these steps to guide your negotiation to a positive conclusion.

■ *Understand your own motivation and that of others.* What are the motivations of those involved in the conflict? Is the basis of the conflict a value difference? Is it an issue of limited resources and the stress caused by the situation? Is it a matter of differing opinions about interventions?

■ *Clarify the issues.* If you and the other person(s) in a conflict do not have a mutual understanding of the issues, you are unlikely to resolve them.

■ *Set your expectations.* This requires examining your ideal solution to the conflict and then tempering it with your understanding of motivations as well as other factors influencing the situation. This step is called *goal setting.*

■ *Discuss each issue involved in the conflict.* Sometimes it is tempting to have a general discussion in which all the issues related to the conflict are raised. The result can be unclear communication and, sometimes, additional conflict.

■ *Make and respond to offers.* This is the part of negotiation that includes give-and-take among participants.

■ *Monitor for ethics and integrity.* Negotiation in conflict situations can only be successful if you work in good faith. If you withhold information or manipulate others' words, you may worsen the situation instead of improving it. At the same time, you should be aware of the ethical issues involved in serving the needs of students with disabilities. Your goal for concluding a negotiation should be to enable everyone to "save face," while at the same time resolving the dilemma in a professional manner.

Consider how each of the foregoing ideas can be applied to the exchange between the teacher and the principal at the beginning of this section. If you use these principles for effective negotiation and think of negotiation as specialized problem solving, you can use steps such as those in Putting Ideas into Practice to respond to conflict positively and constructively. For additional practice, you might consider using the scenario that opened this chapter as a basis for discussing how such conflicts might be addressed by special educators and other professionals.

Resolving Conflict through Mediation

You probably have experienced formal negotiation if you have been involved in the discussion of teacher contracts through your local professional association. Perhaps you have informally negotiated with colleagues concerning the use of planning time or the clarification of roles in a co-taught class. However, what should you do if negotiation fails to resolve the conflict? What strategies remain when you cannot simply retreat from the situation and are not satisfied with the current situation? A specialized form of negotiation, mediation is a process in which a third party who is neutral in regard to the issue at hand guides the individuals in conflict through a voluntary discussion with the goal of settling the dispute (Honeyman, Goh, & Kelly, 2004; Isenhart & Spangle, 2000; Mareschal, 2005). Some authors (e.g., Dana, 2001) even propose that professionals who study mediation and come to understand it and value its role in conflict resolution can learn to mediate even as one of the parties involved in a conflict.

Consider the situation previously mentioned in which you and a colleague are unable to resolve your differences of opinion about the appropriate role for each professional in the co-taught class. The general education teacher is not comfortable with another adult contributing during large-group instruction and prefers that you remain seated and quiet during such times. You maintain that you are highly qualified and experienced and that, with less large-group instruction and more use of small groups, you can actively participate in instruction and better provide a range of supports and services to students in the classroom. At an impasse, perhaps you ask your assistant principal to meet with both of you to discuss possible solutions. Alternatively, perhaps your school district employs a special education coordinator, a nonsupervisory staff member who has the responsibility of fostering collaboration and ensuring that students with special needs receive an appropriate education. This individual also might serve in the role of mediator.

IDEA-04 places a premium on mediation and other strategies to resolve disputes that avoid the need for a due process hearing.

You might also be involved in mediation in a more formal context. As you know, the reauthorization of IDEA in 2004 continued the provision that mediation must be offered to parents who are in conflict with schools concerning their children's special education. Further, it establishes an informal resolution session as part of the due process procedure, and this session can function as a type of informal mediation. Although mediation may not be a successful strategy when the disputed issues concern a legal interpretation of the law or personnel changes (Fiedler, 2000), it has several advantages over due process hearings. For example, mediation is considered a much less formal approach that may prevent an adversarial climate from developing. Further, it is focused on the future, it emphasizes clear and direct communication, it keeps control of the process in the hands of the parties directly involved, and it is far less expensive than a due process hearing (Fiedler, 2000). Of course, if parents do not wish to engage in informal or formal mediation—including a resolution session—or if school professionals have a negative disposition toward the conflict situation and the potential of mediation, it is not the preferred option (Rhoades, Arnold, & Jay, 2001).

Many sources of information exist regarding how to successfully mediate during conflict. Some of the most helpful suggestions include the following (Barsky, 2000; Mareschal, 2005):

1. In any type of mediation, preparation is the key. Whether this involves understanding the context in which a conflict is occurring, the frames of reference of participants, or the impact of the outcome on each individual, an effective mediator has a solid foundation of understanding from the very start.

2. Mediation begins with an orientation—that is, an explanation to all participants of the ground rules. Often, mediators emphasize the importance of clear communication, the priority given to making the situation feel "safe" to everyone, and the optimistic intent to resolve the conflict. A focus on establishing a positive climate of collaboration is particularly helpful.

3. Early in mediation, each party explains his or her perspective, and the specific issues that comprise the conflict are articulated. The rationale for this process is that each person has a unique perspective regarding the conflict and that sharing perspectives sometimes helps to generate solutions.

4. The most critical step of mediation occurs when needs and interests are explored; each party looks for areas of shared needs and interests that might be elements of resolution. If this stage of mediation is not successful, the process is likely to flounder.

5. Once interests are identified, the strategies of negotiation and problem solving are used. An effective mediator will at this point subtlety remind participants of the costs of failing to reach an agreement.

6. When some type of agreement is reached, it should be clearly articulated, either in writing or through an oral point-by-point summary completed during the meeting. This prevents miscommunication.

7. Finally, it is often helpful in mediation for a follow-up meeting to be scheduled so that progress can be reviewed, the current situation assessed, and feedback obtained from the involved parties.

If you think about your roles and responsibilities in schools, you may have numerous opportunities to function informally as a mediator. You might first think of taking this role in assisting students to resolve disagreements. However, you might also serve as a mediator in a conflict among members of a multidisciplinary, a grade-level, or a department team. You could mediate when parents of a student with special needs have a conflict with a teacher or specialist. Finally, you can use the thinking of mediation in your own interactions with your colleagues and the parents and families of the students with whom you work.

Conflict and Diversity

A discussion about conflict would not be complete without mentioning diversity. If you review the information contained throughout this section, you should realize that a key underlying principle for successfully resolving conflict is to analyze it and base your response on that analysis. As part of this process, you should consider culture (Avruch, 2003). That is, you should look beyond race, nationality, or ethnicity to understand more clearly the beliefs, perceptions, and preferences that each person in a conflict holds. Even more than in day-to-day interactions, when you participate in a difficult interaction with professionals, paraprofessionals, parents, or others from a background different from your own, it is essential first that you recognize your own point of view and how it is influenced by *your* culture—your need to preserve harmony, your comfort level with confrontation, the nonverbal cues that you most respond to, your need for formality or informality, and so on. Then you can juxtapose your culture against the cultures of others in order to deliberately communicate and use procedures likely to lead to resolution (Wanis-St. John, 2003). Specific suggestions for doing this are included in Putting Ideas into Practice.

Understanding Resistance

Resistance has been a topic of concern in many fields, including business and the helping professions as well as education (e.g., Erchul, Raven, & Whichard, 2001; Gardner & Cary, 1999; Kampwirth, 1999; Results-Driven Manager, 2005). It most typically occurs as a response to an interpersonal change or an organizational change that has a personal impact. One apt characterization of resistance defines it as the ability to not get what is not wanted from the environment. The use of negatives in the definition is critical: Resistance occurs only in response to a perceived impending change. If no change exists, resistance vanishes.

The use of negatives in the definition, however, should not lead you to conclude that resistance itself is undesirable. In fact, the opposite is true. Resistance is a defense mechanism that prevents individuals from undertaking change that is too risky for their sense of safety. In addition, resistance sometimes leads to an

> ### PUTTING IDEAS INTO PRACTICE
>
> ## Addressing Difficult Interactions in Diverse Groups
>
> Thoughout your professional preparation and practice, you have learned and remained aware of cultural differences in child-rearing practices, importance placed on education, perspectives on time, and many other factors. It is just as important to understand that individuals from various cultures may respond differently when disagreements occur. Here are a few suggestions to consider when faced with such situations.
>
> ■ Most current professional literature on conflict resolution suggests strategies that rely heavily on talk. However, in some cases alternatives may be better. Suggesting a few moments of silence for everyone to think about their needs, creating options for using visual presentations of the points of view being expressed, or identifying a shared emotion a bit removed from the situation at hand may help diffuse the tension and lead to a constructive resolution (Von Glinow, Shapiro, & Brett, 2004).
>
> ■ The sense of urgency for resolution of a conflict may vary by culture (Brew & Cairns, 2004). If you sense that others are feeling pressured to resolve a dispute before they are ready, you might suggest adjourning the meeting and reconvening it at a point in the near future.
>
> ■ Across many cultures, a perceived threat to "face"—that is, a person's social image—can become a significant roadblock to discussion and resolution (White, Tynan, Galinsky, & Thompson, 2004). The implication is that all ideas shared when an interaction is difficult should be thought of in terms of how others will perceive them. For example, some family members may sense they lose face if they follow "orders" from the school professionals on how to address their child's behavior.

appropriate decision not to participate in an activity or change (Charney, 2004). The concern in professional relationships arises when resistance becomes a barrier to effective interactions and needed innovation. Think about the issues that contribute to resistance in the following two examples:

> The team of middle school teachers is discussing options for an upcoming field trip. Mr. Matthews, the science teacher, has an idea he would like the group to consider. He says, "I've been thinking about the opportunities for teaching concepts of physics at an amusement park—you know, riding the roller coaster to explore the effects of gravity. I need to do some more checking, but going to an amusement park would accomplish two goals: keeping the students motivated for the spring and making science concepts come to life." Another team member immediately replies, "Right. There is not a chance that you'll catch me on a roller coaster. I've seen too many news stories recently about problems with safety on them; just thinking about it makes me queasy. And if we go to a park, there'll be too much

pressure to ride. I don't like the idea at all. Besides, how are you going to convince administrators that going to an amusement park is instructionally important?"

Ms. Hill, the school psychologist, is meeting with Mr. Neal, the fifth-grade teacher, shortly before the holidays about a behavioral contract for Reggie, a student with behavior disorders who is inattentive and has been swearing at the teacher and other students. As Ms. Hill explains the contract as a possible intervention, Mr. Neal comments, "You know, I don't mind having Reggie in my class. But I don't know about this contract idea. It's not fair to the other kids to give Reggie special treatment. I predict I'll get parent phone calls about this." After more discussion, Mr. Neal reluctantly agrees to try the intervention.

A week later, Ms. Hill stops by Mr. Neal's classroom to check on Reggie. "How's the contract working for Reggie?"

"Well . . ."

"What's going on?"

"Actually," says Mr. Neal, "I tried it for two days and it just wasn't fitting into my classroom routine. Besides, Reggie probably didn't like being singled out. We need to change it, but for now, with the holidays coming, I just don't have the time to attend to this. Let's talk after the beginning of the year."

In the first example, the resistance to a trip to the amusement park is fairly straightforward: The teacher appears to be concerned about the physical safety of the proposed adventure and is also raising matters of instructional importance. In the second example, the resistance is more difficult to discern clearly, but it is still related to safety: Mr. Neal's response might be interpreted as meaning that he is concerned with his psychological safety. Perhaps he is unfamiliar with the contracting approach Ms. Hill proposed, and he does not want to let her know this. Perhaps he is overwhelmed by the pressures of his job (which might include a new math curriculum, an overcrowded room, or several students with extraordinary needs), and he simply cannot manage one more demand.

Given the amount and pace of change currently taking place in schools, it is not surprising to find resistance common. And when you reflect on the changes occurring in the education of students with disabilities and other special needs, you should conclude that resistance is likely among special services providers as well as between special services providers and general education staff. The fact that many school changes result in increased adult–adult interactions only compounds the issue because such interactions increase the likelihood that each individual's resistance will be known and will affect others.

Causes of Resistance

Although many causes of resistance have been described in the professional literature (e.g., Kampwirth, 2006; Piersal & Gutkin, 1983; Results-Driven Manager, 2005), they can be summarized as addressing just one critical concept:

Resistance is an emotional response based on a rational or irrational fear or concern related to whatever change is proposed or occurring. These fears may pertain to (1) the change itself; (2) the impact of the change on the resistant person; (3) other persons initiating, participating in, or affected by the change; and (4) homeostasis.

Concerns about the Proposed Change

One common source of resistance is professionals' and parents' perceptions of the anticipated outcomes associated with a change. For example, parents may be resistant to moving their children from a separate special education setting to a general education classroom; they believe that their children are receiving excellent services and should not risk those services being diminished.

Another example of fear related to the change itself may be the philosophy or value system associated with the change. If you are a speech/language therapist who believes strongly in the value of therapy offered in separate settings, then the plan to have you work with students primarily in classes may cause you to be resistant. Alternatively, if you believe that integrative therapy should be the standard in your field, you are likely to be resistant to a plan in which you will provide only articulation therapy in a separate clinical setting. For general education teachers, this type of resistance may arise when considering adapting their learning materials and performance standards for students with disabilities. In each example, resistance is attached to a belief system that is associated with a specific change. This form of resistance is particularly likely to occur when change is not clearly explained.

Concerns about the Personal Impact of the Change

According to Fiedler (2000), fear about the personal impact of change is the category into which most professional resistance falls and includes the following issues:

1. Some individuals faced with changing their professional functioning are afraid of failing. They may anticipate that they do not have the skills to participate in the change, and they may perceive that they cannot acquire them.

2. Some professionals fear the frustration that may occur while learning new skills and practices. Whenever changes are undertaken in activities, programs, or services, professionals require time to adjust their practices. Because time is a luxury that simply cannot be afforded in many schools, however, they often are expected to assimilate change rapidly and to immediately function effectively, sometimes beyond the point of reasonable expectations.

3. Personal fear about change also relates to losing autonomy. Many school professionals are accustomed to completing their job responsibilities with little input from others. When a change is proposed, particularly one that appears to threaten this autonomy, fear sometimes results. Resistance is an expected outcome.

Concerns about Others Involved in the Change

The third category of concerns that may lead to resistance focuses on the other individuals. First, concern may be directed at the person initiating the change. Have you ever decided before hearing about a new strategy, service, or program that you probably did not want to participate just because you had a negative perception of the person whose idea it was? Perhaps you did not respect that individual, experienced a great deal of miscommunication with the person, or had discrepant personal styles. It should be noted that this is another example of resistance that, in some cases, has a strongly rational basis.

The second major type of concern included in this category is the threat of change in your relationships with others. If you participate in a change, it may affect how other staff members view you and your status with them. For example, a newly hired special education teacher at the secondary level is asked by the special education director to begin developing a plan for co-teaching with the basic skills teachers. The basic skills teachers are opposed to the co-teaching idea, and the committee they were supposed to have formed to work on the project has met only once. If you were the special education teacher, how would you respond? One approach would be to develop the program alone, hoping to positively influence colleagues in the process. Another would be to let the basic skills teachers know about the request and then to collaborate with them to avoid meeting it. Even if this were inappropriate, the latter option might appeal to the special education teacher if he or she felt unaccepted by the other teachers and had concerns about how they would respond if the program were developed. This type of situation clearly has many alternative solutions. The point here is that the relationship issue may supersede others and lead to resistance.

Homeostasis

The tendency of some individuals and systems to prefer sameness to change is referred to as homeostasis. For individuals, once they become accustomed to a particular way of carrying out responsibilities, working with students, and otherwise fulfilling their professional obligations, they may be unable to consider alternative ways to do those tasks. The degree to which homeostasis plays a part in resistance varies greatly from person to person and with the nature of the change that is at issue.

Organizations also seek to maintain some level of homeostasis and in doing so may encourage resistance. In some school settings, it is considered the norm to resist any change, regardless of its source. We have worked in school settings in which the professionals quickly stated that their schools were difficult places to initiate new programs because staff members simply did not like change. Although this situation relates to individual homeostasis, it is distinguished from it because of its pervasiveness in the school's culture. Several staff in the school may be risk takers or change agents, but their individual characteristics are overshadowed by the norm.

Homeostasis may result from another dilemma referred to as *change fatigue* (Morgan, 2001). That is, in schools where change has been constant, professionals may become very reluctant to participate. A fairly complex example illustrates this concept: An urban high school has had three principals in the past four years. In addition, the school district has changed the high-stakes testing requirements twice during that time. There has been a relatively high staff turnover, and no special educator has more than three years of teaching experience. The school attempted to place more students in general education settings about four years ago, but encountered serious problems related to teacher acceptance, scheduling, and student behavior. When the new principal announces at a meeting for all staff members that her first priority is to improve general education access, teachers roll their eyes and look at each other skeptically. Their reaction, without even hearing about the proposal, is negative. Given the situation, however, it is understandable—they have difficulty comprehending how they can manage yet one more change, one that does not seem feasible.

Indicators of Resistance

Resistance often is indicated through subtle behaviors and can be difficult to clearly recognize. Most behaviors that indicate resistance have alternative, legitimate interpretations, but when examined closely, they actually function as means of avoiding change. Thus, in order to address resistance, you should have a clear picture of how resistance is likely to be manifested. The most common ways include (1) refusing to participate, (2) supporting a change with words but not actions, (3) displacing responsibility, (4) deferring change to a future time, and (5) relying on past practice. Each of these signals of resistance is presented with examples in Figure 11.2.

In considering signals of resistance, it is particularly important to look for patterns of behavior. Anyone can encounter a crisis that leads to the cancellation of a meeting. However, repeated cancellations could indicate resistance. Anyone could have a straightforward reason for delaying a change. However, repeated excuses may be an indicator of resistance. Your role in working with others is to distinguish between legitimate problems and resistance and to base your actions on such distinctions.

Assessing Whether to Address Resistance

The next consideration when you perceive resistance is to decide whether it should be addressed. Your deliberations should examine (1) the appropriateness of the resistance, (2) whether addressing it is warranted, and (3) others' commitment to change.

Determine Whether Resistance Is an Appropriate Response

The concept that resistance is sometimes appropriate has already been mentioned, and overall you may have noticed that this chapter on resistance does

---

Figure 11.2   Indicators of Resistance

Indicator	Explanation
Refusing to participate	Response to change is "No, thank you." Examples: ■ "I figure this is just a fad. By next year it'll be gone." ■ "I just can't deal with doing that right now. I have too many other responsibilities." ■ "I don't want to get involved with this issue. Please ask someone else."
Supporting without substance	Response to change is "puppies-on-the-dashboard" head nodding without meaning. Examples: ■ "Yeah—that's great." ■ "Okay—I see." ■ "That makes sense—uh-huh."
Displacing responsibility	Response to change is claiming others will not permit it. Examples: ■ "The other parents are going to complain." ■ "I understand that the state has said this is not legal." ■ "The principal doesn't allow it."
Deferring to a future time	Response to change is putting it off. Examples: ■ [in September] "Everything is so hectic with the start of the year. Let's give it a little time and then try it." ■ [in November] "The holidays are almost here and you know how disrupted the schedule gets."
Relying on past practice	Response to change is to call on tradition as a reason to retain the status quo. Examples: ■ "We've always done it this way." ■ "If it's not broken, don't fix it." ■ "This way has always been good enough for us." ■ "We can't just rush into this type of intervention. It's too different from what we're used to."

---

not necessarily focus on making it go away. Instead, as you approach resistant interactions, you should first consider the situation from the other individual's point of view. If the change will place too great a burden on the person, resistance may be a positive reaction and should not be addressed. In general, if you remember that addressing resistance should have as a goal respecting it, exploring it, and potentially (but not invariably) responding to it, you will be more effective in your professional relationships. Although our examples tend to make others the resistant people, also keep in mind a point made at the beginning of this chapter: We all resist, given the right circumstances.

Assess Whether Addressing Resistance Is Warranted

Another consideration when deciding whether to respond to a resistant situation is the appropriateness of attempting to address it. The same questions presented in Chapter 2 for deciding whether to problem solve are applicable for resistance. In some instances, the best response to resistance, even if it is not rational, may be no response at all. For example, if a colleague is planning to leave her job at the end of the year, your efforts to address her resistance to a new technique may not be worth the effort. The same could be said for those who are transferring to other schools or retiring. Other situations that may not warrant addressing resistance are those in which administrative support is lacking or contextual variables (such as a lack of resources) make the proposed strategy unrealistic.

Consider the Extent of Others' Commitment to Change

Understanding the likelihood that others will change can assist you in gauging your own commitment to change. Individuals are more likely to participate in a change if they feel they have a moderate or low level of positive or negative feeling about the nature of the change (Fiedler, 2000). They are less likely to change if they have strong negative feelings about it. The implication is that change is less likely to be successful if offered when emotions are intense. A more constructive alternative would be to wait, if possible, until feelings are less intense and then use the strategies discussed in Putting Ideas into Practice on page 312 and in the following section.

Persuasion as a Strategy for Responding to Resistance

One critical strategy for addressing resistant situations is persuasion. Persuasion is your ability to convince another person to agree to your perception or plan regarding an issue or idea (Truscott, Richardson, Cohen, Frank, & Palmeri, 2003). For example, you may be faced with the task of convincing a resistant colleague that change in the daily schedule is necessary and appropriate. Similarly, you may attempt to convince a parent that the educational services proposed by the team are in the best interests of the child. A Basis in Research on page 313 presents an example of research for teachers related to a specific type of persuasion called *rational persuasion*.

Persuasion Approaches

Approaches for persuading are heavily influenced by theories that describe how individuals respond when faced with an idea or activity to which they are resistant (Mason, 2001; Pfau, Szabo, Anderson, Morrill, Zubric, & Wan, 2001; Shelby, 1986). For example, in a *behavioral approach* to persuasion, the goal is to provide

PUTTING IDEAS INTO PRACTICE

Practical Suggestions for Responding to Resistance

Resistance to change and strategies for reducing resistance have captured professionals' attention for many years. Here are some suggestions that can be especially helpful to school professionals who are implementing changes such as inclusive practices, co-teaching, new intervention models, or other new initiatives.

■ Provide as much detailed information about the change as you can. Give specific examples of what the program, service, or model will look like, who it may affect, and the timeline for implementation. This suggestion should involve your administrator, and overall it should be consistent with the principles for program development outlined in Chapter 7.

■ Ask others to describe their perceptions. If you hear misinformation, be sure to replace it with accurate information.

■ If you know someone at another school already implementing the change, ask that person to visit with your colleagues to provide a testimonial about it.

■ Ask specific individuals to assist with clearly identified tasks. If people feel more involvement, they will be more committed to participate.

■ If problems occur, treat them as expected. No complex change occurs without "bumps in the road."

■ Arrange periodic meetings to gather perceptions of the change. Use these as a basis for making refinements as needed.

■ Gather data and present it using clear visuals. In this era of accountability, the most persuasive way to overcome resistance is to demonstrate that initiatives can positively affect student learning.

---

positive reinforcement to resistant individuals in order to convince them to change. This would occur if a teacher were offered a preferred classroom assignment in return for participating in a pilot co-teaching project.

A second theoretical orientation to persuasion is a *consistency approach,* which is based on the notion that individuals are more likely to change if they have a sense of cognitive dissonance (Festinger, 1957). For example, by suggesting to Ms. Boesche that she has already been successful with a student very much like the one she is currently expressing resistance about having in her class, you might plant a seed that eventually prompts her to be more accepting of the new student.

A *perceptual approach* also is considered a means for persuading others. Individuals applying this model recognize that people have a certain tolerance for change. If the proposed change is somewhat close to an activity a person is already comfortable doing, that person is more likely to accept the new activity

A BASIS IN RESEARCH

The Effectiveness of Persuasion: Exploring a Complex Technique

Persuasion is a skill that consultants sometimes use to convince teachers to implement the interventions and strategies identified to address student concerns. Truscott, Richardson, Cohen, Frank, and Palmeri (2003) explored whether one specific approach to persuasion—called *rational persuasion*—was effective with teachers. The researchers examined two essential elements of rational persuasion:

- The importance of identified interventions (RP importance)
- Objections that might be raised and information to overcome those objections (RP objections)

They created nine scripted videotape sequences to describe three common interventions (token economies, contingency contracts, and response cost) and to include neither, one, or both of the RP elements. A total of 71 graduate students who were practicing teachers were divided into four groups. Each group viewed three of the 12.5-minute videotapes (one per week for three weeks). The teachers then rated the acceptability and effetiveness of the intervention portrayed and their level of commitment to try the intervention if they were in that situation. The researchers used accepted procedures to ensure that the order in which the videotapes were viewed was accounted for and the situations described in the videotapes were equivalent.

Truscott and his colleagues found mixed results. That is, in some cases the use of rational persuasion techniques positively influenced teachers' perceptions of the acceptability and effectiveness of the interventions and teachers' willingness to try them. In other cases, this did not occur. The authors noted that, despite the apparent positive effects of rational persuasion in business settings, it may not be a strong enough approach to change teachers' already-held perceptions of interventions for students. That is, if a teacher believes that token economies are not effective for changing student behavior, rational persuasion techniques are not likely to change that teacher's perception. They suggested that a better alternative is collaboration to identify mutually agreeable interventions. However, they also suggested that rational persuasion relies on participants' thinking about the information presented and that the videotapes, being artificial situations for the teachers, might not have activated teacher critical thinking. The researchers concluded that rational persuasion should not be discarded as a technique and that it indirectly influenced teachers, but they acknowledged that a simple relationship between intervention, persuasion, and implementation was unlikely to be found.

This study explored the effectiveness of providing a strong rationale for an intervention and answers to likely objections to the interventions. How do you think those two elements of rational persuasion would influence your thinking? Could they overcome your preconceived notions about an intervention?

Source: Based on S. D. Truscott, R. D. Richardson, C. Cohen, A. Frank, & D. Palmeri, "Does rational persuasion influence potential consultees?" *Psychology in the Schools, 40* (2003): 627–640.

than if it is perceived as radically different. For example, in discussing a new school initiative related to inclusive practices, a principal might explain that teachers in the school are already making many accommodations for students with special needs and that the initiative is simply an extension of the work they are already doing.

Finally, a *functional approach* to persuasion suggests that the process of convincing someone to change must take into account adult learning characteristics. For example, if Ms. Schwartz complained that she dislikes the way students are constantly leaving the room to receive special services, you might suggest that she would prefer to have students stay in the room. This could acknowledge her desire for control over student movement and the sense of classroom community as well as creating an opportunity to discuss integrated, in-class services.

Persuasion Strategies

The knowledge base on theoretical approaches to persuasion leads to a number of suggestions for you to use in encouraging colleagues and others to change.

1. *Seek ways to provide incentives.* For special services providers, incentives could include a trade-off or reduction of workloads; for general education teachers, incentives might involve assistance with classroom chores or opportunities to participate in professional development activities. If you think of any situation in which you need to persuade others, you probably can identify incentives that could be offered to positively affect the outcome.

Persuasion occurs in advertising, but it also helps school professionals when they are responding to colleagues, parents, or others who are resistant to change.

2. *Relate the proposed change issue to a positive image.* To many teachers, the word *change* is a negative stimulus; they immediately associate it with anxiety, stress, more work, and more meetings. One strategy for persuading others is to associate the change with a reduction of anxiety, work, and meetings. Obviously, this strategy is effective only to the extent that the reduction of workload can, in fact, be implemented. The complement to this is to avoid saying anything negative about the change; such messages tend to be remembered and gain strength with time (Kumkale & Albarracin, 2004).

3. *Provide opportunities for others to become familiar with the change through observation.* If a professional observes others successfully carrying out a change, he or she may sense it is feasible after all. For some educators, this could include visiting neighboring school districts where similar activities or services are offered. For others, it may be just an observation period in a nearby colleague's classroom or therapeutic setting.

4. *Create discrepancies that can be brought to the attention of resistant individuals.* Imagine a history teacher who fears that a student with a disability will require too much of the teacher's attention. One strategy would be to arrange an informal meeting between the history teacher and another subject area teacher who has worked with the student and who can share the positive experiences the student had in a general education class. Knowing about the student's success creates a discrepancy and makes resistance less likely.

5. *Link the proposed change with the resolution of the discrepancy.* Persuasion involves more than simply creating dissonance; it also involves efforts to influence how the dissonance will be resolved. In the example just presented, the dissonance exists because of the history teacher's belief that the student cannot be successful and the other teacher's perspective that the student can be successful. To influence the history teacher to resolve the dissonance by agreeing the student could succeed, you might comment on the teacher's ability to work with other difficult students, the fact that he or she would be on the "cutting edge" for the district integration program and in compliance with emerging policy, and the satisfaction experienced by working with the student.

6. *Relate the change to others' knowledge and experience.* Keeping both the nature and the description of the proposed change within others' knowledge and experiential base is a basic strategy of persuasion. A simple illustration of this point concerns the use of technical vocabulary. If you have a strong background in behavioral approaches, you may tend to speak to others in the language of reinforcers, extinction, and punishers. If you change your language so that your message sounds more familiar to your colleagues—rewards, ignoring, and consequences—you may find that less resistance occurs.

7. *Propose changes within the value system of others.* This strategy is a powerful extension of the preceding strategy. Proponents of change should examine participants' value systems and tailor ideas to stay within those parameters.

8. *Gain public commitment.* One strategy for ensuring that a proposed change falls within individuals' tolerance levels is to obtain their overt commitment to the change. Once they have made such a commitment, they are more likely to try to expand their own levels of tolerance for the change. Public commitment raises significantly the probability of implementation.

9. *Involve others early in the planning stages.* Whether you are discussing a single intervention, a modification for a classroom, a program change, or the restructuring of an entire service delivery system, the change will be more readily accomplished if you include others in planning. Doing so enables you to be more responsive to others' needs. Change thus becomes less threatening, and the potential for resistance is decreased.

10. *Be sensitive to adult learning preferences.* Certain conditions may make change for adults easier. In fact, knowledge about adult learning is important when planning for change. Examples of adult learning preferences include incorporating ideas based on the life experiences of participants, using novelty to introduce an idea, and engaging participants in meaningful activities related to accomplishing the change. Although none of these techniques seems strongly persuasive, each has the potential to add enough appeal to the proposed change to make it attractive to the individuals affected by it.

11. *Clarify ownership of the task or activity.* Whenever people are working together toward a goal, they should specify how ownership will be assigned. If change is the issue, the more that individuals feel like they have contributed to designing and implementing the change, the more likely it is that they will participate in it.

12. *Obtain and use feedback from participants.* Feedback is one type of information that participants can contribute to change. The obligation of professionals fostering change is to use this information in a meaningful way. For example, suppose you were working with a general education teacher on accommodations for a student with a mild disability. Before you discuss specific accommodations, you might ask what the classroom goals are, what the teacher's priorities are, and what approaches seem most suited to the class. Based on this input, the discussion of alternatives could proceed. In a second phase, the special educator and general educator should meet to discuss whether the accommodations are being successful. If the general education teacher mentions a problem, the appropriate response from the special education teacher is to explore how that feedback could be used to alter the arrangement. Counterproductive approaches would be for the special education teacher to defend the accommodation or explain how the teacher could make it more effective.

Putting the Pieces Together

At the opening of this chapter, you were alerted to the fact that difficult interactions provide opportunities to learn all the skills that have been presented in this text. Whether conflict or resistance emerges as part of teams, consultation, co-teaching, or interactions with paraprofessionals, your knowledge of problem-solving strategies and communication skills are the tools that enable to you address such situations confidently. Examples of applying your knowledge and skills are provided in Putting Ideas into Practice.

PUTTING IDEAS INTO PRACTICE

Using Communication Skills during Difficult Interactions

When you are faced with responding to conflict or resistance, you have the opportunity to use the communication skills you have learned to good advantage (Guilar, 2001). Consider this example: You have been trying to meet with a classroom teacher to follow up on a self-monitoring strategy you are trying to teach a student to use. The student is to keep an index card taped to her desk, and when she begins a requested task without making a comment out loud in class, she is to make a check on the card. In talking with the student, you realize that the teacher is not encouraging the student to use the strategy and sometimes seems to be going back to a pattern of confronting the student about callouts. In your conversation with the teacher, she claims that she is trying with the student, but that the student will not follow directions or accept guidance.

How might each of these aspects of positive communication help you at some point to talk to the teacher?

- *Frame of reference* (Chapter 8)

  When the teacher says, "I've been really careful about using the strategy and it's not working," what might the teacher mean? What response might you make?

- *Feedback and indirect question* (Chapters 9 and 10)

  You point out to the teacher, "During the period when I had dropped by your class to observe Alesha using the strategy, I noticed that you asked her to not call out four times. I did not notice you direct her to the index card. I wonder if there is something about using the index card strategy that doesn't fit into your classroom routines."

- *Presupposition* (Chapter 10)

  You ask the teacher, "In the two weeks that we've been trying this strategy in your class, what about it has been most effective?" (after a reply) "How does using the strategy break down?"

- *Open question* (Chapter 10)

  You ask the teacher, "What do you think we should do to make this strategy—or some other one that will accomplish the same purpose—more effective for Alesha and more workable for you?"

Summary

As schools continue to emphasize collaboration among professionals, difficult interactions are likely to occur, often because of conflict or resistance. Conflict is any situation in which people perceive that others are interfering with their ability to meet their goals. Although school professionals, including special services providers, traditionally have tended to avoid conflict, it can be constructive and helpful. Conflict generally is caused when two individuals want different outcomes but must settle for the same one, when they want the same outcome but it cannot be available to both, or when one individual internally experiences conflicting reactions to a situation. These causes are influenced by a wide variety of organizational variables. Most individuals have a preferred style for responding to conflict, either competitive, avoiding, accommodative, compromising, or collaborative. Each of these has advantages and drawbacks. You should learn to use each style as appropriate in combination with specific negotiation and mediation strategies that may assist you to create constructive outcomes in conflict situations.

Resistance is the ability to avoid what is not wanted from the environment. It is an emotional response to change based on a variety of professional fears related to the change. Resistance may be demonstrated with many indicators, including refusal to participate, support without substance, displacement of responsibility, deferral to a future time, and reliance on past experience. However, resistance is subtle and should be looked for through patterns of behavior. Four approaches to conceptualizing persuasion—behavioral, consistency, perceptual, and functional—offer many strategies for addressing resistance. Generally, addressing conflict and resistance requires the use of all the knowledge and skills presented throughout this textbook.

Activities and Assignments

1. Many schools and school districts are continuing to make progress toward becoming more inclusive. As you think about the concerns that often are raised about inclusive practices, consider how they might lead to conflict. Try categorizing the conflicts that may arise using the three-part analysis of causes of conflict presented in this chapter. What conclusions does this activity lead you to regarding your school's move toward inclusive practices?

2. Select a conflict situation that is common among your colleagues or class members. First, role-play different styles for managing the conflict. Next, discuss additional strategies for constructively addressing the conflict that are consistent with each style.

3. Special services professionals may not think of themselves as negotiators, despite the importance of negotiation in many of their activities. Using conflict situations identified in the preceding activities or others based on your school experiences, what negotiation techniques might have been helpful for responding to the conflicts? What are the communication skills that seem most helpful during negotiation?

4. What are your state's procedures for mediation and dispute resolution for disagreements related to special education? How do these procedures rely on principles outlined in this chapter? If possible, ask someone who participates in mediation to describe this process and its potential for diffusing conflict.

5. Why is it more common to find resistance among school professionals than conflict? What symptoms of resistance do you find are most common in schools? What are examples of each? On what topics are you resistant to change?

6. Using an example you generated for the preceding activity, analyze it to determine whether it is a situation in which persuasion might be effective. That is, ask yourself these questions: Is resistance an appropriate response to the situation? Why or why not? Does the situation warrant a response to the resistance? Why or why not? How committed to change are the individuals involved? Given your analysis, what is the likelihood that the other person(s) can be persuaded?

7. Have each member of your class spend a few minutes writing about a situation encountered in which resistance played an important role. Then distribute these so that each class member has an unfamiliar situation to address. Using the strategies suggested in this chapter, role-play how to respond to the resistant individual.

8. Think about the topics addressed in this chapter. Write a critical analysis of how effective problem-solving and communication skills affect conflict, resistance, negotiation, and persuasion. Then apply your thinking to teaming, consultation, and co-teaching. What types of conflicts or resistance might occur in each of these service delivery models? How might negotiation and persuasion be effectively used for each?

For Further Reading

Barsky, A. E. (2000). *Conflict resolution for the helping professions.* Belmont, CA: Brooks/Cole.

Christie, D., & Jassi, A. (2002). "Oh no he doesn't!" "Oh yes he does!": Comparing parent and teacher perceptions in Tourette's syndrome [Electronic version]. *Clinical Child Psychology and Psychiatry, 7,* 553–558.

Davidson, J., & Wood, C. (2004). A conflict resolution model [Electronic version]. *Theory into Practice, 43,* 6–13.

Fiedler, C. R. (2000). *Making a difference: Advocacy competencies for special education professionals.* Boston: Allyn & Bacon.

Isenhart, M. W., & Spangle, M. (2000). *Collaborative approaches to resolving conflict.* Thousand Oaks, CA: Sage.

Kosmoski, G. J., & Dennis, R. (2001). *Managing conversations with hostile adults: Strategies for teachers.* Thousand Oaks, CA: Corwin.

Protheroe, N. (2005). Leadership for school improvement. *Principal, 84*(4), 54–56.

Results-driven manager series. (Ed.). (2005). *Managing change to reduce resistance.* Boston: Harvard University Business School Press.

Appendix

Conflict Management Style Survey

This Conflict Management Style Survey has been designed to help you become more aware of your characteristic approach, or style, in managing conflict. In completing this survey, you are invited to respond by making choices that correspond with your typical behavior or attitudes in conflict situations.

The survey identifies 12 situations that you are likely to encounter in your professional life. Please study each situation and the five possible behavioral responses or attitudes carefully and then allocate 10 points among them to indicate your typical behavior, with the highest number of points indicating your strongest choice. Any response can be assigned 0–10 points, so long as all five responses for the given situation add up to 10 total points, as shown in the following example:

Example Situation: In responding to a request from another for help with a problem, you would:

_1_	A.	Clearly instruct him or her how to proceed.
_4_	B.	Enjoy the strategizing and the challenge.
_4_	C.	Help him or her to take responsibility for the problem.
_1_	D.	Find it unnerving but agree to help.
_0_	E.	Avoid the invitation at all costs.
10	Total	

Please choose a single frame of reference (e.g., work-related conflicts, organizational conflicts) and keep that frame of reference in mind when responding to all the situations. As you complete the survey, remember that there are are no right or wrong answers. The survey will be helpful to you only to the extent that your responses accurately represent your characteristic behaviors and attitudes.

Situation 1: Upon experiencing strong feelings in a conflict situation, you:

____	A.	Enjoy the emotional release and sense of exhilaration and accomplishment.
____	B.	Enjoy the strategizing involved and the challenge of the conflict.
____	C.	Become serious about how others are feeling and thinking.
____	D.	Find it frightening because you do not accept that differences can be discussed without someone's feelings getting hurt.
____	E.	Become convinced that there is nothing you can do to resolve the issue.
10	Total	

Situation 2: Consider the following statements and rate them in terms of how characteristic they are of your personal beliefs:

____	A.	Life is conquered by those who believe in winning.
____	B.	Winning is rarely possible in conflict.
____	C.	No one has the final answer to anything, but each has a piece to contribute.
____	D.	In the last analysis, it is wise to turn the other cheek.
____	E.	It is useless to attempt to change a person who seems locked into an opposing view.
10	Total	

Situation 3: What is the best result that you expect from conflict?

_____ A.   Conflict helps people face the fact that one answer is better than others.

_____ B.   Conflict results in canceling out extremes of thinking so that a strong middle ground can be reached.

_____ C.   Conflict clears the air and enhances commitment and results.

_____ D.   Conflict demonstrates the absurdity of self-centeredness and draws people closer together in the commitment to each other.

_____ E.   Conflict lessens complacency and assigns blame where it belongs.

10   Total

Situation 4: When you are the person with the greater authority in a conflict situation, you:

_____ A.   Put it straight, letting the other know your view.

_____ B.   Try to negotiate the best settlement you can get.

_____ C.   Ask to hear the other's feelings and suggest that a position be found that both might be willing to try.

_____ D.   Go along with the other, providing support where you can.

_____ E.   Keep the encounter impersonal, citing results if they apply.

10   Total

Situation 5: When someone you care for takes an unreasonable position, you:

_____ A.   Lay it on the line, telling him or her that you don't like it.

_____ B.   Let him or her know in casual, subtle ways that you are not pleased; possibly distract with humor; and avoid a direct confrontation.

_____ C.   Call attention to the conflict and explore a mutually acceptable solution.

_____ D.   Try to keep your misgivings to yourself.

_____ E.   Let your actions speak for you by indicating depression or lack of interest.

10   Total

Situation 6: When you become angry at a friend or colleague, you:

_____ A.   Just explode without giving it much thought.

_____ B.   Try to smooth things over with a good story.

_____ C.   Express your anger and invite him or her to respond.

_____ D.   Try to compensate for your anger by acting the opposite of what you are feeling.

_____ E.   Remove yourself from the situation.

10   Total

Situation 7: When you find yourself disagreeing with other members of a group on an important issue, you:

_____ A.   Stand by your convictions and defend your position.

_____ B.   Appeal to the logic of the group, in the hope of convincing at least a majority that you are right.

_____ C.   Explore points of agreement and disagreement and the feelings of the group's members, and then search for alternatives that take everyone's views into account.

_____ D.   Go along with the rest of the group.

_____ E.   Not participate in the discussion and not feel bound by any decision reached.

_____

10   Total

Situation 8: When a single group member takes a position in opposition to the rest of the group, you:

_____ A.   Point out publicly that the dissenting member is blocking the group and suggest that the group move on without him or her if necessary.

_____ B.   Make sure the dissenting member has a chance to communicate his or her objections so that a compromise can be reached.

_____ C.   Try to uncover why the dissenting member views the issue differently, so that the group's members can reevaluate their own positions.

_____ D.   Encourage the group's members to set the conflict aside and go on to more agreeable items on the agenda.

_____ E.   Remain silent, because it is best to avoid becoming involved.

_____

10   Total

Situation 9: When you see conflict emerging in a group, you:

_____ A.   Push for a quick decision to ensure that the task is completed.

_____ B.   Avoid outright confrontation by moving the discussion toward a middle ground.

_____ C.   Share with the group your impression of what is going on so the nature of the impending conflict can be discussed.

_____ D.   Forestall or divert the conflict before it emerges by relieving the tension with humor.

_____ E.   Stay out of the conflict as long as it is of no concern to you.

_____

10   Total

Situation 10: In handling conflict between your group and another, you:

_____ A.   Anticipate areas of resistance and prepare responses to objections prior to open conflict.

_____ B.   Encourage your group's members to be prepared by identifying in advance areas of possible compromise.

____ C.   Recognize that conflict is healthy and press for the identification of shared concerns and/or goals.

____ D.   Promote harmony on the grounds that the only real result of conflict is the destruction of friendly relations.

____ E.   Have your group submit the issue to an impartial arbitrator.

____
10 Total

Situation 11: In selecting a member of your group to represent you in negotiating with another group, you would choose a person who:

____ A.   Knows the rationale of your group's position and would press vigorously for your group's point of view.

____ B.   Would see that most of your group's judgments were incorporated into the final negotiated decision without alienating too many members of either group.

____ C.   Would best represent the ideas of your group, evaluate these in view of judgments of the other group, and then emphasize problem-solving approaches to the conflict.

____ D.   Is most skillful in interpersonal relations and would be openly cooperative and tentative in his or her approach.

____ E.   Would present your group's case accurately, while not making commitments that might result in obligating your group to a significantly changed position.

____
10 Total

Situation 12: In your view, what might be the reason for the failure of one group to collaborate with another?

____ A.   Lack of a clearly stated position, or failure to back up the group's position.

____ B.   Tendency of groups to force their leadership or representatives to abide by the group's decision, as opposed to promoting flexibility, which would facilitate compromise.

____ C.   Tendency of groups to enter negotiations with a win/lose perspective.

____ D.   Lack of motivation on the part of the group's membership to live peacefully with the other group.

____ E.   Irresponsible behavior on the part of the group's leadership, resulting in the leaders placing emphasis on maintaining their own power positions rather than addressing the issues involved.

____
10 Total

When you have completed all items, write the number of points you assigned for each of the five responses for the 12 situations in the appropriate columns on the scoring form below. Add the total number of points for each column and make sure that they total 120 points. Then, transfer your column scores onto the style/approach form to discover the extent to which you model the different styles/approaches to managing conflict.

Scoring Form

Situation	Response A	Response B	Response C	Response D	Response E
1	_____	_____	_____	_____	_____
2	_____	_____	_____	_____	_____
3	_____	_____	_____	_____	_____
4	_____	_____	_____	_____	_____
5	_____	_____	_____	_____	_____
6	_____	_____	_____	_____	_____
7	_____	_____	_____	_____	_____
8	_____	_____	_____	_____	_____
9	_____	_____	_____	_____	_____
10	_____	_____	_____	_____	_____
11	_____	_____	_____	_____	_____
12	_____	_____	_____	_____	_____
Total	_____ +	_____ +	_____ +	_____ +	_____ = 120

Column	Points	Style/Approach
A	_____	Controller
B	_____	Compromiser
C	_____	Collaborator
D	_____	Accommodator
E	_____	Avoider

Source: Conflict Management Style Survey. Macon, GA: Mercer University, Center for Student Involvement and Leadership. www.mercer.edu/cs:l/leaps-resource-files.htm. Retrieved February 28, 2002.

CHAPTER 12

Perspectives and Issues

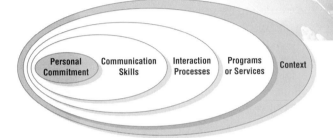

Connections

By studying the chapters of this book thus far, you have learned about the applications in which collaboration occurs and the communication skills and interaction processes that you need in order to collaborate effectively. In this final chapter, you will learn about broader issues that also affect collaborative practice, including considerations related to specific participants and contexts for collaboration that may require special attention. The chapter concludes with a discussion of several ethical issues that may arise in your collaboration with your colleagues.

Learner Objectives

After reading this chapter you will be able to:

1. Describe role-related factors to take into account when collaborating with administrators and professionals from specific disciplines, including related services professionals, transition specialists, and general education teachers.

2. Discuss special considerations that may apply in your collaborative work with families, and analyze your roles and responsibilities for working with parents and other family members, particularly those from diverse groups.

3. Outline special issues that sometimes arise when professionals collaborate in early childhood settings, with private or public agencies other than schools, with vocational and community-based services, in multicultural contexts, and with students.

4. Discuss ethical issues that may arise in professional collaboration.

Brandi knew that many people would be attending Devon's annual review—he is in his final year of high school—but she was still a bit surprised when she entered the conference room. Devon, of course, was present, as were his stepmother and father. In addition, the chair of the vocational arts department, an assistant principal, Devon's counselor, a representative from vocational rehabilitation services, the orientation and mobility specialist, and the transition specialist all were attending. As the itinerant vision specialist, Brandi was concerned that everyone understand both Devon's capabilities and limitations. She listened carefully during the meeting, trying to emphasize Devon's tremendous abilities in computer programming and mathematics, which he plans to study at the community college. She wanted to be sure that everyone encouraged Devon to continue to the university and not be satisfied with a two-year computer technology degree. As the meeting progressed, though, Brandi sensed that different and sometimes competing priorities were represented by the participants. Devon's parents expressed concern about financial aid for college and their fear that he cannot live independently; Devon mentioned his anxiety about obtaining all the support he needs after he leaves high school and not wanting to be treated differently by professors; and the vocational rehabilitation representative discussed eligibility for services. Brandi wondered how to bring all the perspectives together so that Devon can reach his goals.

Introduction

As you have read this book, we hope you have recognized that collaboration is an immensely complex endeavor, in terms of both the subtleties that can make it effective or ineffective and the number of school activities and applications that benefit from it. Because of this complexity, it is often impossible to attend to all the significant factors that can influence collaborative practice, particularly in the typically frenetic daily lives of school professionals.

This chapter is intended to help you integrate what you have learned about collaboration—conceptually and technically—by highlighting five topics that require a clear and sophisticated understanding of it. The first issue concerns collaboration with specific groups of professionals, including general education teachers, related services providers, and administrators. The second topic comprises the special considerations for interacting with families. The third topic encompasses issues that might arise in particular contexts (e.g., interorganizational situations, vocational settings, early childhood settings, multicultural environments). The fourth concern relates to student collaboration. The final issue concerns ethics, including dilemmas that might occur as part of collaboration. As you read this chapter, you might wish to analyze how your collaborative expertise can enhance or constrain your professional interactions in these areas.

Role-Specific Considerations in Collaboration

Although the ideas and skills detailed in this book relate to all your collaborative efforts, their application varies somewhat depending on the roles of those with whom you collaborate (Rogers & Steinfatt, 1999; Shoffner & Briggs, 2001). As you learn about some of the factors that might influence your interactions with administrators, general education teachers, and related services professionals, keep in mind that the information is not intended to form a prescription for your actions. Rather, it is intended to assist you in understanding why you need to make subtle changes in how you respond to different individuals in order to collaborate successfully, an understanding that can be especially critical in situations like the meeting described at the opening of this chapter.

Working with Administrators

Administrators face unique challenges when they are participants in the collaborative efforts at their schools because they have a dual role. They are colleagues and peers in collaboration, but they are also supervisors responsible for evaluating job performance and making other personnel decisions (Brown & Anfara, 2002; Del Favero, 2004). Keeping these two roles separate is often challenging.

For example, sometimes school professionals find it difficult to nurture a collaborative relationship with their administrators because the administrator does not clearly indicate whether the decision making at hand is intended to be collaborative or not. Consider the meeting one principal called to discuss the next steps for Julio, a student with emotional disabilities who, during lunch, had knocked over a table displaying school shirts for sale. The special education and general education teachers, counselor, psychologist, and principal spent most of an hour discussing Julio's needs and the lack of follow-through on recommendations at home, and they considered various options—in-school suspension, a supervised lunch arrangement, and behavior contracts, among others. Both teachers supported the supervision option. Toward the end of the meeting, the principal said, "Thank you for all your input. I have decided that Julio has to be suspended from school—an out-of-school suspension—because of this incident. Nothing you have said has made me change my mind. I'll arrange the necessary procedures, contact the district office since Julio receives special education, and call the parents." Needless to say, the professionals who had attended the meeting felt their time had been wasted.

When teachers and other professionals work with school administrators, it is important to ascertain whether the shared interaction is intended to be collaborative, whether they are functioning in an advisory (but not a decision-making) capacity, or whether they are really just being informed about a decision that has already been made. All of these options are sometimes appropriate. Principals do need information and sometimes advice, even when they have to make decisions based on additional factors of which you may not be aware. They also sometimes inform staff about decisions that have already been reached, and sometimes they collaborate (Jayanthi & Nelson, 2002; Sergiovanni, 2004). Your responsibility is to recognize the place and impact of each type of situation and gauge your communication accordingly. To do this, you might have to ask directly whether an interaction is collaborative or advisory, or you might need to ask your administrator to clarify the purpose of a meeting in which you are to participate; taking these steps can be essential for effective collaboration. In fact, we are sometimes surprised when professionals are frustrated about not having their input used by an administrator, even though the administrator had clearly stated that the input would be considered but not necessarily used as the primary factor in decision making.

The other dilemma that sometimes arises when administrators are participants in collaboration, especially at team meetings, IEP meetings, or conferences attended by several individuals, is inappropriate reliance by professionals on administrative authority (Del Favero, 2004). For example, consider a team meeting in which one professional is insistent in her repeated requests for a specific service; the others are not in agreement, but they do not object strenuously and so the decision is made to accept the vocal teacher's recommendation. Following the meeting the other team members complain to the principal that the teacher had exerted too much influence over the decision. This is an example of a team abdicating responsibility for a group decision and hoping that the administrator would use her authority to "control" the situation—even though this matter would be handled more appropriately through collaborative decision making.

Two other administrative issues related to collaboration merit mention. First, although not common, in some schools the administrator is absent during crucial interactions, especially those requiring a district representative for the purpose of special education decision making. In interactions that require an administrator's participation, your responsibility is to remind the individual of the need for his or her presence, inform your special education supervisor if your administrator does not attend meetings as needed, and document your efforts to ensure this essential participation.

The second issue is much broader and concerns administrators' understanding of topics related to collaboration. For almost two decades administrators have been moving toward greater use of collaborative models (Barth, 1991; Smith & Scott, 1990). It would be difficult to find a leadership text, article, or conference that does not emphasize collaboration as a key element in school success. This includes general understanding of the importance of collaboration, the role of the administrator in fostering a school climate supportive of collaboration, and enough knowledge about collaborative activities to help make them a reality (Billingsley, 2005; Brown & Anfara, 2002; Gabriel, 2005). However, professionals across the country often note that although administrators may be accomplished collaborative leaders in some areas, many of them do not have adequate knowledge regarding collaborative approaches for educating students with disabilities or other special needs.

Perhaps the clearest example of this issue occurs in schools that are beginning co-teaching programs as part of their service delivery system for special education. As noted in Chapter 5, it is essential that principals understand the program philosophy and design, and they need to know that co-teaching involves far more than special educators popping into classrooms to support the students with IEPs. Principals need to recognize the importance of shared planning time, feasible scheduling, and the importance of not assigning huge numbers of students with IEPs or other extraordinary needs into classrooms just because co-teaching is available there. In establishing goals and structures for their collaborative efforts, teachers also should collaborate with principals to ensure the feasibility and desirability of potential activities.

Recognizing that collaboration with its related activities is only one of many items competing for an administrator's attention, one strategy you can use to facilitate your interactions with your administrator is to help provide as much relevant information as you can. Some strategies for providing such information are given in Putting Ideas into Practice on the next page.

Working with General Education Teachers

Much of this textbook includes an emphasis on interacting with general education teachers. However, as with the other specific groups addressed in this section, additional and distinct considerations should be kept in mind when working with them.

Teacher Roles and Responsibilities

Too few general education teachers have been prepared for collaborative roles and responsibilities (Mock & Kauffman, 2002; Slonski-Fowler & Truscott, 2004; Spencer, 2005). Some intuitively understand what is required or actively seek information, and others are receptive to input from colleagues, but a few are uncomfortable working with others in part because they have no orientation to this approach to teaching and related responsibilities. In one middle school, teachers who attended a professional development workshop on co-teaching heard ideas that they later used to rescue and revitalize their failing program. They even contacted the presenter to get additional advice to help them design a promising model for their setting. Contrast that example to an elementary school where a group of teachers met to plan an innovative language arts program in which students work in different classrooms on different days and general educators and special educators share instructional responsibilities. The idea had tremendous potential, but it soon became clear that each teacher firmly believed that he or she had the best approach to teaching language arts and was unwilling to make changes in that approach to accommodate the innovative program. The teachers soon reverted back to their separate programs.

In some respects, special and general education teachers have different languages, and so they often lack the common vocabulary that is necessary for meaningful discussion and planning (Spencer, 2005; Weiner & Murawski, 2005). The example of the unsuccessful collaboration with the elementary school language arts program illustrates how different philosophies can interfere with collaboration. You can easily see how difficult it would be to develop a shared philosophy if those involved do not have a shared vocabulary

General education teachers may experience other challenges based on their perception of their role in interactions involving students with disabilities

PUTTING IDEAS INTO PRACTICE

Strategies for Developing Administrative Support

Principals have many responsibilities that demand their attention. Here are some strategies to help your principal learn about and develop a commitment to collaboration.

- Engage your administrator in initial planning, including planning for communicating about the program to colleagues, parents, and students.

- Discuss with your principal the elements of collaboration you have or wish to include in your program. Decide with your principal what support and resources you can expect for the program.

- Invite your principal or assistant principal to visit another school with you to observe a particularly good program emphasizing collaboration.

- Share journal articles on pertinent topics. You might have as a goal to provide at least one article or clipping each month.

- Alert your administrator to professional development activities related to collaboration. Request permission to attend with a general education teacher, and encourage your principal or assistant principal to accompany you.

- Share with your principal handouts about collaboration received at professional conferences. You might even suggest that particularly relevant ones be distributed to the entire staff for discussion at a faculty, team, or department meeting.

- Take a few moments on a regular basis to chat about the opportunities and challenges of your collaborative activities. This type of face-to-face interaction is sometimes more effective than written communication. Further, it can provide your administrator with enough information that he or she can make better decisions and be more supportive of your collaborative efforts.

- Maintain an ongoing log or list of topics relative to your collaborative efforts that you wish to discuss with your administrator. Determine the priority of each topic, and discuss one or two at each meeting.

- Invite your principal to join you in making presentations about the program to colleagues in other schools or districts.

(Cook, 2001; King & Youngs, 2003). For many reasons, including a long history of general education teachers being told that students with disabilities needed something that only a special educator could provide, some general education teachers are highly collaborative—except when it comes to teaching students with IEPs. Teachers make comments such as, "I don't have a special education credential," "She needs more specialized help than I can give her," or "I can't teach him one thing and the rest of the class something else."

With new emphases in teacher preparation and professional development, comments such as these are becoming less common. Nonetheless, general edu-

The demands for accountability affect all students and their teachers.

cators' concerns about their roles and responsibilities relative to students with disabilities may continue to present roadblocks to productive collaboration. Specific dilemmas may occur around topics that are already issues of concern to all teachers, such as curriculum standards and proficiency assessment as required in the No Child Left Behind Act of 2001. General education teachers often believe that students with IEPs either should not be required to take such tests, or that as classroom teachers they should not be responsible for the achievement of those students. Collaboration may become difficult, especially when general educators learn that their students with disabilities must reach the same standards and that they are accountable for those students' learning in the same way that they are responsible for other students' learning.

Refusal to Collaborate

One final potentially problematic issue raised first in Chapter 11 needs to be mentioned here concerning general education teachers and collaboration. In many schools, one—or perhaps two, three, or more—individual makes it excruciatingly clear through words and actions that he or she will not collaborate on behalf of students with disabilities. Even when special educators make the best use of communication skills and interaction processes and use appropriate strategies for responding to conflict and resistance, such individuals refuse to meet with a team, to co-teach, or to confer for shared problem solving or consultation. Sadly, these few individuals drain a disproportionately high amount of energy from the positive efforts of other staff members, and the rest of the school staff members sometimes plan all their activities around them. We mention this small but critical group of educators for two reasons: First, we wish to acknowledge realistically that even with the best skills some situations that could and should be collaborative will not be. Second, we find that special educators often feel it is their responsibility to convince all colleagues to work collaboratively. We would like to remind you (gently) that collaboration cannot be coerced; it is a professional choice. If a teacher is not carrying out his or her responsibilities in terms of working appropriately with students, it is not the role of a special educator to remedy the situation singlehandedly. That is a supervisory issue and one for which you should seek the appropriate administrative support (Praisner, 2003; Salisbury & McGregor, 2002).

Increasing Understanding

Sometimes when a school staff is working to increase collaborative activities they are helped by taking the time to better understand each other's roles and responsibilities. One way to do this is to spend time at a faculty or department meeting not only discussing the roles of each group and the contributions the groups make in collaboration but also noting the constraints on each group's participation. Another strategy is to experiment with some in-school job sharing, in which teachers "shadow" each other or switch roles for a few periods to get a sense of each other's responsibilities. Both general education and special education teachers should raise any issues on roles and responsibilities—those mentioned here as well as those discussed in Chapter 7 on practical matters—as they occur so that they can be resolved as small matters instead of major professional disagreements.

Working with Professionals from Other Disciplines

Although this book is intended to address a wide range of special services providers, collaboration with professionals who are not teachers often presents several unique issues that need to be considered. These may directly and profoundly influence their interactions (Downing, 2002; Howard, Williams, & Lepper, 2005) among themselves, with general education and special education teachers, and with professionals from other disciplines. These professionals include related services personnel—psychologists, social workers, speech/language therapists, counselors, occupational and physical therapists, itinerant specialists (e.g., orientation and mobility specialists or inclusion facilitators), media specialists, librarians, adaptive physical educators, nurses, and others. Each of these groups is important; few students could develop to an optimal level without the direct or indirect services of several of these specialists. In addition, these professionals have the knowledge and talents to help you fulfill your responsibilities far better than you could independently. When entering professional roles in schools, some of our students tell us how helpful these resource people are and how reassuring it is to know that "We are not in this alone."

Yet, your colleagues in these disciplines do face unique challenges. These have to do with professional preparation and orientation, the limited amount of time that related services personnel are able to spend at a single school, and other role-specific constraints they may experience (Callaghan, 2005; Flannery, Slovic, Treasure, Ackley, & Lucas, 2002; Staton & Gilligan, 2003).

Professional Orientation

Most related services professionals do not have teaching credentials, nor do they have experience in working with large groups of students in a classroom environment. Further, some of them have training that is primarily clinical or medical in its focus. They may have had considerable experience with adults and little coursework or internship experience with school-age children or in education settings. The result is that some related services providers have orientations significantly different from those of general education or special education teachers and other staff members (Spencer, 2005). During collaborative activities, the difference in preparation and orientation can lead to misunderstandings and miscommunication and sometimes to conflict and resistance. For example, an occupational therapist may propose working with a student on grasping and other fine motor skills in a pullout model. The teachers may argue that grasping and related skills can be addressed through writing, cutting, eating, playing with clay, and an entire array of other school activities and do not need to be taught through isolated tasks. Although the occupational therapist might see the value in those practice activities, he or she maintains that only an occupational therapist can really provide the instruction and that this needs to occur in a quiet and separate location. In another example, some speech/language therapists assert that most of their services should be delivered in small, quiet settings away from other students. Many teachers (and many speech/language therapists) note that the classroom, home, and community are the best locations for students to learn speech and language skills.

Time on Site

A second dilemma for collaboration involving related services personnel as well as itinerant teachers is their limited time at a single school site. This factor alone suggests that collaboration will be difficult and sometimes simply not possible. These professionals frequently comment that they never quite know what is happening at any of their schools because they are never there long enough to become part of the school community. This leads to innumerable problems.

For example, sometimes they arrive at a school to provide services only to find that all the students are at a special assembly. Or they are available to meet with a team only on Thursday mornings, and if the team meets at another time, they cannot be present and they miss the discussion. Even when they do attend meetings, they may be late because they have to drive from another location and may be delayed. Conversely, school-based professionals sometimes express frustration with related services and itinerant personnel because of their scarce presence at the school, their rigid scheduling requirements, and their tardiness.

Competing Professional Obligations

A third set of issues for related services professionals, also related to time, concerns their other professional obligations. Many individuals in these professional groups have extremely large caseloads and, as a result, have extraordinary numbers of meetings and conferences to attend and assessments to complete. Some also may be obligated to preserve time in their schedules for writing reports and attending discipline-specific meetings. Some of these professionals may be assigned to help with other school programs and have extensive responsibilities for working with families and community agencies. In addition to creating scheduling difficulties, such responsibilities fragment the attention of these professionals and limit the depth of their involvement in school-based collaboration.

These factors often limit the extent to which related services professionals are able and willing to undertake collaborative endeavors. It may be necessary for these professionals and special and general education teachers to prioritize situations in which active participation on the part of related services professionals is needed. The personnel in a single school also should stay aware of the constraints under which these professionals work and take that into account in scheduling meetings and professional development activities. Finally, if you hear dissatisfaction from other colleagues about related services or itinerant professionals, you might want to find out the nature and extent of the issues and either work to resolve them or assist others in understanding the challenges involved.

Special Considerations for Interacting with Parents

You are likely to have a different relationship with each of the families with which you work depending on the needs of the student and the interests, resources, and needs of the families. Understanding families, including their life cycles and transitions, and having a framework for promoting family participation in educational decision making will assist you in your collaborative endeavors with families.

Understanding Families

When you consider the range of relationships professionals have with families, you will realize that in some cases collaboration is not an appropriate goal. For many reasons it may not be possible for you to get to know the parents well enough or for the parents to know you well enough for collaboration to occur. Similarly, some parents may have so many obligations and demands that collaboration is not a feasible goal. For others, collaboration is appropriate and recommended. A few parents may even want more collaboration than is possible within the time parameters of your schedule. Your responsibility is to gauge your interactions based on the parents' preferences, although in the latter case you may have to refer the parents to other professionals who can further interact with them.

Collaboration is a worthy goal, but your primary responsibilities in working with families are to understand the family and its needs and to facilitate family participation in making decisions about the educational program for their family member with a disability. Facilitating family participation involves providing family members with information about disabilities, educational concerns, and their rights, as well as assisting them to participate in conferences and team meetings.

Systems Theory and Family Life Cycles

Although systems theory has been recognized in related fields since the 1960s (Lambie, 2000), it has become a major influence in how to view and respond to families of children with disabilities only over the last two decades. With systems theory, the family is seen as a complex and interactive social system in which all members' needs and experiences affect the others.

Much like human development, family systems theory views the family as undergoing a series of developmental tasks that vary along several life stages. Nichols (1996) describes the family life cycle as "being concerned with the developmental tasks of the family itself as it deals with the needs of the adult members and the developmental needs of the offspring" (p. 57). Many theorists have proposed family life cycle stages and advanced models with widely varying numbers of cycles. Putting Ideas into Practice on pages 336–337 summarizes typical family functions and tasks (Lambie, 2000) within a four-stage family life cycle framework (Turnbull & Turnbull, 2001).

These family life stages help describe how families change over time. That is, as a family progresses from one stage to the next, family members' responsibilities shift, and the family is said to undergo transition. Transitions are the periods between stages when family members are readjusting their roles and interactions in order to meet the next set of expectations and tasks, and they are characterized by confusion and often by increased stress. As an educator, you can be especially effective in your collaboration with families when you attend to and remain sensitive to the life stages and transitions of families and assist them in taking appropriate steps to support their children. Putting Ideas into Practice on page 338 offers some suggestions for accomplishing this goal.

Unique Factors and Barriers to Collaboration with Families

Consider what the impact might be on a family that has a child with a disability. First, certainly, some family members report that greater affection results

PUTTING IDEAS INTO PRACTICE

Four Family Life Stages and Suggestions for Assisting Families

This description of stages families experience can help you to anticipate the needs of your students' families and how to respond to them.

Birth and Early Childhood

With the introduction of a child through birth or adoption, the primary family functions become nurturing and caring for the infant or young child and providing appropriate behavioral limits. Tasks are to realign family relationships as well as relationships with friends and extended families to accommodate the presence of the young child and the duties of parenthood. Special issues focus on understanding the disability and working through parents' feelings about the diagnosis. Professionals need to provide supportive and accepting environments and help parents begin to see their family life in a new way and to connect parents with support groups.

Childhood

The primary themes for families with children in their elementary school years are affiliation and allowing others to be brought within the family boundaries. The family functions are sensitivity to the child's developmental needs, encouraging the child's independence, and enjoying the child's experiences. Tasks to be accomplished are affiliating with a peer network and establishing family responsibilities and sibling roles. Special issues at this stage are more complex for the family of a child with a disability diagnosis. Deciding on goals, services, and placements are major stressors. Professionals should be empathic listeners, provide objective information as well as connections to family support groups, and help families and the student to talk with siblings and nondisabled peers about the disability.

Adolescence

This stage is characterized by themes of decentralization and the relaxing of boundaries. Parents' essential functions are to tolerate the efforts their child makes to "distance" them and to provide the adolescent with support needed to establish his or her identity, a matter especially important for young people with disabilities (Riley, DeAnda, & Blackaller, in press). The tasks that parents face include managing the adolescent's increasing independence, refocusing their own careers and marriage, and developing more flexible roles. This tumultuous time may be more influenced by a family's cultural context than in any other stage (Groce, 1997). This is a significant period for planning for vocational development, as is described in the upcoming discussion of prevocational and vocational services. Professional support also is needed by families to prepare them for and support them in the student's more active role in IEP planning, the provision of sexuality education, and clarification of the sexuality issues commencing in adolescence.

(continued)

Adulthood

The stage of adulthood is characterized by themes of detachment, dissolving ties, and letting go. Family functions focus on supporting and facilitating independence while encouraging the young adult to accept more responsibility. The primary tasks for families at this time include renegotiating roles and relationships between or among parents and other family members, redefining roles with adult children, re-aligning relationships to include the adult child's housemate, assistant, spouse, and/or in-laws, and dealing with the death of family members. Special issues in accessing postsecondary and supported living services may be family challenges and may require guidance from professionals.

Source: Adapted from six stages presented by R. Lambie, *Family systems within educational contexts: Understanding at-risk and special needs students* (2nd ed.) (Denver: Love, 2000), and from A. P. Turnbull, H. R. Turnbull, E. Erwin, & L. Soodak, *Families, professionals, and exceptionality: Positive outcomes through partnership and trust* (5th ed.) (Upper Saddle River, NJ: Merrill/Prentice Hall, 2006).

(Turnbull, Erwin, & Soodak, 2006). However, some families may have difficulty expressing affection, especially when first learning of their child's disability. And although affection is likely to develop later, that initial response may cause a disruption in the bonding process. For example, the family may have a difficult time helping the child with a disability to develop a positive self-identity. In fact, cultural and peer relations may also intervene, and the self-esteem of the parents or siblings likewise may be affected.

Families also must earn and decide how to spend income. Not surprisingly, they report that they spend more money on a child with a disability, especially if he or she has health care needs or requires special equipment or clothing. Moreover, providing for the other daily care needs—such as transportation, medical procedures, or behavior management—often are so demanding that the parents may not perform as well at work as they would otherwise, and they may lose economic or career opportunities. These same physical and emotional demands also may interfere with family members' recreation and leisure activities.

We do not wish to imply that having a child with a disability is an overwhelming burden. In fact, many family members believe that the child with a disability strengthens their families. Research on the positive contributions of having a child with a disability consistently finds that the child is a catalyst for increased spirituality of family members (Stainton & Besser, 1998; Turnbull et al., 2006). Nevertheless, a child with a disability requires more of a family's physical, emotional, temporal, and fiscal resources than do other children.

A number of variables that may present challenges to any family–professional interactions include family structure, child-care requirements, single-parent families, poverty, and nontraditional families. Two additional types of barriers can be identified (Bailey, Buysse, Edmondson, & Smith, 1992). First, many parents of children with disabilities lack the knowledge and skills needed to contribute

---

PUTTING IDEAS INTO PRACTICE

Enhancing Successful Transitions

Are you wondering what you can do in your professional role to assist families in making successful transitions from one life cycle stage to another? Here are some suggestions.

Early Childhood

- Begin preparing for the separation of preschool children by periodically leaving the child with others.
- Gather information and visit preschools in the community.
- Encourage participation in parent-to-parent programs. ("Veteran" parents are matched in one-to-one relationships with parents who are just beginning the transition process.)
- Familiarize parents with possible school (elementary and secondary) programs, career options, or adult programs so they have an idea of future opportunities.

Childhood

- Provide parents with an overview of curricular options.
- Ensure that IEP meetings provide an empowering context for family collaboration.
- Encourage participation in parent-to-parent matches, workshops, or family support groups to discuss transitions with others.

Adolescence

- Assist families and adolescents to identify community leisure-time activities.
- Incorporate into the IEP skills that will be needed in future career and vocational programs.
- Visit or become familiar with a variety of career and living options.
- Develop a mentor relationship with an adult with a similar exceptionality and an individual who has a career that matches the student's strengths and preferences.

Adulthood

- Provide preferred information to families about guardianship, estate planning, wills, and trusts.
- Assist family members in transferring responsibilities to the individual with an exceptionality, other family members, or service providers as appropriate.
- Assist the young adult and family members with career or vocational choices.
- Address the issues and responsibilities of marriage and family for the young adult.

Source: A. P. Turnbull & H. R. Turnbull, *Families, professionals, and exceptionality: Collaborating for empowerment,* 4th ed. (Upper Saddle River, NJ: Merrill/Prentice Hall, 2001), p. 173.

substantially to the education of their children. For example, parents of students with special needs may have limiting disabilities themselves. Similarly, they may lack the knowledge of programs and service options that are being discussed.

A second type of barrier is attitudinal, such as lack of confidence or assertiveness that prevents parents from active participation in the educational programs of their children. When such barriers are present, professionals must support families and help them feel valued and comfortable participating at whatever level possible in their child's education program. Given the tremendous range of parental abilities and preferences for involvement in interactions with school professionals, asking whether collaboration is a reasonable expectation with particular parents is appropriate.

Ultimately, educators need to be mindful of the many demands on families and consider them when they assess family strengths and set expectations for their work with families. Throughout this chapter and in most books for educators, you will read about the importance of parent participation and collaboration. We concur. But we also encourage you to recognize the very real demands on families as well as the challenges to family–professional interaction and gauge your expectations accordingly. A second admonishment is that you not equate your interpretation of parent involvement with parent investment in their children's education. Many very interested and highly committed parents demonstrate this concern through methods not obvious to school personnel.

Facilitating Family Participation in Decision Making

It is the professional's role to provide families with information they need to support their family member with a disability and to be effective participants in educational decision making. This includes communicating effectively, providing information about disabilities and educational concerns, and reporting evaluation results and student progress—concepts presented in Chapters 8, 9, and 10.

Providing Information to Families

Your first responsibility in providing information to parents is to base your interaction on the family's life stage and related needs. When they learn of a child's disability, they need to understand the nature and consequences of the disability. They may need to learn about medical treatments or other related services as well as other physical care matters. As the child matures, they will need information on social, emotional, physical, and cognitive development. Families need to have clear and accurate information in these areas in order to adjust their expectations and goals for their child. These expectations are central to setting appropriate educational goals.

In addition to basic information about the child's disability and its characteristics, families require procedural information regarding due process, placement, parent rights and responsibilities, and other legal provisions of the laws that affect their child. They further require information about educational and related services that may be appropriate for their child. In early years, the decisions may be focused on whether the toddler or young child receives services in a center or in a home-based program. During elementary and middle school years, choices of specific instructional approaches or different inclusionary practices become more focal. By adolescence, families need information about vocational preparation, postsecondary employment, and educational options so that they can begin planning for them.

Professionals have additional responsibilities for providing families with the results of diagnostic evaluations. This can be a highly sensitive matter, requiring great care in communicating, especially when first informing parents about the possible presence of a disability. However, it remains a potentially emotional issue throughout the child's educational career (Correa, Jones, Thomas, & Morsink, 2005).

Language Matters

One additional communication strategy for providing information merits attention here. Whenever possible, communication with families should be in a language in which they are fluent and preferably in their primary language. The written forms and materials used to communicate or plan programs, announcements from school, and fact sheets for information resources all should be translated into the family's primary language. Many school districts make such materials available, but you also can find websites with materials in languages other than English or links to appropriate resources if you need them.

Every effort should be made to accommodate parents whose primary language is not English. Interpreters and translated papers are helpful.

If the family uses a language other than that of the professionals, interpreters typically should be used. However, particularly for informal communication, interpreters are not needed if the family has some proficiency in English or if the professional has basic proficiency in the family's language. It may be sufficient to speak slowly and clearly and provide the family with written information (Ohtake, Fowler, & Santos, 2001). If an interpreter is needed, several matters should be considered. One of the most important recommendations is that you avoid using the student as the interpreter. This is an inappropriate role for the student because it removes him or her from the appropriate role of participant. Also, be sensitive to confidentiality issues. Although professional interpreters have a code of ethics that honors confidentiality, parents may not fully understand this and may be uncomfortable with the presence of the interpreter. In these cases, you can explain the interpreter's role and responsibility to maintain confidentiality.

Assisting Families to Participate in Student-Centered Meetings

Facilitating effective family participation in educational decision making is sometimes a difficult goal (Lazar & Slostad, 1999). Most of your interactions with families probably focus on understanding, planning for, and making decisions about their family member with a disability. Many of those interactions occur in meetings that are structured to focus on the child and family and to discuss matters such as student progress, behavior, school–home programs, or evaluation results. These meetings are often parent conferences, IEP meetings, or annual review meetings.

Many examples exist of school professionals' failure to ensure that family participation occurs. In some settings, for example, students' IEPs are written prior to conferring with families, with the rationale that it takes too much time to discuss everything and write goals and objectives at a meeting. Sometimes this approach is used in order to have a draft document as an efficient starting point for a full discussion in which all participants will contribute to writing new material or modifying the draft. School professionals using this strategy risk communicating that they know what the student needs better than the family or that they have simply made the decisions as administrative ones. In the worst case of this practice, someone at the meeting says to the parent, after all the prewritten information has been reviewed, "Is there anything else you would like to add?" At best, this approach severely limits participation for most family members.

A second, more indirect example of limiting family participation also is common. School professionals informally (or even formally) touch base prior to a meeting with a family to be sure that everyone agrees with whatever is going to be said. This united front can create an adversarial climate in the interaction. What is even more unfortunate is that it indicates that controversy and alternative perspectives are not part of decision making when families are involved, unless the family member challenges decisions made by the educators as a group.

You should reflect carefully on how the formal and informal procedures for working with families in schools might constrain family participation, especially in interactions at IEP and other group meetings (Wolf & Stephens, 1990) like the one Brandi experienced in the example that opened this chapter. If you can foster participation and collaboration, your interactions with families are more likely to be in the best interests of students.

Many suggestions for structuring and conducting decision-making meetings were presented in the Chapter 3 section on conducting meetings and in the Chapter 10 section on conducting interviews. Additional suggestions are listed in Putting Ideas Into Practice. After reading this section, you might find it helpful to review that material and consider unique applications to families. In addition, individuals and teams should periodically assess themselves and their practices to ensure that they are using strategies that enhance family participation.

Context Considerations for Collaboration

In addition to reflecting on matters of relevance for specific role groups when they are involved in collaboration, in certain contexts, regardless of the professionals involved, collaboration is likely to have distinctive qualities. Three of several contexts in which this is true are interagency collaboration, collaboration in early childhood settings, and collaboration in vocational and community settings.

Interagency Contexts

Schools most certainly provide education and significant services in the community. But they cannot offer all of the services required by children and families, especially those with disabilities and other special needs. The primary mission of schools is to ensure the educational development of children and, at times, this requires collaboration with other community agencies. Through viable interagency collaboration using combined expertise, services provided by different systems can be maximized, problems in services minimized, and costs reduced (Johnson, Zorn, Tam, LaMontagne, & Johnson, 2003). The effectiveness of that collaboration depends in part on the ability of school professionals to convey the educational mission to the representatives of other agencies and to accurately assess and respond to the roles of the other agencies (Schmidt, 2003).

Collaboration is a challenging endeavor when professionals from within the same organization work together. It can be an even more ambitious goal when it involves interacting with individuals from one or sometimes several additional agencies (Fowler, Donegan, Lueke, Hadden, & Phillips, 2000; Hord, 1986). Despite the difficulty, however, interagency collaboration plays an important role in the education of students with disabilities. Examples of interagency collaboration you may experience include working with staff members from a residential or hospital setting to transition a student back into a public school environment; participating on a team that includes professionals from mental health, juvenile justice, public school, and family services to create wraparound options for students for whom no traditional educational approach has been successful; or

PUTTING IDEAS INTO PRACTICE

Suggestions for Enhancing Family Participation in Decision Making

You can maximize family participation in meetings by using ideas such as these.

■ Prepare parents for meetings by sending them in advance a summary of the topics to be addressed and a list of possible questions they might want to ask.

■ Suggest that parents bring examples of their child's work that they would like to discuss, information about their child's friends and responsibilities at home, and other information.

■ At the meeting, have professionals chatting informally near the meeting room until the parent arrives, and have everyone be seated at the same time.

■ Be sure that the professional whom the parents know best accompanies and sits next to them.

■ Use nametags that include the person's role (e.g., math teacher, psychologist).

■ Have a file folder with samples of the student's work, copies of forms being discussed, and blank paper and a pen available for the parents. Unobtrusively providing materials at least helps resolve the inequity that occurs when professionals all have reports and other materials spread in front of them.

■ Structure meetings so that parents have opportunities to provide input throughout by discussing issues related to students by domains. To do this, first address the student's academic strengths and needs, soliciting input from any team members who have pertinent information, including the family members. Then address social and emotional areas, using the same procedure, and so on.

■ Maximize the opportunities for families to make informed decisions. Have a variety of choices for parents and students to make (for example, alternatives for elective classes, communication or self-help priorities, or social skills training options) and actively engage them in decision making. Make sure they understand the choices and how those choices will affect the student's program and future opportunities.

just working with a private practitioner who is counseling or teaching a student you also serve.

A number of issues can arise as part of interagency collaboration. First, the decision to collaborate might be reached by one set of professionals although the implementation of a collaborative effort is the responsibility of a different set of individuals (Quinn & Cumbland, 1994). For example, the director of a private preschool and a special education director may reach an agreement to collaborate in serving students with disabilities in a preschool setting. However, neither the teachers nor the itinerant staff of the preschool have participated in the decision. Some staff members may support the decision and work together enthusiastically, but others may misunderstand the purpose of the decision or disagree with it entirely and undermine it through their actions. Clearly, communication among the staff members within an agency is as important as communication among agencies' administrators who agreed to the collaboration.

A second issue that can arise in this type of collaboration concerns the blending of sometimes very different agencies with very different missions (Callaghan, 2005; Flannery et al., 2002; Morse, 1994). For example, the policies and rules that guide each agency may vary considerably. Teachers in public schools routinely hold meetings with parents and others after the official school day has ended; the clinical staff from a hospital setting often work in a culture in which staff members come to the hospital very early for rounds but leave as soon as their workday has ended. Professionals from the juvenile justice system may be accustomed to enforcing decisions reached by requesting a court order; professionals from public schools and family services more frequently rely on negotiating instructional arrangements and enforcing them by offering encouragement, providing incentives, and staying in close contact. The two approaches are strikingly different, and when professionals share problem solving, they sometimes address the task from almost opposite perspectives.

Many studies and policy analyses have identified benefits from and barriers to interagency collaboration (e.g., Gallagher, LaMontagne, & Johnson, 1995; Mitchell & Scott, 1993; Stegelin & Jones, 1991). A recent study of interagency collaboration at the state level is highlighted in A Basis in Research. This study confirms and expands on many previous findings and offers concrete suggestions for agencies to follow in enhancing their collaboration with other agencies.

Generally, the challenges of interagency collaboration that you will face derive from the differences in organizational cultures that reflect often stark differences in the orientation toward disability, "helping," treatment, and systems operations. However, this type of collaboration has tremendous potential. You are likely to experience both the power and frustration of interagency collaboration as schools and other settings become increasingly collaborative. We encourage you to reflect on the suggestions here, use them, and expand on them by devising even more of your own.

Early Intervention and Preschool Settings

Collaboration is now central to all of special education, but it has been a defining feature of programs that meet the needs of young children with disabilities almost since the inception of that field. Perhaps the best illustration of collaboration at the core of early intervention and preschool services is found in the IDEA rules and regulations that specify who participates on the team to develop the individualized family service plan (IFSP). In addition to the professionals serving the child, the team includes the parents, other family members the parents request, an advocate if requested, the service coordinator who has been working with the family or who has been assigned responsibility by a public agency, professionals who have assessed the child, and professionals who are likely to provide services to the child. The plan developed is designed to meet

A BASIS IN RESEARCH

Factors That Affect Successful Interagency Collaboration

Collaboration is a challenging endeavor when professionals from within the same organization work together. It can become even more daunting when it involves several agencies. A recent study by Johnson and his colleagues (2003) examined public and private interagency collaborations and delineated seven factors related to successful collaborations. They also offered suggestions for strengthening these factors.

■ *Commitment* involves mutual trust and shared sense of responsibility for the goals and visions of the collaboration. Suggestions for fostering and nurturing interagency commitment included maintaining a focus on the potentially positive outcomes and using compromise well—for example, compromise when possible and identify clearly those areas in which compromise is not possible.

■ *Communication* was cited most frequently as the means of overcoming collaboration barriers. Suggestions for enhancing communication focused on proactive strategies such as ensuring frequent use of open communication lines, including written informational updates, regular meetings, phone calls, and e-mail messages. Informal links to promote personal connections were also advised.

■ *Strong leadership from key decision makers* was considered critical, especially by those practitioners and coordinators responsible for implementing the policies and programs. Suggestions were to ensure the commitment of upper management who fully understand their agency and have the authority to make decisions, authorize resource use, and provide direct assistance when needed.

■ *Understanding the culture of collaborating agencies* involves understanding the rules, values, structure, and communication systems of one's own as well as those of the collaborating agency. Findings indicated that by understanding another agency as a *culture,* individuals were less likely to find fault with cultural elements and more likely to search for solutions that were sensitive to the cultures of the involved agencies. Suggestions highlighted learning about the mission, priorities, technical vocabulary, and common terms of the agencies involved and understanding the regulatory context in which they operate.

■ *Providing adequate resources for collaboration* was considered fundamental to supporting individuals who work to establish and maintain an interagency collaboration. Suggestions emphasized the need to provide time and additional resources, even if it required finding additional funding, so that the challenges of collaboration were not an add-on to an already full professional workload.

■ *Minimizing turf issues* occurs by recognizing the inevitability, anticipating these issues, and developing plans to address them as they arise. Suggestions included emphasizing and disseminating examples of positive outcomes of similar collaborations and developing a system of incentives and consequences for individuals involved.

(continued)

■ *Engaging in serious preplanning* is needed to establish a foundation for successful collaboration. Suggestions for planning were to establish a steering committee to articulate goals and anticipated outcomes, and to identify problems, issues, and cultural influences of collaborating agencies.

Source: Based on L. J. Johnson, B. K. Y. Tam, D. Zorn, M. LaMontagne, & S. A. Johnson, "Stakeholders' views of factors that impact successful interagency collaboration," *Exceptional Children, 69*(2) (2003): 195–209.

the needs of the child and his family (Noonan & McCormick, 1993). Howard, Williams, and Lepper (2005) provide guidelines for becoming a valued member of an early intervention or preschool team in Putting Ideas into Practice.

Collaboration in early childhood education simultaneously exists at the professional or personal level and at the interagency or systems level. At the personal level, professionals and parents make joint decisions as they collaboratively plan, implement, and evaluate programs for young children with disabilities. At the systems level, agencies strive for collaboration as they jointly work to provide coordinated and comprehensive programs for children and their families. Both levels of collaboration are needed to provide appropriate and well-designed services.

Services for young children and their families can be classified as belonging to one of three models: center based, home based, or a combination of the two. In all three approaches, cooperation and collaboration are integral (Blue-Banning, Summers, Frankland, Nelson, & Beegle, 2004; Turnbull et al., 2006). For example, center-based services require collaboration as the teacher must work as a member of a team that consists of staff members with expertise in several related disciplines. Typically the team includes speech/language specialists, medical personnel, special education and early childhood teachers, occupational therapists, adaptive physical education teachers, physical therapists, and social workers. These professionals and family members develop a comprehensive program likely to involve a number of service providers from different disciplines. Collaboration with parents and collaboration among professionals are central elements in this model.

In home-based services, professionals work with parents and other family members who become the child's primary teachers. The professional typically goes into the home once or more each week and teaches the parents and other family members to implement the appropriate interventions, monitor the child's progress, and evaluate the outcomes. This has the advantage of teaching the child skills in the natural environment and making skill transfer unnecessary. It may also be more convenient for single-parent homes and for mothers working outside the home (Hallahan & Kauffman, 2003). Being able to collaborate effectively with parents and have them work as partners with the professionals is possibly the most central element in this approach (Cross, Traub, Hunter-Pishgahi, & Shelton, 2004).

Combination services are exactly what the name implies—a combination of home- and center-based services. The children come to a center once or more

PUTTING IDEAS INTO PRACTICE

Becoming a Valued Member of an Early Intervention or Preschool Team

Are you part of a team providing services to young children with disabilities? These tips—which also apply to many other team types—can ensure that you truly are a collaborative team member.

- Be clear about what is known and what is not. One professional is not expected to know other professional orientations, philosophies, and content as well as they know their own.

- Listen—and listen some more. Think carefully about what has been heard and be careful to analyze it correctly. Do not screen out information at an early stage based on past experience or personal biases.

- Consider both the short- and long-term consequences of the other possibilities placed before the group.

- Insist upon clarification. If a goal statement is ambiguous or unclear to one person, it may be unclear to others.

- Check all assumptions underlying a goal before agreeing to support or reject it.

- In setting goals on behalf of an infant or young child be creative. Develop habits of conscience and imagination in order to move beyond personal experiences or the limits of one's education.

Source: V. F. Howard, B. F. Williams, & C. Lepper, *Very young children with special needs: A formative approach for today's children,* 3rd ed. (Upper Saddle River, NJ: Merrill/Prentice Hall, 2005), p. 141.

weekly, and the professionals also visit their homes and work with the families on a scheduled basis. These programs are multifaceted and require flexibility on the part of the teacher. They also require extraordinary collaboration skills on professionals' parts, since they combine the services and demands of the other two models.

From these observations and your understanding of parental participation, you can see that collaboration in early childhood is essential but quite complex. Your role is to recognize the factors of collaboration that are especially important in these situations and to use your communication and interaction process skills to foster appropriate interactions, while at the same time using your knowledge of frame of reference to understand the challenges that may be faced.

Vocational and Community-Based Services

Transition specialists, vocational educators, vocational rehabilitation counselors, secondary teachers, and related personnel in public schools and adult service agencies spend considerable time placing students with disabilities in school and community sites for prevocational and vocational services. Planning, placing, training, and supporting students as they develop functional skills and prepare for adult living and employment are key responsibilities for these educators and related professionals (Harvey, 2001; Johnson, 2002; Kohler & Field, 2003). Increasingly, these specialists are collaborating to plan for and support a student's community-based educational program and transition to postschool employment. There is value to having students involved in all the decisions made about their school programs; their role as team members was discussed in Chapter 3. In the case of transition planning, however, IDEA mandates that students be actively involved in their own program planning, and they need to acquire the knowledge and skills to collaborate in the process.

Prevocational and Vocational Services

The Individuals with Disabilities Education Act (IDEA) requires formal transition planning for students with disabilities beginning at age 16. The importance of these IDEA provisions cannot be overstated. Significant evidence indicates need for effective preparation for postsecondary educational, community, employment, and recreational involvement in order to achieve positive outcomes (Sabornie & deBettencourt, 2004; Wagner & Blackorby, 1996), but the appropriate implementation of this provision is uneven and still evolving in many settings. For the most part, prevocational skills such as following directions, timeliness, completion of assignments, and appropriate group behaviors can be addressed in the school curriculum as can career awareness and exploration activities. However, advanced prevocational skills are best acquired through community-based instructional programs

Although the community is seen as the most effective environment in which students can learn appropriate community-based skills (Wehman, 2001; White & Weiner, 2004), some criticize such programming as promoting isolation and segregation (Sabornie & deBettencourt, 2004; Tashie, Jorgensen, Shapiro-Barnard, Martin, & Schuh, 1996). Therefore, clear communication and collaboration among professionals, parents, and the student during goal setting, program planning, and implementation is especially critical (LaCava, 2005). Successful collaboration in this context is predicated on the articulation of shared goals and expectations and a commitment to honor individual values, needs, and beliefs. As students get older and approach the end of their public school education, they must learn about postschool options, including jobs—how to get, perform, and keep them. They also need to learn how to use public facilities and services, prepare for safe and healthy adult living, and develop leisure and recreational skills. For many students, most notably those with moderate and severe disabilities, this requires community-based instruction.

Appropriate community-based instruction, like appropriate special education, is individualized. It is dependent on student needs and reflects the student's age, abilities and limitations, goals, and the community context. In deciding on the amount of community-based instruction, teams need to determine the appropriate balance of learning skills for successful community living and attending classes with students who do not have disabilities. As the emphasis on integrated recreational activities and service learning increases in the general education community (Kesson & Oyler, 1999), opportunities for integrated community experiences also increase. However, in many cases, teams still must find the most appropriate blend of integrated and potentially isolated settings.

When community-based options are selected, collaborative planning and work are required of secondary teachers, transition specialists, and often related service providers to provide appropriate learning experiences. The teacher and others on the transition team need to plan and conduct career education and community-based instruction, which entails locating placements and then organizing and directing vocational training in local employment sites. School programs that foster independence and smooth transition must still be offered and interagency agreements or cooperative activities must be established (Sabornie & deBettencourt, 2004). A number of challenges face these professionals, and they center largely on coordination of services, communication, and the delineation of responsibilities.

Many of the communication challenges for professionals in community-based settings are similar to those associated with interagency collaboration. For example, the school schedule does not necessarily coordinate with the schedule for community activities. The immediate implication of this is a challenge for the professionals in scheduling real-time communication through meetings or phone calls. Community-based professionals often are working with clients and agencies after school hours when teachers and other school personnel are available for meetings or phone conferences. A vocational specialist or job

Community-based related service providers and itinerant professionals often have to arrange to participate in team conferences by telephone or video connection.

coach is likely to have an irregular work schedule that may include supporting clients who have vocational placements at night or on weekends. In these cases, the professionals should develop communication strategies that allow them to share information regularly without face-to-face interactions. Popular options are using pagers and cellular telephones with scheduled conference times. Asynchronous communication through e-mail or voice mail is also increasingly used. For meaningful collaboration, however, we encourage you to make periodic scheduled face-to-face meetings a priority, especially when problem solving or decision making is needed.

Additional challenges to communication occur as a result of the number and diversity of individuals from the community who are involved in the placement and supervision of students. In developing placements and then placing students, the transition specialist may meet with employers, human resources personnel, and potential co-workers as well as observe the work setting to assess the requisite skills and abilities and to prepare the setting for the student's participation. The logistics of arranging these communications are often daunting, but they are made even more complex by the challenge of understanding the differing cultures, vocabularies, and values of the various professionals and community settings. The transition specialist, knowledgeable about both school and community cultures and expectations, becomes the critical player in facilitating effective communication and understanding among these professionals, the student, and the student's family. The team turns to the transition specialist to ensure that clear and accurate information is being shared across all team members, including the student and family.

Closely related to communication and coordination is the matter of specifying functions and responsibilities for the professionals involved. Clearly described professional roles and responsibilities can facilitate effective communication by identifying the individuals with responsibility and accountability for distinct programmatic functions. Perhaps the area that is most frequently a matter of concern is the assessment and record keeping for community and vocational placements (Dowdy, 1996; Sitlington & Neubert, 1998). Delineation of responsibilities and processes for these and similar functions are likely to facilitate your collaborative efforts with community-based professionals and agencies.

Transition Services

Although state and federal rehabilitation programs have long helped achieve employment for individuals with disabilities, the collaboration of education agencies and rehabilitation services has been limited. Just as the responsibility of schools for transition planning is made clear in IDEA, recent amendments to legislation governing the federal Rehabilitation Services Administration (RSA) include mandates that should lead to greater collaboration with schools in the area of transition. In fact, the Individualized Written Rehabilitation Program (IWRP) has many of the same elements and provisions of the IEP and is developed under a similar process. Since the 1992 Amendments to the Rehabilitation

Act, RSA has used the same definition of *transition services* used in IDEA, and both vocational rehabilitation counselors and school professionals must agree on a coordinated set of activities that comprise an appropriate transition plan for an eligible student. These and many additional provisions require collaboration between the schools and rehabilitation agencies. Yet, the collaboration is not easily achieved, as it is influenced by many of the barriers confronting any interagency collaboration, including differences between IDEA and the Rehabilitation Act requirements relative to eligibility for services, assessment techniques and standards, diagnostic criteria, and availability of services.

Among the immediate concerns for collaborating with vocational rehabilitation colleagues is the need for professionals from both agencies to understand the different contexts in which they operate, the similarities and variations in their governing legislation, and the different professional orientations they bring to their work. In addition to learning definitional, assessment, and eligibility issues, they must understand the transition processes and resources of each agency. Based on this understanding, professionals can develop a shared language and understanding of the opportunities and constraints of both systems.

As is the case with IDEA, the Rehabilitation Act emphasizes collaboration with families and participation of individuals with disabilities. For this reason, school personnel have a responsibility to educate and prepare students and their families for effective participation as partners in the process as they implement transition plans for students. Several suggestions for facilitating collaboration with vocational rehabilitation counselors are offered in the following Putting Ideas into Practice.

Multicultural Contexts

The United States is one of the world's most culturally, ethnically, and linguistically diverse nations, and few professionals practice in school environments in which families of diverse cultures are not represented. The vast majority of professionals interact with families from many different backgrounds and so must be culturally competent (Lynch & Hanson, 2004) and able to offer culturally sensitive and relevant services (Chen, 2001; Trumbull, Rothstein-Fisch, Greenfield, & Quiroz, 2001).

In examining cultural contexts, three points offered by Lynch (2004) are relevant.

■ Culture is dynamic—always changing and evolving; it is not static. What individuals remember from a culture in which they were raised is probably not the way the culture is practiced in the same place today.

■ Culture, language, ethnicity, and race are powerful influences on an individual's values, belief, and behaviors, but they are not the sole influences. One's socioeconomic status, education, socialization, and life experiences greatly influence one's identity and frame of reference. These, in turn, influence how a family functions.

PUTTING IDEAS INTO PRACTICE

Strategies for Enhancing Collaboration with Vocational Rehabilitation Counselors

The collaboration that occurs as students prepare to transition from school to adult services can be particulary complex. These suggestions can enhance the effectiveness of such a process.

- Invite vocational rehabilitation counselors to make presentations for educators, parents, and students, when appropriate, on eligibility and service provision requirements.

- Encourage vocational rehabilitation counselors to become involved with students early. The age at which a student becomes eligible for services varies by state, but school personnel should invite vocational rehabilitation counselors to visit classrooms, interact with students and parents, and become involved in cases at the earliest opportunity.

- Learn about appropriate transition activities for the age levels and needs of the students you teach. Infuse transition activities into subject matter classes and school programs.

- Invite the vocational rehabilitation counselor to speak in classes with a focus on transition to postsecondary options, including educational and employment opportunities.

- Discuss specific disabilities and legal rights guaranteed by IDEA, Section 504 of the Rehabilitation Act, and the Americans with Disabilities Act with students and parents. They need to be able to describe the student's abilities and weaknesses and discuss service options if they are to be co-equal partners in the decision-making processes.

- Prepare students to participate in vocational rehabilitation processes by teaching them to use self-advocacy strategies and equipping them with personal portfolios that include reports of their medical status, academic achievement, work history, career interest inventories, IEPs including transition planning, and other relevant information.

- No cultural, ethnic, linguistic, or racial group is homogeneous. Great diversity exists in the attitudes, values, beliefs, and behaviors within groups of people who share a common culture.

Understanding the culture of a student's family is fundamental to understanding and effectively serving the student because a family's culture is a significant determinant of its structure, values, and beliefs, all critical influences on the student. But how do you go about gaining such knowledge and developing cross-cultural competence? The first step is gaining cultural self-awareness

(Chan, 1990; Harry, 1992). This topic was discussed within the context of understanding one's own frame of reference in Chapter 8.

Learning specific information about other cultures is a second step in the journey toward cultural competence (Chan, 1990; Lynch, 2004). This learning can be achieved through reading, travel, and interactions with representatives of the specific cultural groups. Although many useful resources are available for this purpose, the most enjoyable learning will come from direct interaction and experience. Learning firsthand about the art, music, dance, foods, values, and traditions of a culture different from your own is an exciting and stimulating experience. Learning the language of another cultural group may be the best way of learning about that culture because many traditions and values are conveyed through language. However, although interesting and useful, language learning may not be feasible, and it is not necessary to learn another language for one to become culturally competent.

Developing a culture-generic awareness is the step that follows understanding your own and others' cultures. Many values are shared across cultures and variations in values exist within cultural groups (Kalyanpur & Harry, 1999; Trumbull et al., 2001). This recognition will help you understand that although some values may be more characteristic of one cultural group than another, no culture is monolithic. For example, much is currently written about *African American families* and *Asian American families*. These phrases do not give you an accurate picture of a specific family because they do not take into account the geographic area in which the family lives, their religious preferences, their lifestyles, or their economic status (Tobias, 1993).

Cultural variations are best viewed as continuous, rather than dichotomous, perspectives (Lynch, 2004). This implies that you should recognize that individuals' and family members' positions along the continuum are not static. They may vary at any given time based on such factors as age, education, life experiences, vocation, and socioeconomic status, a point illustrated in Putting Ideas into Practice on page 354.

The final step toward cultural competence is the acquisition of specific information about cultural practices relative to children, child rearing, health, disability, and help seeking (Hanson, Lynch, & Wayman, 1990; Hooper & Umansky, 2004). The views that family members hold toward disability and their beliefs about its causes are likely to affect how they respond to the child's disability and to the interventions that are recommended. You should also expect that families will differ notably in their preferred levels of involvement and collaboration with professionals.

The increasing diversity in U.S. population has an impact on the use of collaborative strategies for educating students with disabilities (Miller, 2002). It is certainly far beyond the scope of this book to adequately explore the interaction issues that occur in multicultural and/or bilingual environments, but two more issues merit attention. First, at the same time that you work to base your collaboration on understanding your colleagues or your students and their families as individuals, you also need to be aware that culture influences individuals' interactions in many ways that can positively or negatively influence collaborative

Cultural Continua

Rather than contrasting lists of values and beliefs to understand cultural differences, Lynch (2004) proposes that educators acknowledge that certain value sets are common across all cultures and are best understood if each is viewed as a continuum.

Family Constellation Continuum

Some families are large and have extended kinship networks that are intimately involved with nearly every aspect of the family's daily life. Others are smaller units with responsibility for all decisions and activities and operate independent of an extended family.

Interdependence/Independence Continuum

Interdependence is the primary value in some families. Contributions to the whole are more highly valued than expressing one's individuality, which could be seen as selfish and rejecting of the family. For other families, individuality, the expression of one's uniqueness, is the greatest value.

Nurturance/Independence Continuum

Although most people nurture young children, the behaviors viewed to be nurturing vary significantly from one individual or group to another. What one group sees as nurturing, another group may see as coddling or overindulgent.

Time Continuum

On one end of the continuum, the amount of time needed for a task or interaction is given to it. At the other end, the task or interaction is given only the amount of time that has been scheduled for it.

Tradition/Technology Continuum

From one perspective, respect for age, tradition, and ritual provide a solid base for contemporary life. The divergent perspective is one that places greater value on the future, technology, and youth.

Ownership Continuum

This reflects whether things are individually owned or are shared broadly.

Rights and Responsibilities Continuum

The concept of equality is the fundamental concern. In some groups, equal and nondifferentiated roles are ascribed to both men and women. In others, women are the caretakers and men the providers and intermediaries between the family and the community.

Harmony/Control Continuum

Some groups primarily value living in harmony and synchrony with their environments; others believe it is more important to control their environments and the events in their lives.

Source: Adapted from E. W. Lynch, "Developing cross-cultural competence," in E. W. Lynch & M. J. Hanson (Eds.), *Developing cross-cultural competence: A guide for working with young children and their families* (3rd ed.) (Baltimore: Brookes, 2004), pp. 49–55.

activities. For example, the directness of your conversations and the topics they address might be influenced by cultural expectations. Some cultural groups turn to their extended families in times of need and may be reluctant to share information with school professionals (Correa & Tulbert, 1993). This could be viewed by school professionals as resistance.

Another example is based on individuals' perceptions of themselves in relation to the rest of society. If colleagues or family members see themselves primarily as part of a minority group, they may interact in a way that conveys powerlessness, thus undermining the essential collaborative characteristic of parity. Conversely, such individuals may interact so assertively that others feel powerless; this may be an attempt to override their own sense of not having control. Most professionals have experienced this in interactions with a family member who begins by making many accusatory statements and extraordinary demands. This can occur because of the family member's sense of powerlessness.

A final consideration about collaboration with ethnically or culturally diverse groups concerns understanding, respecting, and valuing. Every individual who participates in a collaborative activity should begin with the understanding that the only culture one understands is one's own. This critical frame of reference can lead all involved to strive for better understanding and more patience if miscommunication does occur.

In your role as a school professional, the contexts in which you are likely to experience the greatest diversity are in interacting with families and in communities where students live. Many of the challenges or dilemmas you encounter as you collaborate in multicultural settings will reflect your frame of reference and the cultural perspectives you hold as well as those held by the people with whom you interact. Although we encourage you to develop awareness and knowledge of the cultures of families you work with professionally, it is not necessary for you to know everything about a particular culture in order to provide culturally sensitive and responsive services. If professionals are respectful of differences, open to learning, and committed to self-examination and change, they can develop culturally responsive and productive relationships with diverse families.

Student-to-Student Collaboration

When professionals are discussing collaboration, they usually mention its importance for students, too. Certainly, teaching students to interact appropriately with each other is critical, and for many students with disabilities learning peer social skills, including those that foster friendships, can enhance their success in inclusive settings (Bovey & Strain, 2003; Copeland et al., 2004; Fisher, 2001; Kassner, 2002). But social acceptance and friendships are not synonymous with collaboration. For example, we all can think of at least one of our own friends whom we value and enjoy, but might not describe as highly collaborative. Likewise, in schools, many important and supportive student–student interaction activities may not be collaborative, but they nonetheless are supportive of student success. We recommend that you learn about and implement such supports to promote student success (e.g., Frederickson & Turner, 2003), but that you distinguish them from collaboration.

Ethics in Collaborative Practice

A particularly fitting final topic for this chapter is ethics. A number of authors have expressed concern over the past several years about the scant attention paid to ethics in the field of special education (e.g., Howe & Miramontes, 1992; Paul, French, & Cranston-Gingras, 2001). Even though the Council for Exceptional Children, the American Speech and Hearing Association, the National Association for School Psychologists, the American School Counselor Asociation, and other professional organizations have codes of ethics and standards of practice, in schools the topic too often is ignored. When the dimension of working collaboratively is added to the other ethical issues professionals face, it becomes critical to recognize potential ethical dilemmas and to consider how you will address them. Three of several possible ethical issues are confidentiality, feasibility, and accountability.

Common Ethical Issues

One of the most frequent and basic ethical considerations in collaborative practice concerns *confidentiality* (Taylor & Adelman, 1998). Educators have been cautioned for many years about preserving confidentiality related to student and family information, but collaboration brings an entirely new dimension to this ethical issue. For example, suppose that two teachers are co-teaching and the general education teacher shares his favorite teaching idea with the special educator. The latter individual sees that the idea has tremendous potential in several classrooms and enthusiastically but naively shares it with several other teachers. The special educator is startled when the teacher confronts her about giving away "trade secrets." This example of a breach of confidentiality is not so much about teaching or learning as it is about developing and maintaining trusting relationships with colleagues.

A second ethical dilemma concerns *feasibility*. We work in many schools in which professionals express belief in the power of collaboration yet have virtually no time or other supports for collaborative practice. Whether a collaborative effort involves a special education teacher and a general education teacher planning interventions for a student with a mild learning disability, a transdisciplinary team preparing for the inclusion of a student with multiple disabilities, or a multiagency and parental effort to create wraparound services for a high school student with serious emotional disabilities, if time does not exist to meet, the effort is unlikely to be successful. Logically, if the program design, no matter how popular, is not feasible or does not have the support necessary to meet the needs of the student, it may be unethical to create assumptions about positive outcomes of working collaboratively until feasibility issues are addressed.

A third ethical dilemma can occur regarding *accountability* (Cook, Weintraub, & Morse, 1995; Friend & Cook, 1992). Special educators are responsible for ensuring that the needs of students receiving special education and related services are met. All ethical standards in school and child welfare fields include responsibilities to students or clients as central elements. Together, these ethical guidelines assign responsibility to the professionals for promoting the total development of each student/client, including academic, vocational, personal, and social development (Schmidt, 2003). In collaboration, there often can be disagreement on the nature of a student's needs and the strategies necessary to address them. A general education teacher may perceive a student as needing incentives for motivation, whereas a special educator perceives that the student is overwhelmed by the academic environment and needs more structured assignments. A speech/language therapist may see that a language-based program in an inclusive setting would best address a student's needs, but the special educator may identify the priority as offering the student a highly structured, small-group environment such as that found in a special education classroom. What are other ethical dilemmas related to accountability that may occur?

Finally, the ethical standards in special education and related fields require that a professional works collaboratively with other professionals in the school and the community and promotes qualities of fairness, cooperation, respect, and objectivity. In the case of special education, the standards of the Council for Exceptional Children (2002) require that special educators "work cooperatively with and encourage other professionals to improve the provision of special education and related services to persons with exceptionalities" (p. 3).

Professionals need to reflect on and clarify their own ethical standards regarding students with disabilities and their own professional behaviors. By doing this before entering into collaborative interactions and continuing during those interactions, you can recognize practices that you might not be comfortable with but can live with versus those that you cannot justify. By continuing the conversation about ethics as it relates to collaboration, you can balance your commitment to collaboration with your responsibilities to meet the needs of the students you serve.

Summary

Several essential topics affect all dimensions of collaboration. One set of issues relates to individuals in specific role groups, including administrators, general education teachers, related services professionals, and professionals in the community. For each of these groups, collaboration may be influenced by job or role constraints, environmental factors, or the potentially uneven relationships between participants in collaborative activities. Special considerations in working with parents include awareness of family life cycles and strategies for facilitating family participation in decision making. Another set of issues concerns the contexts in which collaboration occurs. Four common contexts that influence collaboration are interagency situations, early childhood settings, vocational settings, and multicultural environments. Professionals who collaborate in these four domains need to be cognizant of the assumptions of their practice and how these assumptions may be problematic for the specific context. One situation that is essential—but not necessarily collaborative—concerns student–student interactions. A final set of issues to consider relates to ethics. Professionals who work closely with one another as well as with paraprofessionals and parents face ethical issues more complex than those that typically occur when professionals work alone.

Activities and Assignments

1. Interview parents of a child with a disability about their expectations for interacting with school professionals. Ask them to relate their most positive and negative experiences. Compare your interview results with those of your classmates. What patterns can you discern? How do parents' perspectives relate to the basic characteristics of collaboration described in Chapter 1? What are the differences between parents whose children were in preschool programs and those who were not?

2. Write a memo to a school administrator outlining the key elements in a collaborative program you are offering or would like to offer. Include a brief description of the program and its rationale and note any fiscal or resource implications. Then suggest the areas in which you will need administrative support and describe the nature of that support. Finally, propose that you meet with the administrator to discuss these points and offer a brief agenda for that meeting. Have classmates or colleagues critique the memo and offer suggestions that clarify it.

3. Make a chart of the roles of individuals who typically participate in collaboration in your setting. For each, list the factors that foster their participation and those that constrain it. What does your analysis suggest about the potential for expanding collaboration in your setting?

4. Select a colleague from another discipline with whom you work. Make a list of your responsibilities for planning and delivering instruction or other services, including interaction with families. Ask your colleague to do the same. Compare your lists, clarify your roles and make plans to eliminate unnecessary overlap, and identify any responsibilities that are not assigned.

5. Investigate services in your community. Use the Internet, school directories or referral sources, the local telephone book, and other sources to compile a list of services that could be appropriate referral sources for the students you serve or plan to serve. Divide the services into family services, health services, rehabilitation services, transition services, and others to determine the range of those available.

6. Write a journal entry about ethical dilemmas you have faced, currently face, or anticipate facing as a school professional. On what basis would you make a decision about whether to take action because of an ethical issue? What supports are provided in your school or school district to help teachers who encounter ethical dilemmas? What assistance might your professional organization provide?

For Further Reading

Al-Hassan, S., & Gardner, R. (2002). Involving immigrant parents of students with disabilities in the educational process. *Teaching Exceptional Children, 34*(5), 52–59.

Dabkowski, D. M. (2004). Encouraging active parent participation in IEP team meetings. *Teaching Exceptional Children, 36*(3), 34–39.

Dunst, C. J. (2002). Family-centered practices: Birth through high school. *Journal of Special Education, 36,* 139–147.

Hanson, M. J., & Lynch, E. W. (2003). *Understanding families: Approaches to diversity, disability, and risk.* Baltimore: Brookes.

Martin, J. E., Marshall, L. H., & Sale, P. (2004). A 3-year study of middle, junior high, and high school IEP meetings. *Exceptional Children, 70,* 285–298.

Nelson, L. G. L., Summers, J. A., & Turnbull, A. P. (2004). Boundaries in family-professional relationships: Implications for special education. *Remedial and Special Education, 25,* 153–166.

Neubert, D. A., & Moon, M. S. (2000). How a transition profile helps students prepare for life in the community. *Teaching Exceptional Children, 33*(2), 20–25.

References

Abelson, M. A., & Woodman, R. W. (1983). Review of research on team effectiveness: Implications for teams in schools. *School Psychology Review, 12,* 125–136.

Achinstein, B. (2002). Conflict amid community: The micropolitics of teacher collaboration [Electronic version]. *Teachers College Record, 104,* 421–455.

Adams, L., Tomlan, P., Cessna, K., & Friend, M. (1995). *Co-teaching: Lessons from practitioners.* Unpublished manuscript, Colorado Department of Education, Denver.

Adler, J. R., & Elmhorst, J. (2002). *Communicating at work: Principles and practices for business and the professions* (7th ed.). New York: McGraw-Hill.

Adler, R. B., Rosenfeld, L. B., & Proctor, R. F. (2004). *Interplay: The process of interpersonal communication.* New York: Oxford University Press.

Agran, M. (1997). *Student directed learning: Teaching self-determination skills.* Pacific Grove, CA: Brooks/Cole.

Akin-Little, K. A., Little, S. G., & Delligatti, N. (2004). A preventative model of school consultation: Incorporating perspectives from positive psychology [Electronic version]. *Psychology in the Schools, 41,* 155–162.

Alessandra, T., & Hunsaker, P. (1993). *Communicating at work.* New York: Fireside.

Allen, R. I., & Petr, C. G. (1996). Toward developing standards for family-centered practice in family support programs. In G. H. S. Singer, L. E. Powers, & A. L. Olsen (Eds.), *Redefining family support: Innovations in public–private partnerships* (pp. 57–86). Baltimore: Brookes.

Allen-Malley, M., & Bishop, P. A. (2000). The power of partners: Two-teacher teams [Electronic version]. *Schools in the Middle, 9*(8), 26–30.

Amatea, E. S., Daniels, H., Bringman, N., & Vandiver, F. M. (2004). Strengthening counselor–teacher–family connections: The family–school collaborative consultation project [Electronic version]. *Professional School Counselor, 8,* 47–55.

American Federation of Teachers. (1999a). AFT renews push for paracertification [Electronic version]. *American Teacher, 83*(4), 3.

American Federation of Teachers. (1999b). Johns Hopkins study shows positive role of paras [Electronic version]. *American Teacher, 84*(1), 3.

Appl, D. J., Troha, C., & Rowell, J. (2001). Reflections of a first-year team. *Teaching Exceptional Children, 33*(3), 4–8.

Argüelles, M. E., Hughes, M. T., & Schumm, J. S. (2000). Co-teaching: A different approach to inclusion [Electronic version]. *Principal, 79*(4), 48, 50–51.

Argyle, M. (1999). *Psychology of interpersonal behavior* (5th ed.). London: Penguin.

Armer, B., & Thomas, B. K. (1978). Attitudes towards interdisciplinary collaboration in pupil personnel service teams. *Journal of School Psychology, 16,* 168–177.

Aronson, E. (2005). *Jigsaw in 10 easy steps.* Social Psychology Network. Retrieved February 8, 2005, from www.jigsaw.org/index.html

Aronson, E., Blaney, N., Stephan, C., Sikes, J., & Snapp, M. (1978). *The jigsaw classroom.* Beverly Hills, CA: Sage.

Ashbaker, B. Y., & Morgan, J. (2001). Growing roles for teachers' aides. *Education Digest, 66*(7), 60–64.

Athanasiou, M. S., Geil, M., Hazel, C. E., & Copeland, E. P. (2002). A look inside school-based consultation: A qualitative study of the beliefs and practices of school psychologists and teachers [Electronic version]. *School Psychology Quarterly, 17,* 258–298.

Attanucci, J. S. (2004). Questioning honor: A parent–teacher conflict over excellence and diversity in a USA urban high school [Electronic version]. *Journal of Moral Education, 33,* 57–69.

Austin, V. L. (2001). Teachers' beliefs about co-teaching. *Remedial and Special Education, 22,* 245–255.

Avruch, K. (2003). Culture. In S. Cheldelin, D. Druckman, & L. Fast (Eds.), *Conflict* (pp. 140–153). New York: Continuum.

Baggs, J. G., Ryan, S. A., Phelps, C. E., Richeson, J. F., & Johnson, J. E. (1992). Collaboration in critical care. *Heart and Lung, 21*(1), 18–24.

Bahamonde, C., & Friend, M. (1999). Teaching English language learners: A proposal for effective service delivery through collaboration and co-teaching. *Journal of Educational and Psychological Consultation, 10,* 1–24.

Bahr, M. W., Whitten, E., & Dieker, L. (1999). A comparison of school-based intervention teams: Implications for educational and legal reform. *Exceptional Children, 66,* 67–83.

Bailey, D. B., Buysse, V., Edmondson, R., & Smith, T. M. (1992). Creating family-centered services in early intervention: Perceptions of professionals in four states. *Exceptional Children, 58*(4), 298–309.

Baker, B. (2005). Diversity matters! [Electronic version] *PM Network, 19*(3), 20–21.

Bangert, A. W., & Cooch, C. G. (2001). Facilitating teacher assistance teams: Key questions [Electronic version]. *NASSP Bulletin, 85*(626), 62–67.

Banks, J. A., & McGee-Banks, C. A. (Eds.). (1999). *Multicultural education: Issues and perspectives.* New York: Wiley.

Banks, J. A., & McGee-Banks, C. A. (Eds.). (2004). *Multicultural education: Issues and perspectives* (5th ed.). New York: Wiley.

Barge, J. K., & Loges, W. E. (2003). Parent, student, and teacher perceptions of parental involvement. *Journal of Applied Communication Research, 31,* 140–163.

Barnett, E. (2004). Characteristics and perceived effectiveness of staff development practices in selected high schools in South Dakota [Electronic version]. *Educational Research Quarterly, 28*(2), 3–18.

Barsky, A. E. (2000). *Conflict resolution for the helping professions.* Belmont, CA: Brooks/Cole.

Bartels, S. M., & Mortenson, B. (2002). Instructional consultation in middle schools: Description of an approach to training teachers to facilitate middle school teams [Electronic version]. *Special Services in the Schools, 18*(1–2), 1–21.

Barth, R. S. (1991). *Improving schools from within.* San Francisco: Jossey-Bass.

Bassi, L. J., & Van Buren, M. E. (1999). Sharpening the leading edge. *Training and Development Journal, 53*(1), 23–33.

Baum, H. S. (2003). *Community action for school reform.* Albany, NY: State University of New York Press.

Bauwens, J., Hourcade, J. J., & Friend, M. (1989). Cooperative teaching: A model for general and special education integration. *Remedial and Special Education, 10*(2), 17–22.

Bay, M., Bryan, T., & O'Connor, R. (1994). Teachers assisting teachers: A prereferral model for urban educators. *Teacher Education and Special Education, 17,* 10–21.

Bazerman, M. H., & Neale, M. A. (1992). *Negotiating rationally.* New York: Free Press.

Beach Center on Disability. (1999). *Effectiveness of parent to parent support* (Beach Center Research Brief). Lawrence: University of Kansas.

Behring, S. T., Cabello, B., Kushida, D., & Murguia, A. (2000). Cultural modifications to current school-based consultation approaches reported by culturally diverse beginning consultants [Electronic version]. *School Psychology Review, 29,* 354–367.

Bell, C. R., & Nadler, L. (1985). *Clients and consultants: Meeting and exceeding expectations* (2nd ed.). Houston, TX: Gulf.

Bell, M. L., & Forde, D. R. (1999). A factorial survey of interpersonal conflict resolution [Electronic version]. *Journal of Social Psychology, 139*(3), 369–377.

Bennis, W., & Biederman, P. W. (1997). *Organizing genius: The secrets of creative collaboration.* Reading, MA: Addison-Wesley.

Bergan, J. R., & Tombari, M. L. (1975). The analysis of verbal interactions occurring during consultation. *Journal of School Psychology, 13,* 209–226.

Bergin, J. W., & Bergin, J. J. (2000). Consultation and counseling strategies to facilitate inclusion [Electronic version]. *Counseling and Human Development, 33,* 1–12.

Berman, P., & McLaughlin, M. W. (1978). *Federal programs supporting educational change: Vol. 8. Implementing and sustaining innovation.* Santa Monica, CA: Rand.

Bernal, C., & Aragon, L. (2004). Critical factors affecting the success of paraprofessional in the first two years of career ladder projects in Colorado. *Remedial and Special Education, 25,* 205–213.

Bickmore, K. (1998). Teacher development for conflict resolution. *Alberta Journal of Educational Research, 44*(1), 53–69.

Billingsley, B. S. (2004a). Promoting teacher quality and retention in special education. *Journal of Learning Disabilities, 37,* 370–376.

Billingsley, B. S. (2004b). Special education teacher retention and attrition: A critical analysis of the research literature. *Journal of Special Education, 38,* 39–55.

Billingsley, B. S. (2005). *Cultivating and keeping committed special education teachers: What principals and district leaders can do.* Thousand Oaks, CA: Corwin.

Bishop, K., & Larimer, N. (1999). Collaboration: Literacy through collaboration [Electronic version]. *Teacher Librarian, 27*(1), 15–20.

Blanchard, K., & Johnson, S. (1982). The one minute manager. New York: William Morrow.

Bloor, M., Frankland, J., Thomas, M., & Robson, K. (2001). *Focus groups in social research.* Thousand Oaks, CA: Sage.

Blue-Banning, M., Summers, J. A., Frankland, H. C., Nelson, L. L., & Beegle, G. (2004). Dimensions of family and professional partnerships:

Constructive guidelines for collaboration. *Exceptional Children, 70* (2), 167–184.

Bondy, E., & Brownell, M. T. (1997). Overcoming barriers to collaboration among partners-in-teaching [Electronic version]. *Intervention in School and Clinic, 33,* 112–115.

Boulter, L. (2004). Family–school connection and school violence prevention [Electronic version]. *Negro Educational Review, 55,* 27–40.

Bovey, T., & Strain, P. (2003). *Promoting positive peer social interactions: What works briefs.* Center on the Social and Emotional Foundations for Early Learning, University of Illinois. Retrieved February 8, 2005, from www.eric.ed.gov/contentdelivery/servlet/ERICServlet?accno=ED481996

Boyd, S. D. (2001). The human side of teaching: Effective listening. *Techniques: Connecting Education and Careers, 76*(7), 60–62.

Braithwaite, C. A. (1997). Sa'ag Naaghai Bik'eh Hozhoon: An ethnography of Navajo educational communication practices. *Communication Education, 46,* 219–33.

Brammer, L. M., & MacDonald, G. (1999). *The helping relationship: Process and skills* (7th ed.). Boston: Allyn & Bacon.

Brammer, L. M., & MacDonald, G. (2003). *The helping relationship: Process and skills* (8th ed.). Boston: Allyn & Bacon.

Brew, F. P., & Cairns, D. R. (2004). Do culture or situational constraints determine choice of direct or indirect styles in intercultural workplace conflicts? [Electronic version] *International Journal of Intercultural Relations, 28,* 331–352.

Briggs, M. H. (1999). Systems for collaboration: Integrating multiple perspectives. *Comprehensive Psychiatric Assessment of Young Children, 8,* 365–377.

Brightman, H. J. (2002). *Group problem solving: An improved managerial approach.* East Lansing: Michigan State University Press.

Brighton, C. M. (2001). Stronger together than apart: Building better models through collaboration and interconnection [Electronic version]. *Journal of Secondary Gifted Education, 12,* 163–165.

Brinkley, R. C. (1989). Getting the most from client interviews. *Performance and Instruction, 28*(4), 5–8.

Broer, S. M., Doyle, M. B., & Giangreco, M. F. (2005). Perspectives of students with intellectual disabilities about their experiences with paraprofessional support. *Exceptional Children, 71,* 415–430.

Brooks, M. (2001). How to resolve conflict in teams [Electronic version]. *People Management, 7*(16) 34–35.

Brown, C. (2004). America's most wanted: Teachers who collaborate. *Teacher Librarian, 32(1),* 13–18.

Brown, D., Pryzwansky, W. B., & Schulte, A. C. (1995). *Psychological consultation: Introduction to theory and practice* (3rd ed.). Boston: Allyn & Bacon.

Brown, D., Pryzwansky, W. B., & Schulte, A. C. (2006). *Psychological consultation and collaboration: introduction to theory and practice* (6th ed.). Boston: Allyn & Bacon.

Brown, K. M., & Anfara, V. A. (2002). The walls of division crumble as ears, mouths, minds and hearts open: A unified profession of middle-level administrators and teachers. *International Journal of Leadership in Education, 5*(1), 33–17.

Brownell, M. T., & Walther-Thomas, C. (2002). An interview with Dr. Marilyn Friend. *Intervention in School and Clinic, 37,* 223–228.

Brownell, M. T., Yeager, E., Rennells, M. S., & Riley, T. (1997). Teachers working together: What teacher educators and researchers should know. *Teacher Education and Special Education, 20,* 340–359.

Bruzzo, T. (2004). Using communication to solve roadblocks to collaboration. *Teacher Librarian, 31*(5), 28.

Bryant, M., & Land, S. (1998). Co-planning is the key to successful co-teaching. *Middle School Journal, 30*(1), 28–34.

Bulach, C. R. (2003). The impact of human relations training on levels of openness and trust. *Research for Educational Reform, 8*(4), 43–57.

Burdette, P. J., & Crockett, J. B. (1999). An exploration of consultation approaches and implementation in heterogeneous classrooms. *Education and Training in Mental Retardation and Developmental Disabilities, 34,* 432–452.

Burns, M. K. (1999). Effectiveness of special personnel in the intervention assistance team model. *Journal of Educational Research, 92*(6), 354–356.

Caffarella, R. S. (2002). *Planning programs for adult learners: A practical guide for educators, trainers, and staff developers* (2nd ed.). San Francisco: Jossey-Bass.

Calder, I., & Grieve, A. (2004). Working with other adults: What teachers need to know [Electronic version]. *Educational Studies, 30,* 113–126.

Callagan, L. (2005). Personal outcomes for people with learning disabilities incorporating the concept of collaboration: Part 2. *Learning Disability Practice, 8*(9), 34–38.

Cambridge, P. (1998) Challenges for safer sex education and HIV prevention services for people with intellectual disabilities in Britain. *Health Promotion International, 13*(1), 67–74.

Cameron, C. A., & Lee, K. (1997). Bridging the gap between home and school with voice-mail technology. *Journal of Educational Research, 90*(3), 182–190.

Canston-Theoharis, J., & Malmgren, K. (2005). Building bridges: Strategies to help paraprofessionals promote peer interaction. *Teaching Exceptional Children, 37*(6), 18–25.

Caplan, G. (1970). *The theory and practice of mental health consultation.* New York: Basic Books.

Capozzoli, T. K. (1999). Conflict resolution: A key ingredient in successful teams [Electronic version]. *Supervision, 60*(11), 14–16.

Carner, L. A., & Alpert, J. A. (1995). Some guidelines for consultants revisited. *Journal of Educational and Psychological Consultation, 6,* 47–57.

Caron, E. A., & McLaughlin, M. J. (2002). Indicators of Beacons of Excellence schools: What do they tell us about collaborative practices? *Journal of Educational and Psychological Consultation, 13,* 285–313.

Carpenter, S. L., King-Sears, M. E., & Keys, S. G. (1998). Counselors + educators + families as a transdisciplinary team = More effective inclusion for students with disabilities, *Professional School Counseling, 2*(1), 9.

Carroll, D. (2001). Considering paraeducator training, roles, and responsibilities. *Teaching Exceptional Children, 34*(2), 60–64.

Cavallaro, C. C., & Haney, M. (1999). *Preschool inclusion.* Baltimore: Brookes.

Chalfant, J. C., Pysh, M. V., & Moultrie, R. (1979). Teacher assistance teams: A model for within building problem solving. *Learning Disability Quarterly, 2,* 85–96.

Chan, S. (1998). Families with Asian roots. In E. W. Lynch & M. J. Hanson (Eds.), *Developing cross-cultural competence: A guide for working with young children and their families* (2nd ed., pp. 251–354). Baltimore: Brookes.

Chan, S. Q. (1990). Early interventionists and culturally diverse families of infants and toddlers with disabilities. *Infants and Young Children, 3*(2), 78–87.

Charalambos, V., Michalinos, Z., & Chamberlain, R. (2004). The design of online learning communities: Critical issues [Electronic version]. *Educational Media International, 41,* 135–143.

Charney, C. (2004). *The instant manager: More than 100 quick tips and techniques and great results.* New York: American Management Association.

Cheldelin, S., Druckman, D., & Fast, L. (Ed.). (2003). *Conflict.* New York: Continuum.

Chen, D. (2001). *Visual impairment in young children: A review of the literature with implications for working with families of diverse cultural and linguistic backgrounds* (CLAS Technical Report #7). Champaign, IL: University of Illinois at Urbana-Champaign, Early Childhood Research Institute on Culturally and Linguistically Appropriate Services.

Chen, D., McLean, M., Corso, R., & Bruns, D. (2001). *Working together in EI: Cultural considerations in helping relationships and service utilization* (Technical Report No. 11) [Electronic version]. Champaign-Urbana, IL: Culturally and Linguistically Appropriate Services for Early Childhood Research (CLAS) Institute.

Chen, M., & Rybak, C. J. (2004). *Group leadership skills: Interpersonal process in group counseling and therapy.* Belmont, CA: Thompson/Brooks Cole.

Chiu, M. M. (2000). Effects of status on solutions, leadership, and evaluations during group problem solving [Electronic version]. *Sociology of Education, 73,* 175–195.

Chopra, R. V., & French, N. K. (2004). Paraeducator relationships with parents of students with significant disabilities. *Remedial and Special Education, 25,* 240–251.

Chopra, R. V., Sandoval-Lucero, E., Aragon, L., Bernal, C., de Balderas, H. B., & Carroll, C. (2004). The paraprofessional role of connector. *Remedial and Special Education, 25,* 219–231.

Chrispeels, J. H., Strait, C. C., & Brown, J. H. (1999). The paradoxes of collaboration [Electronic version]. *Thrust for Educational Leadership, 29*(2), 16–19.

Christie, D., & Jassi, A. (2002). "Oh no he doesn't!" "Oh yes he does!": Comparing parent and teacher perceptions in Tourette's syndrome [Electronic version]. *Clinical Child Psychology and Psychiatry, 7,* 553–558.

Christie, L. S., McKenzie, H. S., & Burdett, C. S. (1972). The consulting teacher approach to special education: Inservice training for regular classroom teachers. *Focus on Exceptional Children, 4,* 1–10.

Clark, D. L., & Astuto, T. A. (1994). Redirecting reform: Challenges to popular assumptions about teachers and students. *Phi Delta Kappan, 75,* 512–520.

Clark, S. G. (2000). The IEP process as a tool for collaboration. *Teaching Exceptional Children, 33*(2), 56–66.

Clark, S. N., & Clark, D.C. (2002). Collaborative decision making: A promising but underused strategy for middle school improvement. *Middle School Journal, 33*(4), 520–57.

Clayton, J., Butrow, P., Tattersall, M., Chye, R., Noel, M., Davis, J. M., & Glare, P. (2003). Asking questions can help: Development and preliminary evaluation of a question prompt list for palliative care patients. *British Journal of Cancer, 89,* 2069–2077.

Cloke, K., & Goldsmith, J. (2000). Conflict resolution that reaps great rewards [Electronic version]. *Journal for Quality and Participation, 23*(3), 27–30.

Coben, S. S., Thomas, C. C., Sattler, R. O., & Morsink, C. V. (1997). Meeting the challenge of consultation and collaboration: Developing interactive teams. *Journal of Learning Disabilities, 30,* 427–432.

Coleman, M. R. (2001). *Conditions of teaching children with exceptional learning needs: The bright futures report* [ERIC Digest E613]. Arlington, VA: ERIC Clearinghouse on Disabilities and Gifted Education. (ERIC Document Reproduction Service No. ED45560)

Coleman, P. T., & Lim, Y. Y. J. (2001). A systematic approach to evaluating the effects of collaborative negotiation training on individuals and groups [Electronic version]. *Negotiation Journal, 17,* 363–392.

Coltrane, B. (2002). Team teaching: Meeting the needs of English language learners through collaboration. *Center for Applied Linguistics Newsletter, 25*(2), 1–5. Retrieved December 27, 2004, from www.cal.org/resources/News/2002spring/team.html

Conderman, G., & Stephens, J. T. (2000). Reflections from beginning special educators. *Teaching Exceptional Children, 33*(1), 16–21.

Conoley, J. C., & Conoley, C. W. (1988). Useful theories in school-based consultation. *Remedial and Special Education, 9*(6), 14–20.

Conoley, J. C., & Conoley, C. W. (1992). *School consultation: Practice and training* (2nd ed.). Boston: Allyn & Bacon.

Constantinides, H. (2001). Organizational and intercultural communication. *Technical Communication Quarterly, 10*(1), 31–59.

Cook, B. G. (2001). A comparison of teachers' attitudes toward their included students with mild and severe disabilities. *Journal of Special Education, 34,* 203–213.

Cook, L. (2005) The principal's role in facilitating collaboration. In B. S. Billingsley, *Cultivating and keeping committed special education teachers: What principals and district leaders can do.* (pp. 140–143). Thousand Oaks, CA: Corwin

Cook, L., & Friend, M. (1990a). *A conceptual framework for collaboration in special education.* Preconvention keynote paper presented at the 68th annual convention of the Council for Exceptional Children, Toronto.

Cook, L., & Friend, M. (1990b). Pragmatic issues in the development of special education consultation programs. *Preventing School Failure, 35*(1), 43–46.

Cook, L., & Friend, M. (1991). Collaboration in special education: Coming of age in the 1990s. *Preventing School Failure, 35*(2), 24–27.

Cook, L., & Friend, M. (1995). Co-teaching guidelines for creating effective practices. *Focus on Exceptional Children, 28*(2), 1–12.

Cook, L., & Hall, K. S. (2004). Making paperwork work for you and your students. In J. Burnette & C. Peters-Johnson (Eds.), *Thriving as a special educator: Balancing your practices and ideals* (pp. 49–61). Arlington, VA: Council for Exceptional Children.

Cook, L. H., Weintraub, F. J., & Morse, W. C. (1995). Ethical dilemmas in the restructuring of special education. In J. L. Paul, D. Evans, & H. Rosselli (Eds.), *Integrating school restructuring and special education reform* (pp. 119–139). Fort Worth, TX: Harcourt Brace.

Cook, R. E., Tessier, A., & Klein, M. D. (1992). *Adapting early childhood curricula for children with special needs.* Upper Saddle River, NJ: Merrill/Prentice Hall.

Copeland, S. R., Hughes, C., Carter, E. W., Guth, C., Presley, J. A., Williams, C. R., & Fowler, S. E. (2004). Increasing access to general education: Perspectives of participants in a high school peer support program. *Remedial and Special Education, 25,* 342–352.

Cornille, T. A., Pestle, R. E., & Vanwy, R. W. (1999). Teachers' conflict management styles with peers and students' parents [Electronic version]. *International Journal of Conflict Management, 10*(1), 69–79.

Correa, V. I., & Tulbert, B. (1993). Collaboration between school personnel in special education and Hispanic families. *Journal of Educational and Psychological Consultation, 5,* 283–308.

Correa, V. I., Jones, H. A., Thomas, C. C., & Morsink, C. V. (2005). *Interactive teaming: Enhancing programs for students with special needs* (4th ed.). Upper Saddle River, NJ: Merrill.

Council for Exceptional Children. (2004). *Parability: The CEC paraeducator standards workbook.* Arlington, VA: Author.

Council for Exceptional Children. (2005). *"Highly qualified" special education teacher requirements frequently asked questions (FAQ).* Alexandria, VA: Author.

Covey, S. (1999). Resolving differences [Electronic version]. *Executive Excellence, 16*(4), 5–6.

Cowan, R. J., & Sheridan, S. M. (2003). Investigating the acceptability of behavioral interventions in applied conjoint behavioral consultation: Moving from analog conditions to naturalistic settings [Electronic version]. *School Psychology Quarterly, 18,* 1–21.

Crespin, B. J. (1971). Means of facilitating education sought. *Education, 92*(2), 36–37.

Cross, A. F., Traub, E. K., Hunter-Pishgahi, L., & Shelton, G. (2004). Elements of successful inclusion for children with significant disabilities. *Topics in Early Childhood Special Education, 24*(3) 169–183.

Crow, J., & Smith, L. (2003). Using co-teaching as a means of facilitating interprofessional collaboration in health and social care [Electronic version]. *Journal of Interprofessional Care, 17,* 45–55.

Cui, G., Van den Berg, S., & Jiang, Y. (1998). Cross-cultural adaptation and ethnic communication: Two structural equation models. *The Howard Journal of Communications, 9*(1), 69–85.

daCosta, J. L., Marshall, J. L., & Riordan, G. (1998, April). *Case study of the development of a collaborative teaching culture in an inner city elementary school.* Paper presented at the annual meeting of the American Educational Research Association, San Diego, CA. (ERIC Documentation Reproduction Service No. ED420630)

Dallmer, D. (2004). Collaborative relationships in teacher education: A personal narrative of conflicting roles [Electronic version]. *Curriculum Inquiry, 34,* 29–45.

Dalton, D. (1999). Ten pointers worth considering in conflict resolution [Electronic version]. *Security: For buyers of products, systems, and services, 36*(10), 72.

Dana, D. (2001). *Conflict resolution.* Washington, DC: McGraw-Hill.

Daniels, V. I., & McBride, A. (2001). Paraeducators as critical team members: Redefining roles and responsibilities [Electronic version]. *NASSP Bulletin, 85*(623), 66–74.

Darling-Hammond, L. (1999). Target time towards teachers. *Journal of Staff Development, 20*(2), 31–41.

Darling-Hammond, L. (2001). The challenge of our schools. *Educational Leadership, 58*(8), 12–17.

DeBoer, A., & Fister, S. (1995). *Working together: Tools for collaborative teaching.* Longmont, CO: Sopris West.

DeJong, P., & Berg, I. K. (2002). *Interviewing for solutions* (2nd ed.). Pacific Grove, CA: Wadsworth.

Del Favero, M. (2004). Bridging the cultural differences between faculty and administrators. *Academic Leader, 20*(3), 4–5.

Delbecq, A. L., Van de Ven, A. H., & Gustafson, D. H. (1986). *Group techniques for program planning: A guide to nominal group and Delphi processes.* Middleton, WI: Green Briar.

DelSignore, T. (2003). Is teaching worth all the trouble? [Electronic version] *English Journal, 92*(4), 23–26.

Denton, C. A., Hasbrouck, J. E., & Sekaquaptewa, S. (2003). The consulting teacher: A descriptive case study in responsive systems consultation. *Journal of Educational and Psychological Consultation, 14,* 41–73.

Dettmer, P., Dyck, N., & Thurston, L. P. (1999). *Consultation, collaboration, and teamwork for students with special needs* (3rd ed.). Boston: Allyn & Bacon.

Dettmer, P., Dyck, N., & Thurston, L. P. (2002). *Consultation, collaboration, and teamwork for students with special needs* (4th ed.). Boston: Allyn & Bacon.

Dettmer, P., Dyck, N., & Thurston, L. P. (2005). *Consultation, collaboration, and teamwork for students with special needs* (5th ed.). Boston: Allyn & Bacon.

Deutsch, M. (2002). Social psychology's contributions to the study of conflict resolution [Electronic version]. *Negotiation Journal, 18,* 307–320.

DeVito, J. A. (2001). *The interpersonal communication book* (9th ed.). New York: Longman.

DeVito, J. A. (2005). *Messages, building interpersonal communication skills* (6th ed.). Boston: Allyn & Bacon.

DeVito, J. A. (2006a). *Human communication: The basic course* (10th ed.). Boston: Allyn & Bacon.

DeVito, J. A. (2006b). *The interpersonal communication book* (10th ed.). Boston: Allyn & Bacon.

DeVoe, D. (1999). Don't let conflict get you off course [Electronic version]. *InfoWorld, 21*(32), 69.

Dieker, L. A. (2001). What are the characteristics of "effective" middle and high school co-taught teams for students with disabilities? [Electronic version] *Preventing School Failure, 46*(1), 14–23.

Dieker, L. A., & Murawski, W. W. (2003). Co-teaching at the secondary level: Unique issues, current trends, and suggestions for success [Electronic version]. *High School Journal, 86*(4), 1–13.

DiGennaro, F. D., Martens, B. K., & McIntyre, L. L. (2005). Increasing treatment integrity through negative reinforcement: Effects on teacher and student behavior [Electronic version]. *School Psychology Review, 34,* 220–231.

Dilworth, M. E., & Imig, D. G. (1995). Professional teacher development and the reform agenda. *ERIC Digest* (ERIC Documentation Reproduction Service No. ED 383694).

Dinkmeyer, D., & Carlson, J. (2001). *Consultation: Creating school-based interventions* (2nd ed.). Philadelphia: Brunner-Routledge.

Dinnebeil, L. A., Hale, L., & Rule, S. (1999). Early intervention program practices that support collaboration [Electronic version]. *Topics in Early Childhood Special Education, 19,* 225–235.

DiSibio, R. A., & Gamble, R. J. (1997). Collaboration between schools and higher education: The key to success [Electronic version]. *College Student Journal, 31,* 532–536.

Dole, R. L. (2004). Collaborating successfully with your school's physical therapist. *Teaching Exceptional Children, 36*(5), 28–35.

Donahue, P. J., Falk, B., & Provet, A. G. (2000). *Mental health consultation in early childhood.* Baltimore: Paul H. Brookes.

Dote-Kwan, J., & Chen, D. (1995). Learners with visual impairments and blindness. In M. C. Wang, M. C. Reynolds, & H. J. Walberg (Eds.), *Handbook of special and remedial education: Research and practice* (2nd ed., pp. 205–228). New York: Elsevier Science.

Dote-Kwan, J., Hughes, M., & Taylor, S. L. (1997). Impact of early experiences on the development of young children with visual impairments: Revisited. *Journal of Visual Impairment & Blindness, 91,* 131–144.

Dougherty, A. M. (2000). *Psychological consultation and collaboration: A casebook* (3rd ed.). Belmont, CA: Brooks/Cole.

Dougherty, A. M. (2004). *Psychological consultation and collaboration in school and community settings* (4th ed.). Belmont, CA: Wadsworth.

Dover, W. F. (2005). Twenty ways to consult and support students with special needs in inclusive classrooms. *Intervention in School and Clinic, 41*(1), 32–35.

Dowdy, C. A. (1996). Vocational rehabilitation and special education: Partners in transition for individuals with learning disabilities. *Journal of Learning Disabilities, 29,* 137–147.

Dowell, D., Abrahamse, D., Houck, J. W., Seal, J., Green, H. J., Cohn, K. C., Ambos, E. L., Isbell, L., Kahl, K., & DeVries, K. (2004). Successful partnerships bridge organizational cultures and unite members around common goals. In J. W. Houck, K. C. Cohn, & C. A. Cohn (Eds.), *Partnering to lead educational renewal: High-quality teachers, high-quality schools* (pp. 20–38). New York: Teachers College Press.

Downing, J. E. (1999). *Teaching communication skills to students with severe disabilities.* Baltimore: Brookes.

Downing, J. E. (2002). *Including students with severe and multiple disabilities in typical classrooms: Practical strategies for teachers* (2nd ed.). Baltimore: Brookes.

Downing, J. E., Ryndak, D. L., & Clark, D. (2000). Paraeducators in inclusive classrooms: Their own perceptions. *Remedial and Special Education, 21,* 171–181.

Doyle, M. B. (2002). *The paraprofessionals' guide to the inclusive classroom: Working as a team* (2nd ed.). Baltimore: Paul H. Brookes.

Doyle, M. B., & Gurney, D. (2000). Guiding paraeducators. In M. S. E. Fishbaugh (Ed.), *The collaboration guide for early career educators.* Baltimore: Brookes.

DuFour, R. (1999). Game plan. *Journal of Staff Development, 20*(2), 61–62.

Duhon, G. J. (2005). Treatment implementation following behavioral consultation in schools: A comparison of three follow-up strategies [Electronic version]. *School Psychology Review, 34,* 87–106.

Earley, P., & Bubb, S. (2004). *Leading and managing continuing professional development: Developing people, developing schools.* Thousand Oaks, CA: Sage, Paul Chapman.

Egan, G. (2001). *Skilled helper: A problem-management and opportunity-development approach to helping* (7th ed.). Belmont, CA: Wadsworth.

Elksnin, L. K., & Elsknin, N. (2000). Teaching parents to teach their children to be prosocial. *Intervention in School and Clinic, 36*(1), 27–32.

Elliott, D., & McKenney, M. (1998). Four inclusion models that work. *Teaching Exceptional Children, 30*(4), 54–58.

Elliott, S. N., & Sheridan, S. M. (1992). Consultation and teaming: Problem solving among educators, parents, and support personnel. *Elementary School Journal, 92,* 315–338.

Ellis, B., Bowman, W. L., Foley, K. C., Gibbons, D., Kerlin, E., Lautzenheiser, T., Lindeman, C. A., Ponick, F. S., Schmid, W., Shafer, A., Turrentine, M., Wilcox, D. K., & Wilcox, E. (2002). Is the clock ticking you off? [Electronic version] *Teaching Music, 9*(5), 40–45.

Emmer, E. T., & Gerwels, M. C. (2002). Cooperative learning in elementary classrooms: Teaching practices and lesson characteristics [Electronic version]. *Elementary School Journal, 103,* 76–91.

Entwisle, D. R. (1994). Subcultural diversity in American families. In L. L'Abate (Ed.), *Handbook of developmental family psychology and psychopathology* (pp. 132–156). New York: Wiley.

Epanchin, B. C., & Friend, M. (in press). The adolescence of inclusive practices: Building bridges through collaboration. In J. McLeskey (Ed.), *Classic articles and inclusion.* Arlington, VA: Council for Exceptional Children.

Ephross, P. H., & Vassil, T. V. (2005). *Groups that work: Structure and process* (2nd ed.). New York: Columbia University Press.

Erchul, W. P. (1999). Two steps forward, one step back: Collaboration in school-based consultation [Electronic version]. *Journal of School Psychology, 37,* 191–203.

Erchul, W. P. (2003). Communication and interpersonal processes in consultation: Guest editor's comments. *Journal of Educational and Psychological Consultation, 14,* 105–107.

Erchul, W. P., & Martens, B. K. (1997). *School consultation: Conceptual and empirical bases.* New York: Plenum.

Erchul, W. P., Raven, B. H., & Ray, A. G. (2001). School psychologists' perceptions of social power bases in teacher consultation. *Journal of Educational and Psychological Consultation, 12,* 1–23.

Erchul, W. P., Raven, B. H., & Whichard, S. M. (2001). School psychologist and teacher perceptions of social power in consultation [Electronic version]. *Journal of School Psychology, 39,* 483–497.

ERIC Clearinghouse on Language and Linguistics. (2000, December). *Examining Latino paraeducators: Interactions with Latino students.* Washington, DC: Author.

Eskaros, M. G. (2004). Fine-tune your listening skills. *Hydrocarbon Processing, 83*(11), 85–87.

Evans, R. (1990). Making mainstreaming work through prereferral consultation. *Educational Leadership, 48*(1), 73–77.

Evans, S. B. (1980). The consultant role of the resource teacher. *Exceptional Children, 46,* 402–404.

Fairhurst, G. T., & Sarr, R. A. (1997). *The art of framing: Managing the language of leadership.* San Francisco: Jossey-Bass/Pfeiffer.

Feldman, R. S. (1985). *Social psychology: Theories, research, and applications.* New York: McGraw-Hill.

Fennick, E. (2001). Co-teaching: An inclusive curriculum for transition. *Teaching Exceptional Children, 33*(6), 60–66.

Fenton, K. S., Yoshida, R. K., Maxwell, J. P., & Kaufman, M. T. (1979). Recognition of team goals: An essential step toward rational decision-making. *Exceptional Children, 45,* 638–644.

Festinger, L. (1957). *A theory of cognitive dissonance.* Stanford, CA: Stanford University Press.

Fiedler, C. R. (2000). *Making a difference: Advocacy competencies for special education professionals.* Boston: Allyn & Bacon.

Fiedler, F. E. (1967). *A theory of leadership effectiveness.* New York: McGraw-Hill.

Fishbaugh, M. S. E. (1997). *Models of collaboration.* Boston: Allyn & Bacon.

Fishbaugh, M. S. E. (2000). *The collaboration guide for early career educators.* Baltimore: Brookes.

Fisher, D. (2001). Cross age tutoring: Alternatives to reading resource room for struggling adolescent readers. *Journal of Instructional Psychology, 28,* 234–240.

Fisher, D., & Frey, N. (2001). Access to the core curriculum: Critical elements for student success. *Remedial and Special Education, 22,* 148–157.

Fisher, R., Ury, W., & Patton, R. (1997). *Getting to yes: Negotiating agreement without giving in* (3rd ed.). Boston: Allyn & Bacon.

Flanigin, A. J., Tiyaamornwong, V., O'Connor, J., & Seibold, D. R. (2002). Computer-mediated group work: The interaction of member sex and anonymity. *Communication Research, 29,* 66–93.

Flannery, K. B., Slovic, R., Treasure, T., Ackley, D., & Lucas, F. (2002). Collaboration and partnership to improve employment outcomes. *Journal of Vocational Rehabilitation, 17*(3), 207–215.

Fleming, G. P. (2000). The effects of brainstorming on subsequent problem-solving. *Dissertation Abstracts International, 61,* 2804.

Fleming, J. L., & Monda-Amaya, L. E. (2001). Process variables critical for team effectiveness. *Remedial and Special Education, 22,* 158–171.

Fleury, M. L. (2000). Confidentiality issues with substitutes and paraeducators. *Teaching Exceptional Children, 33*(1), 44–45.

Foley, G. (1990). Portrait of the arena evaluation. In E. Gibbs & D. Teti (Eds.), *Interdisciplinary assessment of infants: A guide for early intervention professionals* (pp. 271–286). Baltimore, MD: Brookes.

Fowler, S. A., Donegan, M., Lueke, B., Hadden, D. S., & Phillips, B. (2000). Evaluating community collaboration in writing interagency agreements on the age 3 transition. *Exceptional Children, 67,* 1–50.

Fox, N. E., & Ysseldyke, J. E. (1997). Implementing inclusion at the middle school level: Lessons from a negative example. *Exceptional Children, 64,* 81–98.

Frederickson, N., & Turner, J. (2003). Utilizing the classroom peer group to address children's social needs: An evaluation of the Circle of Friends intervention approach. *Journal of Special Education, 36,* 234–245.

Freer, P., & Watson, T. S. (1999). A comparison of parent and teacher acceptability ratings of behavioral and conjoint behavioral consultation

[Electronic version]. *School Psychology Review, 28,* 672–684.

French, N. K. (1998). Working together: Resource teachers and paraeducators. *Remedial and Special Education, 19,* 357–368.

French, N. K. (1999a). Paraeducators and teachers: Shifting roles. *Teaching Exceptional Children, 32*(2), 69–73.

French, N. K. (1999b). Paraeducators: Who are they and what do they do? *Teaching Exceptional Children, 32*(1), 65–69.

French, N. K. (2000). Taking time to save time: Delegating to paraeducators. *Teaching Exceptional Children, 32*(3), 79–83.

French, N. K. (2001). Supervising paraprofessionals: A survey of teacher practices. *Journal of Special Education, 35,* 41–53.

French, N. K. (2003). *Managing paraeducators in your school: How to hire, train, and supervise non-certified staff.* Thousand Oaks, CA: Corwin.

French, N. K. (2004). Maximizing the services of paraeducators. In J. Burnette & C. Peters-Johnson (Eds.), *Thriving as a special educator: Balancing your practices and ideals.* Arlington, VA: Council for Exceptional Children.

French, N. K., & Chopra, R. V. (1999). Parent perspectives on the role of the paraprofessional in inclusion. *Journal of the Association for Persons with Severe Handicaps, 24*(4), 1–14.

Friend, M. (1984). Consultation skills for resource teachers. *Learning Disability Quarterly, 7,* 246–250.

Friend, M. (1988). Putting consultation into context: Historical and contemporary perspectives. *Remedial and Special Education, 9*(6), 7–13.

Friend, M. (2000). Perspectives: Collaboration in the twenty-first century. *Remedial and Special Education, 20,* 130–132, 160.

Friend, M. (2007). *Co-teach! A handbook for creating and sustaining effective classroom partnerships in inclusive schools.* Greensboro, NC: Author.

Friend, M., & Bursuck, W. (1999). *Including students with special needs: A practical guide for classroom teachers* (2nd ed.). Boston: Allyn & Bacon.

Friend, M., & Bursuck, W. (2002). *Including students with special needs: A practical guide for classroom teachers* (3rd ed.). Boston: Allyn & Bacon.

Friend, M., & Cook, L. (1988). Pragmatic issues in school consultation. In J. F. West (Ed.), *School consultation: Interdisciplinary perspectives on theory, research, training, and practice* (pp. 127–142). Austin: Research and Training Project on School Consultation, University of Texas.

Friend, M., & Cook, L. (1990). Collaboration as a predictor for success in school reform. *Journal of Educational and Psychological Consultation, 1,* 69–86.

Friend, M., & Cook, L. (1992). It's my turn: The ethics of collaboration. *Journal of Educational and Psychological Consultation, 3,* 181–184.

Friend, M., & Cook, L. (1997). Student-centered teams in schools: Still in search of an identity. *Journal of Educational and Psychological Consultation, 8*(1), 3–20.

Friend, M., & Cook, L. (2004). Collaborating with professionals and parents without being overwhelmed: Building partnerships and teams. In J. Burnette & C. Peters-Johnson (Eds.), *Thriving as a special educator: Balancing your practices and ideals* (pp. 29–39). Arlington, VA: Council for Exceptional Children.

Friend, M., & Pope K. L. (2005). Creating schools in which all students can succeed. *Kappa Delta Pi Record, 41*(2), 56–61.

Friend, M., Reising, M., & Cook, L. (1993). Co-teaching: An overview of the past, a glimpse at the present, and considerations for the future. *Preventing School Failure, 37*(4), 6–10.

Fullan, M. (1994). Coordinating top-down and bottom-up strategies for educational reform. In R. F. Elmore & S. H. Fuhrman (Eds.), *The governance of curriculum: 1994 yearbook of the Association for Supervision and Curriculum Development* (pp. 186–202). Alexandria, VA: Association for Supervision and Curriculum Development.

Fullan, M. (2001). *Leading in a culture of change.* San Francisco: Jossey-Bass.

Gable, R. A., & Manning, M. L. (1999). Interdisciplinary teaming: Solution to instructing heterogeneous groups of students. *Clearing House, 72,* 182–185.

Gable, R. A., Mostert, M. P., & Tonelson, S. W. (2004). Assessing professional collaboration in schools: Knowing what works [Electronic version]. *Preventing School Failure, 48*(3), 4–8.

Gabriel, J. G. (2005). *How to thrive as a teacher leader.* Alexandria, VA: Association for Supervision and Curriculum Development.

Gallagher, R. J., LaMontagne, M. J., & Johnson, L. J. (1995). Early intervention: The collaborative challenge. In L. J. Johnson, R. J., Gallagher, M. J. LaMontagne, J. B. Jordan, J. J. Gallagher, P. L. Hutinger, & M. B. Karnes (Eds.), *Meeting early intervention challenges: Issues from birth to three* (2nd ed., pp. 279–288). Baltimore: Brookes.

Gallessich, J. (1982). *The profession and practice of consultation.* San Francisco: Jossey-Bass.

Gallivan-Fenlon, A. (1994). Integrated transdisciplinary teams. *Teaching Exceptional Children, 26*(3), 16–20.

Gamble, T. K., & Gamble, M. (1999). *Communication works* (6th ed.). New York: McGraw-Hill.

Gamble, T. K., & Gamble, M. (2001). *Communication works* (7th ed.). New York: McGraw-Hill.

Gamble, T. K., & Gamble, M. (2005). *Communication works* (8th ed.). New York: McGraw-Hill.

Garcia, S. B., Mendez-Perez, A., & Ortiz, A. A. (2000). Mexican American mothers' beliefs about disabilities: Implications for early childhood intervention. *Remedial and Special Education, 21,* 90–102.

Gardner, D. B., & Cary, A. (1999). Collaboration, conflict, and power: Lessons for case managers [Electronic version]. *Family and Community Health, 22*(3), 64–77.

Garmston, R. J., & Wellman, B. M. (1992). *How to make presentations that teach and transform.* Alexandria, VA: Association for Supervision and Curriculum Development.

Gately, S. E., & Gately, F. J. (2001). Understanding co-teaching components. *Teaching Exceptional Children, 33*(4), 40–47.

Gaustad, M. G. (1999). Including the kids across the hall: Collaborative instruction of hearing, deaf, and hard-of-hearing students. *The Journal of Deaf Studies and Deaf Education, 4,* 176–190.

Geen, A. G. (1985). Team teaching in the secondary schools of England and Wales. *Educational Review, 37,* 29–38.

Gentry, M., & Ferriss, S. (1999). StATS: A model of collaboration to develop science talent among rural students [Electronic version]. *Roeper Review, 21,* 316–320.

Gerber, P. J., & Popp, P. A. (2000). Making collaborative teaching more effective for academically able students: Recommendations for implementation and training [Electronic version]. *Learning Disability Quarterly, 23,* 229–236.

Gerlach, K. (2001). *Let's team up! A checklist for para-educators, teachers, and principals* [NEA check list series]. Washington, DC: National Education Association.

Giangreco, M. F. (2003). *Paraprofessional support of students with disabilities in general education: Final report.* Burlington: University of Vermont. (ERIC Document Reproduction Service No. ED483002)

Giangreco, M. F., Edelman, S. W., Broer, S. M., & Doyle, M. B. (2001). Paraprofessional support of students with disabilities: Literature from the past decade. *Exceptional Children, 68,* 45–63.

Giangreco, M. F., Edelman, S. W., Luiselli, T. E., & MacFarland, S. Z. C. (1997). Helping or hovering? Effects of instructional assistant proximity on students with disabilities. *Exceptional Children, 64,* 7–18.

Gilkerson, L. (1990). Understanding institutional functioning style: A resource for hospital and early intervention collaboration. *Young Children, 2*(3), 22–30.

Gladding, S. T. (2003). *Group work: A counseling specialty* (4th ed.). Upper Saddle River, NJ: Merrill/Prentice Hall.

Glazer, C. (2004). Working together: Corporate and community development. In D. Maurrasse (Ed.), *A future for everyone: Innovative social responsibility and community partnerships* (pp. 73–78). New York: Routledge.

Glickman, C. D., Gordan, S. P., & Ross-Gordan, J. M. (1998). The significance of leadership style. *Educational Leadership, 55*(7), 20–22.

Gold, N. (2005). *Teamwork: Multi-disciplinary perspectives.* New York: Palgrave Macmillan.

Goldman, E. (1998). The significance of leadership style. *Educational Leadership, 55*(7), 20–22.

Gomez, G. G. (2001). Sources and information: Creating effective collaboration between high school and community colleges [Electronic version]. *New Directions for Community Colleges, 113,* 81–86.

Gonzalez-Mena, J., & Bhavnagri, N. P. (2000). Diversity and infant/toddler caregiving. *Young Children, 55*(5), 31–35.

Gooden, M. A. (2005). The role of an African American principal in an urban information technology high school [Electronic version]. *Educational Administration Quarterly, 41,* 630–650.

Goodlad, J. (1984). *A place called school.* New York: McGraw-Hill.

Goodman, G. (1978). *SASHA tape user's manual.* Unpublished manuscript, Department of Psychology, University of California, Los Angeles.

Goodman, G. (1984). SASHA tapes: Expanding options for help-intended communication. In D. Larson (Ed.), *Teaching psychological skills: Models for giving psychology away* (pp. 271–286). Monterey, CA: Brooks/Cole.

Goodman, G., & Easterly, G. (1990). Questions—The most popular piece of language. In J. Stewart (Ed.), *Bridges not walls* (5th ed., pp. 69–77). New York: McGraw-Hill.

Graden, J. L., (1989). Redefining prereferral intervention as intervention assistance: Collaboration between general and special education. *Exceptional Children, 56,* 227–231.

Graden, J. L., Casey, A., & Bonstrom, O. (1985). Implementing a prereferral intervention system: Part II. The data. *Exceptional Children, 51,* 487–496.

Graham, D. S. (1998). Consultant effectiveness and treatment acceptability: An examination of consultee requests and consultant responses [Electronic version]. *School Psychology Quarterly, 13,* 155–168.

Granger, J. D., & Greek, M. (2005). Struggling readers stretch their skills: Project maximizes use of paraprofessionals to teach reading. *Journal of Staff Development, 26*(3), 32–36.

Gravois, T. A. (2002). Educating practitioners as consultants: Development and implementation of the instructional consultation team consortium. *Journal of Educational and Psychological Consultation, 13,* 113–132.

Grissom, P. F., Erchul, W. P., & Sheridan, S. M. (2003). Relationships among relational communication processes and perceptions of outcomes in conjoint behavioral consultation. *Journal of Educational and Psychological Consultation, 14,* 157–180.

Groce, N. E. (1997). *Adolescence and disability.* Paper presented at the Thematic Discussion on Childhood Disability, Sixteenth Session of the Committee on the Rights of the Child, Palais des Nations, Geneva.

Guilar, J. D. (2001). *The interpersonal communication skills workshop.* New York: Amacom.

Gursky, D. (2000). From para to teacher [Electronic version]. *American Teacher, 84*(8), 8.

Guskey, T. R., & Peterson, K. D. (1996). The road to classroom change. *Educational Leadership, 53*(4), 10–14.

Gutkin, T. B. (1999). Collaborative versus directive/prescriptive/expert school-based consultation: Reviewing and resolving a false dichotomy [Electronic version]. *Journal of School Psychology, 37,* 167–189.

Hackett, D., & Martin, C. L. (1993). *Facilitation skills for team leaders.* Boston: Thomson.

Hackman, D. G., & Berry, J. E. (2000). Cracking the calendar. *Journal of Staff Development, 21*(3), 45–47.

Hadley, P. A., Simmerman, A., Long, M., & Luna, M. (2000). Facilitating language development for inner-city children: Experimental evaluation of a collaborative, classroom-based intervention [Electronic version]. *Language, Speech, and Hearing Services in Schools, 31,* 280–295.

Hall, E. T. (1966). *The hidden dimension.* Garden City, NY: Doubleday.

Hall, E. T. (1981). *The silent language.* New York: Anchor Books.

Hall, G. E., & George, A. A. (2000). *The use of innovation configuration maps in assessing implementation: The bridge between development and student outcomes.* Paper presented at the Annual Meeting of the American Educational Research Association, New Orleans. (ERIC Documentation Reproduction Service No. ED455099)

Hall, G. E., & Loucks, S. F. (1978). Teacher concerns as a basis for facilitating and personalizing staff development. *Teachers College Record, 80*(1), 36–53.

Hall, L. J., McClannahan, L. E., & Krantz, P. J. (1995). Promoting independence in integrated classrooms by teaching aides to use activity schedules and decreased prompts. *Education and Training in Mental Retardation and Developmental Disabilities, 30,* 208–217.

Hallahan, D. P., & Kauffman, J. M. (2003). *Exceptional learners: Introduction to special education.* Boston: Allyn & Bacon.

Halualani, R. T., Chitgopekar, A. S., Morrison, J. H. T. A., & Dodge, P. S. (2004). Diverse in name only? Intercultural interaction at a multicultural university. *Journal of Communication, 54*(2), 270–286.

Hammeken, P. A. (2003). *Inclusion: An essential guide for the paraprofessional* (2nd ed.). Minnetonka, MN: Peytral.

Hanson, M. J., Lynch, E. W., & Wayman, K. I. (1990). Honoring the cultural diversity of families when gathering data. *Topics in Early Childhood Special Education, 10*(1), 112–131.

Hargie, O., Saunders, C., & Dickson, D. (1994). *Social skills in interpersonal communication* (3rd ed.). New York: Routledge.

Hargreaves, A., & Fullan, M. (1998). *What's worth fighting for in education.* Buckingham: Open University Press.

Haring, N. G., & McCormick, L. (1990). *Exceptional children and youth.* Upper Saddle River, NJ: Merrill/Prentice Hall.

Harlos, K. P. (2001). When organizational voice systems fail: More on the deaf-ear syndrome and frustration effects [Electronic version]. *Journal of Applied Behavioral Science, 37,* 324–342.

Harris, A. M., & Cancelli, A. A. (1991). Teachers as volunteer consultees: Enthusiastic, willing or resistant participants? *Journal of Educational and Psychological Consultation, 2,* 217–238.

Harris, B. M. (1989). *In-service education for staff development.* Boston: Allyn & Bacon.

Harris, K. C. (1995). School-based bilingual special education teacher assistance teams. *Remedial and Special Education, 16,* 337–343.

Harry, B. (1992). Developing cultural awareness: The first step in values clarification for early interventionists. *Topics in Early Childhood Special Education, 12,* 333–350.

Harry, B., Kalyanpur, M., & Day, M. (1999). *Building cultural reciprocity with families: case studies in special education.* Baltimore: Brookes.

Harvey, M. (2001). Vocational-technical education: A logical approach to dropout prevention for secondary special education. *Preventing School Failure, 45*(3), 108–114.

Hawbaker, B. W., Balong, M., Buckwalter, S., & Runyon, S. (2001). Building a strong BASE of support for all students through coplanning. *Teaching Exceptional Children, 33*(4), 24–30.

Hawley, W. D., & Rollie, D. L. (Eds.). (2002). *The keys to effective schools: Educational reform as continuous improvement.* Thousand Oaks, CA: Corwin.

Hayakawa, S. I. (1972). *Language in thought and action* (3rd ed.). New York: Harcourt, Brace, Jovanovich.

Henderson, K. (2002). Collaboration to benefit children with disabilities: Incentives in IDEA. *Journal of Educational and Psychological Consultation, 13,* 383–391.

Heningsen, M. L. M., Heningsen, D. D., Cruz, M. G., & Morrill, J. (2003). Social influence in groups: A comparative application of relational framing theory and the elaboration likelihood model of persuasion [Electronic version]. *Communication Monographs, 70,* 175–197.

Henning-Stout, M., & Meyers, J. (2000). Consultation and human diversity: First things first [Electronic version]. *School Psychology Review, 29,* 419–420.

Heron, T. E., & Harris, K. C. (2001). *The educational consultant: Helping professionals, parents, and mainstreamed students* (4th ed.). Austin, TX: Pro-Ed.

Hersey, P. (1984). *The situational leader: The other 59 minutes.* Escondido, CA: The Center for Leadership Studies.

Hertzog, H. S. (2000, April). When, how and who do I ask for help? Novices' perceptions of learning and assistance. Paper presented at the Annual Meeting of the American Educational Research Association, New Orleans.

Hill, P. T. (2004). The need for new institutions. In P. T. Hill & J. Harvey (Eds.), *Making school reform work: New partnerships for real change* (pp. 8–16). Washington, DC: Brookings Institutions Press.

Hobbs, S. F., & Rose, E. (2000). Dealing with reality. In M. S. E. Fishbaugh (Ed.), *The collaboration guide for early career educators* (pp. 185–200). Baltimore: Paul H. Brookes.

Hobbs, T., & Westling, D. L. (1998). Promoting successful inclusion through collaborative problem-solving. *Teaching Exceptional Children, 31*(1), 12–19.

Hollingsworth, H. L. (2001). We need to talk: Communication strategies for effective collaboration. *Teaching Exceptional Children 33*(5), 4–8.

Honeyman, C., Goh, B. C., & Kelly, L. (2004). Skill is not enough: Seeking connectedness and authority in mediation [Electronic version]. *Negotiation Journal, 20,* 489–511.

Hooper, S. R., & Umansky, W., (2004). *Young children with special needs* (4th ed.). Upper Saddle River, NJ: Merrill/Prentice Hall.

Hord, S. (1986). A synthesis of research on organizational collaboration. *Educational Leadership, 43*(5), 22–26.

Hourcade, J. J., & Bauwens, J. (2001). Cooperative teaching: The renewal of teachers [Electronic version]. *Clearinghouse, 74,* 242–247.

Hourcade, J., Parette, P., & Anderson, H. (2003). Accountability in collaboration: A framework for evaluation [Electronic version]. *Education and Training in Developmental Disabilities, 38,* 398–404.

Houser, B. P. (2005). The power of collaboration: Arizona's best kept secret [Electronic version]. *Nursing Administration Quarterly, 29,* 263–267.

Howard, V. F., Williams, B. F., & Lepper, C. (2005). *Very young children with special needs: A formative approach for today's children* (3rd ed.). Upper Saddle River, NJ: Merrill/Prentice Hall.

Howard, V. F., Williams, B. F., Port, P. D., & Lepper, C. (1997). *Very young children with special needs: A formative approach for the 21st century.* Upper Saddle River, NJ: Merrill.

Howard, V. F., Williams, B. F., Port, P. D., & Lepper, C. (2001). *Very young children with special needs: A formative approach for the 21st century* (2nd ed.). Upper Saddle River, NJ: Merrill/Prentice Hall.

Howe, K. R., & Miramontes, O. B. (1992). *The ethics of special education.* New York: Teachers College Press.

Howells, K. D. (2000). Boldly going where angels fear to tread [Electronic version]. *Intervention in School and Clinic, 35,* 157–160.

Huber, J. J. (2005). Collaborative units for addressing multiple grade levels. *Intervention in School and Clinic, 40,* 301–308.

Huefner, D. S. (2000). The risks and opportunities of the IEP requirements under IDEA 97. *Journal of Special Education, 33,* 195–204.

Hunt, P., Soto, G., Maier, J., & Doering, K. (2003). Collaborative teaming to support students at risk and students with severe disabilities in general education classrooms. *Exceptional Children, 69,* 315–332.

Hunt, P., Soto, G., Maier, J., Liborion, N., & Bae, S. (2004). Collaborative teaming to support preschoolers with severe disabilities who are placed in general education early childhood programs [Electronic version]. *Topics in Early Childhood Special Education, 24,* 123–142.

Hunt, P., Soto, G., Maier, J., Muller, E., & Goetz, L. (2002). Collaborative teaming to support students with augmentative and alternative communication needs in general education classrooms [Electronic version]. *Augmentative and Alternative Communication, 18,* 20–35.

Hutchinson, D. J. (1978). The transdisciplinary approach. In J. B. Curry & K. K. Peppe (Eds.), *Mental retardation: Nursing approaches to care* (pp. 65–74). St. Louis, MO: Mosby.

Huxham, C. (Ed.). (1996). *Creating collaborative advantage.* Thousand Oaks, CA: Sage.

Hymowitz, C. (2006, February 13). Rewarding competitors over collaborators no longer makes sense. *Wall Street Journal.*

Idol, L., Nevin, A., & Paolucci-Whitcomb, P. (1994). *Collaborative consultation* (2nd ed.). Austin, TX: Pro-Ed.

Idol, L., Nevin, A., & Paolucci-Whitcomb, P. (2000). *Collaborative consultation* (3rd ed.). Austin, TX: Pro-Ed.

Imhof, M. (2004). Who are we as we listen? Individual listening profiles in varying contexts. *International Journal of Listening, 18,* 36–45.

Ingraham, C. L. (2003). Multicultural consultee-centered consultation: When novice consultants explore cultural hypotheses with experienced teacher consultees. *Journal of Educational and Psychological Consultation, 14,* 329–362.

Institute of Medicine. (1996). *Healthy communities: New partnerships for the future of public health: A report of the first year of the committee on public health.* Washington, DC: National Academy Press.

Isenhart, M. W., & Spangle, M. (2000). *Collaborative approaches to resolving conflict.* Thousand Oaks, CA: Sage.

Ivey, A. E., & Ivey, M. B. (1999). *Intentional interviewing and counseling: Facilitating client development in a multicultural society* (4th ed.). Belmont, CA: Wadsworth.

Ivey, A. E., & Ivey, M. B. (2003). *Intentional interviewing and counseling: Facilitating client development in a multicultural society* (5th ed.). Belmont, CA: Wadsworth.

Jacobson, J. W., & Mulick, J. A. (2000). System and cost research issues in treatments for people with autistic disorders [Electronic version]. *Journal of Autism and Developmental Disorders, 30,* 585–593.

Jayanthi, M., & Friend, M. (1992). Interpersonal problem solving: A selected literature review to guide practice. *Journal of Educational and Psychological Consultation, 3,* 147–152.

Jayanthi, M., & Nelson, J. S. (2002). *Savvy decision making: An administrator's guide to using focus groups in schools.* Thousand Oaks, CA: Corwin.

Jehn, K. A. (2000). The influence of proportional and perceptual conflict composition on team performance. *International Journal of Conflict Management, 11*(1), 56–73.

Jenkins, J. R., Antil, L. R., Wayne, S. K., & Vadasy, P. F. (2003). How cooperative learning works for special education and remedial students. *Exceptional Children, 69,* 279–292.

Jensen-Campbell, L. A., Gleason, K. A., Adams, R., & Malcolm, K. T. (2003). Interpersonal conflict, agreeableness, and personality development [Electronic version]. *Journal of Personality, 71,* 1060–1085.

Johns, B. H., Crowley, E. P., & Guetzloe, E. (2002). Planning the IEP for students with emotional and behavioral disorders. *Focus on Exceptional Children, 34*(9), 1–12.

Johnson, B. (2004). Local school micropolitical agency: An antidote to new managerialism [Electronic version]. *School Leadership and Management, 24,* 267–286.

Johnson, D. R. (2002). Challenges facing secondary education and transition services for youth with disabilities. *Teaching Exceptional Children, 34*(3) 86–88.

Johnson, D. W. (2003). *Reaching out: Interpersonal effectiveness and self-actualization* (8th ed.). Boston: Allyn & Bacon.

Johnson, D. W. (2006). *Reaching out: Interpersonal effectiveness and self-actualization* (9th ed.). Boston: Allyn & Bacon.

Johnson, D. W., & Johnson, F. P. (1997). *Joining together: Group theory and group skills* (6th ed.). Boston: Allyn & Bacon.

Johnson, D. W., & Johnson, F. P. (2000). *Joining together: Group theory and group skills* (7th ed.). Boston: Allyn & Bacon.

Johnson, D. W., & Johnson, F. P. (2002). *Joining together: Group theory and group skills* (8th ed.). Minneapolis, MN: Pearson.

Johnson, D. W., & Johnson, F. P. (2006). *Joining together: Group theory and group skills* (9th ed.). Boston: Allyn & Bacon.

Johnson, D. W., & Johnson, R. T. (1999). *Learning together and alone: Cooperative, competitive, and individualistic learning* (5th ed.). Boston: Allyn & Bacon.

Johnson, L. J., Zom, D., Tam, B. K. Y., LaMontagne, M., & Johnson, S. A. (2003). Stakeholders' views of factors that impact successful interagency collaboration. *Exceptional Children, 69*(2), 195–209.

Johnson, S. D., & Roellke, C. F. (1999). Secondary teachers' and undergraduate education faculty members' perceptions of teaching-effectiveness criteria: A national survey [Electronic version]. *Communication Education, 48*, 127–138.

John-Steiner, V. (2000). *Creative collaboration.* New York: Oxford University Press.

Johnston, M., Brosnan, P., Cramer, D., & Dove, T. (Eds.). (2000). *Collaborative reform and other improbable dreams.* Albany: State University of New York Press.

Johnston, S. S., Tulbert, B. L., Sebastian, J. P., Devries, K., & Gompert, A. (2000). Vocabulary development: A collaborative effort for teaching content vocabulary [Electronic version]. *Intervention in School and Clinic, 35*, 311–315.

Jolly, A., & Evans, S. (2005). Teacher assistants move to the front of the class: Job embedded learning pays off in student achievement. *Journal of Staff Development, 26*(3), 8–13.

Jordan, J. B., Gallagher, J. J., Hutinger, P. L., & Karnes, M. B. (1988). *Early childhood special education: Birth to three.* Reston, VA: Council for Exceptional Children and Its Division for Early Childhood.

Jordan, L., Reyes-Blanes, M. E., Peel, B. B., & Lane, H. B. (1998). Developing teacher–parent partnerships across cultures: Effective parent conferences. *Intervention in School and Clinic, 33*(3), 141–149.

Jordan, P. J., & Troth, A. C. (2004). Managing emotions during team problem solving: Emotional intelligence and conflict resolution [Electronic version]. *Human Performance, 17*, 195–218.

Joshi, S. V. (2004). School consultation and intervention. In H. Steiner (Ed.), *Handbook of mental health interventions in children and adolescents: An integrated developmental approach* (pp. 885–916). San Francisco: Jossey-Bass.

Joyce, B. R., & Showers, B. (2002). *Student achievement through staff development* (3rd ed.). Alexandria, VA: Association for Supervision and Curriculum Development.

Joyce, B., & Showers, B. (1995). *Student achievement through staff development: Fundamentals of school renewal* (2nd ed.). White Plains, NY: Longman.

Jung, B. (1998). Mainstreaming and fixing things: Secondary teachers and inclusion [Electronic version]. *Educational Forum, 62*, 131–138.

Jung, L. A., & Baird, S. M. (2003). Effects of service coordinator variables on individualized family service plans [Electronic version]. *Journal of Early Intervention, 25*, 206–218.

Kaff, M. S. (2004). Multitasking is multitaxing: Why special educators are leaving the field [Electronic version]. *Preventing School Failure, 48*(2), 10–17.

Kaiser, S. M., & Woodman, R. W. (1985). Multidisciplinary teams and group decision-making techniques: Possible solutions to decision-making problems. *School Psychology Review, 14*, 457–470.

Kalyanpur, M., & Harry, B. (1999). *Culture in special education: Building reciprocal family–professional relationships.* Baltimore: Brookes.

Kampwirth, T. J. (1999). *Collaborative consultation in the schools: Effective practices for students with learning and behavior problems.* Upper Saddle River, NJ: Merrill.

Kampwirth, T. J. (2006). *Collaborative consultation in the schools: Effective practices for students with learning and behavior problems* (3rd ed.). Upper Saddle River, NJ: Merrill.

Karp, H. B. (1984). Working with resistance. *Training and Development Journal, 38*(3), 69–73.

Kassner, K. (2002). Cooperative learning revisited: A way to address the standards. *Music Educators Journal, 88*(4), 17–23.

Katisyannis, A., Hodge, J., & Lanford, A. (2000). Paraeducators: Legal and practice considerations. *Remedial and Special Education, 21*, 297–304.

Kay, P. J., Sherrer, M. K., & Fitzgerald, M. (1992, November). *Involving special educators in school reform: The development of peer leadership.* Paper presented at the conference of the Teacher Education Division of the Council for Exceptional Children, Cincinnati. (ERIC Document Reproduction Service No. 365 029)

Kearns, J. F., Kleinert, H. L., & Kennedy, S. (1999). We need not exclude anyone. *Educational Leadership, 56*(6), 33–38.

Keefe, E. B., Moore, V., & Duff, F. (2004). The four "knows" of collaborative teaming. *Teaching Exceptional Children, 36*(5), 36–42.

Kelker, K. A. (2000). Resolving conflicts. In M. S. E. Fishbaugh (Ed.), *The collaboration guide for early career educators* (pp. 137–163). Baltimore: Paul H. Brookes.

Kenton, S. B. (1989). Speaker credibility in persuasive business communication: A model which explains gender differences. *Journal of Business Communications, 26,* 143–157.

Kersh, M. E., & Masztal, N. B. (1998). An analysis of studies of collaboration between universities and K–12 schools [Electronic version]. *Educational Forum, 62,* 218–225.

Kesson, K., & Oyler, C. (1999). Integrated curriculum and service learning. *English Education, 31,* 135–49.

Kew, D. W. (2000). Middle level teaming—Strength in collaboration [Electronic version]. *Schools in the Middle, 9*(9), 39–40.

Killoran, J., Templeman, T. P., Peters, J., & Udell, T. (2001). Identifying paraprofessional competencies for early intervention and early childhood special education. *Teaching Exceptional Children, 34*(1), 68–73.

King, M. B., & Youngs, P. (2003). *Classroom teachers' views on inclusion.* Research Institute on Secondary Education Reform for Youth with Disabilities (RISER). Retrieved September 10, 2004, from www.eric.ed.gov/content delivery/servlet/ERICServlet?accno=ED4778 78

Kinlaw, D. C. (1993). *Team-managed facilitation.* San Diego, CA: Pfeiffer & Company.

Klapstein, S. (1994). A collaborative interagency diagnostic classroom. *Intervention in School and Clinic, 29,* 180–183.

Kluckhorn, F. R. (1968). Variations in value orientations as a factor in education planning. In E. M. Bower & W. G. Hallister (Eds.), *Behavioral science frontiers in education* (pp. 289–314). New York: Wiley.

Kluwin, T. N. (1999). Co-teaching deaf and hearing students: Research on social integration [Electronic version]. *American Annals of the Deaf, 144,* 339–344.

Knoff, H. M., Sullivan, P., & Liu, D. (1995). Teachers' ratings of effective school psychology consultants: An exploratory factor analysis study [Electronic version]. *Journal of School Psychology, 33,* 39–57.

Knotek, S. (2003). Bias in problem solving and the social process of sudent study teams: A qualitative investigation. *Journal of Special Education, 37,* 2–14.

Knotek, S. E., & Sandoval, J. (2003). Current research in consultee-centered consultation. *Journal of Educational and Psychological Consultation, 14,* 243–250.

Kohler, P. D., & Field, S. (2003). Transition-focused education: Foundation for the future. *Journal of Special Education, 37*(3), 174–183.

Kosmoski, G. J., & Pollack, D. R. (2000). *Managing difficult, frustrating, and hostile conversations: Strategies for savvy administrators.* Thousand Oaks, CA: Corwin Press.

Kosmoski, G. J., & Pollack, D. R. (2001). *Managing conversations with hostile adults: Strategies for teachers.* Thousand Oaks, CA: Corwin Press.

Kotkin, R. A. (1995). The Irvine paraprofessional program: Using paraprofessionals in serving students with ADHD. *Intervention in School and Clinic, 30,* 235–240.

Krajewski, B. (2005). In their own words. *Educational Leadership, 62*(6), 14–18.

Kratochwill, T. R., & Pittman, P. H. (2002). Expanding problem-solving consultation training: Prospects and frameworks. *Journal of Educational and Psychological Consultation, 13,* 69–95.

Kratochwill, T. R., & Stoiber, K. C. (2000). Uncovering critical research agendas for school psychology: Conceptual dimensions and future directions [Electronic version]. *School Psychology Review, 29,* 591–603.

Krebs, C. S. (2000). Beyond blindfolds: Creating an inclusive classroom through collaboration [Electronic version]. *RE:view, 31,* 180–186.

Kroeger, S. D., Leibold, C. K., & Ryan, B. (1999). Creating a sense of ownership in the IEP process. *Teaching Exceptional Children, 32*(1), 4–9.

Kronick, R. F. (2000). *Human services and the full service school: The need for collaboration.* Springfield, IL: Thomas.

Kruger, L. J., Struzziero, J., Watts, R., & Vaca, D. (1995). The relationship between organizational support and satisfaction with teacher assistance teams. *Remedial and Special Education, 16,* 203–211.

Kruk, E. (Ed.). (1997). *Mediation and conflict resolution in social work and the human services.* Chicago: Nelson-Hall.

Kruse, S. D. (1999). Collaborate. *Journal of Staff Development, 20*(3), 14–16.

Kübler-Ross, E. (1969). *On death and dying.* New York: Macmillan.

Kumkale, G. T., & Albarracin, D. (2004). The sleeper effect in persuasion: A meta-analytic review [Electronic version]. *Psychological Bulletin, 130,* 143–172.

Kurpius, D. J., & Brubaker, J. C. (1976). *Psycho-educational consultation: Definition, functions, preparation.* Bloomington: Indiana University.

La Cava, P. G. (2005). Facilitate transitions. *Intervention in School and Clinic, 41,* 46–48.

Lacey, P. (2001). *Support partnerships: Collaboration in action.* London: David Fulton.

Laframboise, K. L., Epanchin, B., Colucci, K., & Hocutt, A. (2004). Working together: Emerging roles of special and general education teachers in inclusive settings [Electronic version]. *Action in Teacher Education, 26*(3), 30–43.

Lamar-Dukes, P., & Dukes, C. (2005). Twenty ways to consider the roles and responsibilities of the inclusion support teacher. *Intervention in School and Clinic, 41*(1), 55–61.

Lambert, L. (1998). How to build leadership capacity. *Educational Leadership, 55*(7), 17–19.

Lambie, R. (2000). *Family systems within educational contexts: Understanding at-risk and special needs students* (2nd ed.). Denver: Love.

Landers, M. F., & Weaver, H. R. (1997). *Inclusive education: A process, not a placement.* Swampscott, MA: Watersun.

Lane, K. L., Mahdavi, J. N., & Borthwick-Duffy, S. (2003). Teacher perceptions of the prereferral intervention process: A call for assistance with school-based interventions. *Preventing School Failure, 47,* 148–155.

Langone, J., Langone, C. A., & McLaughlin, P. J. (2000). Analyzing special educators' views on community-based instruction for students with mental retardation and developmental disabilities: Implications for teacher education. *Journal of Developmental and Physical Disabilities, 12*(1), 17–34.

Larivaara, P., & Taanila, A. (2004). Towards interprofessional family-oriented teamwork in primary services: The evaluation of an education programme [Electronic version]. *Journal of Interprofessional Care, 18,* 153–163.

Lasater, M. W., Johnson, M. M., & Fitzgerald, M. (2000). Completing the education mosaic. *Teaching Exceptional Children, 33*(1), 46–51.

Laud, L. E. (1998). Changing the way we communicate. *Educational Leadership, 55*(7), 23–25.

Laurice, L. M. (2000). Students as strategies participants on collaborative problem-solving teams: An alternative model for middle and secondary schools [Electronic version]. *Intervention in School and Clinic, 36*(1), 47–53.

Lawson, H. A. (1999). Two new mental models for schools and their implications for principals' roles, responsibilities, and preparation [Electronic version]. *NASSP Bulletin, 83*(611), 8–27.

Lazar, A., & Slostad, F. (1999). How to overcome obstacles to parent–teacher partnerships. *Clearinghouse, 72*(4), 206–211.

LeCapitaine, J. (2000). Role of the school psychologist in the treatment of high-risk students [Electronic version]. *Education, 121,* 73–79.

Lee, G. V., & Barnett, B. G. (1994). Using reflective questioning to promote collaborative dialogue. *Journal of Staff Development, 15*(1), 16–21.

Leftwich, S., & Sykes, T. A. (2005). Now hear this. *Black Enterprise 35*(8), 112–113.

Lehr, A. E. (1999). The administrative role in collaborative teaming [Electronic version]. *NASSP Bulletin, 83*(611), 105–111.

Leimu, R., & Koricheva, J. (2005). Does scientific collaboration increase the impact of ecological articles? [Electronic version] *BioScience, 55,* 438–443.

Lenhart, A., Madden, M., & Hitlin, P. (2005). Teens and technology: Youth are leading the transition to a fully wired and mobile nation. Pew Internet and American Life Project. Retrieved from www.pewinternet.org/PPF/r/162/report_display.asp

Leonard, J., Lovelace-Taylor, K., Sanford-DeShields, J., & Spearman, P. (2004). Professional development schools revisited: Reform, authentic partnerships, and new visions [Electronic version]. *Urban Education, 39,* 561–583.

Leonard, L. J., & Leonard, P. E. (1999). Reculturing for collaboration and leadership [Electronic version]. *Journal of Educational Research, 92,* 237–242.

Lewin, K. (1951). *Field theory in the social sciences: Selected theoretical papers.* New York: Harper & Row.

Lieberman, A., & Miller, L. (2002). Transforming professional development: Understanding and organizing learning communities. In W. D. Hawley & D. L. Rollie (Eds.), *The keys to effective schools: Educational reform as continuous improvement.* Thousand Oaks, CA: Corwin.

Little, J. W. (1982). Norms of collegiality and experimentations: Workplace conditions of school success. *American Educational Research Journal, 5,* 325–340.

Littlejohn, S. W., & Domenici, K. (2001). *Engaging communication in conflict: Systemic practice.* Thousand Oaks, CA: Sage.

Lloyd, J. W., Crowley, E. P., Kohler, R. W., & Strain, P. S. (1988). Redefining the applied research agenda: Cooperative learning, prereferral, teacher consultation, and peer-mediated interventions. *Journal of Learning Disabilities, 21,* 43–52.

Logan, K. R., Hansen, C. D., & Neiminen, P. K. (2001). Student support teams: Helping students succeed in general education classrooms or working to place students in special education? *Education and Training in Mental Retardation and Developmental Disabilities, 36,* 280–292.

Lopez, E. C. (2000). Conducting instructional consultation through interpreters [Electronic version]. *School Psychology Review, 29,* 378–388.

Lortie, D.C. (1975). *School teacher: A sociological study.* Chicago: University of Chicago Press.

Loucks-Horsley, S., & Hergert, L. (1985). *An action guide to school improvement.* Alexandria, VA: Association of Supervision and Curriculum Development.

Lovelace, K. A. (2000). External collaboration and performance: North Carolina local public health departments, 1996. *Public Health Reports, 115*(3).

Luckner, J. L. (1999). An examination of two co-teaching classrooms [Electronic version]. *American Annals of the Deaf, 144,* 24–34.

Luft, J. (1984). *Group processes: An introduction to group dynamics* (3rd ed.). New York: McGraw Hill (Mayfield).

Lugg, C. A., & Boyd, W. L. (1993). Leadership for collaboration: Reducing risk and fostering resilience. *Phi Delta Kappan, 75,* 253–258.

Luiselli, J. K. (2002). Focus, scope, and practice of behavioral consultation in public schools [Electronic version]. *Behavior Psychology in the Schools, 24,* 5–21.

Luiselli, J. K., & Diament, C. (2002). *Behavior psychology in the schools: Innovations in evaluation, support, and consultation.* New York: Haworth.

Lustig, M. W., & Koester, J. (1999). *Intercultural competence: Interpersonal communication across cultures* (3rd ed.). New York: Longman.

Lustig, M. W., & Koester, J. (2006). *Intercultural competence: Interpersonal communication across cultures* (5th ed.). Boston: Allyn & Bacon.

Lynch, E. W. (1998). Developing cross-cultural competence. In E. W. Lynch & M. J. Hanson (Eds.), *Developing cross-cultural competence: A guide for working with young children and their families* (2nd ed.). Baltimore: Brookes.

Lynch, E. W. (2004). Developing cross-cultural competence. In E. W. Lynch & M. J. Hanson (Eds.), *Developing cross-cultural competence: A guide for working with children and their families* (3rd ed., pp. 49–55). Baltimore: Brookes.

Lynch, E. W., & Hanson, M. J. (1998). Steps in the right direction: Implications for interventionists.

In E. W. Lynch & M. J. Hanson (Eds.), *Developing cross-cultural competence: A guide for working with young children and their families* (2nd ed, pp. 491–512). Baltimore: Brookes.

Lynch, E. W., & Hanson, M. J. (2004). Steps in the right direction: Implications for interventionists. In E. W. Lynch & M. J. Hanson (Eds.), *Developing cross-cultural competence: A guide for working with young children and their families* (3rd ed, pp. 449–464). Baltimore: Brookes.

Lytle, R. K., & Bordin, J. (2001). Enhancing the IEP team: Strategies for parents and professionals. *Teaching Exceptional Children, 32*(5), 40–44.

MacIver, D. J. (1990). Meeting the needs of young adolescents: Advisory groups, interdisciplinary teacher teams, and school transition programs. *Phi Delta Kappan, 71,* 458–464.

Maeroff, G. (1993). Building teams to rebuild schools. *Phi Delta Kappan, 71,* 512–519.

Magiera, K., Smith, C., Zigmond, N., & Gebaner, K. (2005). Benefits of co-teaching in secondary mathematics classes. *Teaching Exceptional Children, 37*(3), 20–24.

Mainzer, R. W., Deshler, D., Coleman, M. R., Kozleski, E., & Rodriguez-Walling, M. (2003). To ensure the learning of every child with a disability [Electronic version]. *Focus on Exceptional Children, 35*(5), 1–12.

Maital, S. L. (1996). Integration of behavioral and mental health consultation as a means of overcoming resistance. *Journal of Educational and Psychological Consultation, 7,* 291–303.

Mamlin, N. (1999). Despite best intentions: When inclusion fails. *Journal of Special Education, 33,* 36–48.

Man, D. (1999). Community based empowerment programme for families with a brain injured survivor: An outcome study. *Brain Injury, 13*(6), 433–445.

Mancillas, A. (2005, October). Empathic invalidations. *Counseling Today,* pp. 9, 19.

Marans, S., Berkowitz, S. J., & Cohen, D. J. (1998). Police and mental health professionals: Collaborative response to the impact of violence on children and families. *Child and Adolescent Psychiatric Clinics of North America, 7,* 635–650.

Marengo, L., & Dosi, G. (2005). Division of labor, organizational coordination and market mechanisms in collective problem-solving [Electronic version]. *Journal of Economic Behavior and Organization, 58,* 303–326.

Mareschal, P. M. (2005). What makes mediation work? Mediators' perspectives on resolving disputes [Electronic version]. *Industrial Relations, 44,* 509–517.

Margolis, H. (1999). Meditation for special education conflicts: An opportunity to improve family–school relationships. *Journal of Educational Psychological Consultation, 10,* 91–100.

Marks, S. U., Schrader, C., & Levine, M. (1999). Paraeducator experiences in inclusive settings: Helping, hovering, or holding their own? *Exceptional Children, 65,* 315–328.

Martinez, M. E. (1998). What is problem solving? *Phi Delta Kappan, 79,* 605–609.

Mason, L. (2001). Responses to anomalous data and theory change. *Learning and Instruction, 11,* 453–483.

Masters, M. F., & Albright, R. R. (2002). *The complete guide to conflict resolution in the workplace.* New York: American Management Association.

Mastropieri, M. A., Scruggs, T. E., Graetz, J., Norland, J., Gardizi, W., & McDuffie, K. (2005). Case studies in co-teaching in the content areas: Successes, failures, and challenges. *Intervention in School and Clinic, 40,* 260–270.

Mattison, R. E. (2000). School consultation: A review of research on issues unique to the school [Electronic version]. *Journal of the American Academy of Child and Adolescent Psychiatry, 39,* 402–413.

Maurasse, D. (Ed.). (2004). *A future for everyone: Innovative social responsibility and community partnerships.* New York: Routledge.

McCaleb, J. G. (1987). Review of communication competencies used in statewide assessments. In J. L. McCaleb (Ed.), *How do teachers communicate? A review and critique of assessment practices* (pp. 7–28). Washington, DC: American Association of Colleges for Teacher Education.

McCormick, L., Noonan, M. J., Ogata, V., & Heck, R. (2001). Co-teacher relationship and program quality: implications for preparing teachers for inclusive preschool settings. *Education & Training in Mental Retardation & Development Disabilities, 36*(2), 119–132.

McCroskey, J. C., Fayer, J. M., Richmond, V., Sallinen, A., & Barraclough, R. A. (1996). A multicultural examination of the relationship between nonverbal immediacy and affective learning. *Communication Quarterly, 44,* 297–307.

McDonnell, J. (1997). Isn't it about achieving a balance? *TASH Newsletter, 23*(2), 23–24, 29.

McDonnell, J., Thorson, N., Disher, S., Mathot-Buckner, C., Mendel, J., & Ray, L. (2003). The achievement of students with developmental disabilities and their peers without disabilities

in inclusive settings: An exploratory study [Electronic version]. *Education and Treatment of Children, 26,* 224–236.

McGinn, D., & McCormick, J. (1999, February 1). Your next job. *Newsweek,* 42–45.

McKenzie, H. S. (1972). Special education and consulting teachers. In F. Clark, D. Evans, & L. Hammerlynk (Eds.), *Implementing behavioral programs for schools and clinics.* Champaign, IL: Research Press.

McLaughlin, M. J. (2002). Examining special and general education collaborative practices in exemplary schools. *Journal of Educational and Psychological Consultation, 13,* 279–283.

McNamara, K., & Hollinger, C. (2003). Intervention-based assessment: Evaluation rates and eligibility findings. *Exceptional Children, 69,* 181–193.

Medved, M. (2001, August 8). Good teamwork outshines superstar systems. *USA Today,* 13A.

Mehrabian, A. (1971). *Silent messages.* Belmont, CA: Wadsworth.

Mehrabian, A. (1980). *Silent messages* (2nd ed). Belmont, CA: Wadsworth.

Meister, D. G., & Melnick, S. A. (2003). National new teacher study: Beginning teachers' concerns [Electronic version]. *Action in Teacher Education, 24,* 87–94.

Melamed, J. C., & Reiman, J. W. (2000). Collaboration and conflict resolution in education [Electronic version]. *High School Magazine, 7*(7), 16–20.

Menninger, W. C. (1950). Mental health in our schools. *Educational Leadership, 7,* 520.

Meyers, J. (2002). A 30 year perspective on best practices for consultation training. *Journal of Educational and Psychological Consultation, 13,* 35–54.

Miller, H. R., & Hoy, A. W. (2003). A case study of an African American teacher's self-efficacy, stereotype threat, and persistence [Electronic version]. *Teaching and Teacher Education, 19,* 263–276.

Miller, M. D., Brownell, M. T., & Smith, S. W. (1999). Factors that predict teachers staying in, leaving, or transferring from the special education classroom. *Exceptional Children, 65,* 201–218.

Miller, S. P. (2002). *Validated practices for teaching students with diverse needs and abilities* (Chapter 6, pp. 235–285). Boston: Allyn & Bacon

Mitchell, A. (1997). Teacher identity: A key to increased collaboration. *Action in Teacher Education, 19*(3), 1–14.

Mitchell, D. E., & Scott, L. D. (1993). Professional and institutional perspectives on interagency collaboration. *Journal of Educational Policy, 8*(5–6), 75–91.

Mock, D. R., & Kauffman, J. M. (2002). Preparing teachers for full inclusion: Is it possible? [Electronic version] *Teacher Educator, 37,* 202–215.

Monzó, L. D., & Rueda, R. S. (2000, December). *Examining Latino paraeducators: Interactions with Latino students.* Washington, DC: ERIC Clearinghouse on Language and Linguistics.

Moon, M. S., & Inge, K. (2000). Vocational preparation and transition. In M. Snell & F. Brown (Eds.), *Instruction of students with severe disabilities* (5th ed., pp. 591–628). Upper Saddle River, NJ: Merrill/Prentice Hall.

Moon, M. S., & Inge, K. (2005). Vocational preparation and transition. In M. Snell & F. Brown (Eds.), *Instruction of students with severe disabilities* (6th ed., pp. 591–628). Upper Saddle River, NJ: Merrill/Prentice Hall.

Morgan, J., & Ashbaker, B. Y. (2001). Work more effectively with your paraeducator [Electronic version]. *Intervention in School and Clinic, 36,* 230–231.

Morgan, N. (2001). How to overcome "change fatigue." *Harvard Management Update, 6*(7), 1–3.

Morocco, C. C., & Aguilar, C. M. (2002). Coteaching for content understanding: A schoolwide model. *Journal of Educational and Psychological Consultation, 13,* 315–347.

Morris, M. W., & Su, S. K. (1999). Social psychological obstacles in environmental conflict resolution [Electronic version]. *American Behavioral Scientist, 42,* 1322–1349.

Morse, W. (1994). Mental health professionals and teachers: How do the twain meet? *Beyond Behavior, 3*(2), 12–20.

Muchmore, J. A., Cooley, V. E., Marx, G. E., & Crowell, R. A. (2004). Enhancing teacher leadership in urban education: The Oak Park experience [Electronic version]. *Educational Horizons, 82,* 236–244.

Mueller, P. H., & Murphy, F. V. (2001). Determining when a student requires paraeducator support. *Teaching Exceptional Children, 33*(6), 22–27.

Mujis, D., Harris, A., Chapman, C., Stoll, L., & Russ, J. (2004). Improving schools in socioeconomically disadvantaged areas—A review of research evidence [Electronic version]. *School Effectiveness and School Improvement, 15,* 149–175.

Murawski, W. W. (2005). Addressing diverse needs through co-teaching: Take baby steps! *Kappa Delta Pi Record, 41,* 77–82.

Murray, C. (2004). Clarifying collaborative roles in urban high schools: General educators' perspectives. *Teaching Exceptional Children, 36*(5), 44–51.

Nadler, D. J., Hackman, R., & Lawler, E. E. (1979). *Managing organizational behavior.* Boston: Little, Brown.

Naquin, S. S., & Holton, E. F. (2003). *Approaches to training and development* (3rd ed.). Cambridge, MA: Perseus.

Nastasi, B. K., Varjas, K., Bernstein, R., & Jayasena, A. (2000). Conducting participatory culture-specific consultation: A global perspective on multicultural consultation [Electronic version]. *School Psychology Review, 29,* 401–413.

National Joint Committee on Learning Disabilities. (1999). Learning disabilities: Use of paraprofessionals [Electronic version]. *Learning Disability Quarterly, 22,* 23–30.

Nelson, C. M., & Pearson, C. A. (1991). *Integrating services for children and youth with emotional and behavioral disorders.* Reston, VA: Council for Exceptional Children.

Nelson, J. R., Smith, D. J., Taylor, L., Dodd, J. M., & Reavis, K. (1992). A statewide survey of special education administrators regarding mandated prereferral interventions. *Remedial and Special Education, 13*(4), 34–39.

Nelson, M. G. (2001, September). Capitalizing on collaboration [Electronic version]. *Information Week, 855,* 109–111.

Neubert, D. A., & Moon, M. S. (2000). How a transition profile helps students prepare for life in the community. *Teaching Exceptional Children, 33*(2), 20–25.

Neubert, D. A., Moon, M. S., Leconte, P. J., & Lowman, M. (1998). *Transition profile.* Unpublished manuscript, University of Maryland at College Park.

Neus, A., & Scherf, P. (2005). Opening minds: Cultural change with the introduction of open-source collaboration methods [Electronic version]. *IBM Systems Journal, 44,* 215–225.

Nezu, A., & D'Zurilla, T. J. (1981). Effects of problem definition and formulation on the generation of alternatives in the social problem-solving process. *Cognitive Therapy and Research, 5,* 265–271.

Nichols, W. C. (1996). *Treating people in families: An integrative framework.* New York: Guilford Press.

Niebuhr, K. E., & Niebuhr, R. E. (1999). Principal and counselor collaboration [Electronic version]. *Education, 119,* 674–678.

No Child Left Behind Alert. (2005, June). Divvy up classroom instruction and gain twice the teacher quality. *No Child Left Behind Alert, 43,* 46.

Noell, G. H., & Witt, J. C. (1999). When does consultation lead to intervention implementation?

Critical issues for research and practice. *Journal of Special Education, 33,* 29–35.

Noonan, M. J., & McCormick, L. (1993). *Early intervention in natural environments: Methods and procedures.* Pacific Grove, CA: Brooks/Cole.

Norwood, S. L. (2003). *Nursing consultation: A framework for working with communities.* Upper Saddle River, NJ: Prentice Hall.

Nowak, K. L., Watt, J., & Walther, J. B. (2005). The influence of synchrony and sensory modality on the person perception process in computer-mediated groups. *Journal of Computer-Mediated Communication, 10*(3), article 3. Retrieved from http://jcmc.indiana.edu/vol10/issue3/nowak.html

Nunn, G. D., & McMahan, K. R. (2000). "Ideal" problem solving using a collaborative effort for special needs and at-risk students [Electronic version]. *Education, 121,* 305–312.

Ochoa, T. A., & Robinson, J. M. (2005). Revisiting group consensus: Collaborative learning dynamics during a problem-based learning activity in education. *Teacher Education and Special Education, 28,* 10–20.

Ogletree, B. T., Bull, J., Drew, R., & Lunnen, K. (2001). Team-based service delivery for students with disabilities: Practice options and guidelines for success, *Intervention in School and Clinic, 36,* 138–145.

Ohlund, B. J., & Nelson, J. R. (2001). Effective academic and behavioral intervention and supports: A professional development program. *Teacher Education and Special Education, 24,* 267–272.

Ohtake, Y., Fowler, S. A., & Santos. R. M. (2001). *Working with interpreters to plan early childhood services with limited-English–proficient families* (Technical Report No. 12) [Electronic version]. Champaign-Urbana, IL: Culturally and Linguistically Appropriate Services for Early Childhood Research (CLAS) Institute.

Okhuysen, G. A. (2001). Structuring change: Familiarity and formal interventions in problem-solving groups [Electronic version]. *Academy of Management Journal, 44,* 794–808.

Olson, J., Murphy, C. L., & Olson, P. D. (1998). Building effective successful teams: An interactive training model for inservice education, *Journal of Early Intervention, 21*(4), 339.

Orelove, F., & Sobsey, D. (1987). *Educating children with multiple disabilities: A transdisciplinary approach.* Baltimore: Brookes.

Orlovsky, C. (2005). Critical care beyond the bedside: the collaborative effort of the eICU team. *AMN Healthcare News.* Retrieved October 2, 2005, from www.amnhealthcare.com/Features.asp?ArticleID=14299

Ormsbee, C. K. (2001). Effective preassessment team procedures: Making the process work for teachers and students, *Intervention in School and Clinic, 36*(3), 146.

Ormsbee, C. K., & Haring, K. A. (2000). Rural preassessment team member perceptions of effectiveness. *Rural Special Education Quarterly, 19,* 17–26.

O'Sullivan, P. B. (2000). What you don't know won't hurt me: Impression management functions of communication in relationships. *Human Communication Research, 26,* 403–431.

Owings, W. A., & Kaplan, L. S. (2005). *Best practices, best thinking, and emerging issues in school leadership.* Thousand Oaks, CA: Corwin.

Palma, G. M. (1994). Toward a positive and effective teacher and paraprofessional relationship. *Rural Educator, 13*(4), 46–48.

Palmer, J. D. (1988). For the manager who must build a team. In W. B. Reddy & K. Jamison (Eds.). *Team building: Blueprints for productivity and satisfaction* (pp. 137–149). San Diego, CA: University Associates.

Palsha, S. A., & Wesley, P. W. (1998). Improving quality in early childhood environments through on-site consultation [Electronic version]. *Topics in Early Childhood Special Education, 18,* 243–253.

Pandiscio, H. F. (1991). The risky business of collaboration. *School Administrator, 48*(4), 24, 27.

Pardini, P. (2005). Stretching to the next rung: NCLB requirements set the bar for many paraprofessionals, while several states and districts have developed high quality training the surpasses the national law. *Journal of Staff Development, 26*(3), 14–19.

Parett, H. P., & Petch-Hogan, B. (2000). Approaching families: Facilitating culturally/linguistically diverse family involvement. *Teaching Exceptional Children, 32*(2), 4–10.

Park, E. (1999). Making a team effort [Electronic version]. *Schools in the Middle, 8*(7), 35–38.

Parker, C. A. (Ed.). (1975). *Psychological consultation: Helping teachers meet special needs.* Minneapolis: University of Minnesota Leadership Training Institute.

Parsons, M. B., & Reid, D. H. (1999). Training basic teaching skills to paraeducators of students with severe disabilities. *Teaching Exceptional Children, 31*(4), 48–54.

Patterson, K. (2005). What classroom teachers need to know about IDEA '97. *Kappa Delta Pi Record, 41,* 62–67.

Paul, J., French, P., & Cranston-Gingras, A. (2001). Ethics and special education. *Focus on Exceptional Children, 34*(1), 1–16.

Paulus, P. B., & Brown, V. R. (2003). Enhancing ideational creativity in groups: Lessons from research on brainstorming. In P. B. Paulus & B. A. Nijstad (Eds.), *Group creativity: Innovation through collaboration.* New York: Oxford University Press.

Peck, A. F., & Scarpati, S. (2004). Collaboration in the age of accountability. *Teaching Exceptional Children, 35*(6), 7.

Perloff, R. M. (1993). *The dynamics of persuasion.* Hillsdale, NJ: Erlbaum.

Peterson, J. V., & Nisenholz, B. (1998). *Orientation to counseling* (4th ed.). Boston: Allyn & Bacon.

Peterson, K. D. (1999). Time use flows from school culture. *Journal of Staff Development, 20*(2), 16–19.

Peterson, K., & Cosner, S. (2005). Teaching your principal: Top tips for the professional development of the school's chief. *Journal of Staff Development, 26*(2), 28–32.

Petress, K. C. (1999). Listening: A vital skill. *Journal of Instructional Psychology, 26*(4), 261–263.

Pfau, M., Szabo, E. A., Anderson, J., Morrill, J., Zubric, J., & Wan, H. H. (2001). The role and impact of affect in the process of resistance to persuasion [Electronic version]. *Human Communication Research, 27,* 216–252.

Pfeiffer, S. I. (1981). The school based interprofessional team: Recurring problems and some possible solutions. *Journal of School Psychology, 18,* 388–394.

Phillips, V., McCullough, L., Nelson, C. M., & Walker, H. M. (1990). Teamwork among teachers: Promoting a statewide agenda for students at risk for school failure. *Special Services in the Schools, 6,* 3–4.

Pickett, A. L. (1996). *A state of the art report on paraeducators in education and related services* (Report No. SP 398 188). New York: City University of New York, Center for Advanced Studies in Education. (ERIC Document Reproduction Services No. ED398188)

Pickett, A. L. (1997). Paraeducators in school settings: Framing the issues. In A. L. Pickett & K. Gerlach (Eds.), *Supervising paraeducators in school settings: A team approach* (pp. 1–24). Austin, TX: Pro-Ed.

Pickett, A. L. (1999). *Paraeducators: Factors that influence their performance, development, and supervision* (ERIC Digest E587). ERIC Clearinghouse on Disabilities and Gifted Education, Council for Exceptional Children. Retrieved September 17, 2001, from http://ericec.org/ digests/e587.htm

Piersel, W. C., & Gutkin, T. B. (1983). Resistance to school-based consultation: A behavioral analysis of the problem. *Psychology in the Schools, 20,* 311–320.

Pillari, V., & Newsome, M. (1997). *Human behavior in the social environment: Families, groups, organizations, and communities.* Belmont, CA: Wadsworth.

Pipho, C. (1997). The possibilities and problems of collaboration. *Phi Delta Kappan, 79,* 261–262.

Pomplun, M. (1997). When students with disabilities participate in cooperative groups. *Exceptional Children, 64,* 49–58.

Pomson, A. D. M. (2005). One classroom at a time? Teacher isolation and community viewed through the prism of the particular [Electronic version]. *Teachers College Record, 107,* 783–802.

Pounder, D. (1998). *Restructuring schools for collaboration: Promises and pitfalls.* New York: SUNY Press.

Powers, K., Winters, L., Person, D., & Kim, S. (2004). Collecting and using data in a K–16 collaborative. In J. W. Houck, K. C. Cohn, & C. A. Cohn (Eds.), *Partnering to lead educational renewal: High-quality teachers, high-quality schools* (pp. 131–144). New York: Teachers College Press.

Praisner, C. L. (2003). Attitudes of elementary school principals toward the inclusion of students with disabilities. *Exceptional Children, 69,* 135–145.

Prater, M. A., & Bruhl, S. (1998). Acquiring social skills through cooperative learning and teacher-directed instruction. *Remedial and Special Education, 19*(3), 160–172.

Protheroe, N. (2004). Professional learning communities [Electronic version]. *Principal, 83*(5), 39–42.

Protheroe, N. (2005). Leadership for school improvement [Electronic version]. *Principal, 84*(4), 54–56.

Pryzwansky W. B. (1974). A reconsideration of the consultation model for delivery of school based psychological service. *American Journal of Orthopsychiatry, 44,* 579–583.

Pryzwansky, W. B., & Rzepski, B. (1983). School-based teams: An untapped resource for consultation and technical assistance. *School Psychology Review, 12,* 174–179.

Pugach, M. C. (1988). The consulting teacher in the context of educational reform. *Exceptional Children, 55,* 273–275.

Pugach, M. C., & Johnson, L. J. (1995). *Collaborative practitioners, collaborative schools.* Denver: Love.

Pugach, M. C., & Johnson, L. J. (2002). *Collaborative practitioners, collaborative schools* (2nd ed.). Denver: Love.

Putnam, L. L. (2004). Transformations and critical moments in negotiations [Electronic version]. *Negotiation Journal, 20,* 275–295.

Qin, Z., Johnson, D. W., & Johnson, R. T. (1995). Cooperative versus competitive efforts and problem solving. *Review of Educational Research, 65,* 129–143.

Quinn, K., & Cumbland, C. (1994). Service providers' perceptions of interagency collaboration in their communities. *Remedial Special Education, 2,* 109–116.

Quinn, M. M., Jannasch-Pennell, A., & Rutherford, R. B. (1995). Using peers as social skills training agents for students with antisocial behavior: A cooperative learning approach. *Preventing School Failure, 39*(4), 26–31.

Raign, K. R., & Sims, B. R. (1993). Gender, persuasion techniques, and collaboration. *Technical Communication Quarterly, 2*(1), 89–104.

Raven, B. H. (2003). Groupthink, Bay of Pigs, and Watergate revisited. In L. W. Porter, H. L. Angle, & R. W. Allen (Eds.), *Organizational influence processes* (2nd ed.). Armonk, NY: M. E. Sharpe.

Ray, K. P., Skinner, C. H., & Watson, T. S. (1999). Transferring stimulus control via momentum to increase compliance in a student with autism: A demonstration of collaborative consultation [Electronic version]. *School Psychology Review, 28,* 622–628.

Rea, P. J., & Lock, R. H. (2005). Engage your administrator in your collaborative initiative. *Intervention in School and Clinic, 40*(5), 312–316.

Redditt, S. (1991). Two teachers working as one. *Equity and Choice, 8*(1), 49–56.

Reiter-Palmon, R., & Ilies, J. J. (2004). Leadership and creativity: Understanding leadership from a creative problem-solving perspective [Electronic version]. *Leadership Quarterly, 15,* 55–77.

Results-driven manager series. (Ed.) (2005). *Managing change to reduce resistance.* Boston: Harvard University Business School Press.

Reyes, E. I. (1999). Parents, families and communities ensuring children's rights. *Bilingual Review, 24*(1–2), 53–63.

Reynolds, C. R., Gutkin, T. B., Elliott, S. N., & Witt, J. C. (1984). *School psychology: Essentials of theory and practice.* New York: Wiley.

Rhoades, J. A., Arnold, J., & Jay, C. (2001). The role of affective traits and affective states in disputants' motivation and behavior during episodes of organizational conflict. *Journal of Organizational Behavior, 22,* 329–345.

Richardson, J. (2005). Transform your group into a team. *Tools for Schools, 9*(2), 1–8.

Rieck, W. A., & Wadsworth, D. E. D. (2000). Inclusion: Administrative headache or opportunity? [Electronic version] *NASSP Bulletin, 84,* 56–62.

Riggs, C. G. (2001). Ask the paraprofessionals. *Teaching Exceptional Children, 33*(3), 78–83.

Riggs, C. G., & Mueller, P. H. (2001). Employment and utilization of paraeducators in inclusive settings. *Journal of Special Education, 35,* 54–62.

Riley, D. J., DeAnda, D., Blackaller, C. A. (in press). A qualitative study of self-perceptions and interpersonal relationships of persons with significant physical disabilities. *Journal of Social Work in Disabilities and Rehabilitation.*

Riley-Tillman, T. C., & Chafouleas, S. M. (2003). Using interventions that exist in the natural environment to increase treatment integrity and social influence in consultation. *Journal of Educational and Psychological Consultation, 14,* 139–156.

Roach, V., Salisbury, C., & McGregor, G. (2002). Applications of a policy framework to evaluate and promote large-scale change. *Exceptional Children, 68,* 451–464.

Robson, M. (2002). *Problem solving in groups* (3rd ed.). Burlington, VT: Gower.

Rock, M. A., & Zigmond, N. (2001). Intervention assistance: Is it substance or symbolism? *Preventing School Failure, 45,* 153–161.

Rock, M. L. (2000). Effective crisis management planning: Creating a collaborative framework [Electronic version]. *Education and Treatment of Children, 23,* 248–264.

Rock, M. L. (2000). Parents as equal partners: Balancing the scales in IEP development. *Teaching Exceptional Children, 32*(6), 30–37.

Rock, M. L., & Zigmond, N. (2001). Intervention assistance: Is it substance or symbolism? *Preventing School Failure, 45*(4), 153.

Rogers, C. R. (1951). *Client-centered therapy: Its current practice, implications, and theory.* Boston: Houghton Mifflin.

Rogers, C. R. (1972). *On becoming a person.* New York: Dell.

Rogers, C., & Farson, R. (1981). Active listening. In J. A. DeVito (Ed.) *Communication: Concepts and processes* (3rd ed., pp. 137–147). Englewood Cliffs, NJ: Prentice Hall.

Rogers, E. L. (2001). Functional behavioral assessment and children with autism: Working as a team. *Focus on Autism and Other Developmental Disabilities, 16,* 228–232.

Rogers, E. M., & Steinfatt, T. M. (1999). *Intercultural communication.* Prospect Heights, IL: Waveland Press.

Rogers, M. R. (2000). Examining the cultural context of consultation [Electronic version]. *School Psychology Review, 29,* 414–418.

Rosenfield, S. A., & Gravois, T. A. (1996). *Instructional consultation teams: Collaborating for change.* New York: Guilford Press.

Roth, W-M., & Tobin, K. (2004). Coteaching: From praxis to theory [Electronic version]. *Teaching and Teaching: Theory and Practice, 10,* 161–180.

Rothstein-Fisch, C., & Trumbull, E. (in press). The intersection of culture and achievement motivation. *Journal of Applied Developmental Psychology.*

Rowland, G., & Patterson, J. (2004). School-based staff development puts teachers' hands on the controls. *Journal of Staff Development, 25*(2), 27–31.

Rubinson, F. (2002). Lessons learned from implementing problem-solving teams in urban high schools. *Journal of Educational and Psychological Consultation, 13,* 185–217.

Rudawsky, D. J., & Lundgren, D.C. (1999). Competitive responses to negative feedback [Electronic version]. *International Journal of Conflict Management, 10,* 172–190.

Rueda, R., Monzó, L. D., & Higareda, I. (2004). Appropriating the sociocultural resources of Latino paraeducators for effective instruction with Latino students: promise and problems [Electronic version]. *Urban Education, 39,* 52–90.

Russ, S., Chiang, B., Rylance, B. J., & Bongers, J. (2001). Caseload in special education: An integration of research findings. *Exceptional Children, 67,* 161–172.

Sabornie, E. J., & deBettencourt, L. U. (2004). *Teaching students with mild and high-incidence disabilities at the secondary level* (2nd ed.). Upper Saddleback River, NJ: Merrill Prentice Hall.

Salend, S. J. (2001). *Creating inclusive classrooms: Effective and reflective practices* (4th ed.). Upper Saddle River, NJ: Merrill/Prentice Hall.

Salend, S. J., Gordon, J., & Lopez-Vona, K. (2002). Evaluating cooperative teaching teams. *Intervention in School and Clinic, 37,* 195–200.

Salisbury, C. L., Evans, I. M., & Palombaro, M. M. (1997). Collaborative problem-solving to promote the inclusion of young children with significant disabilities in primary grades. *Exceptional Children, 63,* 195–209.

Salisbury, C. L., & McGregor, G. (2002). The administrative climate and context of inclusive elementary schools. *Exceptional Children, 68,* 259–274.

Samaha, N. V., & DeLisi, R. (2000). Peer collaboration on a nonverbal reasoning task by urban, minority students [Electronic version]. *Journal of Experimental Education, 69,* 5–21.

Sanders, M. R., Mazzucchelli, T. G., & Studman, L. J. (2004). Stepping Stones Triple P: The theoretical basis and development of an evidence-based positive parenting program for families with a child who has a disability [Electronic version]. *Journal of Intellectual and Developmental Disability, 29,* 265–283.

Sarason, S. B. (1982). *The culture of the school and the problem of change* (2nd ed.). Boston: Allyn & Bacon.

Schamber, S. (1999). Ten practices for undermining the effectiveness of teaming. *Middle School Journal, 30,* 10–14.

Schmidt, J. J. (2003). *Counseling in schools: Essential services and comprehensive programs* (4th ed.). Boston: Allyn & Bacon.

Schmuck, R. A., & Runkel, P. J. (1994). *The handbook of organizational development in schools* (4th ed.). Prospect Heights, IL: Waveland Press.

Schulte, A. C., & Osborne, S. S. (2003). When assumptive worlds collide: A review of definitions of collaboration in consultation. *Journal of Educational and Psychological Consultation, 14,* 109–138.

Schumm, J. S., Vaughn, S., & Harris, J. (1997). Pyramid power for collaborative planning. *Teaching Exceptional Children, 29*(6), 62–66.

Schwahn, C., & Spady, W. (1998). Why change doesn't happen and how to make sure it does. *Educational Leadership, 55*(7), 45–47.

Scott, J. J., & Smith, S. C. (1987). *Collaborative schools* (ERIC Digest Series No. 22). Eugene, OR: ERIC Clearinghouse on Educational Management, University of Oregon. (ERIC Document Reproduction Service No. ED290233)

Secules, T., Cottom, C., Bray, M., & Miller, L. (1997). Creating schools for thought. *Educational Leadership, 54*(6), 56–63.

Seeley, K. (2005). The listening cure: Listening for culture in intercultural psychological treatments. *Psychoanalytic Review, 92*(3), 431–452.

Sergiovanni, T. J. (1994). *Building community in schools.* San Francisco: Jossey-Bass.

Sergiovanni, T. J. (2004). *The lifeworld of leadership: Creating culture, community, and personal meaning in our school.* San Francisco: Jossey-Bass.

Shapiro, D. R., & Sayers, L. K. (2003). Who does what on the interdisciplinary team regarding physical education for students with disabilities? *Teaching Exceptional Children, 36*(6), 32–38.

Sharan, Y., & Sharan, S. (1994). Group investigation in the cooperative classroom. In S. Sharan (Ed.), *Handbook of cooperative learning methods* (pp. 191–214). Westport, CT: Greenwood Press.

Sharpe, M. N., & Hawes, M. E. (2003). Collaboration between general and special education: Making it work [Electronic version]. *Issue Brief: Examining Current Challenges in Secondary Education and Transition, 2*(1), 1–6.

Shelby, A. N. (1986). Theoretical bases of persuasion. *Journal of Business Communication, 25,* 5–29.

Shell, G. R. (2001). Bargaining styles and negotiation: The Thomas-Kilmann Conflict Mode Instrument in negotiation training [Electronic version]. *Negotiation Journal, 17,* 155–174.

Shen, J. (1998). Do teachers feel empowered? *Educational Leadership, 55*(7), 35–36.

Sheridan, S. M., & Cowan, R. J. 2004). *Consultation with school personnel.* In R. T. Brown (Ed.), *Handbook of pediatric psychology in school settings* (pp. 599–616). Mahwah, NJ: Erlbaum.

Sheridan, S. M., Erchul, W. P., Brown, M. S., Dowd, S. E., Warnes, E. D. Marti, D.C., Schemm, A. V., & Eagle, J. W. (2004). Perceptions of helpfulness in conjoint behavioral consultation: Congruence and agreement between teachers and parents [Electronic version]. *School Psychology Quarterly, 19,* 121–140.

Sheridan, S. M., Kratochwill, T. R., & Bergan, J. R. (1996). *Conjoint behavioral consultation: A procedural manual.* New York: Kluwer/Plenum.

Sheridan, S. M., Welch, M., & Orme, S. F. (1996). Is consultation effective? A review of outcome research. *Remedial and Special Education, 17,* 341–354.

Sherif, M., & Sherif, C. (1956). *An outline of social psychology.* New York: Harper & Row.

Sherry, L., & Chiero, R. (2004). Project TALENT: Infusing technology in K–12 field placements through a learning community model [Electronic version]. *Journal of Technology and Teacher Education, 12,* 265–297.

Shoffner, M. F., & Briggs, M. K. (2001). An interactive approach for developing interprofessional collaboration: Preparing school counselors. *Counselor Education & Supervision, 40,* 193–200.

Simmons, K. H., Ivry, J., & Sletzer, M. M. (1985). Agency–family collaboration. *Practice Concepts, 25,* 343–346.

Sindelar, P. T., Griffin, C. C., Smith, S. W., & Watanabe, A. K. (1992). Prereferral intervention: Encouraging notes on preliminary findings. *Elementary School Journal, 92,* 245–259.

Sitlington, P. L., & Neubert, D. S. (1998). Assessment for life: Methods and processes to determine students' interests, abilities and preferences. In M. Wehmeyer & D. J. Sands (Eds.), *Making it happen: Student involvement in educational planning, decision making, and instruction* (pp. 75–98). Baltimore: Brookes.

Slavin, R. E. (1986). *Using student team learning* (3rd ed.). Baltimore: Center for Research on Elementary and Middle Schools, Johns Hopkins University.

Slavin, R. E. (1991). Synthesis of research on cooperative learning. *Educational Leadership, 48*(5), 71–82.

Slavin, R. E. (1995). *Cooperative learning: Theory, research, and practice* (2nd ed.). Boston: Allyn & Bacon.

Slonski-Fowler, K. E., & Truscott, S. D. (2004). General education teachers' perceptions of the prereferral intervention team process. *Journal of Educational and Psychological Consultation, 15,* 1–39.

Slonski-Fowler, K. E., & Truscott, S. D. (2004). General education teachers' perceptions of the prereferral intervention team process. *Journal of Educational and Psychological Consultation, 15,* 1–39.

Smith, S. C., & Scott, J. S. (1990). *The collaborative school: A work environment for effective instruction.* Eugene: University of Oregon, ERIC Clearinghouse on Educational Management.

Snell, M. E., & Janney, R. (2000a). *Collaborative teaming.* Baltimore: Brookes.

Snell, M. E., & Janney, R. (2000b). Teachers' problem-solving about children with moderate and severe disabilities in elementary classrooms. *Exceptional Children, 66,* 472–490.

Snow, D. A., Zurcher, L. A., & Sjoberg, G. (1982). Interviewing by comment: An adjunct to the direct question. *Qualitative Sociology, 5,* 285–311.

Sodowsky, G. R., & Johnson, P. (1994). World views: Culturally learned assumptions and values. In P. Pedersen & J. C. Carey (Eds.), *Multicultural counseling in schools: A practical handbook* (pp. 59–79). Boston: Allyn & Bacon.

Sparapani, E. R., & Norwood, J. E. (1997). Collaborating with a university [Electronic version]. *Principal, 77*(2), 53–54.

Sparks, D. (1997). Maintaining the faith in teachers' ability to grow: An interview with Asa Hilliard. *Journal of Staff Development, 18*(2), 24–25.

Sparks, D. (1999). Try on strategies to get a good fit. *Journal of Staff Development, 20*(3), 56–60.

Sparks, D., & Hirsch, S. (1997). *A new vision for staff development.* Alexandria, VA: Association for Supervision and Curriculum Development.

Sparks, D., & Loucks-Horsley, S. (1989). Five models for staff development for teachers. *Journal of Staff Development, 10*(4), 40–57.

Sparks, D., Nowakowski, M., Hall, B., Alec, R., & Imrick, J. (1985). School improvement through staff development. *Educational Leadership 42*(6), 59–61.

Sparks, G. (1986). The effectiveness of alternative training activities in changing teaching practices. *American Educational Research Journal, 23*(2), 217–225.

Special Education News. (2000a). Many teachers say they are not prepared to coach paraeducators. Retrieved January 7, 2002, from http://specialednews.com/educators/ednews/parateams051900.html

Special Education News. (2000b). Paraeducator's role is changing amid teacher shortage. Retrieved January 7, 2002, from http://specialednews.com/educators/ednews/paraeds051900.html

Spencer, S. A. (2005). Lynne Cook and June Downing: The practicalities of collaboration in special education service delivery. *Intervention in School and Clinic, 40*(5), 296–300.

Stainton, T., & Bessler, H. (1998). The positive impact of children with an intellectual disability on the family. *Journal of Intellectual and Developmental Disability, 23*(1), 57–70.

Staton, A. R., & Gilligan, T. D. (2003). Teaching school counselors and school psychologists to work collaboratively. *Counselor Education and Supervision, 42*(3), 162–176.

Staw, B. M. (2004). *Psychological dimensions of organizational behavior* (3rd ed.). Upper Saddle River, NJ: Prentice Hall.

Stegelin, D. A., & Jones, S. D. (1991). Components of early childhood interagency collaboration: Results of a statewide study. *Early Education and Development, 2*(1), 54–67.

Sterling-Turner, H. E., Watson, T. S., & Moore, J. W. (2002). The effects of direct training and treatment integrity on treatment outcomes in school consultation [Electronic version]. *School Psychology Quarterly, 17,* 47–77.

Stevens, R. J., & Slavin, R. E. (1995). Effects of a cooperative learning approach in reading and writing on academically handicapped and nonhandicapped students. *The Elementary School Journal, 95,* 241–262.

Stewart, C. J., & Cash, W. B. (2000). *Interviewing: Practices and principles* (9th ed.). New York: McGraw-Hill.

Stewart, C. J., & Cash, W. B. (2006). *Interviewing: Practices and principles* (11th ed.). New York: McGraw-Hill.

Stoessel, S., & Miles, J. A. (n.d.). Co-teaching benefits mainstream and ESL children. *Curricululinks, 2*(1), 1, 3.

Study of Personnel Needs in Special Education. (2001a). *SPeNSE fact sheet: Paperwork in special education.* Rockville, MD: Westat.

Study of Personnel Needs in Special Education. (2001b). *SPeNSE fact sheet: General education teachers' role in special education.* Rockville, MD: Westat.

Sue, D. W., & Constantine, M. G. (2005). Effective multicultural consultation and organizational development. In M. G. Constantione & D. W. Sue (Eds.), *Strategies for building multicultural competence in mental health and educational settings* (pp. 212–226). Hoboken, NJ: John Wiley & Sons.

Sullivan, T. J. (1998). *Collaboration: A health care imperative.* New York: McGraw-Hill.

Sunnafrank, M., & Ramirez, A. (2004). At first sight: Persistent relational effects of get-acquainted conversations. *Journal of Social and Personal Relationships, 21*(3), 361–379.

Supovitz, J. A. (2002). Developing communities of instructional practice [Electronic version]. *Teachers College Record, 104,* 1591–1626.

Taggar, S. (2001). Group composition, creative synergy, and group performance [Electronic version]. *Journal of Creative Behavior, 35,* 261–286.

Tamir, L. (1999). Conflict mediation [Electronic version]. *Executive Excellence, 16*(6), 15–16.

Tarver-Behring, S., & Spagna, M. E. (1999). Counseling with exceptional children. In A. Vernon (Ed.), *Counseling children and adolescents.* Denver, CO: Love.

Tashie, C., Jorgensen, C., Shapiro-Barnard, S., Martin, J., & Schuh, M. (1996). High school inclusion: Strategies and barriers. *TASH Newsletter, 22*(9), 19–22.

Taylor, L., & Adelman, H. (1998). Confidentiality: Competing principles, inevitable dilemmas. *Journal of Educational and Psychological Consultation, 9,* 267–275.

Terry, P. M. (1999). Essential skills for principals. *Thrust for Educational Leadership, 29,* 28–32.

Tharp, R., & Wetzel, R. (1969). *Behavior modification in the natural environment.* New York: Academic Press.

Thomas, C. C., Correa, V. I., & Morsink, C. V. (2001). *Interactive teaming: Consultation and collaboration in special programs* (3rd ed.). Upper Saddle River, NJ: Prentice Hall.

Thomas, K. W., & Kilmann, R. H. (1974). *Thomas–Kilmann conflict mode instrument*. Tuxedo, NY: Xicom.

Thousand, J. S., & Villa, R. A. (2000). Collaborative teaming: A powerful tool in school restructuring. In R. A. Villa & J. S. Thousand (Eds.), *Restructuring for caring and effective education: Piecing the puzzle together* (2nd ed.). Baltimore: Brookes.

Tichenor, M. S., Heins, B., & Piechura-Couture, K. (2000). Parent perceptions of a co-taught inclusive classroom [Electronic version]. *Education, 120,* 546, 569–574.

Tjosvold, D. (1987). Participation: A close look at its dynamics. *Journal of Management, 13,* 739–750.

Tobias, R. (1993). Underlying cultural issues that affect sound consultation/school collaboratives in developing multicultural programs. *Journal of Educational and Psychological Consultation, 4*(3), 237–251.

Toffler, A. (1980). *The third wave.* New York: Morrow.

Tourse, R. W. C., & Mooney, J. F. (Eds.). (1999). *Collaborative practice: School and human service partnerships.* Westport, CT: Praeger.

Tractman, G. M. (1961). New directions for school psychology. *Exceptional Children, 28,* 159–162.

Trenholm, S. (2001). *Thinking through communication: An introduction to the study of human communication* (3rd ed.). Boston: Allyn & Bacon.

Trenholm, S. (2005). *Thinking through communication: An introduction to the study of human communication* (4th ed.). Boston: Allyn & Bacon.

Trenholm, S., & Jensen, A. (2004). *Interpersonal communication* (5th ed.). New York: Oxford University Press.

Trent, S. C. (1998). False starts and other dilemmas of a secondary general education collaborative teacher [Electronic version]. *Journal of Learning Disabilities, 31,* 503–513.

Trentin, G., & Gibelli, C. (1998). Distance collaboration for studying history in lower secondary schools: The storybase project [Electronic version]. *International Journal of Instructional Media, 25*(1), 11–27.

Trumbull, E., Rothstein-Fisch, C., Greenfield, P. M., & Quiroz, B. (2001). *Bridging cultures between home and school: A guide for teachers.* Mahwah, NJ: Erlbaum.

Trump, J. L. (1966). Secondary education tomorrow: Four imperatives for improvement. *NASSP Bulletin, 50*(309), 87–95.

Truscott, S. D., Richardson, R. D., Cohen, C., Frank, A., & Palmeri, D. (2003). Does rational persuasion influence potential consultees? *Psychology in the Schools, 40,* 627–640.

Tuckman, B. W. (1965). Developmental sequence in small groups. *Psychological Bulletin, 63,* 384–399

Tuckman, B. W., & Jensen, M. A. (1977). Stages of small group development revisited. *Group and Organizational Studies, 2,* 419–427.

Turnbull, A. P., & Turnbull, H. R. (2001). *Families, professionals, and exceptionality: Collaborating for empowerment* (4th ed.). Upper Saddle River, NJ: Merrill/Prentice Hall.

Turnbull, A. P., Turnbull, H. R., Erwin, E., & Soodak, L. (2006). *Families, professionals, and exceptionality: Positive outcomes through partnership and trust* (5th ed.). Upper Saddle River, NJ: Merrill/Prentice Hall.

Turnbull, A. P., Turnbull, H. R., Shank, M., & Leal, D. (1995). *Exceptional lives: Special education in today's schools.* Englewood Cliffs, NJ: Merrill/ Prentice Hall.

Ulrich, M. E., & Bauer, A. M. (2003). A closer look at communication between parents and professionals. *Teaching Exceptional Children, 35*(6), 20–23.

Umansky, W., & Hooper, S. R. (1998). *Young children with special needs* (3rd ed). Upper Saddle River, NJ: Merrill/Prentice Hall.

Ury, W. (1991). *Getting past no: Negotiating your way from confrontation to cooperation.* New York: Bantam.

Ury, W. L., Brett, J. M., & Goldberg, S. B. (1988). *Getting disputes resolved: Designing systems to cut the costs of conflict.* San Francisco: Jossey-Bass.

U.S. Department of Education. (2003). *Twenty-fifth annual report to Congress on the implementation of the Individuals with Disabilities Education Act.* Washington, DC: Author.

U.S. Department of Education. (n.d.). *Roles for education paraprofessionals in effective schools: An idea book.* Washington, DC: U.S. Department of Education, Planning and Evaluation Service.

Valle, J. W., & Aponte, E. (2002). IDEA and collaboration: A Bakhtinian perspective on parent and professional discourse. *Journal of Learning Disabilities, 35,* 469–479.

VanGundy, A. B. (2005). *101 activities for teaching creativity and problem solving.* San Francisco: Pfeiffer.

Van Meter, P., & Stevens, R. J. (2000). The role of theory in the study of peer collaboration [Electronic version]. *Journal of Experimental Education, 69,* 113–127.

Vargo, S. (1998). Consulting teacher-to-teacher. *Teaching Exceptional Children, 30*(2), 54–55.

Vaughan, W. (2002). Effects of cooperative learning on achievement and attitudes among students of color. *Journal of Educational Research, 95,* 359–364.

Vaughn, S. (1994, April). *Teachers' views of inclusion: "I'd rather pump gas."* Paper presented at the annual meeting of the American Educational Research Association, New Orleans. (ERIC Document Reproduction Service No. ED370928)

Vaughn, S., Zaragoza, N., Hogan, A., & Walker, J. (1993). A four-year longitudinal investigation of the social skills and behavior problems of students with learning disabilities. *Journal of Learning Disabilities, 26,* 404–412.

Villa, R. A., Thousand, J. S., & Nevin, A. I. (2004). *A guide to co-teaching: Practical tips for facilitating student learning.* Thousand Oaks, CA: Corwin.

Villegas, A. M., & Clewell, B. C. (1998). Increasing teacher diversity by tapping the paraprofessional pool [Electronic version]. *Theory into Practice, 37,* 121–130.

Von Glinow, M. A., Shapiro, D. L., & Brett, J. M. (2004). Can we talk, and show we? Managing emotional conflict in multicultural teams [Electronic version]. *Academy of Management Review, 29,* 578–592.

Waclawski, J., & Church, A. H. (Eds.). (2002). *Organization development: A data-driven approach to organizational change.* San Francisco: Jossey-Bass.

Wade, S. E., Welch, M., & Jensen, J. B. (1994). Teacher receptivity to collaboration: Levels of interest, types of concern and school characteristics as variables contributing to successful implementation. *Journal of Educational and Psychological Consultation, 5,* 177–209.

Wadsworth, D. E., & Knight, D. (1996). Paraprofessionals: The bridge to successful full inclusion. *Intervention in School and Clinic, 31,* 166–171.

Wageman, R., & Mannix, E. A. (2003). Uses and misuses of power in task-performing teams. In L. W. Porter, H. L. Angle, & R. W. Allen (Eds.), *Organizational influence processes* (2nd ed.). Ramonk, NY: M. E. Sharpe.

Wagner, M., & Blackorby, J. (1996). Transition from high school to work or college: How special education students fare. *The Future of Children, 6*(1), 103–120.

Wagner, T. (1998). Change as collaborative inquiry: A constructivist methodology for reinventing schools. *Phi Delta Kappan, 79,* 512–517.

Walcott, D. D. (1997, July–August). Education in human sexuality for young people with moderate and severe mental retardation. *Exceptional Children, 29*(6), 72–74.

Walker, W. (1999). Collaboration: "The faint of heart need not apply" [Electronic version]. *Peabody Journal of Education, 74,* 300–305.

Wallace, T., Anderson, A. R., & Bartholomay, T. (2002). Collaboration: An element associated with the success of four inclusive high schools. *Journal of Educational and Psychological Consultation, 13,* 349–381.

Walsh, J. M., & Jones, B. (2004). New models of cooperative teaching. *Teaching Exceptional Children, 36*(5), 14–20.

Walter, K. E. (2004). *Sustainable school improvement: Making good choices.* Naperville, IL: Learning Point (North Central Regional Educational Laboratory).

Walther-Thomas, C. S. (1997). Co-teaching experiences: The benefits and problems that teachers and principals report over time. *Journal of Learning Disabilities, 30,* 395–407.

Walther-Thomas, C., Korinek, L., & McLaughlin, V. L. (1999). Collaboration to support students' success. *Focus on Exceptional Children, 32*(3), 1–18.

Walther-Thomas, C., Korinek, L., McLaughlin, V. L., & Williams, B. T. (2000). *Collaboration for inclusive education: Developing successful programs.* Boston: Allyn & Bacon.

Wanis-St. John, A. (2003). Thinking globally and acting locally [Electronic version]. *Negotiation Journal, 19,* 389–396.

Warwick, D. (1971). *Team teaching.* London: University of London.

Wasburn-Moses, L. (2005). Roles and responsibilities of secondary special education teachers in an age of reform. *Remedial and Special Education, 26,* 151–158.

Wehman, P. (Ed.). (2001). *Life beyond the classroom: Transition strategies for young people with disabilities* (3rd ed.). Baltimore: Brookes.

Wehmeyer, M. L., & Sands, D. J. (1998). *Making it happen: Student involvement in education planning, decision-making, and instruction.* Baltimore: Brookes.

Weiner, I., & Murawski, W. (2005). Schools attuned: A model for collaborative intervention. *Intervention in School and Clinic, 40*(5), 284–290.

Weiss, M. P., & Lloyd, J. (2003). Conditions for co-teaching: Lessons from a case study. *Teacher Education and Special Education, 26,* 27–41.

Weiss, M. P., & Lloyd, J. W. (2002). Congruence between roles and actions of secondary special educators in co-taught and special education settings. *Journal of Special Education, 36,* 58–68.

Welch, M. (1998). Collaboration: Staying on the bandwagon. *Journal of Teacher Education, 49*(1), 26–37.

Welch, M. (1999). The DECIDE strategy for decision making and problem solving: A workshop template for preparing professionals for educational partnerships. *Journal of Educational and Psychological Consultation, 10,* 363–375.

Welch, M. (2000). Descriptive analysis of team teaching in two elementary classrooms: A formative experimental approach. *Remedial and Special Education, 21,* 366–376.

Welch, M., Brownell, K., & Sheridan, S. (1999). What's the score and game plan on teaming in schools? *Remedial and Special Education, 20*(1), 36–49.

Welch, M., & Tulbert, B. (2000). Practitioners' perspectives of collaboration: A social validation and factor analysis. *Journal of Educational and Psychological Consultation, 11,* 357–378.

Weller, D. R., & McLeskey, J. (2000). Block scheduling and inclusion in a high school: Teacher perceptions of the benefits and challenges. *Remedial and Special Education, 21,* 209–218.

Werts, M. G., Harris, S., Tillery, C. Y., & Roark, R. (2004). What parents tell us about paraeducators. *Remedial and Special Education, 25,* 232–239.

Wesley, P. W., & V. Buysse, V. (2004). Consultation as a framework for productive collaboration in early intervention. *Journal of Educational and Psychological Consultation, 15,* 127–150.

Wesson, L., & Kudlacz, J. M. (2000). Collaboration for change [Electronic version]. *Principal Leadership, 1*(3), 50–53.

Westby, C. E., & Ford, V. (1993). The role of team culture in assessment and intervention. *Journal of Educational and Psychological Consultation, 4,* 319–341.

Westmyer, S. A., DiCioccio, R. L., & Rubin, R. B. (1998). Appropriateness and effectiveness of communication channels in competent interpersonal communication. *Journal of Communication, 48*(3), 27–48.

White, J. B., Tynan, R., Galinsky, A. D., & Thompson, L. (2004). Face threat sensitivity in negotiation: Roadblock to agreement and joint gain [Electronic version]. *Organizational Behavior and Human Decision Processes, 94,* 102–124.

White, J., & Mullis, F. (1998). A systems approach to school counselor consultation [Electronic version]. *Education, 119,* 242–252.

White, J., & Weiner, J. S. (2004). Influence of least restrictive environment and community based training on integrated employment outcomes for transitioning students with severe disabilities. *Journal of Vocational Rehabilitation, 21,* 149–156.

White, R. (2004). The recruitment of paraeducators into the special education profession: A review

of progress, select evaluation outcomes, and new initiatives. *Remedial and Special Education, 25,* 214–218.

Whitehead, B. (1994). The failure of sex education. *American Educator, 18,* 22–29, 44–52.

Whitten, E., & Dieker, L. (1995). Intervention assistance teams: A broader vision. *Preventing School Failure, 40*(1), 41–45.

Whitworth, J. (1999). *Seven steps to successful inclusion.* (ERIC Document Reproduction Service No. ED436040)

Wickstrom, K. F., & Witt, J. C. (1993). Resistance with school-based consultation. In J. Zins, T. R. Kratochwill, & S. N. Elliott (Eds.), *Handbook of consultation services for children* (pp. 159–178). San Francisco: Jossey-Bass.

Widrick, G., Whaley, C., DiVenere, N., Vecchione, E., Swartz, D., & Stiffler, D. (1991). The medical education project: An example of collaboration between parents and professionals. *Children's Health Care, 20,* 93–100.

Wilczynski, S. M., Mandal, R. L., & Fusilier, I. (2000). Bridges and barriers in behavioral consultation. *Psychology in the Schools, 37,* 495–504.

Wilkinson, L. A. (2003). Using behavioral consultation to reduce challenging behavior in the classroom. *Preventing School Failure, 47,* 100–105.

Wilson, G. L. (2005). This doesn't look familiar: A supervisor's guide for observing co-teachers. *Intervention in School and Clinic, 40,* 271–275.

Wineburg, S., & Grossman, P. (1998). Creating a community of learners among high school teachers. *Phi Delta Kappan, 79,* 350–353.

Wolf, J. S., & Stephens, T. M. (1990). Friends of special education: A parent training model. *Journal of Educational and Psychological Consultation, 1,* 343–356.

Wolf, R. (1979). *Strategies for conducting naturalistic evaluation in socio-educational settings: The naturalistic interview.* Kalamazoo, MI: Occasional Series, Evaluation Center, Western Michigan University.

Wolfe, P. S., & Harriott, W. A. (1998). The reauthorization of the Individuals with Disabilities Act (IDEA): What educators and parents should know. *Focus on Autism and Other Developmental Disabilities, 13*(2), 88–95.

Wood, M. (1998). Whose job is it anyway? Educational roles in inclusion. *Exceptional Children, 64,* 181–195.

Yell, M. L., Rozalski, M. E., & Drasgow, E. (2001). Disciplining students with disabilities [Electronic version]. *Focus on Exceptional Children, 33*(9), 1–20.

Index

Photo Credits